PERGAMON INTERNATIONAL LIBRARY
of Science, Technology, Engineering and Social Studies
*The 1000-volume original paperback library in aid of education,
industrial training and the enjoyment of leisure*
Publisher: Robert Maxwell, M.C.

PERGAMON GENERAL PSYCHOLOGY SERIES

Editors: Arnold P. Goldstein, *Syracuse University*
Leonard Krasner, *Suny, Stony Brook*

PREDICTION OF ORGANIZATIONAL BEHAVIOR

PGPS 31

_____Publisher's Notice to Educators_____

THE PERGAMON TEXTBOOK
INSPECTION COPY SERVICE

An inspection copy of any book published in the Pergamon International Library
will gladly be sent without obligation for consideration for course adoption or
recommendation. Copies may be retained for a period of 60 days from receipt and
returned if not suitable. When a particular title is adopted or recommended for
adoption for class use and the recommendation results in a sale of 12 or more
copies, the inspection copy may be retained with our compliments. If after examination the lecturer decides that the book is not suitable for adoption but would like to
retain it for his personal library, then our Educators' Discount of 10% is allowed on
the invoiced price. The Publishers will be pleased to receive suggestions for revised
editions and new titles to be published in this important International Library.

About the Authors...

Norman Frederiksen (Ph.D., Syracuse University) is Senior Research Psychologist and Director of the Division of Psychological Studies at Educational Testing Service. He is author or co-author of two books, over 60 articles in psychology, education, and research, and over 30 psychological papers and research reports. His 35 years of experience include being Associate Professor of Psychology at Princeton University, Research Associate for the College Entrance Examination Board, and Assistant to the eminent psychologists, J.P. Guilford and Floyd H. Allport.

Ollie A. Jensen (M.A., University of California at Berkeley) is Chairman, Department of Special Projects and Vocational-Technical Testing, Test Development Division at Educational Testing Service. At the time of the research here reported he served as Staff Analyst, Examining Standards Section, California State Personnel Board. He is the author or co-author of many publications on testing, personnel, and administration.

Albert E. Beaton (Ph.D., Harvard University) is Director of the Office of Data Analysis Research at Educational Testing Service and Visiting Lecturer at Princeton University. He is the author or co-author of over 20 publications in economics, psychology, education, and statistics and is consultant for numerous organizations.

Bruce Bloxom (Ph.D., University of Washington), a USPHS Postdoctoral Fellow in Personality Research at Educational Testing Service when he contributed to this work, is now Assistant Professor and Director of Undergraduate Study, Department of Psychology, Vanderbilt University.

Prediction of
Organizational Behavior

NORMAN FREDERIKSEN, OLLIE JENSEN,
ALBERT E. BEATON
Educational Testing Service
Princeton, New Jersey

(With a contribution by BRUCE BLOXOM)

PERGAMON PRESS INC.

OXFORD · NEW YORK · TORONTO
SYDNEY · PARIS · BRAUNSCHWEIG

U.K.	Pergamon Press Ltd., Headington Hill Hall, Oxford OX3 0BW, England
U.S.A.	Pergamon Press Inc., Maxwell House, Fairview Park, Elmsford, New York 10523, U.S.A.
CANADA	Pergamon of Canada, Ltd., 207 Queen's Quay West, Toronto 1, Canada
AUSTRALIA	Pergamon Press (Aust.) Pty. Ltd., 19a Boundary Street, Rushcutters Bay, N.S.W. 2011, Australia
FRANCE	Pergamon Press SARL, 24 rue des Ecoles, 75240 Paris, Cedex 05, France
WEST GERMANY	Pergamon Press GMbH, D-3300 Braunschweig, Postfach 2923, Burgplatz 1, West Germany

First edition 1972

Reprinted 1976

Library of Congress Catalog Card No. 72–188309

Printed in Great Britain by A. Wheaton & Co., Exeter

0 08 017189 3 (Flexi)
0 08 016967 8 (Hard)

Contents

Acknowledgments   ix

Chapter 1 **The Person-Situation Interaction Problem**   1
               Experimental and Correlational Approaches
                   to the Study of Behavior   3
               The Concept of Differential Predictability   5
               Evidence of Person-Situation Interactions   6
               Statistical Models for Person-Situation
                   Interactions   19
               What Is a Situation?   21
               Developing a Taxonomy of Situations   22

Chapter 2 **Methods of Data Collection in Social-Psychological**
               Research   37

Chapter 3 **Design for an Experimental Study of Person-**
               Situation Interaction   71
               Choice of Climate Variables   72
               Design of the Study   74

Chapter 4 **The Subjects**   80
               Description of the Sample   80
               Assignment of Subjects to Treatments   82
               Comparison of Treatment Groups with Respect
                   to Predictors   83
               Reports to Subjects   84

Chapter 5   **The Predictor Variables**   87
            Cognitive Ability Tests   88
            Personality Inventory Scales   98
            Background Variables   106
            Climate Ratings   110
            Intercorrelations of the Predictor Scales   112

Chapter 6   **The Situational Tests and the Experimental**
            Manipulation   116
            The Setting for the In-Baskets   116
            The In-Basket Items   121
            Presentation of Organizational Climates   122
            Perception of the Climates by Subjects   135
            Conducting the Research Institute   138

Chapter 7   **The Dependent Variables: Scoring In-Basket**
            Protocols   141
            Scoring the In-Basket Responses   141
            Reliability of In-Basket Scores   153
            Correlations of In-Basket Scores with Ratings
              by Peers and Superiors   160

Chapter 8   **The Criterion Measures: Factor Analysis of**
            In-Basket Scores   164

Chapter 9   **Effects of Organizational Climates on Factor**
            Structure   174

Chapter 10 **Effects of Climates on Means and on Relationships**
            of Performance to Predictor Variables   182
            Effects Due to Personal Characteristics   182
            Effects of Climates on the Relationship of
              Predictors to Performance and on the Means
              of Performance Factor Scores   189

Chapter 11   The Three-Mode Factor Analysis   **199**
Three-Mode Factor Analysis   200
Factor Analysis of the Performance Categories   202
Factor Analysis of the Items   208
The Core Matrix   214
Intercorrelations of the Person-Factor Scores   224
Correlations of Person-Factor Scores with
   Predictors   227
Discussion of the Results   237

Chapter 12   The Findings and Their Implications   **241**
Summary of Major Findings   242
Implications for Personnel Practice   253
Implications for a Model of Human Behavior   257
Methodological Implications   259

References   **266**
Appendix A Group Principal Components Factor Analysis   **275**
Appendix B Within-Group Covariance Factor Analysis   **277**
Appendix C Department of Commerce In-Basket B   **279**
Index   **325**

Acknowledgments

Support for this study came from three major sources: the Office of Naval Research, the California State Personnel Board, and Educational Testing Service. We are especially grateful to Dr. Glenn L. Bryan and Dr. John A. Nagay of the Personnel and Training Branch, ONR, for their encouragement and for their help in arranging for financial support through a contract between ONR and ETS.

The cooperation of Mr. John F. Fisher, Executive Officer of the California State Personnel Board, is gratefully acknowledged. The interest of SPB in the research made it possible for a member of its professional staff to devote a substantial amount of time to the project and for 270 employees of the state to serve as subjects in the experiment. Without the cooperation and support of SPB the experiment would not have been possible. Mr. Vernon R. Taylor, Chief of Examining Standards of SPB, gave generously of his help in making possible the arrangements for data collection and test scoring. Many other members of SPB contributed to the study by serving as subjects for pretesting of situational tests, acting as proctors during the experiment, and by conducting the training activity at the end of the experiment.

Educational Testing Service contributed financially to the research, and the contributions of many members of its staff should be acknowledged. Dr. Herbert Gerjuoy, Research Psychologist, contributed to the early stages of the study, especially in the selection and adaptation of materials for the predictor battery and in the factor analysis of the scores on these measures. Dr. Bruce Bloxom, Post-Doctoral Fellow at ETS in the USPHS Post-Doctoral Training Program in Personality Research, performed the three-mode factor analysis described in Chapter 11 and is the first author of that chapter. This analysis was supported through a grant from the National Institute for Child Health and Human Development to ETS for a Center for Psychological Studies. Dr. L. R Tucker gave advice on statistical problems, particularly in relation to the three-mode factor analysis. Mrs. Sydell Carlton and Mrs. Margueritte Brault were responsible for preparation of the Scoring Manual, and Mrs. Carlton wrote the first draft of Chapter 6. Mrs. Brault recruited, trained, and supervised the scorers of the in-basket protocols. Dr. Norman Wexler was responsible for programming computer work during the early stages of the analysis and for the three-mode factor analysis. Mr. John Barone performed the programming and other computer functions for the regression analysis described in the later chapters. Dr. Fred Damarin and Dr. Bruce Bloxom reviewed the manuscript and made many valuable suggestions; they are not, however, to be held responsible for any errors that may remain. Mrs. Ann King and Mrs. Fay Richardson did the final editing of the report and supervised its preparation; Mrs. Laura Lenz typed and Mrs. Marie Davis and Mrs. Frances Shaffer proofread the final manuscript.

Dr. Carl Helm, now at the City University of New York, was kind enough to adapt his PROTRAN program in the production of the computer-composed reports to subjects.

To all these people, and especially to the subjects who took two days out of their busy lives to perform the duties of an executive in the simulated job, we owe our thanks.

CHAPTER 1

The Person-Situation Interaction Problem

Several years ago a conference was held in Washington to consider the question of how to predict the behavior of a single individual. The government was concerned about the question because a single individual's behavior might be of critical importance to the United States — if he happens to be someone with the power to commit his nation to economic or military acts that affect the welfare and security of Americans. Nikita Khrushchev and Fidel Castro were two individuals whose behavior was at that time thought to be important to the security of the United States.

The fact that the question was posed and that a number of well-known behavioral scientists attended and considered the question very seriously tells us something interesting about the state of psychology as a science. Psychologists have developed a technology of prediction that is widely used in industry and education; the method depends almost wholly on individual differences, with heavy reliance on such characteristics as abilities, attitudes, interests, personality traits, and items of biographical history. The method works reasonably well when the problem is to make comparative statements about probable performance of many individuals — candidates for admission to college or applicants for a job. But the personnel psychologist, at least, is likely to be stumped when asked to make predictions about how a single individual's behavior will vary from one occasion to another over a period of time. Individual differences (at least as usually conceived) do not provide a solution to the problem, since they do not exist for a single individual.

The personnel psychologists' solution to the prediction problem requires that we have a measure of criterion performance, y (e.g., average freshman grade or a rating of job performance), and at least one measure of a personal characteristic, x (e.g., aptitude or interest), that is correlated with y. The regression of y on x provides the basis for prediction of criterion performance. If one wished to follow an analogous procedure for predicting events in the life of a single individual, he would have to consider a domain of the criterion behaviors as measured on each of many occasions, and the predictor variables would have to be personal characteristics that vary over time (e.g., mood states). If it were possible to obtain information about Mr. Castro's mood just prior to the occasions when the criterion behavior was to be exhibited, then one could similarly compute a regression equation for prediction of y on the basis of x.

A more feasible possibility might be to employ another class of predictor variables, that of situational variables. Let us suppose, for example, that the y we wish to predict is Mr. Khrushchev's willingness to compromise in conferences dealing with international problems. Presumably there are, somewhere in Washington, many file drawers full of records of international conferences attended by Khrushchev, and suitable ratings of the criterion variable "willingness to compromise" could be made. Similarly, ratings could be made of each conference with respect to various situational variables that might be predictive of performance—for example, the extent to which the prestige of the USSR is involved in each conference. Given such data, it would be perfectly possible to obtain a regression equation which describes the relationship between y (Khrushchev's willingness to compromise) and x (degree to which the prestige of the USSR is at stake). If the relationship is sufficiently high, one could "predict" the extent to which Khrushchev would compromise at a new international conference; furthermore, given such information, perhaps one could have controlled to some degree Khrushchev's behavior by managing the amount of stress placed on prestige at the conference.

Another approach to the problem of predicting the behavior of the single individual is that of the clinician, who through careful study of the motives of an individual and the "dynamics" of his behavior achieves a degree of understanding that supposedly enables him to predict behavior, even in unique circumstances where the performance has never been observed. Clinical psychologists and psychiatrists are regularly called upon to make predictions of how a patient will respond to a kind of therapy, how a prisoner will adjust to parole, or how a manager will perform in a new position of great responsibility. It is difficult to judge how accurate such predictions are because they are seldom made under conditions which make possible a rigorous evaluation of their accuracy. The clinical judgments are of interest because the clinician makes predictions that do take into account the kind of situation the subject will be concerned with. In doing so, the clinician may make statements that imply interactions between situational and individual variables. He says, in effect, that a patient with a given set of personal characteristics will behave in a particular manner when placed in a certain kind of situation.

From a scientific rather than a clinical point of view, psychologists are interested in generalizations that hold for a large number of people rather than for just one individual. There is the possibility that groups can be identified that are larger than one, but less than all mankind, whose behavior can be described in terms of particular kinds of relationships between performance and situational variables. This report is about an attempt to look systematically for such interactions between personal and situational variables in the prediction of behavior.

EXPERIMENTAL AND CORRELATIONAL APPROACHES TO THE STUDY OF BEHAVIOR

As Cronbach pointed out in his presidential address of 1957 (Cronbach, 1957), psychological research has historically been characterized by two separate streams of thought and method. One stream is experimental psychology. In the experimental method, the scientist systematically changes situations in order to observe the effects of the change on performance. This method permits tight control of situational variables, rigorous tests of hypotheses, and inferences about causation. Individual differences among experimental animals are a source of error, according to this point of view, and the experimental psychologist therefore prefers to deal with homogeneous groups of subjects.

The other stream is correlational psychology. In the correlational method, the scientist is primarily interested in variables on which there are individual differences. The method is to observe relationships between variables that already exist. The method makes possible scientific study of a wide variety of phenomena that the scientist would otherwise not be able to study because (especially with human subjects) conditions and situations cannot be experimentally manipulated. The correlational psychologists have developed a set of analytic techniques that make possible scientific study in domains that are not amenable to rigorous control by experimental procedures. Since variations in scores that are attributable to changes in conditions or situations tend to obscure the relationships between variables, the correlational psychologist tries to obtain measures for all subjects under identical conditions. Variation in situations is viewed as a source of error. Thus the phenomena that constitute the subject matter of psychology for one school are the source of error variance for the other.

Cronbach urged in his presidential address that a federation of the two disciplines is required, in which the experimental psychologists employ correlational methods in order to bring under control variables previously treated as sources of error variance, and in which the correlational psychologists make use of experimental treatments in order to make treatment variance a part of their investigation. As examples of work in which the two disciplines are being brought together, he cited construct validity studies, in which predictions based on theoretical expectations about the construct supposedly measured by a test are verified experimentally, and the work of Fleishman (1956) and of Fleishman and Hempel (1954), who showed that the factorial content of motor tests changes as a function of practice. Cronbach recommends that the correlational psychologists' multivariate conception of the world, a conception that recognizes the inadequacy of any single measure of a construct, be applied to experimental investigations.

Cronbach was not alone. In the same year Eysenck (1957) asserted that a sound theory of personality could not be developed, that a proper theory would have to be a theory of personality *and* situation. Cattell (1957) included in his *Personality and Motivation Structure and Measurement* a section on the taxonomy of situations, a topic that he said was "long overdue in psychological calculation as it affects personality . . . ." More recently (1971) he proposed an extension of the factor analytic model "to enable it to fit the psychological theory of modulation of behavior by ambient situations which change individuals' *state* levels and role involvements . . . . This model is . . . part of a development for integrating the traditional interests of psychometrists, centered in individual differences, with the traditional interests of experimentalists . . . centered on changes in group means." Sells (1963a) also has commented on the unfortunate cleavage between the bivariate-experimental and the multivariate-psychometric approaches.

Psychologists have been slow in following these recommendations, although studies that involve simultaneous attention to experimental treatments and to individual differences are appearing more frequently, especially in educational research, where "aptitude-treatment interaction" (ATI) is becoming a popular subject for investigation. A study by Snow, Tiffin, and Seibert (1965), for example, showed that measures of attitude and aptitude were differentially related to learner performance under different methods of teaching. A later section will review some of the more recent attempts to study behavior as a function of variations of both personal and situational characteristics.   .

THE CONCEPT OF DIFFERENTIAL PREDICTABILITY

There are obvious instances where a test which has predictive power for some individuals has little or no predictive value for others. For example, a mathematics achievement test might be used effectively as a predictor of grades in advanced mathematics courses for people who have studied elementary mathematics, but it would probably have little or no predictive value for people who had not studied mathematics at all. It has been shown that the regression of grades on aptitude tests may be different for men than for women (Abelson, 1952) and different for veteran than for nonveteran students (Frederiksen & Schrader, 1951). There are also more subtle examples of differential predictability. Measures of interest in science correlate with engineering school grades for students who are not "compulsive" but do not correlate for students who are compulsive (Frederiksen & Gilbert, 1960; Frederiksen & Melville, 1954; Stricker, 1966). Motor tests were found to correlate with a criterion involving taxi driving for people with low scores on a measure of occupational aspiration, but the correlation was much lower for those with high occupational aspirations (Ghiselli, 1956). Kogan and Wallach (1964) found that correlations between personality variables (such as impulsiveness) and risk taking were quite low, but when moderator variables (such as test anxiety and defensiveness) were used to identify subgroups of subjects, substantial correlations were found for certain of the subgroups. They conclude that "consideration of potential moderator variables is nothing less than essential in psychological research involving the study of correlations" (page 188).

Saunders (1956) coined the term *moderator variable* for a variable that influences the predictive value of another variable, the predictor; and he has supplied a method for dealing with the moderator as a continuous variable rather than by creating subgroups. Gaylord and Carroll (1948) had suggested earlier a formula for this purpose. Ghiselli (1956, 1960) described a method for developing a test to predict how well individuals could be predicted, and he succeeded in improving prediction considerably by using the new test as a moderator variable. Cleary (1966) presented a model for multiple regression that allows the moderator variables to emerge empirically rather than on the basis of an *a priori* theory.

It is reasonable to suppose that situational variables as well as personal characteristics of subjects might serve as moderators by influencing the relationships between predictors and criteria, as Sells (1963a,b) implies, as do most modern theories of organizational behavior (Schein, 1965). To take an obvious example, correlations between scholastic ability and achievement might well be different in a very noisy classroom than in a quiet one, because of variation in ability of pupils to hear the teacher. When we consider the possibility of experimentally manipulating situational variables, it is apparent that differential predictability becomes a specific example of how experimental methods and correlational methods may be joined. The experiment to be described in this report involves the experimental manipulation of organizational climates, and the effect of these variations in climate on the correlations between predictors and dependent variables is one of the questions to be answered.

EVIDENCE OF PERSON-SITUATION INTERACTIONS

In this section we shall look at a few examples of person-situation interactions that have been demonstrated in two areas: education and organizational behavior.

Aptitude-Treatment Interactions in Education

The importance of individual differences has, of course, long been recognized by educators. One method of dealing with individual differences has been to assign students of different ability levels to programs with different objectives or with different standards. So we have "general" programs, vocational programs, and college preparatory programs in high school, and we have a great variety of "track" systems that may really imply different levels of aspiration as to educational accomplishment. Such ways of coping with individual differences do not recognize the ATI option—the possibility that students with different characteristics (such as general ability level) might attain the *same* standards of achievement if different programs of instruction are made available to students with different characteristics.

Good teachers have always tried to apply the basic idea of ATI by attempting to adapt instructional techniques to the interests and abilities of individual pupils by such methods as varying the language and level of abstractness used in explanations, introducing suitable remedial assignments, varying reading materials, appealing to different interests, and so on. Recent work on ATI introduces the possibility of more systematic large-scale applications of procedures based on empirical evidence rather than intuitive judgments of teachers and supervisors. There is a growing awareness of such possibilities among educators and apparently a greater willingness to consider installing ATI applications on a large scale in school systems.

The most dramatic proposal for a large-scale application of ATI is that of Arthur Jensen (1969), in his controversial article appearing in the *Harvard Educational Review*. Jensen makes a distinction between Level I and Level II types of mental ability (which are really the ends of a continuum, in his scheme). Level I is associative ability, represented by such tests as digit span and serial learning; and Level II is conceptual ability, represented by such tests as Progressive Matrices, tests of arithmetic, and typical intelligence tests. Level I may be thought of as rote learning, while Level II requires elaboration and transformation of stimulus inputs before the subject responds. Large differences in performance on Level II tasks are found between children of middle and low social class, but lower-class children do as well on Level I learning tasks as do the middle-class children, according to Jensen.

Traditional methods of instruction emphasize Level II abilities, Jensen believes, and thus children who are poor at Level II are at a disadvantage, even though they are entirely capable of learning the same material using Level I abilities. He recommends that educators devise teaching methods that will make it possible for lower-class children, who are poor at conceptualization but good at associative learning, to master the basic skills necessary to complete their education and compete for jobs after schooling is complete.

One basic question that must be answered before deciding on the merits of such a proposal is whether the two methods of instruction – the rote and conceptual methods – can in fact enable students to achieve comparable levels of proficiency in the areas represented by the educational objectives of a school. It seems unlikely that they could. One would expect that the use of the two routes to educational achievement would have two undesirable outcomes: (1) the two educational treatments would further separate the two groups with respect to Level I and II abilities, and (2) the rote-learning route would be successful in only some of the desired educational outcomes. An alternative to Jensen's recommendation would be to try to devise educational treatments specifically aimed at improving conceptual abilities in lower-class children.

Cronbach and Snow (1969) have recently reviewed the literature on aptitude-treatment interactions. They conclude that much of the research has been inconclusive and that few interactions have been solidly demonstrated. They believe that weak methodology is largely responsible for the lack of confirmed ATI effects. Some of the experiments cited by Cronbach and Snow do, nevertheless, strongly suggest the existence of ATI, even though there has been little replication of work in the field. A few of the studies judged best by Cronbach and Snow will be reviewed briefly, in order to communicate the flavor of the most successful work on person-situation interactions in the field of education.

Programmed instruction in Spanish   Maier and Jacobs (1964), and Jacobs, Maier, and Stolurow (1966) compared three educational treatments – three methods of teaching Spanish to sixth-grade pupils in the public schools of Denver. One method involved only the use of a semester-long televised self-instructional program; a second method was conventional instruction by teacher only; and the third method was a combination of the televised program and a teacher. In all cases, the time devoted to instruction was the same. All the pupils had studied Spanish as fifth graders by means of a televised course of instruction.

Three kinds of criterion measures were obtained; we shall be concerned with only two of them: Scores on an achievement test in Spanish and scores on a scale for measuring interest in Spanish as something to study and practice. Three measures of personal characteristics were obtained prior to the treatments; these were (1) scores on a Spanish listening test, (2) IQ's based on the Kuhlman–Anderson Intelligence Test, and (3) scores on a brief questionnaire intended to measure interest in Spanish. The purposes of the study were to compare the three treatment methods with respect to criterion performance and to discover if there was an interaction of the treatment methods with personal characteristics – to find out if some methods were superior for certain subgroups of pupils.

The Maier–Jacobs study is unusual in that the class rather than the individual student was used as the unit of analysis. Usable data were obtained for 77 classes, 48 of which were program-taught, 14 teacher-taught and 15 taught by both teacher and program. The means for classes were used in the analysis rather than scores for the 900 or so pupils who participated. Therefore the interpretations of results have to be made in terms of school classes with certain mean scores rather than in terms of individual pupils.

So far as the main effects are concerned, the analysis showed, as would be expected, that achievement in Spanish is related to mean aptitude level of the class; and it also showed that achievement is related to treatment method. The TV program-only classes were clearly inferior to the other treatments, when allowance was made for initial differences in aptitude by using covariance analysis techniques. No interaction of personal characteristics and treatment was found for the achievement criterion. An obvious conclusion might be that the program-only treatment should be dropped.

However, the outcomes involving interest in Spanish as something to study and practice are also important, since further learning is likely to be a function of interest. Using the interest criterion, no significant main effect was found for either aptitude level or treatment. There was, however, a significant person-treatment (or, rather, a class-treatment) interaction. When the teacher-plus-program method was used, high interest was associated with high aptitude and low interest with low aptitude; but when the teacher-only method was used, high interest tended to be associated with the low-aptitude classes. To maximize interest of low-ability classes, it would be somewhat better to use the teacher-only method.

It would be easy to make a recommendation for the high-aptitude classes: one should use the combined teacher-program method to maximize both interest and achievement. For low-ability classes, none of the methods produced high achievement; but since the teacher-only method did at least tend to maximize interest, perhaps it should be used. Still better, one should try to invent another method that might improve both interest and achievement of low-ability classes.

Phonics and whole-word treatments in reading   Cronbach and Snow described in their 1969 summary a study by Stallings and Snow. The evidence of person-treatment interactions is quite striking, considering the small number of cases involved. Twenty first graders were assigned to one or the other of two reading classes; one was taught by a phonics method and the other by look-say (whole-word) method which was supposed to involve meaningfulness to a greater extent. Criterion information included a measure of "learning avoidance," which was based on systematic observations of such indicators as fidgeting, fighting, fooling, distracting neighbors, etc. Other criteria were scores on two reading tests: the California Achievement Test in Reading and the Murphy–Durrell Reading Readiness Analysis. The person variables were various psycholinguistic and memory abilities. The purpose of the study was to see if the effectiveness of the two teaching methods might depend upon the abilities of the children.

In several instances the difference in slopes of regressions is striking, although the number of variables is too large and the amount of data too small to justify firm conclusions without replication. For the regression of learning avoidance on a measure called visual-motor sequencing, the regression lines cross and are almost perpendicular; the more meaningful look-say method was most effective for children who were good visual sequencers, while the phonics method was almost equally effective for children who were poor visual sequencers. Using California reading test scores as the criterion and a measure of auditory sequencing as the predictor, the picture is about the same, with the look-say method best for good sequencers and the phonics method better for poor sequencers. Cronbach and Snow speculate that the look-say method may require the child to depend on his own sequencing abilities and short-term memory, while the phonics method, with its analytic, structured drill, provides a substitute for these abilities and may be boring for the more able children. Replications of this study were reported to be in progress.

Two methods of teaching arithmetic   G. L. Anderson completed a Ph.D. dissertation at the University of Minnesota in 1941 which is unpublished but has been summarized by Cronbach (1967). This research antedated the recent wave of interest in aptitude-treatment interactions, but in many ways it appears to be a model of how to do such research. The study involved a comparison of two methods of teaching arithmetic to fourth graders. One method stressed drill and practice, the other attempted to develop understanding of the meanings of arithmetic operations. Pupils were assigned randomly to the method groups, and instruction continued for a year. Two measures of personal characteristics were employed; one was a test of general ability (the Minneapolis School Ability Test) and the other was a survey test in arithmetic. The criterion measures were a variety of scores reflecting competence in arithmetic. The Johnson–Neyman (1936) method was used in analyzing the data. Results were similar for most of the criterion measures; they showed that the *difference* between the two input measures — general ability and arithmetic achievement — was important in choosing the best treatment for particular children. More specifically, the drill method was better for children who were initially good at arithmetic but of low general ability, while the meaning method was better for pupils who were bright but initially poor at arithmetic. Cronbach and Snow suggest as an interpretation that the children who were initially good at arithmetic were those who had learned to profit from the kind of instruction that characterized schools in the

1930's and which presumably resembled the drill method; while bright students who had failed to learn arithmetic by such methods profited from a new approach which may have been more interesting or may have provided insights that made the enterprise seem more worthwhile. The study is of particular interest because of its demonstration of a somewhat more complex sort of interaction, one involving the relationship between the two person variables that were employed.

Two methods of teaching mathematical concepts   Kropp, Nelson, and King (1967) performed a series of studies that were largely oriented around the idea that certain of the abilities comprising Guilford's structure of intellect model would differentiate students who would profit from different kinds of instruction. In one of their studies, two instructional programs were prepared to teach vector multiplication and the taking of derivatives. One program employed frames in which the ideas were stated verbally (e.g., "The product of two vectors, when the vectors are expressed as ordered pairs of real numbers, is defined by the following three steps") and the other used frames in which the same ideas were stated algebraically. The expectation was that students who do well on tests involving Guilford's semantic abilities would learn better from the verbal programs, while students who do well on the tests of symbolic abilities would do better on the algebraic programs.

The results did not support the hypothesis, but they did reveal an interaction that might be of considerable educational significance. The regression of the criterion score on ability test score was generally steeper for the verbal program than for the algebraic program, regardless of whether the ability test was supposed to measure semantic ability or symbolic ability. Cronbach and Snow offer an interpretation that is based on the notion that both the semantic and symbolic ability tests can best be considered as measures of general ability; thus the findings really show that the verbal program is better for learners of high general ability and the less conventional algebraic method is better for those of low general ability. Thus an alternative method of teaching is available that will permit the less able students to improve their performance.

These studies represent a more-or-less random selection from those that Cronbach and Snow feel were methodologically among the best. They conclude their review by saying that progress toward understanding aptitude-treatment interactions has been slight, that "there are no solidly established ATI relations even on a laboratory scale and no real sign of any hypothesis ready for application and development." But they strongly urge that the search be continued. "To abandon the ATI model," they say, "is to assume that there is only one path toward educational development, and that individual differences have no implication save the fatalistic one of telling the educator that some pupils will advance more rapidly than others no matter what he does." It does, indeed, seem inconceivable that the best methods of learning would not be different for pupils with different patterns of personality, background, and ability.

Person-Situation Interactions in Organizations

The field of organizational psychology deals in general with the performance of individuals working together in groups toward some goal, usually to produce goods or services. The executives and bureaucrats who are responsible for creating and managing organizations must be concerned about such human problems as how to select and train those individuals who are to be a part of the organization, how best to assign work to them, how to create conditions and climates that are conducive to high productivity, and how to create and manage systems of rewards and sanctions that will be effective in controlling the performance of members of the organization. The organizational psychologist of today views the organization as "a complex social system which must be studied as a total system if individual behavior within it is to be truly understood" (Schein, 1965).

Such a conception strongly implies the existence of person-situation interactions, as many organizational psychologists have recognized. Schein states that "We cannot understand the psychological dynamics [of the relationship between the individual and the organization] if we look only to the individual's motivations or only to organizational conditions and practices. The two interact in a complex fashion, requiring us to develop theories and research approaches which can deal with systems and interdependent phenomena." Dunnette (1963) remarked that, "Everyone recognizes the possibility of situational effects on the validity of psychological predictions, but there is a paucity of research designed to estimate systematically the magnitude of such effects." The idea of person-situation interactions came up repeatedly at a conference held in 1959 at the Harvard Business School (Tagiuri, 1961) to discuss the directions in which research should go in studying problems in the selection of executive personnel. Sells' (1963b) report of a conference on the stimulus determinants of behavior emphasized interaction theory, but it gave few specific illustrations of person-situation interactions. In spite of wide recognition of the potential importance of person-situation interactions, it is difficult to find methodologically sound studies that demonstrate such interactions in the domain of organizational performance. Well-established principles involving interactions of personal and situational characteristics are as rare in organizational psychology as they are in education.

A few examples that do imply the existence of person-situation interactions in organizational settings are described briefly below.

The contingency model of leadership   Fiedler (1967a,b) has developed a theory of leadership in which the notion of person-situation interactions is prominent. The person variable he is concerned with may be viewed as a composite of two concepts that have been widely used in studies of administrative behavior— *consideration* and *initiating structure* (Hemphill, 1950). At one end of Fiedler's scale of leadership style is the *relationship-oriented* person who is high on consideration and low on initiating structure: he tends to be considerate of the feelings of members of his group, permissive, and nondirective. At the other end of the scale is the *task-oriented* leader, who is low on consideration and high on initiating structure: he is directive, dictatorial, and tries to "initiate structure" by controlling the behavior of others. Fiedler has developed a test to measure this leadership characteristic and administered it to leaders of a wide variety of groups—basketball teams, surveying parties, military combat crews, small business concerns, and laboratory teams. The correlation between scores on the leadership test and measures of group performance have been high, he reports; but sometimes the correlation is positive and sometimes negative. For some situations, high performance of the group is associated with the relationship-oriented style of leadership, and for other situations high group performance is associated with the task-oriented style of leadership.

The situational variable that determines whether the correlation shall be positive or negative, according to Fiedler's contingency model of leadership, is the favorableness of the situation for the leader. Favorableness is defined in terms of three characteristics of the situation: group atmosphere, position power, and task structure. By dichotomizing on each of these three characteristics, Fiedler generates eight categories of groups; these groups can be arranged in order of favorability for leadership. The most favorable group is one characterized by good leader-member relations, a structured task, and a strong leader position; the least favorable group is characterized by poor leader-member relations, and unstructured task, and a weak leadership position.

Fiedler's evidence in support of the contingency theory consists of correlations (Spearman's *rho*) between measures of group performance (e.g., accuracy of bombing) and the measure of leadership style preferred by the group leaders. For groups that are intermediate with respect to favorability for leadership, the median *rho* is found to be in the neighborhood of 0.50, while for groups that are at the extremes (either very favorable or very unfavorable for leadership), the median *rho* is about −0.50. Thus the evidence would appear to constitute quite striking evidence of a person-situation interaction in the area of leadership.

Research dealing with the contingency model of leadership has recently been reviewed by Graen, Alvares, Orris, and Martella (1970). They distinguish between the antecedent and the evidential studies − those used by Fiedler in developing the contingency model of leadership and those used in testing it. Using data from the antecedent studies, a plot of the mean *rhos* against the measure of favorableness for leadership shows that negative correlations between leadership style and group performance do occur in situations that are favorable and are unfavorable for leadership, and positive correlations occur in situations that are intermediate with regard to the favorableness-for-leadership scale. The *eta* (nonlinear correlation) between *rho* and favorability for leadership is 0.59. But a similar plot based on data from the evidential studies shows no such tendency, and the *eta* turns out to be 0.04. The authors criticize Fiedler for certain of his research procedures and conclude that the evidential data they review cast grave doubts on the plausibility of the contingency model of leadership effectiveness. The possibility remains, however, that still other situational variables of a broader and more general nature influence the operation of the person-situation interaction itself; in other words, it is possible that the contingency model of leadership is appropriate only in certain varieties of organizational situations.

Effects of participation in decision making on attitudes and performance
Vroom (1959, 1960) hypothesized that the attitudes and performance of supervisors might vary with their opportunity to participate in decision making regarding company operations, and that the effects of such participation might also be a function of certain personal characteristics of the supervisors.

The subjects in his investigation were 108 supervisors employed by a company whose business was the delivery of parcels from department stores. The personal characteristics that Vroom thought might interact with amount of participation in decision making were Need for Independence and Authoritarianism. Authoritarianism was measured by means of 25 items from the F scale (Adorno, Frenkel–Brunswik, Levinson, & Sanford, 1950), and Need for Independence was measured by a 16-item questionnaire (e.g., "When you have a problem, how much do you like to think it through yourself without help from others?"). The situational variable, amount of Participation in Decision Making, was also measured by a questionnaire (e.g., "Does your immediate superior ask your opinion when a problem comes up which involves your work?"). Vroom defends the use of a self-report method for measuring participation on the grounds that one's *perception* of the amount of participation is more important than the actual amount, so far as the interaction effects are concerned. The danger, of course, is that experimental dependencies may be introduced by the use of self-report measures for both the personal and situational variables in the investigation.

Criterion measures included both an attitude or job satisfaction measure and ratings of job performance by supervisors. Attitude was measured by means of still another questionnaire (e.g., "How well do you like supervisory work?"). Ratings were made by the immediate superiors of the subjects and produced two scores — an overall performance evaluation and a summary appraisal.

The hypothesis to be tested was that participation in decision making would have different effects on attitudes for people with different personality characteristics. The hypothesis was tested by comparing the correlation of participation scores with each criterion measure for subgroups of subjects representing thirds of the score distribution for Need for Independence and for Authoritarianism. Thus the method of analysis is similar to the one frequently employed in studying moderator variables. In this case, the Participation score is considered to be the predictor variable, and the personal characteristics are the moderator variables.

For the total group, correlations between amount of participation in decision making and the criterion measures were low and positive, indicating a slight tendency for participation to be associated with favorable attitude and with high performance ratings. The correlations computed for the subgroups demonstrated the expected moderator effects; for example, the correlations with attitude for the three levels of Need for Independence were 0.55 for the high group, 0.31 for the middle group, and 0.13 for those in the lowest third on Need for Independence. Assuming a causal relationship, opportunity to participate in decision making was especially effective in improving attitude toward the job for those with high need for independence. The corresponding correlations for the three subgroups on Authoritarianism were 0.03, 0.35, and 0.53, indicating that opportunity for participation in decision making improves attitude particularly for those who are low on the Authoritarian scale. Similar but less striking differences were found for the ratings of performance. Although the N's are small, the results do suggest that person-situational interactions exist, and the interactions appear to make psychological sense. The results would have been more convincing, however, if the measures of participation, personality, and attitude had not all been self-report instruments filled out by the same individuals.

Perceptions of innovative behavior and organizational climate   A study by Forehand (1963) deals with the area of person perception in an organizational context. Since evaluation of performance in real organizations is likely to require an investigator to use rating procedures of some sort, a study of factors that influence the perception by peers and superiors of a worker's performance is an important area of research in organizational psychology. Forehand was concerned particularly with the effects of the rater's attitude on ratings of performance, and the effects of the organizational climate on ratings of performance. In other words, he was looking for interactions involving attitudes of raters, organizational climate, and perceptions of performance.

The subjects in his investigation were 188 administrators employed by 30 different agencies of the federal government. Each subject filled out a questionnaire describing the climate of his organization, and he was rated on a variety of characteristics by one peer and by his immediate superior. The dependent measure of primary interest was a forced-choice inventory intended to measure innovative behavior of the subjects; it was filled out by the peers and superiors. The peers and superiors also responded to a forced-choice measure of attitude toward innovation that required them to choose adjectives describing an "ideal government executive."

Two hypotheses were tested. The first hypothesis was that the correlation between a rating on innovative performance of subjects and a global rating of their administrative ability would be higher for raters who claim to value innovation highly than for those who do not. The second hypothesis was that the correlations between the innovation ratings and the global ratings would be higher in organizations whose climate is perceived by the subjects as democratic or group centered than in organizations perceived as bureaucratic or rule centered.

The method involved comparison of correlations based on high and low groups of 60 persons each. In the case of the first hypothesis, the 60 highest and 60 lowest subjects were selected on the basis of the attitude-toward-innovation scores of their superiors. Similarly, the highest and lowest group of subjects were selected on the basis of attitude-toward-innovation scores of their peers. Correlations between the innovation rating and the global rating of subjects were computed for each group of 60 subjects. As predicted, the correlation between ratings of innovation and global administrative ability is higher if the raters value innovation highly than if they do not. The correlations are 0.51 and 0.12 for superiors with favorable and those with unfavorable attitudes toward innovation, respectively; and the corresponding correlations for peers are 0.46 and 0.02. Presumably the results can be interpreted in the light of different conceptions of what constitutes a good administrator in the global sense: raters who value innovation are more likely to give a high subjective weight to innovation in making their global rating.

The results for the second hypothesis were less striking and were in fact not consistent. A subgroup of 60 subjects was selected whose ratings indicated they worked in democratic, or group-centered, organizations; and another subgroup was selected who worked in bureaucratic, or rule-centered, organizations. The magnitude of the correlation between ratings of innovation and global administrative ability were higher for subjects in rule-centered than in group-centered organizations if the ratings were made by superiors; but if ratings were made by peers, the correlation was higher for group-centered organizations. (The correlations were 0.12 and 0.27 for group- and rule-centered organizations, respectively, with ratings by superiors; and the corresponding correlations were 0.35 and 0.14 with ratings by peers.) Thus a more complex interaction involving both kind of rater and kind of organization is found. Persons perceived as innovative by peers will be given high global evaluations if the climate of the organization is seen as democratic; but persons perceived as innovative by superiors will be given high global evaluations if the climate is seen as bureaucratic. Forehand proposed the following interpretation: in democratic organizations there is opportunity for peers to cooperate in developing solutions to problems, the solutions then being passed on to the superior for review; thus the peers but not the superior have an opportunity to observe the innovative behavior. In bureaucratic organizations, on the other hand, there is less likelihood that peers will collaborate in solving problems, and problem solving will therefore be an individual activity; thus the superior and not the peers will have an opportunity to observe and evaluate innovative ability. The evidence for such a complex interaction involving type of judge as well as type of organization is tenuous indeed; but it is interesting to note the possibility that the role of a situational moderator can be reversed by another situational variable.

These are some of the more familiar examples of studies purporting to demonstrate person-situation interactions in organizational psychology. Although many psychologists have given lip service to the idea, few have produced persuasive evidence that such interactions exist in important areas of behavior. There seems to have been almost no attempt to replicate studies, with the notable exception of the contingency model of leadership, where the results of replication attempts have been discouraging. One might conclude that this line of work is doomed to failure and go on to other things. But the idea of person-situation interaction seems so reasonable, and we see (or think we see) so many instances of interactions in the lives of people around us, that we recommend continuation of the search. Cronbach and Snow concluded their review of aptitude-treatment interaction research in a similar vein. Their advice as to how to proceed seems as applicable to organizational and other areas of psychology as it does to education.

The reasons for inconclusive results in studies of ATI, according to Cronbach and Snow, include inadequate formulation of problems, inadequate instructional treatments (often because they are too brief or too artificial), too few experimental subjects, and inadequate statistical analysis. What we need most of all, Cronbach and Snow feel, is a better theoretical conception of the phenomenon under investigation, and one way to achieve a better theory is through detailed analysis of process. Process analysis would undoubtedly be improved by spending a good deal of time observing and engaging in clinical investigations of individuals who are performing the tasks under investigation.

The statistical models employed in evaluating ATI were in general considered inadequate by Cronbach and Snow; but the educational researchers have generally employed more appropriate and sophisticated methods of analysis than have the organizational psychologists. The next section will review some statistical models that would be appropriate for analyzing data from the point of view of discovering person-situation interactions. The final section in this chapter will discuss the need for better ways of conceptualizing the domain of situational variation and will present suggestions for the development of a taxonomy of situations.

STATISTICAL MODELS FOR PERSON-SITUATION INTERACTIONS

The analysis method typically used in the organizational research seems to have consisted merely in comparing correlations between contrasting groups of subjects, often without even looking to see if differences in correlations might be accounted for by differences in variability or reliability of measures. The educational research has in general employed more appropriate methods of analysis, such as the analysis of covariance techniques in which significance tests are employed in evaluating differences in regressions. But in a complex multivariate experiment in which a number of predictors, criterion variables, and situations are employed, still more sophisticated analytical methods may be required. We may, for example, need to investigate the effects of experimental treatments on the pattern of interrelationships among a set of dependent variables as well as upon slopes and intercepts of regressions, and we may find it necessary to inquire how the moderating effect of one situational variable is influenced by another more general situational condition.

The simplest kind of evidence for the existence of a personal-situational interaction is merely a significant difference in correlation between two measures of performance for groups that differ with respect to a situational factor of some sort. For example, if the correlation between a mathematical aptitude test score and achievement in a statistics course is zero for students taught by means of a teaching machine and 0.60 for students taught in a conventional classroom, one might conclude that teaching method interacts with mathematics ability in the learning of statistics. This would be called an instance of ATI (aptitude-treatment interaction) by educational psychologists.

One must of course do more than judge that the two correlations look different in magnitude before concluding that he has discovered a moderator variable, since correlations can differ for many reasons. For example, the low correlation for one of the groups might result from low variability or low reliability of one or both of the measures. An analysis of covariance model would be a better procedure for comparing the relationships for the two groups. The Gulliksen–Wilks (1950) method, for example, provides successive tests for three null hypotheses: equal errors of estimate, equal slopes, and equal intercepts of the regression lines. Beaton (1964) has extended the analysis of covariance procedure to cross-classified designs. The existence of a moderator effect would be demonstrated by finding that the regressions differed significantly with regard to slope. An analysis of variance provides analogous information in cases where the data are not continuous.

Saunders (1956) proposed a somewhat more elaborate model for moderator effects, which is a multivariate curvilinear regression based on a polynomial expansion. Since it assumes that the moderator variable is a continuous variable, it would probably be more often useful for moderator variables that correspond to personal characteristics than those that correspond to situations; but theoretically the model is applicable to any kind of continuous variable. The model is curvilinear in that it includes in the regression equation the product of the predictor and moderator variable scores as well as the variables themselves. It is a curvilinear model in a limited sense, since no squares or higher powers of the variables are employed. What this amounts to, in the case of one predictor and one moderator, is a prediction formula in which the weight assigned to the predictor depends upon the magnitude of the moderator score. In spatial terms, the model produces a curved regression surface rather than a regression plane, but it is curved only in the sense that the slope of the linear regression of criterion on predictor variable changes systematically as one moves from low to high values on the moderator variable.

Rock, Barone, and Linn (1967) have provided a method for identifying multiple moderators. Their computer program can form subgroups of individuals who are homogeneous with respect to scores on a set of moderator variables and who are maximally predictable on the basis of one or more predictor variables. In the case where the predictors are personal variables and the moderators are situational characteristics, the existence of a multiple moderator effect would demonstrate a person-situation interaction, just as in the case of a single moderator; in addition, it provides an empirical method for searching systematically for situational variables that jointly define a subgroup of individuals who differ in predictability from other subgroups.

Tucker's (1963, 1964, 1965, 1966) three-mode factor analysis provides still another statistical method for studying person-situation interactions. The method can be applied to instances where data can be classified in three ways or modes. For example, it would be possible to obtain data describing behaviors classified in terms of (1) subject displaying the behavior, (2) the nature of the behavior, and (3) the situation in which the behavior occurred. Ordinary factoring methods can be applied if the data are collapsed to form a two-mode matrix. If the data are collapsed across situations, we have a subject by behavior matrix, and factors in the domain of the behaviors may be identified. If the data are collapsed across people, we have a behavior by situation matrix, and factors in the domain of situations may be identified. A factor, in this case, would be defined as a cluster of situations that resemble one another with respect to the kinds of behavior they elicit. The next step in a three-mode factor analysis produces a reduced three-mode matrix showing relationships between behavior factors, situation factors, and person factors. If person factors are found, the existence of an interaction between persons and situations has been demonstrated. Each person factor can then be interpreted in terms of its slice through the reduced three-mode matrix; this slice contains "loadings" that describe what behavior factors are associated with each situation factor for an idealized subject who represents the particular person factor. Chapter 11 describes the results of a three-mode factor analysis of a person by behavior by situation data matrix based on data from the present investigation.

In addition to "first-order" interactions of the sort described above, where the behavior displayed by an individual depends upon both his personal characteristics and the nature of the situation in which he behaves, it is at least possible that higher-order interactions exist. A higher-order interaction would exist when the nature of the person-situation interaction varied, depending upon other conditions (situations) that might be more general or more extensive in time than those involved in the first-order interaction. In a later chapter, data will be presented that appear to demonstrate such a higher-order interaction.

WHAT IS A SITUATION?

At some point it is going to be necessary to face the problem of defining *situation*, if we are to consider seriously how to deal with variance attributable to both subjects and situations in predicting behavior. A situation is usually thought of as a particular combination of circumstances that persists for a short time. The hero in a novel faces a "situation" when the door to his room bursts open and in storms a man with blazing guns. But other uses of the term imply much greater stability; we say a house is well situated on a lot, or a man has a good situation in his company. If there is to be any generality to scientific work involving situational variables, it will obviously be necessary to rule out situations that are so temporary and so characterized by a large number of elements that they are unique. Our definition will have to be sufficiently general to permit many instances of a particular situation to occur, if we are to obtain data from many subjects and if the definition is to be useful in prediction. It will also be necessary somehow to identify the salient aspects of a many-faceted situation in order to deal with the parts that are the important determiners of behavior. The design in the wallpaper was probably not salient in the situation where our hero faces the man with blazing guns. For purposes of psychological investigations, the following definition is proposed: a situation is a set of circumstances that is likely to influence the behavior of at least some individuals, and that is likely to recur repeatedly in essentially the same form.

The following section will discuss more fully the problem of identifying such classes of situations that are likely to be of scientific value and empirical methods that might be used in developing taxonomies of situations.

DEVELOPING A TAXONOMY OF SITUATIONS

A taxonomy is merely a useful way of classifying phenomena, whether they be books, plants, people, or ideas. It is a way of simplifying a complicated universe in order to make it easier to deal with, both conceptually and practically. Scientific advances are greatly facilitated by the availability of comprehensive and unambiguous classificatory systems.

Any classification system is to some degree arbitrary. One might sort the books in his library on the basis of size, so that they will fit on particular shelves; he might sort them on the basis of color in order to create esthetic effects; or he might sort them into categories of books he might want to consult for particular purposes, to reduce the amount of searching he would have to do in finding appropriate references. Taxonomies can be purely descriptive, or they can to various degrees represent a theoretical orientation. The periodic table represents not only a classification of the elements but also what has proved to be a useful theory about the nature of matter.

In psychology we have few well-established taxonomies except in the domain of individual differences. We do not have accepted taxonomies of situations. In this section we shall consider some possible criteria for choosing one taxonomic system rather than another and some empirical procedures that might be employed in constructing taxonomies.

Taxonomies of Attributes and Taxonomies of Individuals

In thinking about development of taxonomies, it is important to distinguish between taxonomies of *attributes* and taxonomies of *individuals*.

The taxonomies employed to describe individual differences in psychology are classifications of attributes of people, not classifications of the people themselves. The categories in the classifications are entities like *ideational fluency* and *extroversion*, not groups of people. In biological taxonomies, on the other hand, the elements are categories composed of the organisms themselves, such as oak, maple, pine, and hemlock trees. The difference is surely not accidental. The analog of *species* in biology would be *types* in psychology, and many attempts by psychologists to develop typological classifications of people have not survived, presumably because as many people fall between the idealized types as fit them. Such is not the case in dendrology: oaks, maples, and pines can all be identified, even by a novice, and no individuals are found that fall between the oak and the maple. Such a claim cannot be made for distinctions between extroverts and introverts (Jung, 1922), among theoretic, economic, esthetic, social, political, and religious types (Spranger, 1928), or among erotic, compulsive, and narcissistic types (Freud, 1932).

Both taxonomies of attributes and taxonomies of individuals would presumably be useful, but since the criteria and the procedures for developing classificatory schemes might differ, it will be well to discuss them separately.

Taxonomies of Attributes in Psychology

In psychology we have reasonably satisfactory taxonomies in the domain of individual differences, even though there are competing and overlapping classificatory systems based on different methods of observation. In the realm of cognitive abilities, for example, we have J. P. Guilford's (1956, 1967) structure-of-intellect model, represented by a $4 \times 5 \times 6$ solid. The three dimensions of the solid correspond to (1) four kinds of *content* (figural, symbolic, semantic, and behavioral), (2) five kinds of psychological *operations* (cognition, memory, divergent production, convergent production, and evaluation), and (3) six kinds of *products* (units, classes, relations, systems, transformations, and implications). The model thus implies the existence of 120 unique abilities (e.g., the ability required to "evaluate semantic transformations"). This classification of cognitive abilities is based more on observation and logic than on empirical procedures and might be described as "facet theory," a term used by Guttman (Guttman & Schlesinger, 1965) to describe the use of facets, or logical dimensions, to guide the development of tests. The existence of many of the abilities defined by the cells in the structure-of-intellect model have been verified empirically, and the model has proven to be very useful. The distinction between convergent and divergent thinking, for example, has been widely employed by psychologists and has contributed to clarifying the research problems in such areas as creative behavior.

Another taxonomic system in the realm of cognitive ability is based on the work of L. L. Thurstone and his many students, who used empirical methods (factor analysis) in their search for independent cognitive abilities. A number of separate (but usually correlated) abilities, such as induction, deduction, perceptual speed, spatial ability, verbal meaning, and ideational fluency, have been identified. The number of such separate abilities is not known, but French, Ekstrom, and Price (1963) selected tests to measure 24 of these abilities in preparing their *Manual for Kit of Reference Tests for Cognitive Factors*. They might have chosen more. The kit has been widely used in investigations involving cognitive abilities, and the use of a common set of measuring instruments has made it possible to draw inferences based on studies done by many different investigators.

An interesting feature of the taxonomy of abilities based on factor studies is that, since factors are usually correlated, it is possible to demonstrate a hierarchical arrangement of abilities. By factoring the intercorrelations of first-order factors, second- and third-order factors may be found. These higher-order factors provide a still more parsimonious way to categorize the universe under consideration, just as in classifications of plants and animals one may proceed from family through genus to species —from very broad to more narrow and possibly overlapping categories.

In the domain of personality there similarly exists a classification system based largely on the work of factor analysts —Cattell (1957), Guilford (1959), Eysenck (1953), Norman (1963), and many others. One may choose from a relatively short list of personality variables such as Eysenck's (introversion, neuroticism) or from a much longer list, such as Cattell's. Cattell has, in fact, developed an atlas of personality traits designated by a Universal Index numbering system (e.g., Exuberance is UI 21). Again, a hierarchical classification system is possible, based on second- and third-order factors.

The development of taxonomies in the area of individual differences has been pursued more or less independently by psychologists interested in cognition and those interested in personality. A major task is to determine empirically the relationships between factors in these two domains. The problem is made more difficult because of a major difference in the testing methods that are typically used: cognitive measures are generally based on tests of performance (e.g., solving arithmetic problems), while the personality measures are generally based on self-report inventories (answering questionnaires containing items like "Do you sometimes think that people are talking about you behind your back?"). Scores based on the two methods may appear to be more independent than they really are because different methods of measurement are used. A spelling test based on self-report items (e.g., "Are you usually considered a good speller?") would probably correlate more highly with the self-report measures of personality than do the usual tests of spelling that require one to demonstrate his spelling performance.

The multitrait-multimethod approach of Campbell and Fiske (1959) provides one way to find out how much of the variance in scores is based on method. In such an experiment, both kinds of "traits" (ability and personality) would be measured by both methods (performance tests and self-report). Suitable methods of analysis would enable one to find out how much of the test variance is attributable to method and how much to the traits. Such studies need to be done before we have a unified taxonomy of individual differences.

But in spite of such defects and in spite of the fact that our knowledge about individual differences is continually in flux, the two taxonomies of individual differences have proved to be extremely useful in psychological prediction studies. Different investigators can use similar operations to measure a particular facet of individual differences, relationships found by one investigator can be confirmed by another, and the categories in the taxonomic system can be used in the development of theory about human performance.

Taxonomies of Situations

We do not have a comparable taxonomy of situations. The lack of a taxonomy to represent the stimulus side of the S-R formula is interesting in view of the fact that individual differences as a topic in psychology was a relatively late arrival. The early behavioristic stimulus-response notion implied that all the variance in behavior was attributable to the various stimuli impinging on the organism; yet no systematic study of variation in stimuli was made except in very circumscribed domains such as in psychophysics, where sensory experiences (such as hue or pitch) were related to aspects of the physical stimulus (frequency of light or sound waves).

Sociologists have provided us with descriptions of bureaucracies (Weber, 1946) and organizations (March & Simon, 1958), but such descriptions do not contribute as much as one might expect to the development of a taxonomy of situations because they commit the same error that many of the early psychologists did—they ignore individual differences. Max Weber's brilliant description of a bureaucratic organization does not provide information about variations among bureaucracies, and thus descriptions of the variations in situations that might interact with individual differences to produce variations in performance are lacking.

Experimental psychologists of all stripes, including experimental social psychologists, have shown great ingenuity in devising situations for use as experimental conditions in their investigations. But the guiding principle in devising these experiments has, naturally enough, usually been the hypothesis or theory being tested. Such work has not led to the construction of a taxonomy of situations. Perhaps the development and testing of theories would have progressed more rapidly if a taxonomy of situations had been available to guide the work of various investigators and to facilitate the drawing of inferences based on many studies by many independent investigators.

Sells (1963a) states the problem very well: "The most obvious need in evaluating the manifold encounter of organism and environment is a more satisfactory and systematic conceptualization of the environment. This implies a taxonomic, dimensional analysis of stimulus variables comparable to the trait systems that have been developed for individual difference variables.... While work proceeds actively to extend the exploration of individual differences, however, the equally important frontier of situational dimensions is virtually ignored.... Experimenters must have systematic information about relevant dimensions of the environment beyond the piecemeal, concrete, immediate variables customarily observed on the basis of experience."

Methods for Developing Taxonomies

How does one go about developing a taxonomy? The methods historically used in botany seem to have been based on careful observation and good judgment. They certainly cannot be characterized as "armchair" methods, since the field work must have been enormous. At the age of 25 Linnaeus, a student at Uppsala in Sweden, became interested in the classification of plants. He was sent to Lapland in 1732 as a collector of specimens, and in the next five months he traveled almost 5000 miles in Lapland, Norway, and Sweden (at a total cost, we are told, of £25) observing, making notes and drawings, and collecting specimens. He developed a classification of plants based principally on characteristics of stamens and pistils. He sorted plants into 24 classes, primarily on the basis of the number and variations in the stamens, and the 24 classes were divided into orders on the basis of the number and variations in the pistils. The system is thus based on sexual characteristics, with the female parts determining the orders and the male parts the classes. The method seems somewhat arbitrary, at least to a psychologist today. Why were stamens and pistils chosen rather than other morphological characteristics involving leaf, stem, roots, fruit, etc.? What criteria *should* be employed in choosing a taxonomic system?

The aim of the plant taxonomist was then, and still is, to find a classification of plants that would accurately reflect their evolutionary development. The evaluation of taxonomies from that point of view requires information based on fossil remains, geographical distribution, immigration pathways, and chromosomal and biochemical relations as well as morphological features. The course of evolutionary development would seem to be an unlikely reason for seeking a taxonomy of situations. If we are to attempt to develop a taxonomy of situations for use in the behavioral sciences, what criteria can appropriately be used for choosing among the large number of classification systems that are possible?

Development of Taxonomies of Attributes

The empirical method most commonly used for empirically developing a taxonomy of attributes is factor analysis. The procedure involves (1) obtaining a list of variables that encompass the domain of investigation (e.g., cognitive abilities), (2) finding or developing satisfactory methods of measuring these variables (or a sample of the variables), (3) administering the resulting battery of tests to a sample of individuals representative of those possessing the attributes, (4) computing the intercorrelations of the tests, and (5) carrying out the various steps involved in the factor analysis, including rotation of axes. All these are fairly familiar procedures except the first: how does one obtain a list of variables comprising the domain of investigation?

In his early work on personality, Cattell (1946) solved the problem by going to the dictionary. He assumed that any important aspect of human personality would have a name; on this reasonable assumption, he identified the words in the dictionary that were descriptive of personality and used this list to represent the domain. The Thurstones apparently used a variety of methods in assembling their batteries of cognitive tests. They chose items and item types that had previously been used by psychologists in tests of intellectual abilities, but they also made use of what Guttman would now call facet analysis and were guided by a general hypothesis as to what the emerging factor structure might be. They put into the battery tests to represent such facets as verbal, numerical, and visual abilities, and they included tests that would help answer such specific questions as "whether reasoning involves a distinct mental ability which transcends the detailed form on which it is exercised" (Thurstone, 1938, page 11), such as verbal, numerical, or spatial material.

There is no prescription that can be given to the would-be developer of a taxonomy of attributes of situations with regard to how to proceed. Sampling from a population of attributes would be desirable but impractical, since we do not have the necessary roster from which to draw a sample. One should certainly try to take advantage of any existing classification that can be found, and he should make as much use as he can of facet design. In the initial stages of the investigation it would be prudent, one would think, to delimit the search to subtypes of situations, such as classrooms or typing pools, rather than situations in general. Classifying attributes of trees would be a far more feasible undertaking than classifying all living organisms. Ultimately, a taxonomy of situations, if we ever have one, will surely not be the work of any one investigator.

Sells (1963b) has employed a scheme proposed by Sherif and Sherif (1956) to develop an "outline of basic aspects of the total stimulus situation" that should be consulted by anyone embarking on a project to develop a taxonomy of attributes of situations. The outline is quite extensive (it occupies nearly five pages of small type) and it includes such categories as weather (temperature, humidity, oxygen, climate, atmospheric changes), social institutions (family, religion, language, law, etc.), socioeconomic status (social status, income, residence, debts, savings, employment, education, etc.), informal group structure (definiteness, clarity, relation to basic objectives, what the goals are, etc.), regulation of group procedure, etc., etc.

Krause (1970) proposes the following as subclasses of social behavior settings: (1) *Joint working* (which involves a mutual goal and some promise of mutual compensation), (2) *Trading* (which aims to compromise conflict of interest through exchange), (3) *Fighting* (any means of settling a conflict without compromise), (4) *Sponsored teaching* (involves modification of a learner's behavior), (5) *Serving* (one participant receives from another some satisfaction of a need for which the second participant receives some compensation), (6) *Self-disclosure* (revelation of one's opinions to another), and (7) *Playing* (a nonserious approximation of other situations merely for the pleasures of the performance). As Krause points out, wide ranges of variation within these categories are possible, involving physical environments, roles, institutional contexts, and other aspects of the setting as suggested by Sells' outline described above.

One area of empirical investigation that has produced several classifications of attributes of situations is the measurement of college environments (Pace, 1968). An instrument developed by Pace called *College and University Environment Scales* (CUES) is currently in use. Its items are statements that might describe a particular college (e.g., "There is a lot of group spirit"). The items were administered to students, who are presumed to be aware of the college environment, and they respond by judging whether each statement is *true* or *not true*. A statement is assumed to be true about the college if two-thirds or more of the students endorse it, and a score for the institution is obtained by using this standard. A factor analysis of such scores obtained from 50 colleges and universities produced five factors which are the basis for the five scales employed in the current version of CUES. College environments can, according to these studies, be described in terms of measures of five attributes: (1) *Practicality* (characterized by enterprise, organization, material benefits, and social activities), (2) *Community* (friendly, cohesive, group oriented), (3) *Awareness* (concern about personal, poetic, and political meaning), (4) *Propriety* (politeness and decorum), and (5) *Scholarship* (intellectual and scholastic discipline).

Another factor analytic study of college environments (Astin, 1962) was based on 33 items of information obtainable from public sources, such as size, proportion of men, number of fields in which degrees are offered, percentage of Ph.D.'s on the faculty, and budget. Data from 300 schools were obtained. The five factors obtained were named *affluence, size, masculinity, homogeneity of offerings*, and *technical emphasis*. Other attempts to construct taxonomies of college characteristics have been based on subjective categories. The number of categories obtained is typically small, as is true of the factor studies. Surely the diversity among American colleges cannot be adequately described by only five dimensions. A beginning has been made toward the development of a taxonomy of attributes, but we have a long way to go.

Development of Taxonomies of Situations

Combining attributes   Given a list of attributes of a situation, it is possible to generate a classification of the situations themselves merely by taking all the possible combinations of attributes. A description of trees in terms of three dichotomous attributes would generate eight categories of specimens. The three dichotomies might, for example, be broad leaves vs. needle- or scale-like leaves, coniferous vs. nonconiferous trees, and deciduous vs. nondeciduous trees. One of the eight categories defined by these attribute categories contains trees that are deciduous, coniferous, and have needle-shaped leaves and would include the larch and the tamarack; the category formed by deciduous, nonconiferous, and broad-leaved trees would include the so-called hardwoods. An objection to such a procedure is that if there are a large number of attributes, the number of categories of individuals generated would become very large indeed. However, if a large number of these categories turn out to be empty cells, the method still might be feasible. In the tree example, the category defined by deciduous, coniferous, and broad-leaved would turn out to be an empty cell because there is no known tree possessing this combination of attributes. Another problem with the method has to do with how to treat attributes that are continuous measures (such as height). Presumably it would be necessary to dichotomize, trichotomize, or otherwise subdivide such continuous measures.

The Center for the Study of Evaluation at UCLA has used this method of constructing a taxonomy (Hoepfner & Klein, 1970) in developing differentiated norms for schools on verbal and nonverbal tests. The data came from the Coleman study of equality of educational opportunity (Coleman, *et al.*, 1966). Eight attributes of schools were employed, all of which are continuous measures; one was trichotomized and the others were dichotomized. The eight attributes are based on the following questionnaire items:

1. What is the racial balance in your school?
2. How many families of your students are represented at a typical meeting of the PTA or similar parent group?
3. How many volumes do you have in your school library?
4. About what percentage of the students who attended your school last year are now attending a different school? Do not count those who moved because of graduation or promotion.
5. Which best describes the location of your school? (Small town, city, rural, etc.)
6. Which best describes the pupils served by your school? (Parents' occupations)

7. What percentage of the students in your school have mothers who are employed outside the home?
8. Which of the following indicates the area of the country in which your school is located?

Three hundred and eighty-four categories of schools are generated by this classification of attributes (3×2^7). For each category, Hoepfner and Klein report two verbal and two nonverbal scores. A school principal could use the school attribute classification to find which one of the 384 school categories his school belongs in; and by comparing the mean score for his school with the norms for that category, he could find out whether the mean for his school is low, middle, or high in comparison with other schools like his own.

With the large number of attributes that one would ordinarily expect to be associated with situations, the method would undoubtedly generate an astronomical number of categories, and it would be useful only if some further method of data reduction were used.

Cluster analysis   We have suggested that the factor analytic procedures that have been employed in developing taxonomies of personal attributes might also be useful in developing taxonomies of situational attributes, and several examples have been cited of such applications of the method. What empirical methods are available for developing taxonomies of the situations themselves? One of the earliest attempts to develop a measure of similarity was that of Pearson (1926), who developed a "coefficient of racial likeness." R. A. Fisher (1936) developed discriminant analysis for use in taxonomy, reported in an article entitled "The use of multiple measurements in taxonomic problems." This approach is mainly useful, however, if the categories are already known and one wants to minimize error in using variables in assigning individuals to those categories. It is not useful in exploratory studies aimed at the discovery of the categories. Discriminant analysis was generalized by Rao (1948).

A method that is useful for exploratory studies is inverse factor analysis. In any factor study one begins with a vector of attribute scores for each of a sample of individuals. In conventional factor analysis, correlations between all the pairs of attributes are computed and factored. In inverse factor analysis one begins with the same kind of matrix, but computes correlations between all the pairs of *individuals*. A high correlation means that two individuals are similar with respect to their scores on the attributes, and a factor then represents a cluster of individuals all of whom tend to be alike with regard to their attribute scores. Thus, an inverse factor analysis based on a matrix of morphological attributes for a population of trees would presumably yield factors interpretable as oaks, maples, pines, etc.

More generally, there are a variety of methods that are potentially useful in developing taxonomies; these methods are called cluster analysis methods (e.g., Johnson, 1967; McQuitty, 1956; Rubin, 1967; Tryon & Bailey, 1966). Such methods begin with vectors of attribute scores for individuals, as in inverse factor analysis, but the measure of similarity or distance for a pair of individuals is not usually a correlation coefficient. It might be simply the number of characteristics shared by two individuals, a pooled judgment of the similarity of two objects, the Euclidean distance between two vectors (Cronbach & Gleser, 1953; Osgood & Suci, 1952) or a generalized distance measure of a more sophisticated sort (Mahalanobis, 1936). The cluster analysis methods have in common the identification of groups of similar individuals. The clusters themselves may be grouped hierarchically (Friedman & Rubin, 1967; Ward, 1963). Nonmetric multidimensional scaling methods (Kruskal, 1964; Shepard, 1962) may be used to search for clusters if one is unwilling to make metric assumptions about his data. The interpretation of a cluster or hierarchy of clusters (like the interpretation of a factor in conventional factor analysis) depends ultimately on a judgment regarding the characteristics common to the individuals (or attributes) that comprise the cluster (or factor).

The use of numerical methods in plant and animal taxonomy has been increasing in recent years (Sokal & Sneath, 1963), with applications in a wide variety of areas of biology and anthropology. An interesting application of cluster analysis was recently reported in *Science* (True & Matson, 1970) that comes a little closer to our problem of classifying situations. Twenty archeological sites in Chile were described in terms of 74 characteristics, mainly based on bead and stone artifacts found at the sites. Similarity coefficients were computed for the pairs of sites, and a cluster analysis was carried out by one of the methods described by Sokal and Sneath. The method first selects the pairs of sites that are most similar to each other, then progressively adds other sites to the pairs, thus building up clusters of similar sites. Four main clusters were found; they tended to confirm grouping of sites that had previously been made judgmentally. One cluster, for example, contained artifacts suggesting utilization of vegetable foods and a minimum concern with hunting.

A more direct attempt to develop a taxonomy of situations is Hemphill's

(1959) study of characteristics of executive positions. Hemphill developed a questionnaire containing a large number of statements that might be descriptive of some aspect of an executive's position (e.g., "negotiate bank loans for the company"). These items were obtained from literature describing executive behavior, from interviews with executives, and from job descriptions of executive positions. Executives from several companies responded to each item by rating the degree to which it was a part of his position. An inverse factor analysis was performed, using the correlations between pairs of executives who responded to the questionnaire. Ten orthogonal factors were identified, and the interpretation of each factor was based on an investigation of the activities of the executives comprising that factor. The factors did not closely correspond to job titles. The executive positions were classified as follows:

1. Providing a staff service
2. Supervision of work
3. Business control
4. Technical — markets and products
5. Human, community, and social affairs
6. Long range planning
7. Exercise of broad power and authority
8. Business reputation
9. Personal demands
10. Preservation of assets

Since these interpretations of the factors were written in terms descriptive of the executive positions, the statements resemble *attributes* of situations (jobs) in which executives might find themselves rather than the jobs themselves. But methodologically the study fits the cluster analysis rather than the factor analysis design. This classification would obviously be useful in studying interactions of personal characteristics of executives with the characteristics of the positions themselves in predicting performance.

Classification of situations based on elicited behavior   The criterion for determining taxonomic categories implied by the factor and cluster analysis methods so far considered is mutual similarity of the members of the factor or cluster. Such a criterion can be defended on such grounds as objectivity and empirical feasibility. But another criterion for classification could be proposed in the case of a taxonomy of situations. Instead of assigning situations to clusters on the basis of their mutual possession of various attributes, it is possible to group situations on the basis of their tendency to elicit similar behaviors. Such a criterion would seem to be especially appropriate when one's ultimate purpose is the investigation of person-situation interactions in predicting behavior.

The kind of data that is necessary for the empirical development of taxonomic categories by this criterion is rarely obtained. What is needed, for each of a large number of persons, is a record of which of many behaviors are displayed in response to each of many situations. In other words, a three-dimensional data solid is required, the three dimensions representing subjects, behaviors, and situations. Given such a data matrix, our usual practice would be to collapse across situations to form a subject-by-performance matrix and to factor the matrix of intercorrelations of the behaviors. Such a procedure would yield a basis for a classification of behaviors. (We could also collapse across situations and factor the inter-correlations of subjects—an inverse factor analysis. This would yield clusters of people and possibly a basis for a typology.)

Still another possibility is to collapse the data matrix across people, yielding a situation-by-performance matrix. We are suggesting that the correlations between all the pairs of *situations* be computed and that a factor analysis of this intercorrelation matrix be performed. A high correlation between two situations means that they elicit similar behaviors; thus a factor represents a cluster of situations that tend to evoke the same responses. Such factors would constitute the categories in a taxonomy of situations, using the criterion of *similarity of behaviors elicited* rather than the criterion of similarity with respect to attributes.

The steps described above are preliminary to a three-mode factor analysis (Tucker, 1965, 1966). Once factors in the domain of performance and in the domain of situations are obtained, one can go on to the computation of factors in the domain of the subjects, as described in an earlier section. Subject factors may be interpreted on the basis of the relationship between performance factors and situation factors that characterizes each person factor. Thus the model permits one to investigate the role of individual differences as well as performance factors and situation factors.

Data that permit one to perform such an investigation are rare because we do not in one investigation ordinarily evaluate many aspects of performance in each of many situations; more typically, one or two dependent variables are recorded for a control condition plus one or two experimental conditions. Data reported in a monograph by Endler, Hunt, and Rosenstein (1962) are relevant, although the basic datum is a self-report of what the subject *thought* his response would be to each hypothetical situation, rather than a record of actual behavior.

The data were obtained by administering an "S-R Inventory of Anxiousness" to 169 college students. The inventory required the respondent to report the probable intensity of each of 14 possible responses in each of 11 different situations. The responses included, for example, "heart beats faster," "perspire," "enjoy the challenge," "become immobilized"; and the situations included such things as "You are going to meet a new date," "You are starting out in a sailboat into a rough sea," and "You are going into an interview for an important job." A three-mode factor analysis of the data was done by Levin (1965) and reported by Tucker (1965) at the 1964 Invitational Conference on Testing Problems.

The analysis revealed three factors in the domain of the responses reported. These factors are interpreted as General Distress (with high loadings on "get an uneasy feeling," "heart beats faster," "emotions disrupt actions"), Exhilaration ("enjoy the challenge," "seek experiences like this," "feel exhilarated and thrilled"), and Autonomic Responses ("have loose bowels," "need to urinate frequently," "get full feeling in stomach").

The situational factors were also three in number and were interpreted as Interpersonal Stress situations (speech before large group, interview for important job, competitive contest), Dangerous Inanimate situations (on a ledge high on a mountainside, alone in woods at night, sailboat on rough sea), and "Unknown" situations (going into a psychological experiment, starting off on a long automobile trip, going to a counseling bureau to seek help in solving a personal problem). Thus if one uses the criterion of similarity of responses elicited, the taxonomy for this very limited domain of situations and responses would comprise the three categories of interpersonal stress situations, dangerous inanimate situations, and "unknown" situations.

The interpretation of the core matrix that resulted from the three-mode factor analysis showed that there are individual differences with respect to the relationship of response categories to the situational categories. Three person factors were found, each of which can be interpreted in terms of the response made to the situation factors. The idealized person representing Person Factor I tended to report distress and autonomic responses, particularly to the interpersonal stress and dangerous inanimate situations, and he reported little exhilaration. The Person Factor II individual was likely to report exhilaration to all three types of situations, but particularly the inanimate danger situation. The Person Factor III individual reported exhilaration in the interpersonal stress situations and distress and autonomic responses to the inanimate danger situations. These are somewhat oversimplified interpretations of the person factors.

This analysis illustrates quite well how taxonomic categories of situations can be identified by using the criterion of similarity with regard to responses elicited, although in this instance the domain sampled is very small both in terms of situations and responses. It also illustrates how one can handle the problem of how to deal with the problem of individual differences.

The foregoing discussion has contrasted two possible kinds of taxonomies — taxonomies of attributes and taxonomies of individuals — and the discussion may have created the impression that these are competing ideas and that one should choose between the two methods. On the contrary, they may both be useful, and each may be of scientific interest. The effects of cultural and educational influences on the structure or organization of cognitive abilities, for example, is an important kind of problem for psychologists and educators. The development of a classification of attributes, furthermore, might be useful as a first step in the search for a taxonomy of individuals, or types. We are often overwhelmed with the number of variables that are available for use in scientific investigations, and the availability of the attribute categories might enable us more economically to systematically cover a wide variety of attributes in an investigation.

CHAPTER 2

Methods of Data Collection in Social-Psychological Research

Methods of Gathering Information

The problems involved in gathering information about behavior of subjects in a social-psychological experiment are analogous to the problems of measurement in any field of psychology. We should be just as concerned about the standard psychometric questions of reliability and validity when the measures in question are the dependent measures obtained in a psychological experiment as when they are tests of aptitude and achievement for use in personnel selection or in a classroom. Our willingness to reject a hypothesis because of negative experimental findings may be considerably different if we learn that the reliability of the dependent measure is zero.

A proposed classification of methods for measuring the outcomes of training (Frederiksen, 1962b) seems useful also in considering methods for measuring outcomes of experiments in social or organizational psychology. Seven methods were distinguished:

1. Solicit opinions
2. Administer attitude scales
3. Measure knowledge
4. Elicit related behavior
5. Elicit "what-I-would-do" behavior
6. Elicit lifelike behavior
7. Observe real-life behavior

Solicit opinions This method usually involves asking observers to fill out questionnaires or rating scales of one kind or another; the method has been widely used in personality research and in social and organizational psychology, as well as many other areas of behavioral research. It has been shown that it is possible to obtain high reliabilities with rating scales. It is more difficult, however, to demonstrate the validity of rating scales, since they tend to be used when more objective measures of performance are unobtainable.

Rating scales are the method of choice when one is primarily interested in obtaining opinions, impressions, or perceptions of the performance of others. The use of such scales would be especially appropriate, for example, in person-perception studies. Aside from their utility in such investigations, the principal virtues of rating scales are probably their speed and economy. One can seldom be confident that rating scales accurately reflect consistencies in behavior such as one might wish to observe in social-psychological study, particularly if the behaviors are complex or are supposed to be manifestations of some internal state. The common tendencies for raters to be generous in attributing good qualities to people (the generosity error) and their inability to differentiate accurately among various characteristics of people (the halo effect) are well known. If one's purpose is limited to obtaining information about the opinions or perceptions claimed by a subject, the method is face valid, and objections having to do with the lack of correlation with a behavioral criterion are irrelevant. Usually, however, rating scales are used as a device to find out about consistencies in someone's behavior, and for such purposes the method has little to recommend it except economy.

It is not an uncommon practice for investigators to administer to the same subjects rating scales intended to provide both the independent and the dependent measures in a study. For example, ratings of job satisfaction may provide the dependent variable and ratings of the climate of the organization the independent variable. When both ratings are made by the same individuals, an experimental dependency is introduced that admits the possibility that, for example, the raters' conception of the relationship between job satisfaction and climate will determine the relationship found by the researcher. When rating scales are used, it would be prudent to avoid such experimental dependencies by insuring that different judges are used to evaluate the different variables.

Administer attitude scales   The dependent measure in studies of organizational behavior is often an attitude, such as job satisfaction, liking for a particular instructor or supervisor, or approval of a supervisory practice. In its simplest form, attitude measurement is just a way of soliciting opinions, with all the drawbacks mentioned above. But more sophisticated methods of scale construction are available that may result in instruments that are superior to the typical rating scale.

In a Thurstone scale (Thurstone, 1928), each item is a statement that expresses some degree of favorableness to the attitude in question, and one can respond to the item by expressing agreement or disagreement. The scale is composed of items that have been selected on the basis of data that reveal the degree of favorableness to the attitude shown by each item and the accuracy with which the item can be placed on the scale of favorableness. One's score on the attitude scale is merely the average of the scale values corresponding to the items with which he agrees.

The other widely used type of scale is the Likert scale (Likert, 1932), which is based on a quite different approach. No prior judgment about the favorableness or unfavorableness of items is required; the method is merely an application of the techniques of item analysis that are ordinarily employed in building tests of intelligence and educational achievement. The respondent indicates his degree of agreement with each statement in the scale by choosing one of several response alternatives (e.g., strongly agree, agree, undecided, disagree, strongly disagree). Scoring weights of 1 to 5 would generally be applied to these response alternatives. Items are selected on the basis of their discriminating power as measured by their correlation with the total score on the attitude scale, thus insuring some degree of internal consistency among the items.

Attitude scales are susceptible to various kinds of bias due to response sets. One kind of bias that has been demonstrated is an acquiescent response set—a tendency to agree with propositions presented. It has been shown, for example, that positive, rather than negative, correlations are sometimes obtained between scores based on one set of attitude items and another set composed of the same items restated to express the opposite idea. One way of reducing the effect of acquiescence on a scale is to write items in such a way that half are keyed for the *yes* or *agree* response and half for *no* or *disagree*.

Another even more pervasive bias is that due to a social-desirability response set—the tendency to choose those responses that seem most desirable socially, that put the respondent in the best light (Edwards, 1953). Such biases would be a less serious problem if they occurred equally for all subjects; but of course they do not. Some people are much more prone to put themselves in a favorable light than others by choosing socially desirable alternatives; thus the measure of attitude is confounded with the response set. To make matters worse, there may even be different notions among respondents as to what constitutes a socially-desirable response (Messick, 1960).

An obvious way to investigate the validity of an attitude scale is to see if the spontaneous behaviors of subjects are consistent with their scores on the attitude scale. Relatively few studies of this sort have been done (Festinger, 1964). In some cases validities have been found to be strikingly high (Thurstone & Chave, 1929) and in others near zero (Corey, 1937; LaPiere, 1934). The answer undoubtedly depends upon the specifics of a given situation. The related question of the extent to which *change* in attitude is reflected in change in behavior has also received very little attention. Festinger (1964) was able to find only three relevant studies, one dealing with attitudes of mothers regarding the proper age to begin toilet training, one with attitudes of foremen toward employees, and one with attitudes involved in care of teeth and gums. He concluded that "we cannot glibly assume a relationship between attitude change and behavior." It is risky to assume that overt behavior can be predicted from attitude scales and still more risky to assume that change in behavior can be predicted from change in scores on attitude scales. It would seem reasonable to use attitude scales when one is interested in getting information only about opinions (Green, 1967). If one wishes to make generalizations about performance, it would be prudent to try to devise behavioral measures of the variable rather than to use attitude scales.

Measure knowledge   The measurement of knowledge of facts, rules, and principles pertaining to a domain of investigation is of course employed on a massive scale in educational research and practice. Such tests are of value in evaluating educational outcomes as well as in motivating students, informing students (and teachers) of what constitutes the domain to be taught and learned, and for providing feedback to students and teachers with regard to the success of their joint endeavor. Tests to measure knowledge may make use of a great variety of item types — true-false, multiple-choice, matching, fill-in, essay, and many others. Such tests are relatively easy to construct, many can be scored by machine, and they are easily administered to large numbers of people.

The assumption that possession of knowledge will predict performance of tasks related to that knowledge is not always justified. One might, for example, know the principles of good grammatical construction without being able to write fluent and understandable reports. To the extent that measures involved in investigations of social behavior have to do with performance, it seems preferable to try to devise direct measures of that performance rather than measures of knowledge of facts and principles, if one wants to be more confident of the validity of his findings. Scores on a written test of knowledge of good administrative practices will not necessarily correlate highly with performance as an administrator.

Elicit related behavior   For many reasons it may be difficult or impossible to elicit or evaluate behavior that closely corresponds to the ultimate criterion one wishes to measure, and therefore one may resort to the observation of behavior thought to be logically related to that behavior. The evaluation of creativity provides an example. The ultimate criterion of creativity no doubt lies in the production of architectural designs and structures, novels, plays, poems, music, and paintings, or scientific insights and theories. Direct observation of these behaviors is obviously impractical in an experimental setting; even evaluation of the products is exceedingly difficult, especially when comparisons must be made across artistic and scientific domains. The solution to the problem that has been widely adopted by researchers in the area of creativity is to devise tests that elicit behaviors that are thought to be logically related to the grander sorts of creative performance. Getzels and Jackson (1962), for example, in their well-known study of highly intelligent and highly creative adolescents, used five measures of creativity, most of which were originally developed by Guilford (1967). These measures were based on tasks in which the subject was required to (1) give as many definitions as possible to common words like *bark* and *sack*; (2) give as many uses as possible for objects such as a brick and a paper clip; (3) find a given geometric form hidden in more complex geometric figures; (4) provide humorous or sad endings to fables in which the last line was missing; and (5) make up mathematical problems that could be solved using information included in a passage on, for example, the cost of building a house. All these tasks seem to require a good deal of verbal and ideational fluency, ability to change sets, to overcome the powerful associations arising from the customary contexts of words and objects, as well as a certain amount of persistence and willingness to keep trying. All of these things are logically related to production of the truly creative products—the great novel, painting, or scientific discovery. But since the relationship of these "related" behaviors to the ultimate criterion must be inferred, the validity of tests in this category cannot be taken for granted. It is possible, for example, that high production of responses to the five tasks used by Getzels and Jackson is partly a function of one's having low standards with regard to what constitutes a satisfactory response (Klein, Frederiksen, & Evans,

1969), which is an interpretation *not* logically related to the ultimate criterion of creativity.

The method of eliciting related behavior is feasible and practical as a substitute for measuring the criterion behavior itself whenever it is possible to think of behaviors that seem logically related to the criterion and that can be measured more easily than the criterion itself. But since the relationship of the related behavior to the criterion behavior is inferred, validity can never be taken for granted. Evidence of a high relationship between the related behaviors and the criterion behaviors would help to establish the validity of the method, but this is often difficult to do for the very reasons that lead one to use the technique of eliciting related behaviors in the first place.

Elicit "What-I-would-do" behavior   This technique usually involves the presentation of brief descriptions of problem situations each followed by a question or by a set of multiple-choice alternatives. In the multiple-choice form, the respondent answers by choosing the alternative that seems to him to represent the best thing to do in the situation. In the free-response form the question might be, "What would you do?" and the response consists in describing in words what would be a good response to the problem. For example, the situation described in an examination for prospective teachers is as follows: "A student begins working on his homework during a class discussion." A possible response would be to say that you would try to involve the student in the discussion by asking him questions. In multiple-choice form, this response might be presented along with several other possible courses of action.

An objection to the multiple-choice version of such a test is, of course, that the candidate does not have to devise a solution — he merely has to evaluate those presented to him. In real life, problems do not usually present themselves in multiple-choice form and it is necessary to invent the solution rather than to choose one. The free-response form of such a test would be better, from this point of view.

Several other criticisms of the "what-I-would-do" format may be mentioned. One is that the problem situation is typically described so briefly that it is difficult to justify scoring standards; one solution can hardly be defended as clearly better than another in the absence of more detailed information. It might sometimes be claimed that the only defensible answer to the question, "What would you do?" is "It depends." Another criticism is that the free response to the question turns out to be an essay, and the difficulty of evaluating essay material is well known. The respondent of course devises an answer with the aim of earning a high mark from the examiner, and it may or may not represent what his behavior would actually be. The role of verbal facility will probably be greater than it ought to be if we want to get a measure of the examinee's performance in actual problem situations.

Elicit lifelike behavior   In this category are situational tests, or "simulations," that approach the realism of real life but can still be standardized so that all subjects are presented with identical problems under identical conditions. Such tests have the characteristic that the subject is behaving as though he were in a real-life situation rather than saying what he would do or displaying characteristics that are thought to be logically related in some way to the behaviors the experimenter really wants to assess.

The term "simulation" has been applied to those instances in which one attempts to build a laboratory model of a natural or real-life phenomenon of considerable complexity (Guetzkow, 1962). Simulation, in this sense, has been employed in studying reactions to bureaucratic authority (Evan & Zelditch, 1961), performance of school administrators (Hemphill, Griffiths, & Frederiksen, 1962), inter-nation relations (Guetzkow, 1959), business decision making (Cohen, Cyert, Dill, Kuehn, Miller, Van Wormer, & Winters, 1960), and operation of an air defense direction center (Chapman, Kennedy, Newell, & Biel, 1962), to name a few. But simulation has also been used in a different sense, as in computer simulation, to represent a model or a theory of how variables or constructs are supposed to interact in producing certain outcomes. Because of the ambiguity of the term *simulation*, we prefer to call tests in this category *situational tests*.

In a real-life situation, one must wait for suitable opportunities for the behavior we wish to observe to be displayed. These opportunities may be rare, and they almost never appear in equal numbers or in similar contexts for different people. In a situational test, such opportunities are provided equally to all candidates, in similar contexts. If scores can be obtained that have satisfactory properties from a psychometric point of view, they may be acceptable as measures to be used as dependent variables in a psychological experiment. This is the method employed in the investigation reported in later chapters. We shall return to a more detailed description of the situational tests employed.

Observe real-life behavior   This category is often viewed as the "ultimate" measure of performance, the validity of which cannot be questioned. But when examined closely, the process of making observations of performance in real life does not have much to commend it.

A basic requirement for good measurement is that testing conditions be standardized — that all subjects have equal opportunities to display the appropriate behaviors and that there be no unfair constraints that put some subjects at a disadvantage. In real life such conditions are rarely found, even in a work situation where many people are performing similar tasks in the same room. Variations in observed behavior may be attributable to all sorts of situational variations. For example, opportunities for certain kinds of problem solving may arise rarely for some subjects because hard problems are given to those who have displayed a capacity to deal with them. Systematic observation of real-life behavior may also be difficult and costly to carry out. It is for such reasons that in many studies investigators resort to the use of rating scales. Thus we come full circle in our consideration of methods of collecting data in social-psychological investigations.

Use of Laboratory Methods in Social-Psychological Research

It is perhaps paradoxical that observation of behavior in real life is not an ideal method for the scientific study of human behavior. Such a method is generally unsatisfactory not only because of its inadequacies from a measurement point of view, but also because it does not permit the scientist to control conditions in such a way as to permit him to rigorously attribute variation in performance to situational variables. It also does not give him the ability to assign subjects to treatments according to a prearranged plan; consequently he can never be sure that covariation of behavior with situations is attributable to the situations or to some sort of selective factors that tended to put different kinds of people in the different situations. For such reasons the psychologist often prefers to take his problem into the laboratory where he can control the experimental variables and randomly assign subjects to treatments.

Realism   Laboratory methods ordinarily involve a good deal of simplification. In studying certain kinds of problems, especially in the areas of personality and social psychology, it may be necessary to employ situations involving considerable complexity. If one wishes to study experimentally variations in social climate, for example, the laboratory setting cannot be simple. Or in situations where the behavior under study (courtesy, for example) could easily be produced voluntarily but we wish to know to what extent it will occur spontaneously, we may need a very lifelike laboratory situation. The development of an elaborate situational test may provide a way to retain an adequate amount of complexity and realism in an experimental situation while still permitting the experimenter to control conditions rigorously and to assign subjects to treatments in a manner consistent with the design of his study.

Campbell (1957) has made a distinction between *internal validity* and *external validity*. The first refers to consistency or replicability of results within an experimental situation, while *external validity* refers to the generalizability of results — the extent to which results of an experiment can be extended from artificial laboratory settings to complex real-life situations. External validity, according to Campbell, can be maximized by (among other things) increasing the realism of the experimental situation. Vroom (1969), in discussing a similar point, suggests that the most promising approach is "to increase the authenticity of laboratory simulations of organizations . . . ."

Aronson and Carlsmith (1969) make another distinction — that between what they call *experimental realism* and *mundane realism* in a social-psychological experiment. A "simulation" can be realistic in the sense that it accurately mirrors some aspect of the real world, but if it is at the same time boring and dull, it may merely put the subject to sleep. Such realism they call *mundane realism*. But if the situation is realistic in the sense that it interests and captivates the subject, they call it *experimental realism*. They obviously feel that experimental situations should be realistic in the latter sense. The laboratory situation ought to be realistic both with regard to accurately mirroring the world and captivating the subject, if it is to yield externally valid results in Campbell's sense.

Deception and role-playing   There are at least two ways in which a subject may serve in a social-psychological experiment. One method involves some degree of role-playing. The subject in a psychological experiment typically knows that he is serving as a subject and that his behavior is being observed, although he would not ordinarily be told the true purpose of the experiment. One extreme of role-playing would result from his being instructed to pretend to be someone else, such as an employment interviewer or a shop steward, and try to behave as that person would behave. At the other extreme, he would be assigned no such specific role, but he would nevertheless by implication play some role by virtue of his being an experimental subject and thus representing mankind, or college sophomores, or some other population, for the benefit of the experimenter. Role-playing must be involved to some degree whenever a person knows that he is a subject in a psychological experiment, and his behavior may therefore be influenced to some degree by his conception of how the person he is representing ought to act.

There is evidence that such conceptions can influence behavior in experiments, either because the subject wants to make a good impression (Riecken, 1962) or wants to help the experimenter get the results the subject thinks he is seeking. It has been shown that in certain experimental settings subjects will display behaviors that they would be very unlikely to carry out in a real-life situation (Milgram, 1963; Orne, 1962).

In order to avoid contaminating the results of an experiment with subjects' "lay theories" or conceptions about how people ought to behave in certain roles, or how the experimenter expects them to behave, psychologists sometimes employ deception, so that subjects can be put into standard experimental situations without their being aware that they are experimental subjects. Thus behavior can be elicited that is spontaneous and free from any influences attributable to prior conceptions about how people ought to behave in a particular role.

Use of deception is of course not without its problems, including the ethical problems involved in misrepresenting situations to individuals. Even what appears to be an innocuous deception may at least cause some loss of dignity on the part of subjects and may in some instances result in emotional upset or discomfort, even when attempts are made to alleviate such reactions by attempts at debriefing. In addition to the ethical question, there is the question of how successful an attempted deception is in misleading subjects as to the nature of an experiment. A survey by Stricker (1967) of experiments involving deception showed that in many experiments where deception was used, no attempt was made to find out how successful the deception was; and in those cases where such investigations were made, the deception was often only partly successful. Deception is potentially useful, but the experimenter must weigh any possible harm or discomfort to subjects against the presumed scientific value of the study. He must also judge the probable success of the deception and should at the end of the study attempt to find out how well it had succeeded.

Role-playing experiments should be considered as a possible alternative to deception. It is possible that, at least under certain conditions, instructions and experimental tasks can be planned in such a way as to minimize the influence of lay theories and social desirability bias on the results. Brown (1962) favors the use of such methods; he writes, "We believe that a role-playing subject will behave in a way that corresponds more closely to the life situation than a hoodwinked subject will." Probably neither point of view is always right or always wrong; but, as we shall attempt to show, a method of eliciting lifelike behavior can be devised that does not

require deception and that appears to be relatively free from the undesirable aspects of the role-playing experiment.

The in-basket test   The type of situational test employed in this study is
the so-called in-basket test. An in-basket test is a rather elaborate, realistic situational test that simulates certain aspects of an administrator's
paper work. It consists of the letters, memoranda, records of incoming
telephone calls, and other materials that have supposedly collected in the
in-basket of an administrative officer. The examinee is given appropriate
background information about the organization in which he is to be
employed and appropriate office materials, such as memo pads, routing
slips, letterheads, pads of paper, pencils, and paper clips. He is instructed
that he is the incumbent of the administrative job and that he is to respond
to the materials in his in-basket as though he were actually on the job, by
writing letters and memoranda, preparing agenda for meetings, writing
notes or reminders for himself, arranging conferences, or doing anything
else that he deems appropriate. He is asked *not* to pretend to be someone
else, but to behave as though he were actually the incumbent of the new
job.

Scoring methods have been developed that yield reasonably reliable
scores on a number of variables that are of psychological interest. Scores
reflect, for example, tendencies to take final action, to be informal, to use
the discussion method, to interact with superiors, and to procrastinate.

In-basket tests appear to be potentially useful in providing behavioral
measures of personality. Cronbach (1960) makes the point that in contrast
to ability tests, which attempt to measure *maximum* performance, personality tests should measure *typical* performance. Most behavioral
manifestations of personality are under easy voluntary control, at least for
short periods of time, so that if a subject knows or guesses that a certain
characteristic is being measured by a test, he can easily change his behavior in whatever way he considers desirable. The typical personality
inventory is even more obviously susceptible to bias in self-report. Performance tests may provide a better method of eliciting "typical" behavior
that is relevant to the measurement of aspects of personality.

Performance tests of personality have typically required deception of
the subject so that he will be misled as to the real purpose of the test.
In-basket tests, on the other hand, would seem to be capable of eliciting
typical behavior without the need to deceive the subject, because the
range of possible responses is very broad and the instructions provide
such little structure that the subject is not likely to guess what is to be

measured. The subject is asked merely to "be the executive" and do what he deems appropriate, as though he were actually on the job. While the subject may guess that it is desirable to get a lot done and generally to use "good judgment," he cannot possibly know or guess the variety of scoring categories that may be employed in scoring the protocols.

Furthermore, in-basket tests are well adapted to certain kinds of experimental applications, specifically those that can be manipulated by varying the background information presented before the test begins. One can vary the organization experimentally in many ways—for example, by changing the form of organization as portrayed by the organization chart; by changing the personalities of the subjects' superiors or peers as depicted in the background materials; or by changing the purposes or nature of the organization, for example, from commercial to nonprofit. In the present study, the experimental modifications of the simulated organization had to do with its climate. The organizational climates were communicated in many ways, both subtle and overt, and the perceptions of the climate were reinforced during the test by including suitable materials in the in-basket itself.

The next section of this chapter describes the development of in-basket tests and some of the research in which in-baskets were used.

Air Force In-Baskets

The first in-basket tests were developed for use in training evaluation. The Officer Education Research Laboratory of the Air Force Personnel and Training Research Center contracted with Educational Testing Service to study the desired outcomes of training in the Command and Staff School of the Air University and to develop prototype methods to determine how well these objectives were achieved.

A careful study of the curriculum of the Command and Staff School was first undertaken. The method primarily involved asking instructors for statements about changes in performance they hoped to produce in their students. An armchair analysis of several hundred statements obtained from the instructors yielded a classification of behaviors into 12 categories (Findley, Frederiksen, & Saunders, 1954). Six of the categories involved behaviors that are primarily *individual*, that could be exhibited by a person working alone; and the other six were primarily *interactive*, behaviors that involved interrelationships with other people. Four of the individual categories were selected as the primary focus of the evaluating instruments to be developed. These categories had to do with *efficient use of routines* (standard operating procedures, regulations), *flexibility, foresight,* and *effective evaluation of data.* These behaviors seemed to represent important aspects of executive performance.

It was thought desirable to develop as the prototype instrument a test that would tend to elicit the relevant kinds of behavior in a situation that resembled as closely as possible the real job of an Air Force officer. Discussions with Air Force officers revealed that a good deal of the work that they do alone (as contrasted with the interactive behaviors) centers around the contents of one of the two baskets labelled *IN* and *OUT* usually found on the desk of an Air Force officer. Accordingly, it was decided to try to develop a realistic situational test that required the examinee to deal with items in his in-basket.

The first attempts at writing in-basket items were criticized by Air Force officers on the grounds that it was not reasonable to take action on the items because too little information was available, that the "correct" action depended upon a great many unknown factors in the situation. Furthermore, the concept of "completed staff action" was involved; the Commanding Officer required that a proposal for action be evaluated by all the appropriate members of his staff before he decided what to do. Such criticisms showed the necessity of a more elaborate test than had first been envisaged. It appeared to be necessary to provide a rather complete indoctrination of the candidate with regard to the setting of his assignment, a description of the organization, its history, mission, and physical characteristics, as well as tables of organization and equipment, etc. Such a complete indoctrination might take days — far too much time for the prototype test under consideration. The final compromise was a test which involved the device of suddenly placing the examinee in a new position ostensibly because of an emergency, such as the sudden death of his predecessor, and allowing only an hour or so before the test itself to study the background materials. This procedure simulates the not-uncommon requirement that a new executive must begin making decisions before he is fully prepared for his assignment.

The in-basket tests that were prepared and tried out at Maxwell Air Force Base required the candidate to play four roles in succession. In one two-hour period he was Commanding Officer of a hypothetical 71st Composite Wing, located at a fictitious Pine City Air Force Base. In subsequent two-hour periods, on different days, he served as Director of Material, Director of Personnel, and Director of Operations. In each role he was given an in-basket containing incoming letters, memoranda, staff studies, letters prepared for his signature by subordinates, and other similar material. An aide had attached to many of the documents materials from the files that showed what staff action had already been taken. The examinee was given pencils, paper, buck slips, and memo pads and was instructed to work as though he were actually on the job, writing letters or memos, calling meetings, or anything else he deemed appropriate.

The Air Force in-baskets were disappointing from the standpoint of their psychometric properties (Frederiksen, Saunders, & Wand, 1957). In subsequent studies different methods of scoring have been employed that yield more satisfactory reliabilities for many scoring categories.

School Administration In-Baskets

The purpose of the study of school administration (Hemphill, Griffiths, & Frederiksen, 1962) was to try to identify some major dimensions of administrative performance and to investigate the relationships of these major dimensions to a variety of other measurable characteristics of people. Subjects were 232 elementary school principals from a wide variety of elementary schools across the country.

The background material was much more elaborate than for the Air Force study. A day and a half of the five-day test period was spent by subjects in learning about a simulated elementary school (of which each was to serve as the principal) and the community in which it was located. Training materials included a film strip, a sound color motion picture film, and tape recordings of events such as school board meetings, as well as printed materials – a school survey, personnel folders for teachers and staff, floor plans, staff rosters, a staff handbook, the school census, etc. At the end of the orientation period the subjects had about as much information as could reasonably be expected of a new principal in an actual situation.

The balance of the week was devoted to work sessions in which each subject performed the duties of the principal of the Whitman School. His tasks involved participating in committee work (with other subjects), observing and commenting on the performance of teachers (recorded on kinescopes), and reacting to conference situations (presented by means of tape recordings). But the primary means of presenting problems was the in-basket. Four in-baskets were presented, each requiring a half-day session. One of the in-baskets, given at the end of the experimental session, was the Bureau of Business in-basket, about which more will be said later. The other three represented the paper work of the principal on three very busy days of the school year. At the end of the week, each principal left an envelope full of memos, letters, reminders, instructions to his secretary, appointment calendars, and the like, that he had written in response to the problems posed by the items in his in-basket. Methods for scoring these protocols were required, methods that would be reliable and that would reflect important attributes of the work of a school administrator.

The scoring methods that were developed for scoring the in-baskets were essentially the same as those employed in the present study; they are described in detail in Chapter 7. In brief, the scoring method considers each in-basket item as pioviding an opportunity for each listed category of performance (e.g., asking a subordinate for information) to occur; the score is the number of times it did occur. Some of the categories required the scorer to make a judgment about the purpose of the behavior; such judgments were based in part on information provided by a Reasons for Action form filled out by the subject at the end of the in-basket. This form required the examinee to state briefly for each item (1) what he did and (2) why. The information thus provided was of considerable help in scoring some of the categories of performance.

The Air Force and the school administration studies differed in another important way. Each item in the Air Force in-baskets was prepared specifically to elicit a certain preselected kind of behavior judged relevant to the purposes of the training program. The school study, on the other hand, started out with the question of how to identify some important aspects of behavior in administration. This led to a quite different approach in the development of testing materials. Rather than write items to elicit predetermined kinds of behavior, the investigators in the second study tried to build in-baskets that would be representative of the work required in school administration. Items were written to fit a grid that presumably described the job of a school administrator in terms of a set of descriptive concepts. The records of performance in this "representative" job provided the raw material for developing the scoring categories.

The procedure of selecting scoring categories began by examining a number of protocols to see what kinds of variation in performance seemed to be observable. By pooling the observations of a number of people, a large number of cards were collected, each containing a statement of some kind of difference observed in the way principals behaved. The cards contained phrases like "compulsive," "postpones decisions," and "makes unwarranted assumptions." Other ideas for categories came from theories of administration and leadership (e.g., Griffiths, 1959; Hemphill, 1958).

Eventually, by sorting and recombining cards, 68 scoring categories were selected. Reliabilities of the scores based on these categories ranged from zero to 0.97. (The method used for estimating reliability reflected both the degree of reliability of the scorers and consistency in performance of the subjects.) Forty scores were selected for use in subsequent analyses; the reliabilities of these scores ranged from 0.52 to 0.97, with median of 0.78.

The intercorrelations of the 40 scores were computed, and the matrix of intercorrelations was factored. Eight factors were retained; they accounted for most of the common variance in the scores. Rotations were made graphically to produce an oblique factor matrix. The eight factors proved to be interpretable and seemed to make a good deal of psychological sense. The eight primary factors are as follows:

1. *Exchanging information.* Scoring categories with high loadings on this factor included "Asks subordinates for information, opinion, or advice," "Gives information to subordinates," and "Requires further information for deciding."

2. *Discussing before acting.* Those who are high on this factor plan many discussions, tend to use face-to-face communication; and tend *not* to take precipitate action.

3. *Complying with suggestions made by others.* Those who are high on this factor tend to take prompt action on problems, but the actions consist in following suggestions made by others, such as their subordinates or their superiors.

4. *Analyzing the situation.* This factor appears to involve situational analyses of the problems posed by the in-basket items.

5. *Maintaining organizational relationships.* The scoring categories with high loadings on this factor imply concern about superiors and people outside the organization.

6. *Organizing work.* This factor is characterized by care in specifying in advance quite exactly when various things are to be done.

7. *Responding to outsiders.* The four scores with highest loadings in this factor all have to do with people outside the organization; in the school setting, this presumably reflects concern with community relations.

8. *Directing the work of others.* The key to this interpretation is a high loading for "Gives directions and/or suggestions." Other loadings suggest that giving directions to subordinates is likely to be done courteously and in writing.

A second-order factor analysis of the intercorrelations of the eight primary factors yielded two factors. At this higher level of generality one can describe performance on in-basket items in terms of *Amount of work done in handling items* and in terms of a bipolar factor *Preparation for decision vs. taking final action.* The latter has negative loadings in "Concluding decisions" and "Terminal action" and positive loadings on a variety of scores having to do with deciding how to proceed, getting information, and having discussions.

The study of school administration also involved administering to the 232 elementary school principals a large battery of tests, inventories, and questionnaires and investigating the relationships of cognitive abilities, personality, and biographical information to the factors in school administration. It is not appropriate to summarize the findings here, except to state that a number of relationships were found that seem to make psychological sense and that tend to show some consistency in performance across a domain that includes ability tests, personality inventories, and ratings as well as performance in the simulated school.

The Bureau of Business In-Basket

The "Bureau of Business" is a fictitious organization of businessmen and business firms something like the Chamber of Commerce. It was selected as the setting for an in-basket because it requires little technical training or specific job knowledge. Background information about the Bureau is brief, consisting only of a brochure called "The Bureau of Business—What it is and what it does," a table of organization, a job description, and a calendar. The instructions ask the examinee to assume that he has just become the Executive Officer of the Northeastern Division of the Bureau, that he is replacing on short notice a man who died suddenly of a heart attack, and that the boss is out of town. He is further instructed to deal with the items in his in-basket as though he were actually on the job, to take as much action as possible with the information available, to "behave as though you were really on the job." Although the subjects were quite varied in training and experience, they apparently had no difficulty in assuming the duties of the Executive Officer.

Factor analysis studies   The BB in-basket (Frederiksen, 1962a) was administered to 335 individuals, including a few undergraduate students, graduate students of business administration, government administrators (the largest subgroup), business executives in an advanced management seminar, and the faculty of an army logistics management training program. Scoring was done by the same group of scorers and with essentially the same scoring categories used in the school administration study. Reliabilities ranged from zero to 0.87. Forty variables whose reliabilities ranged from 0.19 to 0.87 were chosen for use in a factor analysis; the median reliability of the selected variables was 0.52. The variables used in this analysis overlapped considerably with those in the school administration study, but there were some important differences that no doubt contributed to certain differences in factor structure.

The 40×40 matrix of intercorrelations was factored; 10 factors were initially retained, of which eight proved to be interpretable. Rotation to oblique structure was accomplished through use of Carroll's (1957) oblimin rotation program. The eight factors could be interpreted as dimensions of performance that were meaningful both psychologically and in terms of administrative behavior. Some, but not all, appeared to be very similar to factors from the study of school administration.

A comparison of primary factors from the two analyses shows that only two factors appeared in both studies in substantially the same form: *Acting in compliance with suggestions* and *Discussing*. Four factors were similar in that a few scores had high loadings in both studies; using the names assigned in the BB study, these four are *Preparing for action by becoming informed, Concern with public relations, Concern with superiors*, and *Directing subordinates*. Two factors unique to the BB study were *Procrastinating* and *Informality*, and two that were unique to the school study are *Analyzing the situation* and *Organizing work*. The two studies employed the same scorers and the same scoring rules. They differed in that different kinds of subjects were used, different in-baskets were used (although the school analysis was based on four in-baskets including the BB), slightly different sets of scoring categories were used, and different methods were used for rotating axes. The information available does not permit any conclusions as to which of these differences might be responsible for the differences in factor structure; all may have had some influence.

Consideration of the two sets of findings suggests that at least 10 and possibly more factors would be found in scores based on Bureau of Business protocols if data were combined from the two studies. A factor analysis was carried out using the BB in-basket scores of 620 cases—the 232 elementary school principals and the 335 subjects in the study just described. It was hoped that the more diverse group of subjects and the large sample would make possible a better determination of the factorial structure of in-basket scores than has previously been possible. The study will be described in a little more detail because it has not been reported elsewhere.

The scores and scoring categories are those from the original investigations. The data were pooled; reliabilities and intercorrelations were computed for 620 cases that resulted from combining the two groups.

Reliabilities are the correlations between scores based on odd- and even-numbered items, corrected for double length by the Spearman–Brown formula. Since different scorers scored the odd and even halves of the test, the reliabilities reflect both interscorer agreement and consistency of performance. The reliabilities and intercorrelations of 60 scoring categories were computed; the remaining eight scores were dropped because of extremely low means and standard deviations. A list of the 60 scoring categories is shown in Table 2-1 with their reliability coefficients. Reliabilities tend to be slightly higher for the combined group, presumably because of the more diverse collection of subjects.

Table 2-1   Reliabilities, Means, and Standard Deviations of Bureau of Business In-Basket Scores ($N = 620$)

Scoring Category	Reliability	Mean	Standard Deviation
Imaginativeness	0.63	6.7	3.6
Organizational change	0.58	3.5	2.3
Number of courses of action taken	0.75	44.2	11.0
Number of items attempted	0.88	31.6	5.1
Estimated number of words written	0.84	80.5	17.4
Number of subordinates involved	0.74	36.0	8.8
*Number of subordinate groups involved	0.13	1.0	1.3
Number of superiors involved	0.46	2.9	2.2
Number of outsiders involved	0.41	9.8	3.4
*Number of outside groups involved	0.18		
Number of unusual actions	0.32	4.1	2.6
*Recognizes good work	0.13		
Aware of poor work	0.38	3.5	2.3
Carelessness or minor error	0.44	0.7	1.5
Socially insensitive	0.42	2.1	1.5
Relates to background information	0.57	6.5	4.0
Conceptual analysis	0.29	1.8	2.2
Prejudges, unwarranted assumption	0.23	1.7	1.3
Uses human values	0.20	0.3	0.6
Uses program values	0.45	1.1	1.6
Discusses with subordinates	0.66	5.6	3.3
Discusses with superiors or outsiders	0.33	2.0	1.7

Table 2-1   (*Continued*)

Scoring Category	Reliability	Mean	Standard Deviation
Asks subordinates for information or opinion	0.56	5.7	3.4
Asks superiors for information or opinion	0.18	0.2	0.5
Asks outsiders for information or opinion	0.20	0.5	0.7
Requires further information for deciding	0.45	3.9	3.0
Delays, postpones	0.68	1.2	1.9
Arrives at a procedure for deciding	0.63	9.6	4.2
*Contingent decision	0.01		
Concluding decision	0.69	19.3	4.9
Plans only	0.64	1.6	2.4
Work scheduled for same or next day	0.57	2.6	2.3
Work scheduled for same or next week	0.41	1.7	1.7
Work scheduled, no time specified	0.42	5.5	3.4
Leading action	0.69	11.8	4.5
Terminal action	0.69	16.6	4.6
Follows lead by subordinate	0.58	8.3	3.2
Follows lead by superior	0.59	4.3	2.1
Follows preestablished structure	0.30	8.5	2.5
*Coordination	0.16		
Initiates a new structure	0.63	13.0	4.2
Delegates partially with control	0.33	0.6	0.9
*Delegates partially without control	0.09		
Gives directions or suggestions	0.61	15.5	5.0
Refers to superiors	0.32	0.3	0.6
Communicates face-to-face	0.68	6.6	3.7
Communicates by telephone	0.62	3.2	2.5
Communicates by writing	0.82	26.3	5.8
Gives information to subordinates	0.19	2.3	1.8
Gives information to superiors	0.18	0.4	0.7
*Gives information to outsiders	0.09		
Explains actions to subordinates	0.43	1.3	1.6
Courtesy to subordinates	0.80	5.8	4.8
*Courtesy to superiors	0.10		
Courtesy to outsiders	0.20	1.0	1.1
Informality to subordinates	0.87	4.2	5.1
Informality to superiors	0.52	0.2	0.6
Sets a deadline	0.23	0.4	0.7
*Follow-up or feed-back planned	0.16		

*Not used in factor analysis.

The factor analysis was based on the intercorrelations of 50 of the 60 variables named in Table 2-1; 10 (identified by asterisks) were dropped because of low reliabilities. Two additional variables were included in the analysis as extension variables; these variables did not influence the factor structure in any way, but the method permitted their loadings on the factors to be obtained. These variables are actually dichotomies. One of the added dichotomies is male vs. female and the other is principal vs. nonprincipal. The relationship of these dichotomies to other variables unfortunately cannot be revealed fully because of their confounding in the data: all nonprincipals are males; all females are also principals. The principals were divided about equally between the sexes.

Factor extraction was performed by an iterative principal axis procedure involving successively improved estimates of the number of significant factors and of the communalities of the 50 variables (Saunders, 1960). Initially 14 factors were retained. Rotation was accomplished according to the normal equamax criterion.

Two of the 14 factors proved to be uninterpretable. The next step in the analysis was to rotate 12 factors to oblique structure. The two uninterpretable factors were set orthogonal to all the other factors, and the oblique rotations were accomplished by choosing one variable to represent each of the remaining 12 factors and putting the axis of the corresponding factor through that variable. Plots of the factor loadings showed that reasonably good simple structure had been attained by this procedure. The intercorrelations of the oblique factors shown in Table 2-2 range from 0.61 to −0.30.

In interpreting the factors we will make use of the loadings of the variables on both the orthogonal and oblique factors. Loadings of 0.35 or higher will be considered in the following interpretations; where the variables are listed in the discussion below, the first column will contain the orthogonal and the second the oblique factor loading. The 12 factors identified are as follows:

> **Discussing** The factor loadings of 0.35 or more for this factor are as follows:
>
> | | | |
> |---|---|---|
> | Discusses with subordinates | 0.81 | 0.65 |
> | Communicates face-to-face | 0.77 | 0.61 |
> | Arrives at a procedure for deciding | 0.54 | 0.31 |
> | Initiates a new structure | 0.51 | 0.48 |
> | Leading action | 0.47 | 0.27 |
> | Work scheduled for same or next day | 0.46 | 0.34 |

Table 2-2 Intercorrelations of Factors

Factor	I	II	III	IV	V	VI	VII	VIII	IX	X	XI	XII
I. Discussing		0.41	-0.30	0.14	0.51	0.22	0.38	-0.06	0.33	0.32	0.14	0.14
II. Constructive action	0.41		-0.13	-0.05	0.37	0.27	0.40	0.31	0.05	0.29	0.20	0.18
III. Final action	-0.30	-0.13		0.61	-0.38	-0.04	0.09	0.10	-0.34	0.21	0.06	0.05
IV. Following suggestions	0.14	-0.05	0.61		0.03	0.29	0.15	0.04	-0.14	0.54	0.25	0.24
V. Preparatory action	0.51	0.37	-0.38	0.03		0.44	0.12	0.16	0.29	0.25	0.05	0.14
VI. Analyzing the situation	0.22	0.27	-0.04	0.29	0.44		0.06	-0.03	0.02	0.35	0.06	0.34
VII. Concern with superiors	0.38	0.40	0.09	0.15	0.12	0.06		0.20	0.18	0.20	0.10	0.02
VIII. Controlling subordinates	-0.06	0.31	0.10	0.04	0.16	-0.03	0.20		-0.11	0.01	0.01	0.01
IX. Procrastination	0.33	0.05	-0.34	-0.14	0.29	0.02	0.18	-0.11		-0.18	-0.20	-0.18
X. Orderly work	0.32	0.29	0.21	0.54	0.25	0.35	0.20	0.01	-0.18		0.53	0.10
XI. Informality	0.14	0.20	0.06	0.25	0.05	0.06	0.10	0.01	-0.16	0.53		0.03
XII. Concern with outsiders	0.14	0.18	0.05	0.24	0.14	0.34	0.02	0.01	-0.18	0.10	0.03	

This is clearly the same factor that has appeared in the two earlier studies. The "procedure for deciding" is usually to have a discussion, and the "new structure" is likely to be a committee. Use of discussion as a method of solving administrative problems is clearly one dimension of performance on which there are consistent individual differences.

Constructive action   The loadings are as follows:

Imaginativeness	0.68	0.62
Number of courses of action taken	0.66	0.51
Organizational change	0.63	0.52
Follows lead by superior	0.43	0.25
Aware of poor work	0.40	0.32

This factor was not identified in the previous analyses, and could not have been because the variables that best define the factor were not included. The first three variables shown above are based on a method of "content" scoring that is different from that used for other scores. The method will be described in more detail in Chapter 7. Briefly, lists of courses of action taken by examinees were prepared, and the scorer marked the score sheet to indicate all the courses that had been taken by each subject. The score "Number of courses of action taken" is of course the total number so marked for each examinee. The "Imaginativeness" score is the number of these courses of action taken that had previously been designated as imaginative solutions to the problem, as "good ideas"; and the "Organizational change" score was the number of courses of action taken by an examinee that had previously been designated as making some sort of permanent change in the organization. These three scores have the highest loadings, especially in the case of the oblique rotation, and they no doubt are to some extent a method factor. But the factor is retained because of its interesting implications, and it has been named *Constructive action*.

Final action   Here are the factor loadings:

Terminal action	0.75	0.58
Concluding decision	0.65	0.46
Number of items attempted	0.56	0.45
Communicates by writing	0.54	0.41
Number of subordinates involved	0.36	0.32
Initiates a new structure	0.36	0.35
Estimated number of words written	0.35	0.27

In the previous studies, "Terminal action" and "Concluding decision" contributed to a factor called *Acting in compliance with suggestions*. With the present data and with the factor analytic methods employed, it was possible to separate out the two components—*acting* and *complying*. We have called this factor *Final action*, and the one described below *Following suggestions*. The correlation between the two obliquely rotated factors is 0.61.

Following suggestions   The loadings are as follows:

Follows lead by subordinate	0.74	0.47
Social insensitivity	0.51	0.18
Concluding decision	0.47	0.08
Communicates by writing	0.44	−0.02
Terminal action	0.44	−0.00
Number of items attempted	0.42	0.01
Follows lead by superior	0.42	0.29
Makes unwarranted assumptions	0.41	0.17

This factor represents the "compliance with suggestions" part of the old "acting in compliance" factor. The "social insensitivity" score represents an attempt to measure the subject's tendency to notice and prevent actions that are unnecessarily offensive to individuals; but since most of the items were put in the form of an action suggested by a subordinate, it turned out to load on *Following suggestions*. Especially in the oblique solution, the factor quite clearly represents tendencies to follow suggestions made by others.

Preparatory action   The loadings follow:

Arrives at a procedure for deciding	0.65	0.51
Requires further information for deciding	0.63	0.51
Asks subordinates for information		
or opinion	0.56	0.38
Leading action	0.48	0.33
Work scheduled for same or next day	0.35	0.25

This factor is similar to the factors in the previous studies that were called *Preparing for action by becoming informed* and *Exchanging information*. It clearly represents actions short of the final determination of a solution to a problem, but goes beyond merely planning. It represents overt action directed at making a decision. Discussion is not a part of preparation for action as defined by this factor; in the oblique rotation, the correlation between this factor and *Discussing* is 0.51.

Analyzing the situation   The loadings are as follows:

Conceptual analysis	0.84	0.71
Uses program values	0.59	0.42
Explains actions to subordinates	0.55	0.42
Uses human values	0.45	0.34

"Conceptual analysis" is scored if the subject shows in his response that he has seen more than the immediate implications of a problem or a proposed solution to a problem. The scores involving program or human values are usually based on statements in the Reasons for Action form that relate his action to general institutional goals or to welfare of individuals. Thus the factor represents tendencies to act in ways that imply perceiving the problem in a cognitively complex way. The factor had appeared only in the school administration study.

Concern with superiors   The loadings:

Number of superiors involved	0.78	0.75
Discusses with superiors or outsiders	0.49	0.48
Asks superiors for information or opinion	0.44	0.41
Follows lead by superior	0.36	0.34

This factor represents a tendency to involve one's superiors in his actions and presumably to try to please the boss. (The combining of superiors and outsiders in the second scoring category listed above resulted from an attempt during the early development of the scoring procedure to reduce the number of scores. The attempt was misguided, as it turned out, because some of the factors hinge on tendencies to involve superiors and outsiders. The mistake was not repeated in the present study.) The factor is similar to the one given the same title in the BB study and has some resemblance to the factor *Maintaining organizational relationships* that was found in the school study.

Controlling subordinates   Loadings of 0.30 or higher are reported for this factor; they are as follows:

Delegates partially with control	0.52	0.48
Aware of poor work	0.41	0.22
Estimated number of words written	0.38	0.16
Number of subordinates involved	0.33	0.24
Gives directions or suggestions	0.33	0.18
Sets a deadline	0.32	0.24

This factor is relatively small, but the interpretation seems clear that this dimension of performance in the in-basket situation has to do with assigning work to one's subordinates and with techniques for controlling them. A somewhat similar factor was found in both of the earlier studies.

Procrastination   The loadings are as follows:

Tentative or definite plans only	0.75	0.63
Delays, postpones, or temporizes	0.48	0.48
Communicates by telephone	0.36	0.25

Examinees who are high on this factor are characterized by a tendency to avoid action, not to go beyond the planning stage. (In the oblique rotation, the loading of "Leading action" is -0.34.) A very similar factor was found in the BB analysis.

Orderly work   The loadings are as follows:

Follows preestablished structure	0.51	0.38
Work scheduled for same or next week	0.43	0.29
Communicates by writing	0.42	0.23
Courtesy to subordinates	0.36	0.29
Gives directions or suggestions	0.35	0.14

Any response that indicates that the subject has decided to follow a formal regulation, rule, or policy is scored as "Follows preestablished structure"; also such responses as initialing standard forms, instructing a subordinate to file something, and referring problems appropriately to existing channels are all scored here. The factor is small but has some similarity to the *Organizing work* factor found in the school administration study.

Informality   The loadings:

Informality to subordinates	0.61	0.50
Relates to background information or other items	0.57	0.46
Informality to superiors	0.43	0.32

The "informality" scoring categories have to do with use of first names, slang, colloquial language, and the like. The loading for "Relates to background information" is no doubt accounted for by the necessity to look up first names in the Table of Organization. The interpretation of the factor is clear; it corresponds closely to a factor with the same name found in the BB study.

Concern with outsiders   The loadings:

Courtesy to outsiders	0.60	0.54
Number of outsiders involved	0.48	0.32
Estimated number of words written	0.37	0.19
Number of courses of action taken	0.35	0.08
Discusses with superiors or outsiders	0.35	0.27

The interpretation of this factor as *Concern with outsiders* seems quite clear. The loadings on number of words and number of actions suggest that this concern is associated with a high level of productivity, although these loadings are much reduced in the oblique solution. The loading on the last item listed would no doubt have been greater if superiors had not been included in the scoring category. A factor similar to this one was found in both of the other analyses.

The 12 factors resulting from the analysis thus represent the 10 factors found in the two preceding studies, including the two that matched well, the four that matched quite imperfectly, and the two that were unique for each of the two studies. The two additional factors are *Constructive action* and *Final action*. *Final action* resulted from splitting apart two highly correlated ($r = 0.61$) components of the earlier *Acting in compliance with suggestions* factor. The only entirely new factor resulted from putting additional scores into the correlation matrix, the three scores based on the records of courses of action taken. Performance on the BB in-basket can thus be described reasonably satisfactorily in terms of 12 factors.

The loadings of the two extension variables, sex and principalship status, are shown in Table 2-3. The largest loadings are found in the last two columns, those showing the extension loadings of the dichotomy principal vs. nonprincipal. High positive loadings indicate that non-principals are more likely than principals to display in their paper work the kind of behavior defined by the factor.

We see that the nonprincipals (who are for the most part experienced administrators in government or business settings) are more likely than elementary school principals to take constructive action and to control subordinates, and they are less likely to act precipitately on problems and to analyze situations. Except for the loadings on *Analyzing the situation*, these are probably the kinds of differences we might expect between experienced government and business administrators and elementary school principals. Elementary school principals actually have few sub-ordinates to help with administrative work except for a secretary, since

Table 2-3   Extension Loadings of Sex and Principalship Status on In-Basket Scores

Factor	Loading			
	Sex[a]		Principalship[b]	
	Orthogonal Rotation	Oblique Rotation	Orthogonal Rotation	Oblique Rotation
Discussing	0.02	0.02	−0.03	−0.04
Constructive action	−0.22	−0.20	0.41	0.39
Final action	0.11	0.09	−0.21	−0.20
Following suggestions	0.13	0.01	−0.19	0.05
Preparatory action	0.04	0.08	0.03	−0.10
Analyzing the situation	0.20	0.13	−0.36	−0.30
Concern with superiors	−0.02	−0.04	−0.05	−0.03
Controlling subordinates	−0.22	−0.11	0.45	0.31
Procrastination	−0.02	−0.00	0.06	0.02
Orderly work	−0.03	0.02	0.08	0.03
Informality	−0.15	−0.12	−0.06	−0.04
Concern with outsiders	0.01	0.03	0.07	0.01

[a] 0 = male, 1 = female
[b] 0 = principal, 1 = nonprincipal

teachers have essentially full-time responsibility for their classrooms. With respect to *Analyzing the situation*, we may speculate that the background and training of administrators in public education encourages a tendency to be vocal about the "program values" and goals associated with a school program, and that this tendency may account for the loading.

Differences between men and women are less marked and may merely reflect the differences between principals and nonprincipals, since all the women in the study were elementary school principals. The confounding of sex and principalship makes an unambiguous interpretation of the extension loadings impossible; but the fact that fairly high extension loadings do occur suggests that the method is at least sensitive enough to reveal relationships between factors in in-basket performance and biographical information.

Validity of In-Basket Scores

We have proposed that simulated jobs rather than real jobs might be used as the basis for social-psychological experiments, in order to overcome some of the disadvantages of real life as a setting for scientific study of behavior. It seems clear that the use of a situational test as a simulation device does permit one to do a technically superior experiment; but the question of the external validity (Campbell, 1957) of the simulation remains to be answered. Validity, in this context, has to do with the question of our ability to generalize from the experiment to behavior in real-life settings. Do generalizations or scientific "laws" based on performance in a simulated situation enable one to predict behavior in the real world?

The validity of a simulation, one would suppose, depends largely upon the extent to which subjects in experiments involving simulation respond to problems and social influences in a way that characterizes their "typical" behavior. But no one is ever perfectly consistent, even in real life; rather he tends to play roles that are appropriate to various contexts. Therefore we cannot expect perfect correspondence between behavior in simulated and in real situations. In addition to the limitations in consistency across situations in real life, we have the further question of the special effects of being a subject in an experiment where one is instructed to behave as usual ("as though you were really on the job"). We know from work both with personality inventories and with conventional tests that various response sets or biases influence performance (Cronbach, 1946; Cronbach, 1950; Edwards, 1957; Frederiksen & Messick, 1959; Messick, 1960; Messick & Jackson, 1961), and it is quite reasonable to expect that such biases would also be present in a situational test. Of particular concern is the bias toward giving the response thought to be most socially desirable, the response that will put the respondent in the best light. It has, as a matter of fact, been shown that there are substantial correlations between measures thought to reflect the extent of social desirability bias in a questionnaire and scores on the BB in-basket (Frederiksen, 1966). However, it is also reasonable to suppose that the effort to make a good impression in taking the in-basket test would also characterize one's performance in a real job, and that effects of desirability bias on categories of behavior would be similar in the simulated job and in a real job. The fact that examinees in the in-basket situation do not know the scoring categories makes it impossible for them to bias responses deliberately to get high scores on certain performance categories. The examinee presumably guesses only that he should do well, accomplish a lot, and show good judgment, and this is just about what he would be likely to try to do in a real job as well.

Data are available from the study of school administrators (Frederiksen, 1961) on consistency of performance across in-baskets. Such information would usually be thought of as bearing on the question of reliability rather than validity; but it is relevant to this discussion, since a lack of consistency between different simulated situations would certainly make questionable the consistency in performance from a simulated to a real-life situation. The information available consists of comparisons of odd-even and alternate-form reliabilities for four in-baskets. Three of the in-baskets, designated A, C, and D, involved the simulated elementary school of which the examinee served as principal; and the fourth was the BB in-basket. Scores on 34 categories of behavior were selected for study. Distributions of reliability coefficients and median reliabilities are shown in Table 2-4. It was concluded that there is clearly more consistency of

Table 2-4 Distribution of Reliability Coefficients for School and Bureau of Business In-Baskets

	Frequency									
	Odd-Even Reliability				Alternate-Form Reliability					
Interval	A	C	D	BB	A vs. C	A vs. D	C vs. D	A vs. BB	C vs. BB	D vs. BB
0.90–0.99	1									
0.80–0.89	2	3	2	3						
0.70–0.79	6	3	4	6						
0.60–0.69	4	10←	4	8	3		5	1		1
0.50–0.59	4←	6←	5←	3	3	5	2	1	2	1
0.40–0.49	7	3	9	4	4	6	7←	3	2	5
0.30–0.39	4	5	1	5	9←	6←	12	7←	10←	8←
0.20–0.29	3	2	7	2	10	7	2	13←	10	10
0.10–0.19	1	1	2	2	5	9	5	7	8	6
0.00–0.09	2	1		1	1	1	1		2	3
(−0.01)–(−0.10)	—	—	—	—				1		
Median	0.49	0.56	0.47	0.59	0.33	0.29	0.38	0.25	0.27	0.28

performance *within* an in-basket than *between* in-baskets, i.e., odd-even reliabilities are noticeably higher than "alternate form" reliabilities. This greater consistency of performance within an in-basket might be due to temporary sets or attitudes which persist through a single session but vary from day to day for individual subjects. The "alternate form" reliabilities are generally higher (but only slightly so) for pairs which include two school in-baskets than for pairs involving a school in-basket and the BB in-basket. In other words, there is a little more consistency in performance between two school situations than between a school and a business situation. The fact that there is some consistency across in-baskets taken at different times and with quite different settings and problems at least suggests that it is not hopeless to find some consistency in performance between real and simulated situations. The fact that there is a difference suggests that it may be feasible to make use of experimental variations in settings as dependent variables in social-psychological experiments.

Another approach to the problem of validity would be to demonstrate that the dependent variables obtained in the simulated situation are related in logically sensible ways to measures obtained in a variety of other situations and through use of other kinds of instrumentation. The finding that performance in the simulated situation is consistent with biographical information and with scores obtained from tests and inventories would make more plausible the judgment that findings from experiments using simulation have some generality. This approach to the problem considers the in-basket as a test, and the question has to do with the construct validity of the test.

As was mentioned earlier, the school administration study provided some information that is relevant. The procedure involved the factoring of a large matrix containing both in-basket scores and scores on a large number of ability tests, personality and interest inventories, ratings, and items of biographical information. An orthogonal factor matrix composed of the first 10 factors was rotated obliquely to form a factor matrix resembling as closely as possible the original in-basket factor structure. Coefficients were computed that reflect the relative relationship of each of the 120 variables to each of eight oblique reference vectors, each vector corresponding to one of the eight in-basket factors. These coefficients are proportional to the correlations of the variables with the unique part of each factor — that part not included in the second-order domain. Similar coefficients with second-order factors were computed. This procedure revealed a number of interesting relationships that are described in detail elsewhere (Hemphill, Griffiths, & Frederiksen, 1962). A few of the most interesting results are summarized here. The sex of the principal was related to several factors: female principals were more likely than males to exchange information and to respond to people outside the school system, while males were more likely to comply with suggestions and to analyze the situation. Older principals were more likely to respond to outsiders, and young principals were more likely to comply with suggestions (but there is a confounding of age and sex, since the younger principals tended to be males). Years of academic training was not substantially related to any of the factors.

The personality inventory employed in the study was the 16 Personality Factor (16 PF) questionnaire of Cattell. The general findings in the area of personality were that principals who are anxious, insecure, and characterized by nervous tension tend to be high on organizing work (which is consistent with the interpretation of this factor as a pattern of compulsive behavior) and low on maintaining organizational relationships. Principals who are friendly and "adventurous" (not shy), according to the 16 PF, on the other hand, are high on maintaining relationships with others in the organization. Principals who earned high scores on cognitive tests such as reasoning, arithmetic and vocabulary, and on a test of school administration tended to be high on exchanging information, complying with suggestions, and amount of work accomplished, but low on directing the work of others.

A somewhat similar study involving the government administrators who took the BB in-basket was also carried out (Frederiksen, 1966). Zero-order correlations between in-basket scores and predictor variables, and extension loadings of the predictor variables on in-basket factors, were reported. The predictors included items of biographical information, scores on cognitive tests, and scores on the Strong Vocational Interest Blank (SVIB) and the Thurstone Temperament Schedule. A few of the highlights are as follows: High level in government service was associated with a high level of work output (as indicated by number of subordinates involved, for example) and with the giving of directions and suggestions, and was negatively associated with the *Procrastination* factor. High vocabulary score was associated with many imaginative courses of action. Those who resembled sales managers and life insurance salesmen in the way they answered the SVIB items tended to schedule face-to-face discussions, while those who resembled forest service men tended to avoid discussions and asking for information. Those with high scores on the Active scale of the Temperament Schedule were active in taking in-baskets: they wrote a lot, attempted many items, involved many people, and took many leading actions (but not necessarily terminal actions). Those who had supervisory responsibilities in their real jobs tended to be high in directing subordinates in their in-basket work.

Industrial Applications

In-baskets have been widely used in industrial settings, primarily for training but also for assessment. The work in this area has been summarized by Lopez (1966) in a publication of the American Management Association.

After the development and tryout of the first in-basket tests at the Air University, the behavioral research staff of the American Telephone and Telegraph Company, working with research people at ETS (L. B. Ward, 1959), constructed an in-basket to be used for training at the middle-management level. The test required candidates to play the role of a district plant manager. Those responsible for executive training were apparently pleased with the results, and the AT & T in-basket was used widely as a training device. Other companies, including IBM, Dayton Rubber Company, The Boeing Company, The Port of New York Authority, and Procter and Gamble, developed their own versions for use in their training programs. More recently, The University of Michigan's Bureau of Industrial Relations constructed a series of training in-baskets which are offered for sale, and the American Management Association has developed in-basket exercises for use in its Management Course. In-baskets have apparently been widely accepted as training devices because of their face validity and their acceptance by trainees. But no objective evaluation of the in-basket as a training device has been carried out.

The industrial applications of in-baskets to selection and assessment are of more interest in the present context, because any evidence that in-basket scores are useful for selecting executives implies just the kind of evidence of external validity that we need — evidence that performance in a simulated work situation is consistent with performance in a real job. Unfortunately, much of the work in this area makes use of subjective judgments of in-basket performance rather than scores. A common technique (one employed by the Personnel Relations Department of AT & T (Bray & Grant, 1966)) involves an interview with the examinee upon completion of the in-basket, on the basis of which a report describing his administrative performance is written. Such methods do not lend themselves to statistical statements about relationships of criteria to in-basket scores of the sort used in this study.

Other companies, notably the Port of New York Authority, have used the "psychometric" approach in which scoring methods and categories similar to those described earlier have been used. Lopez summarizes a number of studies of this sort, but for many of the studies he provides only verbal summarizations ("the in-basket scoring factors correlated significantly with many criteria"). The work of the industrial psychologist often does not find its way into the psychological literature. Except for a few modest correlations with supervisors' ratings reported by Lopez, we find little quantitative information that bears on the question of consistency of performance between situational test and the job.

A body of information is accumulating that seems to say that measures of performance in the simulated administrative job have logical and sensible relationships with a wide variety of measures from other domains of behavior, that involve different measurement techniques, and that include items of a biographical nature. The evidence of validity of in-basket tests is, we judge, sufficient to justify performing social-psychological experiments in a laboratory situation that involves the simulation of an administrative position.

CHAPTER 3

Design for an Experimental Study of Person-Situation Interaction

In this chapter we shall present a brief overview of an experiment dealing with person-situation interactions in an organizational setting. In subsequent chapters, the subjects in the experiment, the independent and dependent variables, the experimental treatments, the methods of analysis, and the findings and interpretation will be described in detail.

A reasonably alert reader of the preceding two chapters will have little difficulty in anticipating, at least in general outline, the nature and purposes of the experiment to be described, since the methodological and philosophical groundwork has been presented there. The general purpose of the study, of course, is to investigate interactions of personal and situational variables in the prediction of performance. More specifically, the purpose is to attempt to answer three kinds of questions: (1) What are the effects of some situational variables on the interrelationships (factor structure) of a number of dependent variables? (2) What are the effects of the situational variables on the regressions of dependent variables on a set of predictor variables? (3) What are the effects of the situational variables on the means of the dependent variables? The "laboratory" setting for the study is a simulated organization in which each subject is the incumbent of a particular job. The dependent variables are scores based on records of the subjects' performance in that simulated job, the predictor variables are measures of cognitive abilities and personal characteristics, and the situational variables are organizational climate conditions that were made to vary systematically, according to the experimental design.

The study attempts to be experimentally rigorous. All subjects were

71

employed in the same job in the same organization, and all subjects served under the same executives, had the same subordinates, and faced identical problems. The only variations were in the experimental treatments—the organizational climates. Subjects were assigned in an unbiased manner to climate conditions; these climates had to do with (1) encouragement of innovation and originality vs. following rules, regulations, and standard procedures; and (2) a type of supervision in which freedom in carrying out assignments was permitted vs. a type of supervision that involved monitoring the details of a subordinate's performance. Such an experimental approach to the study of climates in a complex organization was possible only because the organization was a simulated one. In other words, the experimental procedure required the use of a long, complex, and realistic situational test.

The research is a multivariate correlational study as well as an experimental study. While it attempts to be rigorous in controlling conditions and assigning subjects to treatments, it also attempts to employ additional statistical controls on unwanted sources of variation; it employs not one but many dependent variables; it looks for joint effects of experimental treatments as well as for main effects; and it looks not only for effects of experimental treatments on the means of the dependent variables, but also for variations in slopes of regression planes and variations in the factorial structure in the domain of the dependent variables. The study also examines the possibility that situational variables defined in terms of clusters of related *problems* (rather than in terms of the more general and pervasive organizational climates) will interact with personal characteristics in influencing performance.

CHOICE OF CLIMATE VARIABLES

The lack of a taxonomy of situations and situational attributes is no less a problem in dealing with organizations than in any other area of behavioral science. Studies of organizations have involved a wide variety of concepts and constructs; autocratic vs. democratic leadership styles, consideration and initiating structure as attributes of executive performance, degrees of supervision of performance, kinds of delegation of authority, informal and formal channels of communication, centralization vs. decentralization of authority, and participatory management have all been the subject of investigation in studies of organizational psychology. The organizational characteristics most frequently studied, according to Forehand and Gilmer (1964), are size, organizational structure, systems complexity, leadership patterns, and goal direction. They use the term *organizational climate* to refer to such attributes of organizations, and they define the term as "the set of characteristics that describe an organization and that (a) distinguish the organization from other organizations, (b) are relatively enduring over time, and (c) influence the behavior of people in the organization." Other investigators stress the latter part of this definition; Kahn, Wolfe, Quinn, Snoek, and Rosenthal (1964), for example, find that much of an organization's climate consists of "those overarching shalts and shalt nots which govern the actions, imply the sanctions and in time permeate the souls of organization members" (pages 150–151).

The climate of an organization, as we conceive of it in this investigation, is a set of expectations or understandings, held in common by most of the members of an organization, as to a kind of uniformity in behavior that is seen as appropriate in that organization; these expectations presumably result from perceptions of uniformities in behavior on the part of the organization's members, from overt or subtle declarations of policy on the part of the leaders, from a uniform background of training and experience on the part of the members, or from some combination of these. Ultimately, the climate presumably results from manipulations of reinforcements or sanctions by people in positions of power and through policies having to do with selection and retention of personnel. This definition excludes the more prosaic kinds of organizational variation, such as mere size or type of physical plant, and suggests ways of representing climates in a simulated organization.

The two climate dichotomies used in this research were chosen partly because it seemed feasible to represent them clearly in a simulated organization and partly because they seemed to represent the variety of concepts that have been used in much research on organizations. Two climate conditions were chosen instead of one in order to make it possible to discover any interactions between the two climate dichotomies that might occur.

One dichotomy was called *innovation vs. rules*. In the *innovation* climate, information was presented in the simulation of the organization that was intended to give subjects the impression that in the organization employees were expected to be creative and original and to invent new and better ways of doing work; rules existed, but they might be disregarded if better ways could be found for accomplishing an objective. In the contrasting *rules* climate, materials were included that were supposed to show that employees were expected to follow rules and SOP; an employee who failed to do so could expect some indication of disapproval.

The other dichotomy had to do with supervision of subordinates. One climate condition was called *global supervision* and the other *detailed supervision*. Under the *global* supervision climate, it was expected that work would be assigned to subordinates with freedom as to how the assignment was carried out, but also with the expectation that performance would be evaluated by the supervisor. Under the *detailed* supervision climate, on the other hand, the supervisor was supposed to monitor the performance of his subordinates at all times so that mistakes could be prevented before they occurred. The climate conditions were supposed to apply to the subject in his simulated job as well as to his subordinates. The two climate dichotomies were assigned to subjects in such a way as to form a 2×2 treatment design, as will be described in the following section.

DESIGN OF THE STUDY

The experiment was carried out in a simulated department – the "Department of Commerce" – of the State of California. Subjects in the experiment were 260 male executives who were employed by the State of California in a wide variety of positions, ranging from forestry to prison service, and from the heads of departments (appointed by the Governor) to people at a middle-management level. The simulated job was that of Chief of the Field Service Division of the Department of Commerce, a job that required little technical skill or information beyond that already known to all of the subjects by virtue of their experience as employees of the State of California.

Most of the experimental data were obtained at a two-day "Research Institute" held in Sacramento. During the institute each subject served as Chief of the Field Service Division; all subjects faced exactly the same in-basket problems, worked under the same superiors, had the same colleagues and subordinates, and (except for the experimental variations in climate) worked under the same conditions. The scores obtained from the records of performance made by the subjects – the letters, memoranda, notes, plans, and reminders they wrote as responses to problems found in their in-baskets – provided the dependent measures of the study.

Prior to the institute, subjects responded to the items in a biographical questionnaire and a personality inventory, and during the first day of the institute they took a battery of tests of cognitive abilities under standard conditions and timing. These tests, questionnaires, and inventories provided the predictor variables of the study.

After the institute, a portion of the subjects were asked to nominate peers and superiors to serve as raters; these nominees were later asked to fill out rating forms describing the behavior of the subjects in their real jobs. A large majority of those asked to make ratings did so. These data made possible an investigation of consistency in performance between simulated and real job situations, at least as performance in real jobs is perceived by peers and superiors.

As the subjects came to the registration desk on the morning of the first day of the Research Institute, every fourth subject was assigned to a different group. The members of each group assembled for each session in their own room with their own supervisor. Each group was given a different experimental treatment—a different combination of organizational climates.

As we have seen, there were two dichotomies, representing two kinds of climate conditions. One dichotomy had to do with being creative and original vs. following rules, regulations, and standard procedures. The other had to do with a global type of supervision in which the supervisor was mainly concerned with assigning work and evaluating the final products of the subordinate's work vs. a type of supervision in which the supervisor was expected to monitor the details of the work of a subordinate. Half the subjects were assigned to the rules climate and half to the innovation climate; similarly, half were assigned to the detailed supervision climate and half to the global supervision climate. The two treatment dichotomies overlap, as shown in Fig. 3-1, to form four treatment

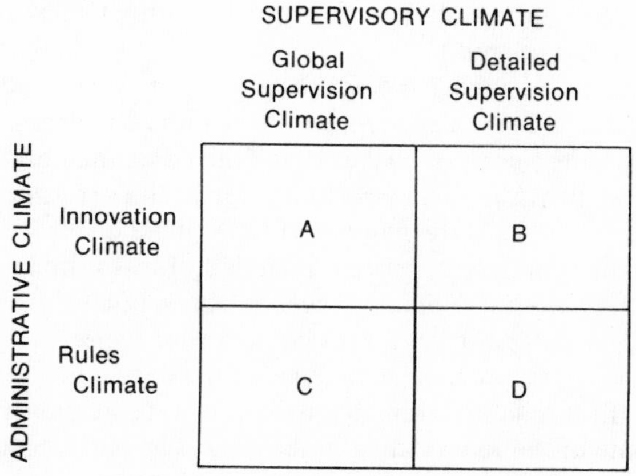

Fig. 3-1   The climate combinations.

combinations. Cell A, for example, contains subjects to whom was presented a climate in which both innovation and global supervision were emphasized, while Cell D represents subjects to whom was presented the rules climate and the climate in which supervision stressed monitoring details. This design makes it possible to study joint effects of the climate conditions as well as their main effects.

The climate conditions were presented to the subjects by varying the material used to describe the Department of Commerce (CDC). This material was presented to the subjects just before the in-basket work was assigned. The background materials were intended to inform the subjects about the nature of the CDC generally and the Field Services Division in particular. The items included such items as an organization chart, a copy of the statute founding the CDC, a draft of the next CDC annual report, and a series of administrative memoranda that constitute the rules and regulations in force. One method of presenting the several climate conditions was to have Mr. Veep (who is second in command of CDC) add annotations and underlining to these administrative memoranda. For the rules climate, for example, the subject found that Mr. Veep had underlined statements calling attention to deadline dates, use of forms, and standard procedures to be followed; while for the innovation climate Veep had underlined statements calling attention to goals and general policies of the organization. Other communications, both direct and subtle, were intended to make clear to the subjects how they were expected to perform as Chief of the Field Services Division with respect to the climate dichotomies. Additional materials were included in the in-baskets to reinforce the perception of the climate. (Any direct responses to such materials were not scored.)

The dependent variables are scores based on various categories of performance that are revealed in responses to in-basket items. The method of scoring considers each in-basket item (such as a memorandum from a subordinate) as providing an opportunity for each performance category to occur, and the score is the number of times it did occur. The categories of performance that were scored included, for example, *conceptual analysis of problems, informality to subordinates, having discussions with peers, postponing decisions,* and *taking terminal action.*

The first step in the statistical analysis of the data was a series of factor analyses of the predictor variables aimed merely at data reduction, at removing some of the redundancy in the data. The aim was to find a small number of factors that would represent most of the variance in the scores on the various predictor measures used in the study and that would reflect common variance while minimizing the influence of uniqueness in the specific tests making up the factor. Such analyses were done separately for three groups of predictor variables—cognitive tests, inventory scores, and biographical data. The result in each case was a much smaller number of factors than variables; the factors were used as predictors in subsequent analyses in the form of factor scores.

In the statistical analysis of the effects of experimental treatments, there are three pairs of contrasting groups to be considered. One pair of contrasting groups is the innovation climate group vs. the rules climate group—the rows in Fig. 3-1. The second pair is the global supervision group vs. the detailed supervision group—the columns in Fig. 3-1. The third pair represents the interactions of the climate conditions—a contrast of the diagonal cells in Fig. 3-1. One of the pairs of groups is composed of the subjects in cells A and D; the subjects in this group may be thought of as having been presented with a *consistent* picture of an organization— either rules combined with detailed supervision or innovation combined with global supervision. The other group is composed of the subjects in cells B and C. The members of the BC group were given a rather inconsistent picture; they were asked to believe that, for example, their organization simultaneously required innovation and detailed supervision of subordinates' work.

The first major question asked of the data has to do with the effects of the variations in organizational climate on the factor structure of the dependent variables. Is the factor structure of the in-basket performance scores the same for the rules climate as for the innovation climate, for example? The method employed was one proposed by L. R Tucker called within-group covariance factor analysis. Its principal advantage is that it does not confound differences in factor loadings with differences in the groups of subjects, since a single matrix of factor loadings is obtained for both groups combined. A matrix of variances and covariances of factor scores is then computed for each group by multiplying scores by factor loadings for each group separately. Differences in variances and covariances thus reflect group differences in scores but not group differences in loadings. Identical factors may be identified even though they differ in variance or in their correlations with other factors. If a factor does not exist for one of the groups, it will have zero variance.

The second major question is the question of comparability of "validity" coefficients. Are the relationships of factors in the domain of the dependent variables to factors of ability, personality, and personal history the same for groups working under different organizational climates? This question was answered by comparing the slopes of regression planes in predicting performance factor scores for two contrasting treatment groups from all the predictor factor scores obtained from the ability tests, inventories, and questionnaires. Each performance factor was used as a criterion. An analysis of covariance procedure was used to test the hypothesis that the slopes of the regression planes are the same for the two contrasting treatment groups.

The third question has to do with the effects of the experimental treatments on the means of the dependent variables — the in-basket performance factor scores. It is not appropriate to ask this question unless the regressions of scores for a given in-basket factor on the predictors are parallel, because the lack of parallel regression planes means that the treatments do not have a uniform effect on all subjects, but rather have different effects for subjects with different personal characteristics. For those in-basket factors and those pairs of treatment groups that have parallel regression planes, the statistical evaluation of differences in means was accomplished by the test of equality of intercepts of regressions, another part of the analysis of covariance procedure.

These statistical operations provide answers, with significance tests, to our questions about effects of experimental treatments on means and intercorrelations of dependent variables and about possible roles of the treatments in person-situation interactions. The factoring procedures reduce the number of variables, relative to the number of subjects, in order to increase the power of the statistical tests.

Another method of analyzing the data is three-mode factor analysis. In this method, the response to an in-basket *item* was used as the basic datum rather than score across items. Three kinds of factors result: (1) in-basket performance factors (similar to those obtained in the conventional factor analysis); (2) item factors, which are clusters of items that are similar in the sense that they elicit similar categories of performance; and (3) person factors, which represent clusters of subjects who tend to behave similarly in response to particular item factors. The intercorrelations of person-factor scores under different climate conditions were compared, as were the correlations of person-factor scores with predictors. The results of the three-mode factor analysis thus provide additional information relevant to our general question about how situations interact with personal characteristics in influencing performance. In the three-mode analysis we go to a different level in classifying situations — the clusters of items — and we learn something about how two kinds of situations — the item clusters and the organizational climates — interact with each other and with personal characteristics in determining behavior.

Subsequent chapters will describe in greater detail the various aspects of this research plan. Chapter 4 describes the subjects in terms of biographical information, and it discusses the results of the procedure used in assigning subjects to treatments from the point of view of similarity of the groups with respect to predictor variables. Chapter 5 describes the predictor variables. Chapter 6 describes the Department of Commerce, the CDC in-baskets, the organizational climates and how they were presented, and the conduct of the Research Institute. Chapter 7 describes the dependent variables: the scoring of in-baskets, the reliability of scores, and the correlations of in-basket scores with ratings by peers and superiors. Chapter 8 describes the criterion variables — the factors that resulted from a factor analysis of the dependent variables. Chapters 9, 10, and 11 present the results of the data analysis.

CHAPTER 4

The Subjects

The subjects who attended the Research Institutes and who provided the data of the study were all employed as administrators by the State of California. Since the main object of the research was to study inter-relationships among variables, it was not considered necessary to try to draw a sample that would be representative of the state management population. It was important, however, to make the sample quite varied with respect to the measures to be employed in the study.

DESCRIPTION OF THE SAMPLE

At the time the subjects were selected, there were 1530 positions listed in the state service Management Directory. These management positions are divided into two major categories and four echelons. The two cate-gories are (1) civil service and (2) statutory or exempt (appointee) posi-tions. The exempt positions tend to be high-level jobs, some of which require appointment by the Governor. The four echelons, in order from highest to lowest, are the following:

1. Director of a department or agency
2. Deputy Director of a department
3. Head of a major subdivision of a department or Superintendent of a large institution
4. Head of a major function or unit within a major subdivision

Each department in state service was asked by the State Personnel Board to enlist the participation of one-fifth of its management personnel as subjects in the experiment. It was suggested that, to the extent possible, the participants should be from all four managerial echelons and should represent all levels of competency.

Only six of the more than 50 departments in the state declined the invitation, and only one of these six, the Department of Education, is a large department by state service standards. Most of the participating departments met or exceeded their quota, and more than 300 managers agreed to participate. Of this number, approximately 270 actually came to at least one of the two institutes. Several participants were later eliminated from the study because they did not return the questionnaire and inventory or because they were called away from the institute to meet an emergency (the State Legislature was in session at the time). The data obtained from three female participants were not used in any of the analyses, in order to avoid the problem of dealing with sex differences. The remaining 260 participants are the subjects of the research here reported.

Table 4-1 shows the percentage of the Management Directory population and of the sample who are in the two major categories and in the four echelons. So far as echelons are concerned, the sample matches the population fairly well. The principal difference is to be found in the civil service and exempt categories; the sample contains relatively fewer employees in the exempt category—those who are appointees rather than civil service employees.

Table 4-2 compares the research sample with the Directory population in terms of the departments in which individuals are employed. To simplify the presentation, the 50-odd departments have been combined into five "agencies" and an "all others" category; e.g., the Health and Welfare agency is composed of the departments of Mental Hygiene, Public Health, Social Welfare, and Rehabilitation. The Health and Welfare agency is somewhat underrepresented in the sample, as are the departments in the "all others" category; the remaining agencies are somewhat overrepresented.

Table 4-1 Percentage of the Management Directory Population and the Research Sample in Civil Service Categories (Population $N = 1530$; Sample $N = 260$)

Echelon	Civil Service		Exempt		Totals	
	Population	Sample	Population	Sample	Population	Sample
1 and 2	3.3	4.9	7.5	5.5	10.8	10.4
3	21.6	26.2	4.2	2.2	25.8	28.4
4	60.6	60.6	2.8	0.6	63.4	61.2
Totals	85.5	91.7	14.5	8.3	100.0	100.0

Table 4-2   Percentage of the Management Directory Population and the Research Sample Departmental Categories

Agency in Which Employed	Population	Research Sample
Health and Welfare	17.2	13.1
Youth and Adult Corrections	10.8	13.8
Resources	11.8	17.3
Highways and Transportation	17.9	19.6
Revenue and Management	10.4	14.2
All Others	31.9	22.0
Total	100.0	100.0

The median age of those in the research sample is 49; the median age of those listed in the Management Directory is 51. This difference is probably caused by two factors: (1) the Department of Education, which has a median manager age of 55, did not choose to participate in the research; and (2) the Department of Mental Hygiene enlisted a disproportionate number of Echelon 4 subjects (including a few whom the department was trying to upgrade to level four but who had not yet been officially placed in that category).

The model subject is married, has two children, and has spent over three years in military service. He is a college graduate or is within a year of graduation, and his major educational background is in an area related to business or government or is in applied physical science. He has had from 6 to 11 years of experience in administrative work, and his current position is a job classified in the Fiscal, Management, or Staff Service category.

ASSIGNMENT OF SUBJECTS TO TREATMENTS

The objectives of the procedure for assigning subjects to treatments were (1) a random assignment of the subjects to experimental treatments, (2) an equal number of subjects in each treatment category, and (3) operational simplicity. The procedural steps used in assigning subjects to treatments were as follows: The Institute schedules were printed on four colors of paper, one for subjects in each treatment category. These schedules were sequentially interleafed, i.e., pink, yellow, blue, green, pink, yellow, blue, green, etc. The collated schedules were then divided into equal stacks, one for each Institute, and each stack was divided into three equal packets, one for each of three registration desks. The alphabetical listing of participants for each Institute was divided into three equal segments, one of which was assigned to each registration desk. As participants approached the registration area, they were directed to the appropriate registration desk on the basis of the initial letter of the last name. The assignment of a participant to a particular treatment was accomplished by handing him the schedule on top of the packet; the color designated the treatment condition. Thus order of appearance, within alphabetic segments, was the basis of assignment to an experimental condition.

COMPARISON OF TREATMENT GROUPS WITH RESPECT TO PREDICTORS

A number of personality inventories, biographical data items, and cognitive ability tests were administered to subjects prior to their participation in the Department of Commerce situational test and its associated experimental climate conditions. As is described in the following chapter, three factor analyses were carried out for the purpose of reducing the number of predictor variables. The result of the data reduction was a set of 23 predictor variables, 21 of which are factor scores representing factors in the personality, biographical information, and cognitive test domains. A complete description of the 23 variables will be found in Chapter 5.

Our interest in the predictor variables at this point is to see how successful was the method of assigning subjects to treatments, from the point of view of randomization. Subjects were dichotomized in two ways: assignment to *innovation* vs. *rules* climate conditions, and assignment to *detailed supervision* vs. *global supervision* climate conditions. These two dichotomies are the rows and columns in Fig. 3-1. Another dichotomy can be constructed by using the diagonally opposite cells in Fig. 3-1. One part of this dichotomy consists of the subjects who were in the *rules-detailed supervision* cell and in the *innovation-global supervision* cell; the other half of the dichotomy is the group composed of people who were in the *rules-global supervision* cell and in the *innovation-detailed supervision* cell.

The *t* tests were computed to test the significance of differences between means. Five of the 69 differences are significant at the 5% level,[1] and none

[1]The significant differences were as follows: for the *rules* vs. *innovation* groups, *Theoretical Education* and *Years of Military Service*; for the *global* and *detailed supervision* groups, *Global Evaluation Climate Rating*; and for consistent and inconsistent climate groups, *Test S*, *Conservative Strategy* and *Rules Climate Rating*. (*See* Chapter 5 for definitions of these variables.)

are significant at the 1% level. One would expect to find three or four differences significant at the 5% level by chance when making such a large number of t tests. It appears that the methods employed resulted in a reasonably unbiased assignment of subjects to experimental treatments.

REPORTS TO SUBJECTS

At the final meeting of the Research Institute, a general briefing session was held, at which time the purposes of the experiment and the methods of scoring and analysis to be used were explained to the subjects. The participants were given assurance that all data would be treated as strictly confidential, that numbers rather than names would be used to identify subjects as soon as data were collated, and that no information on specific individuals would be revealed to anyone, including anyone in the state service. They were also informed that each subject would be sent a report of scores based on his in-basket performance.

Helm (1965) had been experimenting with a computer program that could be used to prepare individual verbal reports on profiles of test scores, and it was decided to use his program to print computer-composed reports of performance on in-basket problems for mailing to the participants.[2]

It was decided that the reports to subjects should be based on composite scores, rather than raw scores, in order to summarize the information more succinctly, and that the composite scores should be based on the anticipated results of a factor analysis. At the time, reliability information was available for all the in-basket scoring categories, but the factor analysis had not been completed. The best prediction of the outcome of the factor analysis seemed to be the factors obtained in the Bureau of Business factor analysis of data for 620 subjects that is described in Chapter 2.

When the reliability information was taken into account, it seemed desirable to drop the factor identified as *Orderly work*. The remaining 11 factors, plus an anticipated second-order factor involving amount of work, were used as the basis for judgmentally combining variables to produce 12 composite scores from the CDC in-baskets.

A verbal description of the behavior involved in each composite score was written for use in the computer report to subjects, and lists of modifiers were prepared to designate the frequency of the behavior. Five such

[2]The assistance of Dr. Carl Helm in adapting the program to the IBM 7044 computer is gratefully acknowledged.

COMPUTER GENERATED INTERPRETATION FOR SUBJECT X00049

THE AMOUNT OF WORK YOU DID IN THE SIMULATED JOB WAS
UNUSUALLY LARGE , AS INDICATED BY SUCH SIMPLE MEASURES AS
THE NUMBER OF ITEMS YOU ATTEMPTED,   THE AMOUNT OF WRITING
YOU DID, AND THE NUMBER OF ACTIONS YOU TOOK. IN ADDITION ,
A LARGE NUMBER OF THE COURSES OF ACTION YOU TOOK WERE OF
THE SORT THAT WE JUDGED TO BE IMAGINATIVE OR THAT SHOWED
AWARENESS OF NEED FOR BETTER PERFORMANCE IN THE
ORGANIZATION. COMPARED WITH THE AVERAGE PARTICIPANT, YOU
HAD A SMALLER TENDENCY TO SEE THE BROAD IMPLICATIONS OF THE
INBASKET PROBLEMS.
    YOU VERY FREQUENTLY DELAYED OR POSTPONED ACTION ON
PROBLEMS OR MERELY MADE PLANS WITHOUT TAKING ACTION. YOU
OFTEN DEALT WITH PROBLEMS BY MAKING FINAL DECISIONS OR
TAKING TERMINAL ACTIONS, AND YOU RARELY FOLLOWED
SUGGESTIONS MADE BY OTHERS. YOU INFREQUENTLY PREPARED FOR
ACTION BY, FOR EXAMPLE, ASKING FOR MORE INFORMATION, AND
YOU SELDOM PLANNED TO HAVE DISCUSSIONS WITH SUBORDINATES
AND OTHERS ABOUT PROBLEMS.
    ATTEMPTS TO CONTROL SUBORDINATES, BY SUCH MEANS AS
GIVING DIRECTIONS AND SETTING UP CHECKS AND DEADLINES,
OCCURRED VERY FREQUENTLY .YOU SHOWED SOME CONCERN ABOUT
YOUR SUPERIORS BY OCCASIONALLY INVOLVING THEM IN YOUR WORK,
AND YOU SHOWED MUCH CONCERN FOR PEOPLE OUTSIDE THE
DEPARTMENT OF COMMERCE. YOUR STYLE OF DEALING WITH OTHERS
WAS RARELY INFORMAL.

COMPUTER GENERATED INTERPRETATION FOR SUBJECT X00040

THE AMOUNT OF WORK YOU DID IN THE SIMULATED JOB WAS
RELATIVELY SMALL , AS INDICATED BY SUCH SIMPLE MEASURES AS
THE NUMBER OF ITEMS YOU ATTEMPTED,   THE AMOUNT OF WRITING
YOU DID, AND THE NUMBER OF ACTIONS YOU TOOK. IN ADDITION ,
AN AVERAGE NUMBER OF THE COURSES OF ACTION YOU TOOK WERE OF
THE SORT THAT WE JUDGED TO BE IMAGINATIVE OR THAT SHOWED
AWARENESS OF NEED FOR BETTER PERFORMANCE IN THE
ORGANIZATION. COMPARED WITH THE AVERAGE PARTICIPANT, YOU
HAD A SMALLER TENDENCY TO SEE THE BROAD IMPLICATIONS OF THE
INBASKET PROBLEMS.
    YOU OCCASIONALLY DELAYED OR POSTPONED ACTION ON
PROBLEMS OR MERELY MADE PLANS WITHOUT TAKING ACTION. YOU
OFTEN DEALT WITH PROBLEMS BY MAKING FINAL DECISIONS OR
TAKING TERMINAL ACTIONS, AND YOU OCCASIONALLY FOLLOWED
SUGGESTIONS MADE BY OTHERS. YOU VERY FREQUENTLY PREPARED
FOR ACTION BY, FOR EXAMPLE, ASKING FOR MORE INFORMATION,
BUT YOU SELDOM PLANNED TO HAVE DISCUSSIONS WITH
SUBORDINATES AND OTHERS ABOUT PROBLEMS.
    ATTEMPTS TO CONTROL SUBORDINATES, BY SUCH MEANS AS
GIVING DIRECTIONS AND SETTING UP CHECKS AND DEADLINES,
OCCURRED VERY FREQUENTLY .YOU SHOWED LITTLE CONCERN ABOUT
YOUR SUPERIORS BY INFREQUENTLY INVOLVING THEM IN YOUR WORK,
AND YOU SHOWED SOME CONCERN FOR PEOPLE OUTSIDE THE
DEPARTMENT OF COMMERCE. YOUR STYLE OF DEALING WITH OTHERS
WAS RARELY INFORMAL.

Fig. 4-1   Sample computer-generated reports.

modifiers were prepared for use in connection with the description of each composite score. The computer was instructed to choose one of these modifiers on the basis of the magnitude of the subject's score. The first description, for example, was as follows: "The amount of work you did in the simulated job was _____, as indicated by such simple measures as the number of items you attempted, the amount of writing you did, and the number of actions you took." The computer selected one of the following phrases to go in the blank: unusually large, relatively large, about average, relatively small, quite small. The score distribution was divided into equal fifths, and the computer selected the modifier which was associated with the subject's position in the score distribution. The computer was also instructed to choose connectives on the basis of the amount of contrast between certain pairs of related composite scores. Connectives like *and*, *but*, and *however* were inserted as appropriate.

The computer-generated report was mailed to each subject with a form letter that explained how the report was prepared. Samples of reports generated by the computer are shown in Fig. 4-1.

CHAPTER 5

The Predictor Variables

The predictor variables employed in the study include cognitive ability tests, scores on personality inventories, and items of biographical information. The following three sections will describe the tests of each type, will present statistical information about them, and will describe the results of three factor analyses that were conducted for the purpose of reducing the number of predictor variables.

More instruments were included in the battery than could be used in the main statistical analysis. It was intended from the beginning that factor analytic techniques would be used for preliminary data reduction, and the batteries were planned with this in mind. Thus in a number of instances several tests or inventories were included to represent a variable expected to emerge from the factor analysis. Use of a composite score based on the factor has the advantage of representing the common variance of the factor while reducing the influence of unique aspects of particular tests or questionnaires.

Several tests to represent each factor could not be used as a general rule, however, for a couple of reasons. One is that in the area of biographical information there is no well-established set of constructs based on factor analytic studies that could be used to choose instruments. A second reason is that testing time was limited because of practical considerations; in several instances it was necessary to choose one test to represent a factor, rather than two or more tests.

87

COGNITIVE ABILITY TESTS

Description of Tests

The cognitive tests included several tests selected from the *Manual for Kit of Reference Tests for Cognitive Factors* (French, Ekstrom, & Price, 1963) and two experimental tests devised by one of the authors for possible use by the California State Personnel Board in personnel selection. Each of these tests is briefly described below.

Gestalt Completion Test   This is one of the two tests selected by French, Ekstrom, and Price to measure Speed of Closure. They define this factor as "The ability to unify an apparently disparate perceptual field into a single percept." A test item is a number of black blotches formed by cutting away parts of a silhouette of a familiar object (*see* Fig. 5-1). The subject's task is to write the name of the object below the picture. Two separately timed parts were administered. Each part contained 10 items, and three minutes were allowed for each part.

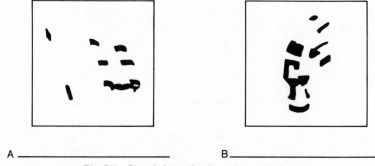

A ————————————   B ————————————

Fig. 5-1   Sample items for Gestalt completion test.

Concealed Words Test   This is the other test chosen to measure the Speed of Closure factor. Each item is a word printed in large lower case letters with parts of the letters missing (*see* Fig. 5-2). The items are thus

north

north _____   *north* _____

Fig. 5-2   Sample item for concealed words test.

similar to those in the Gestalt Completion Test except that printed words rather than silhouettes of objects are the stimulus materials. The task is to write the correct word for each item. Two separately timed parts, each with 25 items and a three-minute time limit, were administered.

Hidden Patterns Test   This test was used to represent the Flexibility of Closure factor, which is defined by French, Ekstrom, and Price as "The ability to keep one or more definite configurations in mind so as to make identification in spite of perceptual distractions." The test is an adaptation of the Gottschaldt Figures Test used by Thurstone. Each item is a geometrical pattern (*see* Fig. 5-3). A simpler figure, used as a model, is em-

How quickly can you recognize a figure that is hidden among other lines? This test contains rows of patterns. In each pattern you are to look for the model shown below:

The model must always be in this position, not on its side or upside down.

In the next row, when the model appears, it is shown by heavy lines:

( )   (X)   ( )   ( )   (X)   ( )   ( )

Your task will be to place an X in the space below each pattern in which the model appears. Now, try this row:

1.   2.   3.   4.   5.   6.   7.   8.   9.   10.

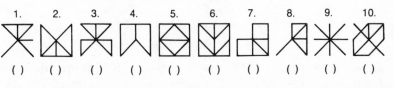

( )   ( )   ( )   ( )   ( )   ( )   ( )   ( )   ( )   ( )

Fig. 5-3   Sample items for hidden patterns test.

bedded in some of the patterns and not in others. The task is to mark all items that contain the model. There are two separately timed parts, each containing 200 items. Two minutes are allowed for each part.

The Hidden Patterns Test is substantially correlated with the rod and frame test and is thought to provide a reasonably good measure of field independence (Jackson, Messick, & Myers, 1964; Witkin, Dyk, Faterson, Goodenough, & Karp, 1962). It was included in the test battery primarily because of the theoretical relevance of the field dependence-independence cognitive style variable to the organizational climates used as experimental variables in the experiment. Cronbach and Snow (1969), however, in the light of their review of ATI research, are inclined to interpret tests such as Hidden Patterns as measures of fluid intelligence (Cattell, 1963).

Thing Categories Test   The Thing Categories Test was chosen to represent the Ideational Fluency factor, defined by French, Ekstrom, and Price as "The facility to call up ideas wherein quantity and not quality of ideas is emphasized." The subject is asked to write the names of as many things in a given category as he can think of in the time allowed. There are two parts to the test; for one part the category is "things round" (baseball, wheel), and for the other part the category is "things blue" (sky, overalls). Three minutes are allowed for each part.

Locations Test   This test was chosen to represent Induction — "Associated abilities involved in the finding of general concepts that will fit sets of data, the forming and trying out of hypotheses." The test was adapted by French, Ekstrom, and Price from Thurstone's Marks test. Each item consists of five rows of dashes, separated into groups by spaces (*see* Fig. 5-4). In each of the first four rows, one dash has been replaced by an

Example A:
```
Row 1    --------------   --x  ------
Row 2    -----   --x--    ------------
Row 3    -------------    --x   ------
Row 4    -----   --x----    ----------
Row 5    -----1--   --2--3-4  5---
```

Fig. 5-4   Sample item for locations test.

x, according to some rule. The task is to figure out what the rule is and to apply the rule in the fifth row by deciding where the *x* belongs. The subject indicates his answer by marking a number to indicate the correct position of the *x*. Six minutes are allowed for each part; each part has 14 items.

First and Last Names   This is a test of the Associative or Rote Memory factor, the ability to remember bits of unrelated material. The subject is given a list of 15 names (first and last) to study for three minutes. Then the 15 last names are presented in a different order, and he is given two minutes to supply the correct first name. There are two parts, each involving 15 names.

Mathematics Test Each item of this test requires the subject to compare two quantities, one in Column A and one in Column B, and respond by choosing one of four alternatives:

A — the quantity in Column A is greater
B — the quantity in Column B is greater
C — the two quantities are equal
D — the size relationship cannot be determined
  from the information given

In the sample item, for example, subjects were required to compare "N^2" and "N^4"; it was keyed D because N might be less than 1, 1, or greater than 1. The items varied considerably in difficulty and involved numerical and simple algebraic expressions. The test was chosen as a measure of mathematical aptitude because it seemed to require a fairly high level of understanding of quantitative relationships and a minimum of computational skills. Ten minutes were allowed for the 30-item test.

Vocabulary Test This is the V-5 Advanced Vocabulary Test from the *Manual for Kit of Reference Tests for Cognitive Factors*, adapted from a test by John B. Carroll. It is a four-choice synonyms test with rather difficult items. Four minutes were allowed for each of two parts, each part containing 18 items.

Test S, Analogies This test is one of the experimental tests developed for the State Personnel Board. It consists of 30 five-choice verbal analogies items of a conventional sort. The unusual feature of the test is that the subject is required to indicate his degree of confidence in his answer to each item by choosing an answer with *full commitment* or *partial commitment*, or by making *no commitment*. The directions include the following paragraphs:

In this test you are to demonstrate how effectively you can use your ability to perceive relationships.

The test consists of thirty analogies.
Example. cloth: dye::house: ?
  (A) brush (B) door (C) paint (D) shade (E) wood

The answer is (C) because paint colors a house in much the same way dye colors cloth.

In marking an answer to an item you can choose from several courses of action.

You may make a FULL COMMITMENT, a PARTIAL COMMITMENT, or NO COMMITMENT.

If you make a FULL COMMITMENT and the answer you have chosen is

right, you receive   8 credits

wrong, you receive   0 credits

If you make a PARTIAL COMMITMENT and the answer you have chosen is

right, you receive   7 credits

wrong, you receive   3 credits

If you make NO COMMITMENT, you receive————————————— 5 credits

You may mark NO COMMITMENT to any item—do so whenever you believe it is to your advantage to mark NO COMMITMENT.

Several items have *no one* right answer; thus, NO COMMITMENT is the best response for some items in the test.

Sample Answer Sheet

	A		B		C		D		E		No
F| | |P		F| | |P		F| | |P		F| | |P		F| | |P		| |

If you believe that the answer to an item is C and want to make a FULL COMMITMENT, you should mark the answer space on the answer sheet that is under the "F" to the left of C.

If you think that the answer is C but want to make only a PARTIAL COMMITMENT, you should mark the answer space that is under the "P" to the right of C.

If you are uncertain as to the answer or believe that there are either *more than one or no* right answer, you should mark the answer space under the "NO" (NO COMMITMENT).

As each item marked "NO COMMITMENT" and each item left blank (omitted or not reached) will be scored for 5 credits, you are, in effect, starting the test with 30×5 or 150 credits.

Each *Right* FULL COMMITMENT will *increase* this total by 3 credits.

Each *Wrong* FULL COMMITMENT will *decrease* this total by 5 credits.

Each *Right* PARTIAL COMMITMENT will *increase* this total by 2 credits.

Each *Wrong* PARTIAL COMMITMENT will *decrease* this total by 2 credits.

Your goal in this test is to take the series of actions that gives the highest possible total number of credits.

Several methods of scoring, in addition to the one described to the examinee, were devised in an attempt to measure various decision strategies and their effectiveness. The seven scores obtained from the Analogies Test are as follows:

1. *Strategy Score.* This is the score obtained by using the "credits" for correct answers as described above in the directions to examinees.

2. *Number Right.* This is merely the number of items answered correctly, including the items where *No Commitment* is keyed as the correct answer.

3. *Efficiency Index.* This is a ratio obtained by dividing the subject's Strategy Score by his *optimum* strategy score. The optimum strategy score is defined as eight times the number of correct answers (other than those keyed No Commitment) plus five times the remaining items. This is the strategy score the person would have received if he had always chosen the optimum level of commitment.

4. *Confidence Index.* This score is intended to reflect the subject's willingness to take risks to maximize his score. The formula is

$$\frac{5(FC) + 3(PC)}{\text{No. items attempted}} \times 100$$

where FC is the number of full commitments and PC is the number of partial commitments. The weights are proportional to the amount of risk per unit of potential gain in score.

5. *Conservatism Index.* This score is supposed to be a measure of one's tendency to sacrifice potential gain in order to minimize losses. The score is

$$\frac{3(NC) + (PCR)}{\text{No. items attempted}} \times 100$$

where NC is the number of no commitments recorded and PCR is the number of partial commitments on items answered correctly. The weights are proportional to the amount of potential gain sacrificed.

6. *Plunger Index.* As the name indicates, this score is supposed to reflect a tendency to take unjustified risks. The formula is

$$\frac{5(FCW) + 2(PCW)}{\text{No. items attempted}} \times 100$$

where FCW is the number of full commitments to items answered incorrectly and PCW is the number of partial commitments to items answered incorrectly. The weights are again proportional to the number of penalty points.

7. *Accuracy Score.* This score reflects a general tendency to make appropriate commitments in responding to items. High scores are assigned when (1) the proportion of full commitments that are correct is high, (2) when the proportion of partial commitments that are correct is moderate, (3) when the proportion of no commitments that are correct is low, (4) when the proportion of full commitments that are correct is greater than the number of partial commitments that are correct, and (5) when the proportion of partial commitments that are correct is greater

than the number of no commitments that are correct. The complete procedure for scoring is rather long and complicated and will not be presented more fully.

Multiple Analogies Test   This is the second State Personnel Board experimental test. Each item is in the form of a verbal analogy in which the first element is given and a choice for each of the other three elements must be made from a list of four words provided. Two analogies are to be made for each item. Here is a sample item and an excerpt from the instructions:

Boy is to _____ as _____ is to _____.

(A) gang	(E) child	(I) adult	B F L
(B) girl	(F) man	(J) ride	
(C) man	(G) group	(K) Rotary	C E I
(D) run	(H) walk	(L) woman	

In the example, one set of relationships is "*boy* is to (B) girl as (F) man is to (L) woman." Therefore, the choices to be marked at the right of the item are BFL.

Another set of relationships is "*boy* is to (C) man as (E) child is to (I) adult." Therefore, the choices to be marked at the right are also CEI.

These choices have been marked correctly in the example above. Of course, it does not matter which set of three letters is marked first; if CEI were marked on the top line and BFL below, this would be equally correct. Mark your answers in capital letters, please.

Remember that a given choice such as "(C) man" may be used only once. On the other hand, as in the example, both choice "(C) man" and choice "(F) man" may be used.

Since this test is designed to measure your ability to make multiple interpretations and associations, credit will be given *only if your answers to both* of the items based on a given sentence are correct.

The test was scored in accordance with the instructions, i.e., giving credit only for items for which two satisfactory analogies were produced. The test proved to be rather difficult with this method of scoring; so a second score was also obtained based on the total number of satisfactory analogies.

Statistical Information

The statistical information obtained for the tests in the cognitive domain are shown in Tables 5-1 and 5-2, which present intercorrelations, means, standard deviations, and, where available, reliability coefficients.

The reliability coefficients for the tests from the factor kit are in general reasonably high. These correlations are all based on the correlations

Table 5-1 Intercorrelations of Cognitive Tests ($N = 260$)

	1	2	3	4	5	6	7	8	9	10	11	12	13	14	15	16	17	18
Multiple Analogies Test																		
1. Regular Score		0.50	0.31	0.29	0.24	-0.08	0.07	-0.25	0.29	0.23	0.22	0.22	0.08	0.13	0.37	0.11	0.34	0.29
2. Modified Score			0.01	0.15	-0.08	0.05	-0.05	0.02	0.03	0.11	0.08	0.12	0.07	0.14	0.13	0.09	0.11	-0.02
Test S. Analogies																		
3. Strategy Score				0.68	0.88	-0.33	0.30	-0.86	0.63	0.25	0.21	0.19	0.08	0.05	0.29	0.29	0.40	0.25
4. Number Right					0.28	0.24	-0.25	-0.33	0.38	0.25	0.18	0.22	0.14	0.12	0.27	0.19	0.31	0.19
5. Efficiency Index						-0.64	0.58	-0.95	0.57	0.17	0.18	0.12	0.01	0.00	0.22	0.25	0.33	0.19
6. Confidence Index							-0.94	0.75	-0.20	-0.02	-0.08	-0.06	0.05	0.04	-0.12	-0.15	-0.12	0.03
7. Conservatism Index								-0.68	0.16	-0.00	0.07	0.06	-0.02	-0.03	0.12	0.16	0.13	0.04
8. Plunger Index									-0.56	-0.18	-0.19	-0.15	-0.02	-0.01	-0.26	-0.27	-0.33	-0.18
9. Accuracy Score										0.23	0.15	0.15	0.07	-0.01	0.29	0.12	0.31	0.18
Factor Kit Tests																		
10. Gestalt Completion Test											0.44	0.28	0.14	0.15	0.19	0.15	0.17	-0.01
11. Concealed Words Test												0.22	0.14	0.16	0.23	0.24	0.21	0.17
12. Hidden Patterns Test													0.22	0.10	0.23	0.17	0.19	0.06
13. Things Round														0.42	0.13	0.12	0.05	0.11
14. Things Blue															0.10	0.17	0.05	0.20
15. Locations Test																0.10	0.42	0.14
16. First and Last Names																	0.13	0.10
17. Mathematics Test																		0.21
18. Vocabulary Test																		

Table 5-2   Means, Standard Deviations, and Reliabilities of Cognitive Tests

		Mean	SD	Reliability
	Multiple Analogies Test			
1.	Regular Score	1.8	1.7	
2.	Modified Score	7.4	3.5	
	Test S, Analogies			
3.	Strategy Score	151.4	17.4	0.90
4.	Number Right	12.8	3.2	
5.	Efficiency Index	83.8	8.4	
6.	Confidence Index	264.8	76.6	
7.	Conservatism Index	93.3	39.4	
8.	Plunger Index	92.0	54.5	
9.	Accuracy Score	2.7	1.6	
	Factor Kit Tests			
10.	Gestalt Completion Test	11.7	4.9	0.84
11.	Concealed Words Test	21.4	6.0	0.80
12.	Hidden Patterns Test	145.9	35.3	0.86
13.	Things Round	18.8	5.6 ⎱	0.59
14.	Things Blue	7.5	3.1 ⎰	
15.	Locations Test	8.7	5.2	0.76
16.	First and Last Names	14.8	6.9	0.86
17.	Mathematics Test	17.1	4.8	0.80
18.	Vocabulary Test	25.9	5.9	0.81

between separately timed parts, which are then corrected for double length by means of the Spearman–Brown formula. In the case of the Thing Categories Test, the reliability for a single test, based on Things Round and Things Blue, is shown. Separate reliability coefficients for the two parts were not obtainable.

No reliability is reported for the Multiple Analogies Test. This test was highly speeded and was not administered with separately timed parts. Its reliability may be presumed to be quite low. Test S was not so highly speeded; the mean number of items attempted was 27.1 (of 30 items). The estimated reliability of the strategy score, based on an intra-class correlation, is 0.90.

Factor Analysis of Cognitive Test Scores

The intercorrelations shown in Table 5-1 were factored by the group principal components method. A description of the method is presented in Appendix A.

The rotated factor loadings that resulted from the factor analysis are shown in Table 5-3. Six common factors were identified, and the rotation

Table 5-3 Reference Factor Loadings for Cognitive Tests

Cognitive Variable	I	II	III	IV	Factor V	VI	(VII)	(VIII)	(IX)
Multiple Analogies Test									
1. Regular Score	0.74	0.08	-0.00	0.03	-0.03	0.07	0.01	-0.04	0.13
2. Modified Score	0.86	-0.08	0.00	-0.03	0.03	-0.07	-0.01	0.04	-0.13
Test S, Analogies									
3. Strategy Score	0.00	0.82	-0.23	-0.01	0.01	0.01	0.01	0.04	0.01
4. Number Right	0.06	0.54	-0.65	-0.00	0.04	0.07	0.06	0.05	-0.01
5. Efficiency Index	-0.04	0.73	0.14	-0.00	-0.01	-0.03	-0.02	0.01	0.02
6. Confidence Index	-0.02	-0.16	-0.80	-0.01	0.01	-0.00	-0.01	-0.01	0.01
7. Conservatism Index	0.01	0.09	0.83	-0.01	0.02	0.03	0.02	0.02	0.00
8. Plunger Index	-0.01	-0.67	-0.25	-0.00	-0.00	-0.00	-0.00	-0.02	0.01
9. Accuracy Score	0.04	0.67	-0.20	0.01	-0.00	0.03	0.00	-0.08	-0.02
Factor Kit Tests									
10. Gestalt Completion Test	0.02	0.07	-0.06	0.75	0.01	-0.04	0.03	-0.05	-0.10
11. Concealed Words Test	-0.02	-0.07	0.06	0.76	-0.01	0.04	-0.03	0.05	0.10
12. Hidden Patterns Test	0.00	-0.00	-0.00	0.00	-0.00	-0.00	0.93	0.00	-0.00
13. Things Round	-0.04	0.03	-0.02	-0.02	0.80	0.01	0.06	-0.03	-0.05
14. Things Blue	0.04	-0.03	0.02	0.02	0.79	-0.01	-0.06	0.03	0.05
15. Locations Test	0.02	-0.05	0.03	0.01	0.04	0.73	0.02	-0.02	-0.04
16. First and Last Names	0.00	-0.00	0.00	0.00	-0.00	-0.00	0.00	0.94	-0.00
17. Mathematics Test	-0.02	0.05	-0.03	-0.01	-0.04	0.71	-0.02	0.02	0.04
18. Vocabulary Test	0.00	-0.00	0.00	0.00	0.00	0.00	-0.00	-0.00	0.94

gave quite good simple structure. The factors are easily identifiable. Three unique variables were retained and factor loadings are shown for them, also.

The first factor is obviously the Multiple Analogies Test. Factors II and III are both based on the experimental Test S, Analogies. The seven scores can be represented adequately by two factors. Factor II is called Successful Strategy; it has high loadings on all the scores from the test except the Confidence Index and the Conservatism Index. All the scores with high loadings on this factor take into account in one way or another the extent to which answers were correct, and most of them also reflect successful choice of "commitments." The factor thus seems to reflect both high ability in doing the analogies and good judgment in using the options to increase one's score. The factor is therefore called Successful Strategy in Analogies. The other Test S factor has a high positive loading for the Conservatism Index and negative loadings on the Confidence Index and on Number Right. It reflects a tendency to make partial or no commitments rather than high commitments and is associated with low ability to choose correct answers. It is called Conservative Strategy.

The other factors came out as expected; the two speed of closure tests loaded on one factor, as did the two Thing Categories Tests. Locations and Mathematics loaded on a factor we call Inductive Reasoning. Hidden Patterns, First and Last Names, and Vocabulary tests are retained as unique variables. The 18 cognitive tests are thus reduced to nine variables for use in the main statistical analysis.

The intercorrelations of the nine factors are shown in Table 5-4. Correlations are in general quite low. The highest correlation (0.40) is between Inductive Reasoning and Test S, Successful Strategy. Inductive Reasoning also correlates positively with the Multiple Analogies Test (0.33). The two factors from Test S correlate 0.38. All other correlations are lower than 0.30.

PERSONALITY INVENTORY SCALES

Description of the Scales

After considering a large number of available personality inventories, it was decided to choose scales from various sources and to adapt and combine them into a new instrument for use in this study. A total of 16 scales were chosen from various sources. Since most of the scales in these inventories were not balanced with respect to the proportion of items

Table 5-4 Intercorrelations among Cognitive Test Factors

Factor	I	II	III	IV	V	VI	(VII)	(VIII)	(IX)
I Multiple Analogies Test		0.16	−0.04	0.22	0.14	0.33	0.19	0.12	0.15
II Test S, Successful Strategy			0.38	0.26	0.04	0.40	0.17	0.26	0.23
III Test S, Conservative Strategy				−0.01	−0.07	0.06	0.01	0.10	−0.01
IV Speed of Closure					0.21	0.28	0.29	0.23	0.09
V Ideational Fluency						0.12	0.19	0.17	0.19
VI Inductive Reasoning							0.25	0.14	0.21
(VII) Hidden Patterns								0.17	0.06
(VIII) First and Last Names									0.10
(IX) Vocabulary									

keyed *true* and *false*, it was necessary to rewrite some of the items in reversed form in order to reduce the likelihood of acquiescence response bias. Items were also rewritten as necessary to fit a consistent format; each item in the inventory is a statement that can be answered *true* or *false*. Where appropriate, items were made into "*I*" statements, e.g., "I am always in a hurry." The option of omitting an item was allowed but discouraged. The instructions told the subject to read each statement and "encircle *T* if you agree with a statement or feel that it is true about you. Encircle *F* if you disagree with a statement or feel that it is not true about you." The inventory that resulted from putting all the items together in scrambled order contains 292 items and yields scores on 16 nonoverlapping scales. The scales used are described below.

Acquiescence   The Acquiescence scale contains 24 items. Since the purpose of this scale is to measure any general tendency that may exist for one to acquiesce to propositions placed before him in a personality inventory, all items are keyed *true*. The items chosen span all the scales of the Personality Research Inventory (Saunders, 1955b) in an attempt to wash out the effects of any common content, and all were near the median with respect to percentage of endorsement. Sample item: "I am more idealistic than most people."

Activity   This is the "A" scale from the Thurstone Temperament Schedule. The items have been recast in "I" form, and a number were rephrased in order to balance those keyed *T* and *F*. There are 19 items, 10 keyed *T* and 9 keyed *F*. Sample item: "I usually work fast."

Anxiety   These items were originally from the Minnesota Multiphasic Personality Inventory; many of them were subsequently used in the Taylor Manifest Anxiety Scale (Taylor, 1953). There are 20 items in the scale, half keyed *T* and half keyed *F*. Sample item: "I work under a great deal of strain."

Authoritarianism   This is the California "F" scale (Adorno, Frenkel-Brunswik, Levinson, & Sanford, 1950), with one item omitted because of overlap with the Preference for Complexity scale. There are 28 items, all keyed *T*. Sample item: "An insult to our honor should never go unpunished."

Dominance   This is the "D" scale from the Thurstone Temperament Schedule with items balanced—10 are keyed *T* and 10 *F*. Sample item: "I do not hesitate to assume responsibilities."

Impulsiveness   This is the Thurstone Temperament Schedule "I" scale, with 10 items keyed T and 10 F. Sample item: "I like to take chances just for the sake of excitement."

Maladjustment   These items are from the Heron (1956) personality measure; some of the items derive from the MMPI, the Taylor MAS, and the Edwards SD scale. Ten items are keyed T and 10 F. Sample item: "I am a rather nervous person."

Preference for Complexity   This is a form of the Barron (1953) complexity-simplicity scale, with the items balanced by members of the ETS Division of Psychological Studies, Personality and Social Behavior Research Group. One item is from the "F" scale. There are 22 items, half keyed T and half keyed F. Sample item: "I enjoy discarding the old and accepting the new."

Reflectiveness   The items are from the "R" scale of the Thurstone Temperament Schedule; 10 items are keyed T and 10 F. Sample item: "When I have an important problem, I prefer to think it through by myself."

Rigidity   This is the Gough-Sanford (1952) rigidity scale. There are 22 items, half keyed T and half F. Sample item: "If I start a task, I finish it, even if it is not very important."

Self-Sufficiency   This is Wolff's (1958) self-sufficiency scale with Grayson's (1951) critical items deleted. The items originally are from the MMPI. Twelve items are keyed T and 11 F. Sample item: "I seldom ask for advice."

Sociability-H   This is from the Heron (1956) personality measure. There are only 12 items, half keyed T and half F. Sample item: "I find it easy to act naturally at a party."

Sociability-T   This is the "S" scale of the Thurstone Temperament Schedule. Eleven items are keyed T and 9 F. Sample item: "I quickly get to know my neighbors."

Social Desirability   These items were selected from the Personality Research Inventory to measure social desirability response bias. They span all the scales of the PRI, to minimize the effect of item content. Nine items are keyed T, 11 F. Sample item: "I am generally patient when someone delays me."

Stability   These items are from the "E" scale of the Thurstone Temperament Schedule. There are 20 items, equally divided between T and F. Sample item: "I can relax in a noisy room."

Tolerance for Ambiguity   This is the Budner (1962) tolerance of ambiguity scale. There are 16 items, half keyed T and half F. Sample item: "A good teacher is one who makes you wonder about your habitual way of looking at things."

Ghiselli Self-Description Inventory

In addition to the inventory described above, Ghiselli's (1954) *Self-Description Inventory* was administered. This instrument contains 64 pairs of words, and for each pair of words the subject is instructed to "check the one you think *most* describes you." Sample pairs are *realistic, tactful*; *sincere, calm*; *weak, selfish*; *noisy, arrogant*. Seven scores are obtained. The scoring keys overlap by varying amounts, and the keyed items are given weights varying from *1* to *5*. The names of the seven scales are Intelligence, Supervisory Qualities, Initiative, Self-Assurance, Perceived Occupational Level, Decision-Making Approach, and Sociometric Popularity. The inventory was included partly because of interest on the part of the State Personnel Board in the instrument and partly because of the face validity of the scales.

Statistical Information

The intercorrelations of the 16 scales and their means, standard deviations, and reliabilities are presented in Tables 5-5 and 5-6. The reliabilities are based on correlations between odd- and even-numbered items, corrected for double length by the Spearman–Brown formula. Most of the reliabilities are only moderately high, although a few are near 0.8. The scales intended to measure response bias were quite low in reliability (0.27 for acquiescence and 0.20 for social desirability); perhaps the subjects took seriously the assurances about confidentiality and the scientific purposes of the study and thus relatively little variance in responses can be attributed to response bias.

The Acquiescence scale correlated 0.22 with the "F" scale and 0.21 with Rigidity, which compared with the reliability of the Acquiescence scale (0.27) is quite high. All the "F" scale items are keyed *true*, but the Rigidity scale was balanced. The Social Desirability scale correlated with several scales substantially higher than its reliability; correlations were

Table 5-5 Intercorrelations of Inventory Scales

Scale	1	2	3	4	5	6	7	8	9	10	11	12	13	14	15	16
1. Acquiescence		0.15	0.06	0.22	0.09	0.09	0.13	-0.12	0.06	0.21	0.03	-0.02	0.12	0.01	-0.10	-0.05
2. Activity			-0.04	0.09	0.37	0.40	0.04	0.01	-0.09	-0.08	-0.04	0.27	0.23	0.06	0.05	0.09
3. Anxiety				0.03	-0.20	-0.25	0.57	0.04	0.21	0.06	-0.08	-0.24	-0.23	-0.23	-0.47	-0.02
4. Authoritarianism					-0.09	0.02	0.09	-0.52	0.05	0.45	0.14	-0.06	-0.11	0.14	-0.18	-0.37
5. Dominance						0.56	-0.21	0.15	-0.23	-0.11	-0.27	0.57	0.69	0.24	0.19	0.17
6. Impulsiveness							-0.15	0.14	-0.22	-0.09	-0.13	0.51	0.53	0.11	0.22	0.16
7. Maladjustment								0.04	0.24	0.01	0.04	-0.23	-0.27	-0.32	-0.55	-0.00
8. Preference for Complexity									0.07	-0.53	-0.19	0.15	0.11	-0.22	-0.04	0.49
9. Reflectiveness										0.09	0.28	-0.34	-0.33	-0.03	-0.17	0.05
10. Rigidity											0.21	-0.14	-0.09	0.25	-0.06	-0.44
11. Self-Sufficiency												-0.23	-0.41	0.03	0.12	-0.11
12. Sociability-H													0.57	0.05	0.18	0.13
13. Sociability-T														0.26	0.25	0.11
14. Social Desirability															0.17	-0.07
15. Stability																0.03
16. Tolerance for Ambiguity																

Table 5-6   Means, Standard Deviations, and Reliabilities of Inventory Scales

Scale	Maximum Possible Score	Mean	SD	Reliability
1. Acquiescence	36	19.6	4.2	0.27
2. Activity	38	25.3	5.7	0.64
3. Anxiety	20	4.2	3.7	0.62
4. Authoritarianism	56	15.6	8.2	0.79
5. Dominance	40	26.8	8.2	0.82
6. Impulsiveness	40	23.2	6.1	0.57
7. Maladjustment	40	11.8	5.4	0.63
8. Preference for Complexity	44	21.0	6.0	0.61
9. Reflectiveness	38	20.8	5.5	0.47
10. Rigidity	44	21.3	6.1	0.57
11. Self-Sufficiency	22	8.6	4.3	0.58
12. Sociability-H	24	11.4	4.5	0.61
13. Sociability-T	40	24.2	7.3	0.80
14. Social Desirability	30	21.7	3.5	0.20
15. Stability	40	28.1	5.8	0.63
16. Tolerance for Ambiguity	32	21.8	3.8	0.28

positive for Dominance, Rigidity, and Sociability-T, and negative for Anxiety, Maladjustment, and Preference for Complexity.

The reliabilities for the Ghiselli instrument ranged from 0.06 to 0.50, with a median of 0.36. The correlations of any score with other scores in the inventory were typically as high or higher than its reliability; the item overlap would of course tend to produce such high intercorrelations. These results suggest that one factor would account for most of the reliable variance in the instrument. Because of the low reliabilities of most of the scales, the probability that they contained relatively little unique variance, and the uncertainty of the meaning of a single score based on all items, it was decided to drop the instrument from further analysis.

Factor Analysis of Personality Inventory Scales

The intercorrelations of the 16 scales of the personality inventory were factored by the group principal components method. Four factors were retained and rotated; the factor loadings that resulted are shown in Table 5-7.

Table 5-7   Personality Inventory Factor Loadings

Scale	Factor			
	I	II	III	IV
1. Acquiescence	0.15	0.15	0.21	0.13
2. Activity	0.50	0.13	0.03	0.57
3. Anxiety	−0.00	0.76	0.03	−0.03
4. Authoritarianism	0.09	0.11	0.75	0.10
5. Dominance	0.77	−0.02	−0.03	0.14
6. Impulsiveness	0.69	−0.02	−0.01	0.33
7. Maladjustment	0.02	0.82	0.02	0.12
8. Preference for Complexity	0.04	0.10	−0.81	0.03
9. Reflectiveness	−0.44	0.09	−0.11	0.50
10. Rigidity	−0.02	−0.00	0.76	0.04
11. Self-Sufficiency	−0.47	−0.20	0.08	0.64
12. Sociability-H	0.72	−0.01	−0.02	0.01
13. Sociability-T	0.76	−0.08	0.02	−0.15
14. Social Desirability	0.07	−0.44	0.22	0.04
15. Stability	−0.03	−0.74	−0.08	0.07
16. Tolerance for Ambiguity	0.03	0.00	−0.72	0.10

The highest loadings on Factor I are for Dominance, Impulsiveness, and the two Sociability scales, with Activity also showing a moderate positive loading. Loadings are negative for Reflectiveness and Self-Sufficiency. It seems reasonable to think of this factor as *Social Extroversion*.

Factor II is *Maladjustment*. It has high positive loadings on scales for maladjustment and anxiety, and a high negative loading for stability. Social desirability has a moderate negative loading.

Factor III has two high positive and two high negative loadings. The positive loadings are for rigidity and authoritarianism and the negative loadings for preference for complexity and tolerance for ambiguity. We have named the factor *Rigid Authoritarianism*.

The last factor has only three moderately high loadings, all positive, for self-sufficiency, activity, and reflectiveness. There is also a loading of 0.33 for impulsiveness. The factor seems to represent an independence of thought and action, and we have chosen to call it *Independence*.

The 16 scales thus seem to be represented quite well by the four factors. Their intercorrelations are quite low, as is shown in Table 5-8; the highest correlation (−0.31) is between *Social Extroversion* and *Maladjustment*. In the analysis to be reported in later chapters, the personality inventory domain will be represented by the four factor scores.

Table 5-8   Intercorrelations of Personality Inventory Factors

	I	II	III	IV
I Social Extroversion		−0.31	−0.18	0.00
II Maladjustment			−0.01	−0.01
III Rigid Authoritarianism				0.07
IV Independence				

BACKGROUND VARIABLES

The principal source of information about background characteristics of the subjects was a one-page questionnaire which, like the inventories, was filled out and returned to the research office by subjects before the Research Institutes were held. The description of the subjects presented in Chapter 4 is largely based on tabulations from this questionnaire. From the questionnaire data, 13 variables were generated. The 13 variables are as follows:

1. *Institutional (1) vs. noninstitutional (0) department.*   This dichotomy has to do with whether or not a person works in an institutional setting. The "institutional" employees may be physicians, psychologists, engineers, lawyers, accountants, managers, or anyone else employed in a hospital, prison, or other institutional setting.

2. *Job level.*   There are three job levels that have been defined; from high to low they are called (3) administrative (top policy-influencing positions), (2) managerial (responsible for more than one unit and function), and (1) supervisory (responsible for a single organizational entity or function, or a professional-technical position). The frequencies for the three categories are as follows: Administrative, 27; Managerial, 74; and Supervisory, 159.

3. *Civil service (1) vs. exempt (0) status.*   This is a dichotomy with *civil service* and *exempt* categories. The exempt employees are those who are appointees rather than regular civil service employees. Only 23 subjects were in exempt positions.

4. *Professional (1) vs. managerial (0) job.*   The two categories in this dichotomy are those whose training and experience are primarily in a professional area, such as engineering, and those whose training and/or experience are primarily in the area of administration.

5. *Outdoor (1) vs. indoor (0) job.*   This dichotomy obviously depends primarily on whether one ordinarily works indoors (in an office, hospital, or laboratory) or outdoors. In the latter category are technical public

service occupations such as agriculture, conservation, engineering, regulatory, and public safety jobs.

6. *Management service occupations (1) vs. all other jobs (0).* Management service occupations include those with fiscal, administrative, personnel, and training functions.

7. *Birthdate.*

8. *Years of education.*

9. *Theoretical (1) vs. applied (0) education.* This dichotomy contrasts a theoretical with an applied orientation in higher education. Included in *theoretical* were such fields of graduate training (or undergraduate major, if there was no graduate training) as physics, chemistry, mathematics, geology, biology, genetics, anthropology, psychology, economics, history, music, and literature, as contrasted with engineering, architecture, medicine, veterinary medicine, agriculture, forestry, animal husbandry, sanitation, education, social work, public health, accounting, and business administration.

10. *Engineering or science education (1) vs. other (0).* This dichotomy contrasts the engineering and natural science fields (both applied and theoretical) with other fields. The engineering and science category includes engineering, architecture, physics, chemistry, geology, biology, genetics, mathematics, medicine, veterinary medicine, agriculture, forestry, animal husbandry, etc. The "other" category includes all the other areas of concentration, such as education, social work, public health, industrial arts, sociology, psychology, political science, economics, humanities, accounting, business administration, and public administration.

11. *Years of military service.*

12. *Years of administrative experience.*

13. *Number of children.*

The intercorrelations of the 13 variables are shown in Table 5-9. The intercorrelations were factored, using the group principal components method. The factor loadings are shown in Table 5-10, and the intercorrelations of the factors are presented in Table 5-11. The factor structure is essentially orthogonal, as shown by the very low factor intercorrelations in Table 5-11. Four factors were retained, as were three additional variables which shared very little variance with other variables.

Factor I has only two high loadings, one indicating Educational Level and the other employment in an Institutional vs. a Noninstitutional setting. There is also a small negative loading for outdoor job. Those who are high

Table 5-9 Intercorrelations of Background Variables

	1	2	3	4	5	6	7	8	9	10	11	12	13
1. Institutional (1) vs. Non-institutional (0) Department		-0.11	0.13	0.06	-0.48	0.01	0.09	0.29	-0.00	-0.15	-0.02	-0.02	-0.09
2. Job Level			-0.53	0.03	0.12	-0.15	-0.33	0.04	-0.03	-0.11	-0.05	0.28	-0.02
3. Civil Service (1) vs. Exempt (0) Status				0.04	-0.22	0.18	0.18	-0.05	-0.06	0.13	-0.04	-0.20	0.04
4. Professional (1) vs. Managerial (0) Job					0.43	-0.78	-0.05	0.15	-0.06	0.40	-0.12	-0.08	0.00
5. Outdoor (1) vs. Indoor (0) Job						-0.68	-0.12	-0.12	-0.04	0.51	-0.03	-0.01	0.05
6. Management Service Occupations (1) vs. All Other Jobs (0)							0.10	-0.04	0.03	-0.40	0.05	0.03	0.01
7. Birthdate								0.13	0.06	-0.06	0.10	-0.64	0.24
8. Years of Education									0.05	0.12	0.14	-0.06	0.04
9. Theoretical (1) vs. Applied (0) Education										-0.07	0.04	-0.15	-0.10
10. Engineering-Science Education (1) vs. Other (0)											-0.04	-0.03	0.13
11. Years of Military Service												0.04	0.05
12. Years of Administrative Experience													-0.16
13. Number of Children													

Table 5-10 Reference Factor Loadings for Background Variables

Background Variable	Factor						
	I	II	III	IV	(V)	(VI)	(VII)
1. Institutional (1) vs. Noninstitutional (0) Department	*0.79*	-0.04	0.08	0.11	-0.03	-0.08	-0.05
2. Job Level	0.02	*0.72*	-0.45	0.02	-0.03	-0.04	0.03
3. Civil Service (1) vs. Exempt (0) Status	0.01	*-0.61*	*0.63*	0.01	-0.02	-0.04	0.03
4. Professional (1) vs. Managerial (0) Job	0.19	-0.06	0.04	*-0.83*	-0.02	-0.06	-0.04
5. Outdoor (1) vs. Indoor (0) Job	-0.32	0.06	-0.10	*-0.77*	0.01	0.05	-0.00
6. Management Service Occupations (1) vs. All Other Jobs (0)	-0.09	-0.07	0.09	*0.89*	-0.02	-0.01	0.04
7. Birthdate	0.04	*-0.74*	*-0.47*	0.07	-0.05	0.06	0.04
8. Years of Education	*0.80*	0.04	-0.08	-0.11	0.03	0.08	0.05
9. Theoretical (1) vs. Applied (0) Education	-0.00	-0.00	0.00	-0.00	*0.98*	-0.00	0.00
10. Engineering-Science Education (1) vs. Other (0)	0.03	-0.09	0.19	*-0.69*	-0.01	0.00	0.11
11. Years of Military Service	-0.00	0.00	-0.00	0.00	-0.00	*0.99*	-0.00
12. Years of Administrative Experience	0.03	*0.74*	*0.48*	0.07	-0.04	0.07	0.03
13. Number of Children	-0.00	-0.00	-0.00	-0.00	-0.00	-0.00	*0.96*

Table 5-11   Intercorrelations of Background Factors

		I	II	III	IV	(V)	(VI)	(VII)
I	Educated Institutional Man		−0.10	−0.04	0.08	0.03	0.07	−0.03
II	Power and Seniority			0.00	−0.07	−0.07	−0.03	−0.17
III	Dead-End Seniority				0.06	−0.12	−0.02	−0.14
IV	Staff Officer					0.06	0.08	−0.05
(V)	Theoretical Education						0.04	−0.10
(VI)	Years of Military Service							0.05
(VII)	Number of Children							

on Factor I undoubtedly tend to be professionally trained people who work in hospitals or other institutional settings such as prisons. We identify the factor as representing the *Educated Institutional Man*.

Factor II has high positive loadings on age (−0.74 for Birthdate), Job Level, and Years of Administrative Experience, and a negative loading on Civil Service Status. Those with high scores on Factor II thus tend to be older, experienced people in high level, appointive positions. We call the factor *Power and Seniority*.

Factor III loadings tend to be somewhat lower; the highest is for Civil Service (rather than exempt) status (0.63). The loadings for Years of Administrative Experience and age (−0.47 for date of birth) are also positive, but the loading for Job Level is negative. Subjects with high loadings on Factor III thus tend to be older, experienced people in the civil service who did not reach a high level in the state service. We call the factor *Dead-End Seniority*.

Factor IV has a high positive loading (0.89) for Management Service Occupations and negative loadings for Professional and Outdoor jobs and for Engineering-Science Education. This factor thus seems to represent the person whose specialty is administration rather than some substantive professional area. The factor is therefore called *Staff Officer*.

The three variables retained because of high uniqueness were Theoretical vs. Applied Education (loading = 0.98), Years of Military Service (0.99), and Number of Children (0.96). The factor analysis has thus reduced the number of personal history variables to seven and has eliminated most of the redundancy in the biographical data by yielding a nearly orthogonal set of factors.

CLIMATE RATINGS

Another task completed by the subjects before their participation in the Research Institutes was to fill out a rating form concerned with the

organizational climates of their real jobs. It was thought that this information might be especially useful because there might be interactions between experimental organizational climates and ratings of real-job
climates. There might, for example, be contrast effects; the experimental
rules climate might be perceived as more extreme if the subject came from
an organization that did not emphasize rules and regulations.

The instructions given the subjects for marking the form were as
follows:

> Organizations differ with respect to their organizational climates. Make a
> vertical mark on each of the rating scales below to indicate where your own
> state service organization (department or division, whichever is the natural
> unit in your case) falls in relation to the labels on the scales.
> For example, on the following scale a line has been marked at the far right,
> since state service is public rather than private. In some of the scales below,
> however, an intermediate response may be more appropriate for you.

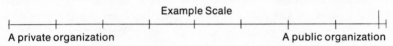

Example Scale

A private organization   A public organization

There followed seven scales, only two of which are relevant to the
study. The other scales were presented to help conceal the nature of the
experimental variables from the subjects; these had to do with autocratic
vs. democratic organizations, high vs. low standards of performance,
stress on quality vs. quantity of production, and the like. The two scales
that are relevant and were used in the analysis are shown below:

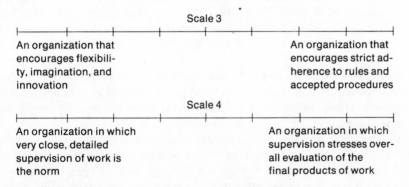

Scale 3

An organization that   An organization that
encourages flexibili-   encourages strict ad-
ty, imagination, and   herence to rules and
innovation   accepted procedures

Scale 4

An organization in which   An organization in which
very close, detailed   supervision stresses over-
supervision of work is   all evaluation of the
the norm   final products of work

These two scales of course represent the two organizational climate conditions that were manipulated to form the experimental variables.

The marks made by subjects were translated into numerical scores by numbering the spaces on the rating scales from 1 to 9, starting at the left. The mean rating on the *innovation-rules* scale turned out to be 4.4, a little toward the innovation end of the scale, and the standard deviation was 2.1. The mean of the *detailed supervision–global supervision* scale was 6.3 with a standard deviation of 1.7; the mean rating tends toward the global end of the scale. The correlation between the two scales was -0.34, showing a tendency for perceptions of innovation and global supervision climates to be associated.

INTERCORRELATIONS OF THE PREDICTOR SCALES

The factor analyses of the predictor variables were done in three parts, treating cognitive, personality, and personal history variables separately. This was done in order to minimize the possibility of getting factors that were primarily attributable to method or type of instrument employed. When a matrix of intercorrelations based on both cognitive tests and personality inventory scales is factored, one is likely to get factors that are influenced by method of collecting data. In our case, it would not be surprising to find factors reflecting inventory method, cognitive test method, and biographical data.

Partitioning the matrix and factoring the submatrices separately avoids this problem, but it is possible that the intercorrelations of all the factors that result may show more redundancy than we would like. The purpose of this section is to examine the interrelationships among factor scores based on all the submatrices described above. The intercorrelations of the 23 predictor scores are shown in Table 5-12 (*see* pages 114–115). The correlations are based on factor scores in standard score form (mean of 0 and standard deviation of 1), except that the climate ratings were used in raw score form.

Inspection of the table shows that the factor scores tend to have rather low correlations across the domains of personality, cognitive ability, and biographical information. There are, however, a few statistically significant correlations that may be worth commenting on.

In the block of correlations between biographical factors and inventory factors, we note a correlation of -0.28 between *Rigid Authoritarianism* and *Educated Institutional Man*, which is consistent with the findings often reported about the authoritarian personality (Adorno, *et al.*, 1950; Christie, 1954). The same personality factor correlates positively (0.21) with *Dead-End Seniority*; its correlation with *Power and Seniority* is also positive but not significant, suggesting that the age component is only partly responsible for the correlation with *Dead-End Seniority*.

There are also a number of low positive correlations between biographical factors and cognitive abilities. Correlations of cognitive factors with both *Dead-End Seniority* and *Power and Seniority* are quite consistently negative, the highest being about −0.28. Negative correlations between ability tests and age are commonly found in samples of employed people, and they probably can be accounted for, at least in part, by changes in hiring practices over the years, so that the younger people out-perform the older ones on cognitive ability tests. The highest of these negative correlations, for the Speed of Closure factor, may also represent superiority of younger men on a highly speeded test. The only other correlation in this block of any consequence is a correlation of 0.23 between *Vocabulary* and *Educated Institutional Man*.

The highest correlation in the matrix containing correlations between Inventory Factors and Cognitive Factors is −0.26, between *Vocabulary* and *Rigid Authoritarianism*. This personality factor correlates negatively with all the ability measures, which is the direction of the relationship usually found for the authoritarian personality. *Vocabulary* also correlates negatively with *Social Extroversion* (−0.22) and positively with *Independence* (0.22). Correlations in this submatrix are generally quite low.

The organizational climate ratings have very low correlations with other variables, as might be expected. The highest correlation (0.24) is between Acquiescence and the Rules climate rating, which conceivably could be accounted for in terms of a response bias. All other correlations are lower than 0.17.

The 23 variables resulting from the data-reduction procedures are thus only moderately correlated in a few instances. These are the measures that will be employed as predictors of performance in the simulated job, and in a later chapter we will be interested in seeing to what extent the relationships between predictors and dependent measures will be influenced by the experimental manipulation of organizational climates.

Table 5-12   Intercorrelations of Predictor Measures ($N = 260$)

	1	2	3	4	5	6	7	8	9	10
Background										
Noncomposite:										
1. Theoretical Education		0.04	−0.10	0.03	−0.07	−0.12	0.06	−0.04	0.02	−0.11
2. Years of Military Service			0.05	0.07	−0.03	−0.02	0.08	0.08	0.00	0.09
3. Number of Children				−0.03	−0.17	−0.14	−0.05	−0.03	0.06	0.05
Composite:										
4. Educated Institutional Man					−0.10	−0.04	0.08	−0.01	−0.01	−0.07
5. Power and Seniority						0.00	−0.07	0.05	0.02	0.00
6. Dead-End Seniority							0.06	0.01	−0.04	−0.06
7. Staff Officer								−0.05	−0.04	0.09
Personality										
Noncomposite:										
8. Acquiescence									0.08	0.14
Composite:										
9. Social Extroversion										0.00
10. Independence										
11. Maladjustment										
12. Rigid Authoritarianism										
Cognitive										
Noncomposite:										
13. Hidden Patterns										
14. First and Last Names										
15. Vocabulary										
Composite:										
16. Multiple Analogies Test										
17. Test S, Successful Strategy										
18. Test S, Conservative Strategy										
19. Speed of Closure										
20. Ideational Fluency										
21. Inductive Reasoning										
Real Job Organizational Climate Rating										
22. Rules										
23. Global Supervision										

11	12	13	14	15	16	17	18	19	20	21	22	23
−0.07	−0.05	−0.09	0.06	0.07	−0.07	0.03	0.10	−0.04	0.01	−0.06	−0.05	−0.01
0.03	0.04	0.01	0.11	0.00	0.04	0.09	−0.04	0.04	0.02	0.06	−0.00	−0.06
−0.02	−0.11	0.10	−0.04	−0.06	0.07	0.04	−0.08	0.15	0.12	0.15	−0.01	−0.11
0.05	−0.28	−0.05	0.06	0.23	−0.04	0.06	0.04	−0.03	0.14	−0.08	−0.11	−0.09
−0.11	0.12	−0.14	−0.15	0.07	−0.09	−0.28	−0.07	−0.28	−0.04	−0.23	0.05	0.04
0.04	0.21	−0.17	−0.14	−0.02	−0.03	−0.16	−0.08	−0.23	−0.03	−0.08	−0.03	0.17
−0.02	−0.05	−0.06	0.09	0.16	−0.08	0.01	0.02	−0.04	0.05	−0.08	−0.00	−0.09
0.10	0.19	0.09	−0.01	0.04	0.02	−0.06	−0.05	−0.00	0.10	−0.01	0.24	−0.14
−0.31	−0.18	−0.09	0.03	−0.22	−0.11	−0.15	−0.01	−0.06	0.01	−0.15	0.04	−0.02
−0.01	0.07	0.06	0.01	0.22	0.08	−0.08	−0.17	0.09	0.10	0.13	0.10	−0.08
	−0.01	0.06	0.06	0.18	0.19	0.16	0.06	0.17	0.18	0.07	−0.04	−0.03
		−0.08	−0.04	−0.26	−0.12	−0.18	−0.03	−0.09	−0.13	−0.15	0.13	0.14
			0.17	0.06	0.19	0.17	0.01	0.29	0.19	0.25	0.13	−0.12
				0.10	0.12	0.26	0.10	0.23	0.17	0.14	0.02	−0.16
					0.15	0.23	−0.01	0.09	0.19	0.21	−0.01	−0.14
						0.16	−0.04	0.22	0.14	0.33	−0.15	0.03
							0.38	0.26	0.04	0.40	−0.12	−0.15
								−0.01	−0.07	0.06	−0.03	−0.03
									0.21	0.28	−0.08	−0.04
										0.12	−0.04	−0.14
											−0.06	−0.10
												−0.34

CHAPTER 6

The Situational Tests and the Experimental Manipulation

THE SETTING FOR THE IN-BASKETS

During the in-basket exercise, each subject assumed the name and position of Art Dodd, newly appointed Chief of the Division of Field Services of the California Department of Commerce (CDC). Since each subject was actually employed by the State of California, he was already familiar with the state organization — its policies, rules, protocols, forms, terminology, and so on. But because the Department of Commerce is a fictional agency, the subjects had to be given information about the department in which they were to work during the two days of the Research Institute.

The Department of Commerce was (supposedly) set up in 1959 by Senate Bill No. 43. It is the responsibility of the Department of Commerce to gather, analyze, and disseminate statistics useful to industry, commerce, and agriculture; to conduct studies of factors affecting the growth of economic activity; to promote the development of new business and industry in California; to advise and aid local business concerns in the state; to prepare long-range plans for the growth of the state; and to encourage the formation of local and regional planning agencies. In addition, CDC is to foster domestic and international trade and to improve facilities for trade, to work toward the maximum use of California harbors, and to operate world trade centers. It is to promote and encourage tourism in California by encouragement of the private development of tourist facilities, dissemination of tourist literature, and facilitation of travel of visitors throughout the state.

The Director of the Department of Commerce is Mr. Apex; he was appointed by the Governor and serves as the Governor's chief staff adviser on economic development and planning. The Deputy Director of the Department is John Veep. Apex and Veep, then, are Art Dodd's superiors, but it is with Veep that Dodd interacts more.

Dodd is Chief of the Division of Field Services of CDC, with offices in Sacramento. He has five principal peers, the chiefs of the other five divisions that make up CDC: Ora Sellers, Chief of Economic Development; Tom Hiroshima, Chief of Planning and Redevelopment; Al Einstein, Chief of Economic Research and Statistics; Joe Madison, Chief of Public Information; and Mary Staffer, Chief of Administrative Services.

Dodd's immediate subordinates are the three regional managers of the Field Services Division: Ralph Chavez, Southern Regional Manager (based in Los Angeles); Herb Bay, Coast Regional Manager (based in San Francisco); and Jay Capitola, Valley and Out-of-State Manager (based in Sacramento). Each of these Field Offices is staffed by three or more Business Development Agents, responsible for industrial development, business services, travel, and data collection; a Trade Specialist, responsible for trade center management and domestic and world trade promotion; and a Planner, responsible for planning and redevelopment. In all, Dodd has 22 subordinates, including his secretary, Marjorie Sperry.

In constructing the in-baskets, care was taken to keep the personalities of the various staff members consistent within each in-basket and from one in-basket to the other. As Dodd goes through the in-basket items, he rapidly learns that some of these subordinates are excellent, some mediocre, and some inefficient—much like the employees of any other organization. And, as in real-life situations, there are frictions and problems as these members interact with each other and with people outside the Field Services Division.

A number of factors make it clear that Dodd is to be thrust right into the middle of a hectic schedule. His predecessor has recently resigned to take a position with an Eastern firm and has had to leave sooner than he had expected. Therefore, Dodd has not been able to receive much of the job orientation that had been planned for him, and work has been piling up in his office. In addition, there is an overlap between his leaving his former job in the Governor's office and his starting his new job in the Department of Commerce. The first in-basket takes place on a Sunday afternoon. Because of the backlog of work in the office and because Dodd has just returned from one trip and is leaving that evening for another, he has come into his office to familiarize himself with the background material and to try to take care of as much paper work as he can. Since it is a Sunday, there is no one around with whom he can consult.

Instructions for the second in-basket also convey a sense of urgency. This in-basket, too, takes place on a weekend day, this time four months after Art Dodd has been in his position. He has just returned from a vacation and is scheduled to leave in less than two days for a business trip that will keep him out of the office for about a week and a half. Once again, work has been piling up and he must take care of as much of it as possible before his trip. And again, since it is a Saturday, he is alone in his office and can consult with no one. In both in-baskets the fact that he is alone forces him to use writing as the only immediately available method of communication. The background materials he has been given provide him with enough basic information to deal with many of the in-basket materials presented to him.

Reasons for the State Setting

Setting Dodd's position in the California state system ensured some measure of homogeneity among the subjects with respect to familiarity with the situation and injected a note of realism that enabled the subjects to slide into the role more easily. The use of a familiar setting presumably helped the subjects to identify with Art Dodd and therefore to respond as they typically would in dealing with their in-basket problems. The use of the California state setting significantly reduced the amount of descriptive and explanatory material that had to be incorporated into the simulation.

A further reason for the choice of the California setting was the fact that the State of California contributed subjects as well as other support for the project and was naturally interested in obtaining data that would be as applicable as possible to the state employees.

The Department of Commerce

The decision to use a fictitious agency rather than an existing agency as the specific setting for the situational test was based on a number of considerations, the most important of which was the desire to present all subjects with an equally novel situation. The use of the fictional agency, it was hoped, would also minimize the influence of any preconceived notions or biases that the subjects might have had toward any specific department that exists in the California state system.

Another advantage of the fictional agency is that it gives the subjects more freedom to behave forthrightly. Subjects might be unwilling to criticize an actual department or its members, but if the agency is fictional, they presumably have fewer qualms about voicing their opinions. The state service aspect of the setting is of course real, but it is large, remote, and far more impersonal than any of its specific departments.

The Department of Commerce was selected as the fictional department because it appeared to encompass an optimum combination of the novel and the familiar. At the time the fictional act was drawn that set up the CDC, a California Development Agency, a State Planning Office, and a state governmental entity called the World Trade Center Authority actually existed; furthermore, there was a bill before the State Legislature that would create an Office of Tourism. "Senate Bill No. 43" draws all these functions into one organization. This bill and other background materials thus provided a bridge from the familiar to the unfamiliar.

The configuration of functional diversity, along with a requirement that limited CDC to supplementing and coordinating such services as were already provided by local agencies, was deliberately manufactured in order to simulate institutional interaction complexities typical of medium to large departments, while keeping the cast of characters no greater than that found in small departments.

Chief of the Division of Field Services

Chief of the Division of Field Services was chosen as the role position in the simulation because (1) the division chief level represented a reasonable (first or second level) promotion for over half of the subjects and the *status quo* or a nonderogatory demotion for most (but not all) of the remainder; (2) the Field Service Division could logically encompass a cross-section of departmental functions and problems; (3) the physical separation of the Chief from the majority of his subordinates (in field offices throughout the state and nation) made the restriction to written communication less artificial; (4) the chief-at-headquarters vs. Indians-in-the-field structure is a common one in state service; (5) such a position would enable the subject to interact with a wide variety of people, both inside and outside the state system, and with superiors, peers, and subordinates; and (6) mastery of a technical area of knowledge was not necessary in order to undertake the position.

Presentation of the Setting

Two months before the Research Institute was held at Sacramento, the participants were sent memos that described in general terms the purposes of the study. They were given a general statement of some problems of executive performance and were presented with a very general overview of the research project. They were assured that individual test performance would be held confidential.

About a month before the Research Institute was to take place, the subjects were sent a packet of background materials they could use to familiarize themselves with the organization and functions of the Department of Commerce and with the responsibilities of the simulated position they were to fill. A covering letter informed the subjects that at the "Research Institute on Executive Selection" each participant would be asked to perform the work of Arthur Dodd, that he was to assume that he had accepted the appointment a week ago and would start work on the date that the incumbent's resignation became effective. He was further told that the enclosed background material had been sent to him by his predecessor, Frank Fields, in order to familiarize him with his new position.

The background material itself consisted of six documents. The first contained organization charts of the California Department of Commerce and of its three field offices (Los Angeles, San Francisco, and Sacramento). The second document was a single sheet of paper that listed the classes of jobs within the Department of Commerce by salary range and by division. A third was a copy of the Senate Bill that set up the Department of Commerce. Scrawled in the margins of this were notes that Frank Fields had written to summarize the main points of the bill for Art Dodd. A three-page list of the functions of the Department of Commerce was yet another piece of background material. Frank Fields had annotated this document, too, to call attention to what he considered to be the main points. The fifth item was a short Class Specification (job description) for the Chief of the Division of Field Services. The final document was a rough draft of the next Annual Report of the Department of Commerce.

The only other materials (except questionnaires and inventories) sent to the participants before they assembled in Sacramento were concerned with instructions for reporting to the Research Institute.

At the Research Institute itself, a half-hour study period preceded the administration of the first CDC in-basket test. During this study period each subject was given three sets of materials for immediate study and for subsequent reference.

The first set contained copies of the documents that had been sent to each subject a month earlier, for use as reference material during the in-basket exercise. The second set consisted of two climate-setting documents (to be discussed below). The third was an abbreviated personnel file that contained a short work history on each subordinate, a short duties statement for each class of subordinate positions, a chronological record of civil service employment lists established for each subordinate class, and a copy of the current employment list for the Regional Manager class, with notes regarding its usage to date.

In order to reduce the subjects' memorizing chores, the total number of people involved by name in all in-basket items kept below 50, and names repeatedly appeared in conjunction with appropriate job and organizational subdivision titles. The names used were, for the most part, mnemonic; e.g., Apex is the CDC Director, Veep is the Deputy Director, the Los Angeles Trade Specialist is Dodger, while the one in San Francisco is Giant.

THE IN-BASKET ITEMS

One of the main objectives of an in-basket test is the presentation of realistic job-related situations that elicit responses typical of on-the-job behavior; realism, therefore, was a major objective of the simulation development. In the selection and development of materials, no attempt was made to reflect a particular theoretical framework or a particular kind or level of management job. Instead, the contents of agency files and previously used in-baskets were gleaned for items with general applicability, for situational variety, and for ease of transformation to the CDC setting.

A total of 70 items were used in the two CDC in-basket tests. Twelve of these items are climate-reinforcing items, none of which was used in the scoring.

On the average, three persons are explicitly involved per in-basket item, at least to the extent of being named in the documents presenting the item. One-half of those thus involved are subordinates in the Field Services Division, one-third are superiors and peers in the CDC, and one-sixth are other CDC employees, employees in other departments, or people outside of state service. There are five problem situations that recur and keep building in intensiveness throughout the two tests. There are five sets of items for which the details of the problem situation given in a single item are misleadingly incomplete or biased and for which a full picture can be obtained only through relating the contents of two or more items in the set. The items vary widely in significance, in complexity, in the overtness of problem statement, and in the source and nature of suggestions concerning desirable courses of action.

The first of the two CDC in-baskets is presented in Appendix C; the reader may want to deal with some of these items as though he were Art Dodd, in order to get some feel for the task.

PRESENTATION OF ORGANIZATIONAL CLIMATES

An organizational climate, as we have defined it in Chapter 3, is a set of attitudes or expectations held in common by a majority of the members of an organization, as to a kind of uniformity in behavior that is seen as appropriate in that organization. These expectations presumably result from perceptions of uniformities in the behavior of the organization's members, from overt declarations of policy by the leaders, from a uniform background of training and experience on the part of the members, or from any combination of these. Ultimately, the climate presumably results from manipulations of reinforcements or sanctions by the people in positions of power in the bureaucracy and through policies having to do with selection and retention of personnel. In simulating organizational climates in this experiment we tried to include, both in the background and in the in-baskets, materials that realistically and clearly showed that Mr. Apex and Mr. Veep had certain preferences with regard to styles of behavior in the organization.

As described in Chapter 3, the four experimental treatment conditions involved two dichotomies representing extremes of two organizational climates. One dichotomy had to do with following rules, regulations, and standard procedures vs. being creative, innovative, and original. The other dichotomy had to do with supervisory styles; in one climate condition the supervisor was expected to monitor closely the details of the work of a subordinate and in the other the supervisor was supposed to give subordinates considerable freedom in carrying out assignments and to evaluate the final products of the subordinate's work. Half the subjects were randomly assigned to the rules climate and half to the innovation climate and, similarly, half were assigned to the detailed supervision and half to the global supervision climate. The combination of the climates resulted in four treatment conditions: (1) rules plus detailed supervision, (2) rules plus global supervision, (3) innovation plus detailed supervision, and (4) innovation plus global supervision. Approximately one-fourth of the subjects were assigned to each treatment combination. These climates were presented to the subjects both in the background materials and in the actual in-baskets.

Climate Presentation in Background Materials

Attached to the Administrative Memoranda given to the subjects shortly before the first in-basket was a brief office memo addressed to Art Dodd from John Veep. The first paragraph of the memo states the following:

> The attached Numbered Administrative Memoranda, although concerned mainly with personnel management, reflect in their tone and points of emphasis the general management philosophy that Mr. Apex has set for the Department.

The remainder of the memo has two different versions, one of which was given to subjects in the "rules" climate and the other to subjects in the "innovation" climate. The two versions are given below.

Rules Climate

Service is our stock-in-trade.

We serve best when internal conflicts, cross-purpose actions, and duplications of effort are least.

Internal conflicts, etc., are least when well-conceived rules, policies, and precedents are known and followed by all.

We can continue to grow and improve our service only if we eliminate friction by following the approved procedures. Rules are the distillation of years of experience. Let's know them and follow them!

I've added some underlines to call attention to certain specifics that I'm sure Apex is especially concerned about.

Innovation Climate

Service is our stock-in-trade.

Continual development and utilization of fresh, well-conceived approaches to new and old problems is the only way to prevent stagnation.

We can continue to grow and improve our service only if we are constantly seeking new and better ways of doing our work — whether it is filing, keeping attendance records, planning surveys, or bringing General Motors to California. Do it the old way only if the old way is best!

I've added some underlines to call attention to things that I'm sure Mr. Apex is especially concerned about.

Although the basic information given in the Administrative Memoranda is identical in all four climate combinations, the style of presentation and the emphases communicated by Veep's underlining vary. Each version of the first Administrative Memorandum, for example, merely lists the title, contents, and distribution of various notices, handbooks, and guides; but the accompanying material is quite different in the "rules" climate than in the "innovation" climate. The titles are different ("Directives" vs. "Guides"), and the underlined passages give quite different impressions. Figure 6-1 represents the memorandum for the "rules" climate, and Fig. 6-2 represents the memorandum for the "innovation" climate. Similar differences in flavor and underlining appear in all the Administrative Memoranda.

```
┌────────────────────────────────────────────────────────────────────┐
│                     ADMINISTRATIVE DIRECTIVES                        │
│                                                                      │
│ Administrative directives will take one of the following forms:      │
│     Title                  Contents                   Distribution   │
│ Numbered          Departmental organization and     All divisions and│
│ Administrative    management, fiscal and personnel   their major      │
│ Memoranda         rules, and procedures              subdivisions     │
│                                                                      │
│ Departmental      Department-wide instructions       All divisions    │
│ Memoranda         concerning interim or temporary    and their major  │
│                   procedures, information of general  subdivisions    │
│                   interest, and transmittals for Numbered             │
│                   Administrative Memos.                               │
│                                                                      │
│ Department        Basic overall rules and procedures  All divisions and│
│ Operations        concerning line operations          their major     │
│ Notices                                               subdivisions     │
│                                                                      │
│ Division          Operating instructions for a specific As required by the│
│ Operations        subdivision of the organization     division        │
│ Notices                                                               │
│                                                                      │
│ Automobile        Instructions concerning operation,  All custodians of│
│ Handbook          service, and repair of vehicles owned Department cars│
│                   by the Department                                   │
│                                                                      │
│ Travel Guide      Instructions as to travel authoriza- All divisions and│
│                   tions, advances, and allowances;     their major     │
│                   "transportation of persons"          subdivisions    │
│                                                                      │
│ Records, Forms    Departmental records management;    All divisions and│
│ Control, and      forms control procedures and        their major     │
│ Communication     standards; communication media and  subdivisions    │
│ Manual            standards                                           │
│                                                                      │
│ Equipment and     Instructions concerning equipment   All divisions    │
│ Supply            control, service, and repairs; supply and their major│
│ Handbook and      and equipment requisitioning; forms  subdivisions    │
│ Catalogue         and supplies stocked by the Dept. in                │
│                   Sacramento; "transportation of things"              │
│                                                                      │
│ The purposes served by administrative directives are                 │
│     1. to provide administrators with the rules and regulations needed for main-│
│        taining a smooth running organization with a minimum of lost motion,│
│     2. to provide supervisors with specific rules and procedures for (a) maintaining│
│        department-wide personnel and business management standards and│
│        (b) evaluating and improving the work of each subordinate,     │
│     3. to provide every employee (a) with approved procedures and standards for│
│        using them and (b) with criteria for evaluating his own work and conduct.│
│ Admin. Memo. #1                    1(1)                  Rev. 1/2/62  │
│ Directives                                                           │
│                                                    CDC-A(A)-3:37-3    │
└────────────────────────────────────────────────────────────────────┘
```

Fig. 6-1 "Rules" version of administrative memo. # 1.

```
┌─────────────────────────────────────────────────────────────────────────┐
│                        ADMINISTRATIVE GUIDES                              │
│                                                                           │
│ In most instances administrative guides are intended to serve as          │
│    1.  reminders of the variety of goals of business and personnel        │
│        management,                                                        │
│    2.  reminders of the range of factors to be considered when            │
│        evaluating, in a par-                                              │
│        ticular situation, the relative importance of possible goals       │
│        and the relative                                                   │
│        desirability of available means for achieving a specific goal,     │
│    3.  stimulators to constructive, imaginative thinking.                 │
│ The exceptions are those instances where the course of action is          │
│ prescribed by law                                                         │
│ or the regulations of a central control agency.                           │
│                                                                           │
│ To date the following kinds of Administrative Guides have been            │
│ developed for use                                                         │
│ within the Department:                                                    │
└─────────────────────────────────────────────────────────────────────────┘
```

Title	Content	Routine Distribution
Numbered Administrative Memoranda	Departmental organization and business and personnel management policy and procedural guides	All divisions and their major subdivisions
Departmental Memoranda	Department-wide guides concerning interim or temporary procedures, information of general interest, and transmittals for Numbered Administrative Memos.	All divisions and their major subdivisions
Department Operations Notices	Basic overall policy or procedural guides concerning line operations	All divisions and their major subdivisions
Division Operations Notices	Intra-divisional procedural guides for other than one-time procedures	As required by the division
Automobile Handbook	Information concerning operation, service, and repair of vehicles owned by the Department	All custodians of Department cars
Travel Guide	Information concerning travel authorizations, advances, and allowances; "transportation of persons"	All divisions and their major subdivisions
Records, Forms Control, and Communication Manual	Information concerning departmental records management and forms control procedures and communication media	All divisions and their major subdivisions
Equipment and Supply Handbook and Catalogue	Equipment control, service, and repairs; supply and equipment requisitioning; list of forms and supplies stocked by the Dept. in Sacramento; "transportation of things"	All divisions and their major subdivisions

Admin. Memo. #1   1(1)
Admin. Guides   Rev. 1/2/62
                                                           CDC-A(B)-3:36-3

Fig. 6-2   "Innovation" version of administrative memo. # 1.

The other climate dichotomy (detailed supervision vs. global supervision) was presented in a similar manner. John Veep has sent Art Dodd a cartoon and has commented on the message of the cartoon (one cartoon and set of comments for the "detailed supervision" climate and another for the global supervision climate). The two cartoons and two sets of comments are shown in Figs. 6-3 through 6-6.

In addition to the presentation of the climates in the written background materials, a tape recorded message was used at the time of the administration of the second in-basket. When the proctor read the instructions for the in-basket, the subjects found that four months had elapsed since Art Dodd started to work as the Chief of the Division of Field Services in the Department of Commerce and that once again Dodd was coming to the office on a weekend to get some work done before a business trip. As Dodd is waiting for the elevator (the subjects are informed) he runs into four members of the Department of Institutions and Agencies and is present during a brief conversation among the four of them as the elevator ascends. The taped message presents this conversation, in which these employees discuss their problems in adjusting to the demands of their organization and the differences between their department and the Department of Commerce.

Once again, the basic structure of the "conversation" is identical for all four climate conditions. But, depending upon which climate is being presented, sentences here and there differ. At the end of the conversation, for example, there are different versions of the final remarks. The four versions are given below.

Climate *AC* (innovation; detailed supervision):
> "I'll bet Bill wishes he were in the Commerce Department. Today Bill needs their brand of administration: nice and loose when it comes to rules, and every detail spelled out when it comes to supervision."

Climate *AD* (innovation; global supervision):
> "I'll bet Bill wishes he were in the Commerce Department. Today Bill needs their brand of administration: nice and loose when it comes to rules, and emphasis on the broad picture when it comes to supervision."

Climate *BC* (rules; detailed supervision):
> "I'll bet Bill wishes he were in the Commerce Department. Today Bill needs their brand of administration: the tried and true when it comes to rules, and every detail spelled out when it comes to supervision."

Climate *BD* (rules; global supervision):
> "I'll bet Bill wishes he were in the Commerce Department. Today Bill needs their brand of administration: the tried and true when it comes to rules, and emphasis on the broad picture when it comes to supervision."

STATE OF CALIFORNIA
OFFICE MEMO

DATE _____

TO _____ Art Dodd _____

FROM ____ John Veep _____

SUBJECT _____

The attached cartoon depicts the kind of supervision
that I am trying to discourage in the Department of
Commerce. I feel you must give a subordinate concrete,
constructive criticism on specific details. You have to
let him know exactly what he did right and what he did
wrong and how whatever is wrong can be corrected.
General brick-bats may bowl the subordinate over;
overall commendations may blow him to Cloud 9--either
way, he doesn't know exactly what hit him. No real
learning has taken place. Good management requires
close, detailed supervision of the work of each
subordinate.
And you can expect the same from me!

CDC-A(C)-1:2-4

STD FORM 100

Fig. 6-3 Veep's note for detailed supervision climate.

127

CDC-A(C)-2:2-4

Fig. 6-4   Veep's cartoon for detailed supervision climate.

Climate Presentation in the In-Baskets

In addition to the climate presentation in the background materials, each in-basket contained six "climate items." These were generally quite short and required little or no response from the subjects; any response made to these items was not scored. They were included in the in-baskets solely for the purpose of keeping the climate perceptions alive. As in the background materials, the basic information conveyed in these items is identical for all four climate conditions; the items differ only with regard to the additional comments on them. One of these items in the first in-basket, for example, takes the form of a memo from John Veep to all staff members. In it Veep says that he has been requested to transmit a message from Administrative Services on the rapid depletion of stock items. The message, identical for all climates, requests each staff member to limit himself to a minimum of pencils, writing pads, etc. Following the message, there is a short comment by Veep. In the "rules" climate, Veep's comment is simply: "We should, of course, cooperate as fully as possible."

STATE OF CALIFORNIA
OFFICE MEMO

DATE _____

TO _____Art Dodd_____

FROM ___John Veep_____

SUBJECT _____

The attached cartoon depicts the kind of supervision
that I am trying to discourage in the Department of
Commerce. I feel a supervisor should give his subordinate
plenty of room for self-expression and plenty of
opportunity to perform the job in his own way. So a
subordinate's report isn't wirtten the way you would
write it! --You didn't write it, and you shouldn't
rewrite it.

Soft-pedal the details; focus on the goals. --Is the
point of the communication clear? Is the tone of the
communication appropriate for the situation? Is the job
successfully accomplished? Good management requires that
you know how well your subordinate does his job, not that
you interfere with how he does his job.

And you can expect the same from me!

CDC-A(D)-1:2-4

STD FORM 100

Fig. 6-5   Veep's note for global supervision climate.

129

CDC-A(D)-2:2-4

Fig. 6-6   Veep's cartoon for global supervision climate.

But in the "innovation" climate, his comment is as follows: "We should, of course, cooperate as fully as is practical, but for heaven's sakes, don't let a million dollar idea get lost to save a five-cent pencil!"

Similarly, in the second in-basket there is a memo from Veep to Art Dodd, in which Veep comments on a talk recently given by Alden Bee, one of Dodd's men. In the "details" climate, Veep chooses to comment on some of the minor details of the speech, saying such things as: "His choice of terms could be improved. He used the word 'allure' rather than 'attract' . . . and 'preclude' rather than 'prevent' . . . . With the addition of a little more material and with some coaching as to changes in details, I think the Industrial Managers would also be favorably impressed." In the "global supervision" climate, on the other hand, Veep's comments have a distinctly different flavor. Here, he makes such remarks as: "I think Bee gave a little too much emphasis to our function of negotiating with companies to prevent moves to out-of-state locations"; and "with the addition of a little more material and a modification of general emphasis, I think the Industrial Managers would also be favorably impressed."

Figures 6-7 and 6-8 provide an additional example of items related to the innovation-rules climate dichotomy, and Figs. 6-9 and 6-10 are detailed and global supervision climate items.

CALIFORNIA DEPARTMENT OF COMMERCE

California
FIRST
In Population

DATE: April 9, 1965

MEMO TO: Art Dodd

FROM: John Veep

SUBJECT: Request to reinstate Mike Johnson.

Last week Sellers submitted a memorandum to Administrative Services Division in which he inquired about the possibility of reinstating Mike Johnson, a former Sr. B.D.A. in Field Services Division. This memo is to inform you of the action taken on this request and to remind you that in the future, whenever the individual being considered for reinstatement is a former employee of your division, you will be asked to participate in the reinstatement determination.

Previous to coming to work for us Johnson was employed as a B.D.A. with the San Francisco Port Authority. We appointed him as a Sr. B.D.A. in August 1962. Johnson resigned in November of 1963 in order to accept a job in private industry. This job was eliminated in a reorganization following a recent merger.

While he was employed by the Department, Johnson was most noteworthy for his by-the-book approach to all assignments. If there was a rule, policy, or precedent which could be forced to apply to the problem at hand, he would always apply it in preference to applying common sense or ingenuity. While this adherence to the book occasionally got him and us through a major storm undamaged, most of the time it left a broad wake of frustration and extra work. The request for reinstatement was denied.

Employees who can follow directions imaginatively -- we need.

Employees who always must have a set of directions to follow -- we can do without

Fig. 6-7 In-basket memorandum for innovation climate.

131

CALIFORNIA DEPARTMENT OF COMMERCE

California
FIRST
In Population

MEMO TO: Art Dodd

DATE: April 9, 1965

FROM: John Veep

SUBJECT: Request to reinstate Mike Johnson.

Last week Sellers submitted a memorandum to Administrative Services Division in which he inquired about the possibility of reinstating Mike Johnson, a former Sr. B.D.A. in Field Services Division. This memo is to inform you of the action taken on this request and to remind you that in the future, whenever an individual being considered for reinstatement is a former employee of your division, you will be asked to participate in the reinstatement determination.

Previous to coming to work for us Johnson was employed as a B.D.A. with San Francisco Port Authority. We appointed him as a Sr. B.D.A. in August 1962. Johnson resigned in November of 1963 in order to accept a job in private industry. This job was eliminated in a reorganization following a recent merger.

While he was employed by the Department, Johnson was most noteworthy for his continual preference for generating his own blue sky approaches to assignments -- rather than following established standards and authorized procedures. While he was often quite ingenious and on occasion got the job done well, most of the time he left a broad wake of turmoil and confusion. The request for reinstatement was denied.

Geniuses who will both work within a given framework and submit suggestions for changing the framework through channels -- we can use.

Geniuses who continually remake the framework without authorization -- we can do without.

Fig. 6-8 In-basket memorandum for rules climate.

CALIFORNIA DEPARTMENT OF COMMERCE

California FIRST In Population

MEMO TO: Chief FSD and Chief EDD   **DATE:** April 5, 1965

FROM: John Veep

SUBJECT: New Office Procedure.

As the operations of the Department continue to expand, the necessity for establishing a procedure to facilitate the supervisors' function of overseeing the work of their units has become more and more urgent. There is a general consensus that it is becoming increasingly difficult for the line supervisors to control adequately the details of their subordinates' work. We have had a few unhappy experiences lately -- witness the recent Chalmers fiasco.

Such incidents could quite probably be avoided if we had an adequate system by which line supervisors could keep on top of the details of the work in their units. We are therefore planning to institute the following procedure: beginning July 1, 1965, a copy will be made of all work (including correspondence, memos, summary of telephone conversations, etc.) relating to key projects specifically assigned by the supervisor, and a file of these copies kept in constant good order by the clerical staff. Copies of mail coming in regarding these projects will also be made. Each supervisor will be expected to establish a schedule for reviewing this file which will allow him to alter the direction, style or content of the work being done on the key projects for which he is accountable before commitments are made. (Note: additional filing cabinets will not be available before July 1.)

Supervisorial attention to detail is essential in a department which must handle sensitive and complex problems. If any of you have further ideas on this subject, let's have them!

Fig. 6-9 In-basket memorandum for detailed supervision climate.

133

CALIFORNIA DEPARTMENT OF COMMERCE

California
FIRST
In Population

MEMO TO: Chief FSD and Chief EDD

DATE: April 5, 1965

FROM: John Veep

SUBJECT: Change of office practice.

Ever since this Department was established, it has been the practice of the line division staffs to make a third copy of all correspondence, memos, etc., for the unit supervisor's file. We have finally realized that this practice is unnecessary and wasteful -- the duplication of filing chores and the failure of the staff to make significant use of these files should have resulted in the abandonment of this practice long ago.

Another point is relevant. The implication involved in requiring the third copy -- the implication that the staff needs to have every detail checked and managed by the supervisor -- is derogatory to the staff and could lead to a significant decline of effort. Let's continue to maintain check points and be available for advice, remembering that the development and expansion of the staff's overall competence is our most vital concern.

Each supervisor is expected to take the steps necessary to stop the practice of making third copies and to purge third copy files.

Abolishing the supervisor's third copy is a concrete action in line with our principles of supervisor-employee relationships. If any of you have other suggestions, please submit them.

Fig. 6-10 In-basket memorandum for global supervision climate.

134

PERCEPTION OF THE CLIMATES BY SUBJECTS

At the end of the second CDC in-basket, after the Reasons for Action form had been completed, subjects were asked to make judgments on a brief rating scale that had to do with their perception of the organizational climates in the simulated job. One of the rating scale items required the subject to rate the climate of his CDC position on a scale of *1* to *9*, where *1* was defined as a climate that encouraged innovation and *9* a climate that encouraged one to follow rules and standard procedures. The other rating scale similarly required the subject to rate the climate of his CDC job on a scale extending from *1* to *9*, where *1* represented a climate that encouraged detailed supervision and *9* a climate that encouraged global supervision and overall evaluation of the performance of a subordinate. The purpose of the ratings was to provide information as to how effective were the efforts to create organizational climates experimentally.

Table 6-1 presents frequency distributions and means of ratings of the innovation-rules dichotomy. The first two columns show the distributions of judgments for subjects in an innovation climate. For those in the first column the innovation climate was combined with global supervision, and for those in the second column it was combined with the detailed supervision climate. The last two columns show the distributions of judgments for subjects in the rules climate. Those in the third column were in the

Table 6-1   Frequency Distributions and Means of Ratings on the Innovation-Rules Climate Scale

		Subjects in Innovation-Global Supervision Climate	Subjects in Innovation-Detailed Supervision Climate	Subjects in Rules-Global Supervision Climate	Subjects in Rules-Detailed Supervision Climate
Rules	9	1		4	17
	8	1	2	8	15
	7	1	1	17	18 ← Mean
	6		3	9	4
	5		6	5 ← Mean	2
	4	9	4	5	3
	3	8 ← Mean	15 ← Mean	5	1
	2	22	14	5	4
Innovation	1	16	16	5	
Mean		2.48	2.89	5.52	7.12
No response		7	3	3	1
N		65	64	66	65

climate combination that included global supervision with the rules climate, and those in the fourth column were in a climate combination that included detailed supervision with the rules climate. (The nonrespondents were subjects who were inadvertently allowed to leave before their work was checked for completeness.)

It is clear that the climates were correctly perceived by a great majority of the subjects. It is also apparent that the two climate dichotomies interacted with each other to a certain extent. Innovation and global supervision are mutually consistent, and when the innovation climate was combined with global supervision, only three subjects failed to mark 1, 2, 3, or 4, the innovation end of the rating scale. But when the innovation climate is combined with detailed supervision, the innovation climate is somewhat less clearly perceived. Similar effects are found for the rules climate. The rules climate is not perceived as uniformly as the innovation climate, especially when it is combined with global supervision.

Table 6-2 presents, in comparable form, the frequency distributions and means for ratings of the detailed-global supervision climate dichotomy. The perception of the supervision climates is quite clear when they are reinforced by the appropriate climate from the innovation-rules dichotomy (Columns 1 and 4); but when inconsistent climates are presented in combination, the perception is much less uniform. In the case where detailed

Table 6-2   Frequency Distributions and Means of Ratings on the Detailed-Global Supervision Climate Scale

		Subjects in Global Supervision-Innovation Climate	Subjects in Detailed Supervision-Innovation Climate	Subjects in Global Supervision-Rules Climate	Subjects in Detailed Supervision-Rules Climate
Global	9	11	2	4	1
	8	22 ← Mean	3	17	
	7	15	15	15 ← Mean	4
	6	5	4	15	7
	5	1	7 ← Mean	4	4
	4	2	5	2	6
	3	1	8	3	8 ← Mean
	2	1	11	2	16
Detailed	1		6	1	17
Mean		7.38	4.56	6.48	3.11
No response		7	3	3	2
N		65	64	66	65

supervision is combined with innovation there is a bimodal distribution of judgments on the supervision scale. Some subjects obviously found it difficult to discriminate between the climate dichotomies.

Tables 6-3 and 6-4 show the results of two-way analyses of variance. Table 6-3 presents the results for ratings on the innovation-rules scale. The row effect, which is produced by the experimental attempts to create innovation and rules climates, is highly significant ($p < 0.001$); there was a strong tendency for subjects to report the climate condition that had been presented to them. The column effect is also highly significant ($p < 0.001$) although the F value is much lower than for the row effect. The column effect is no doubt produced by the similarity of the innovation climate to the global supervision climate and of the rules climate to the detailed supervision climate; subjects to some extent confused these climates. Table 6-3 also reveals a significant interaction ($p < 0.05$) which is apparently due to the fact that perception of the rules climate was distorted by the supervision dichotomy more than was the innovation climate.

As shown in Table 6-4, which presents results for the supervision climate ratings, the column effect was highly significant ($p < 0.001$); the subjects tended strongly to report the supervision climate condition that had been presented to them. The row effect was also significant ($p < 0.001$), although the F value was much lower than for the column

Table 6-3 Analysis of Variance of Innovation-Rules Climate Ratings

Source	SS	df	MS	F
Row	813.906	1	813.906	210.1*
Column	61.659	1	61.659	15.9*
Row × Column	22.047	1	22.047	5.7†
Within Cell	937.394	242	3.874	

*Significant at the 0.001 level of confidence.
†Significant at the 0.05 level of confidence.

Table 6-4 Analysis of Variance of Detailed-Global Supervision Climate Ratings

Source	SS	df	MS	F
Row	83.266	1	83.266	21.4*
Column	588.490	1	588.490	151.4*
Row × Column	4.772	1	4.772	1.2
Within Cell	936.672	241	3.887	

*Significant at the 0.001 level of confidence.

effect. The row effect was, again, no doubt due to the similarity between the two climate dichotomies. In the case of supervision climate ratings the interaction was not significant.

The results strongly support the conclusion that subjects did in general correctly perceive the organizational climates that were intended. If the treatment conditions that were combined were mutually reinforcing, the climate condition was correctly perceived more often than if they were inconsistent; but interactions were otherwise of marginal importance.

CONDUCTING THE RESEARCH INSTITUTE

Well before the subjects arrived at the Research Institute, they had been sent memos that, in a general way, described the purposes of the study. They were also sent background information on the job they were to assume and a short battery of biographical and personality inventories. When the actual testing period began, then, they were not totally unfamiliar with what to expect. They did not know, however, the details of the study nor the specific organizational climates that were to be investigated.

For the sake of the convenience of dealing with smaller numbers of subjects, two Research Institutes were held, both on the campus of Sacramento State College. Subjects were assigned to one or the other of the Institutes randomly, and the two Institutes were as nearly identical in all respects as possible.

As each subject arrived at the testing site, he was assigned to one of the four treatment groups, as described in Chapter 4, by a procedure that was intended to randomize the placement of the participants in the various groups. In order to ensure confidentiality, the subjects themselves were identified by number only. As each subject registered at the testing site, he was assigned an identification number. It was this number rather than his name that appeared on all his written work. The subjects were told that during the first morning and part of the first afternoon, all four groups would be treated alike and that during the remainder of the afternoon and during the next morning, treatment of the groups would differ. The subjects of course were not informed about how the treatment of these four groups would differ.

Before any of the work of the Institute was begun, the subjects were told the following: "In order to minimize the likelihood of contamination of research data, we ask that tonight and tomorrow morning you refrain from discussing details of the Institute with anyone here. Tomorrow, after lunch, there will be opportunity to discuss the various phases of the Institute in the training sessions."

After a short briefing session, the subjects proceeded to their respective assigned areas. The four groups met in four different rooms of the cafeteria. In charge of each group, which numbered between 30 and 35 subjects, was a staff supervisor and a staff proctor.

The first task given to the subjects consisted of two short-answer tests in a multiple-choice format (*see* Chapter 5). Then the Bureau of Business In-Basket Test was administered. (This test is described in Chapter 2. It was intended for use in providing control variables, but for various reasons it was not used in the analysis.) The subjects were allowed two hours and 15 minutes to do as much work as they could on the 32 items in the in-basket. After this, they were given 45 minutes to fill out a Reasons for Action (RFA) form: for each item in the in-basket, they were asked to give a brief summary of what they did and why.

This task was followed by a one-hour lunch break, during which all four of the treatment groups met together in the cafeteria. After lunch each group returned to its assigned room and spent an hour and 15 minutes working on nine brief short-answer tests, ranging in duration from three to 12 minutes (*see* Chapter 5). These nine short-answer tests were followed by a short break, after which the subjects were given the background materials for the California Department of Commerce in-baskets. They were allowed a half hour to study these materials and were then given the first CDC in-basket. They were allowed two hours and 15 minutes to work on the 30 items in the in-basket and an additional 45 minutes to complete the corresponding RFA form. The completion of the RFA form ended the subjects' work for the first day.

On the following morning the subjects once again reported to their assigned areas and were given the introduction to the second CDC in-basket. They were told that about four months had elapsed since they had started working as Art Dodd, the Chief of the Division of Field Services of the Department of Commerce, and that once again Dodd was coming to the office on a weekend day. While waiting for the elevator, they are told, Dodd is present during a conversation among other employees of the California state system. The subjects then heard this conversation, which was presented to them by means of a taped recording. The purpose of the tape was to provide the subjects with further material designed to convey the various "climate" atmospheres. Directly after the tape, the subjects started work on the second CDC in-basket. For this in-basket, which consisted of 40 items, the subjects were allowed three hours plus an additional hour for filling out the RFA form and the rating scales for evaluating the "climate" of their simulated job. This completed the subjects' formal work at the Research Institute.

In the afternoon of the second day the subjects participated in discussions of the in-basket work, conducted by departmental Training Officers and members of the Training Division of the State Personnel Board, and then assembled in an auditorium for a final meeting at which the nature of the climate conditions and purposes of the research study were discussed.

CHAPTER 7

The Dependent Variables:
Scoring In-Basket Protocols

The dependent variables are the scores based on records of performance in the simulated job. They include (1) scores based on inspection of the actual letters, memoranda, and other responses written by subjects, (2) scores based on tabulations of the courses of action taken by subjects, and (3) subjective ratings made by scorers upon completion of the scoring of each protocol. This chapter will describe the scoring procedures, present evidence pertaining to the reliability of the scores, and report correlations of scores obtained from the in-basket responses with ratings made by peers and superiors of the in-basket respondents.

SCORING THE IN-BASKET RESPONSES

At the end of the Research Institute, each participant left behind all his written responses to the items in his in-basket: all the letters and memoranda he had written, the notes on his calendar and reminders to himself, agenda he had prepared for meetings, and his plans for discussions, interviews, and telephone calls. This material constituted the record of his performance in response to a standard set of administrative problems as influenced by whatever organizational climate conditions he had perceived to exist. The task of the research staff was to reduce all this material to a set of scores that represent the performance of each participant.

In the development of scoring procedures, a distinction was made between *stylistic* and *content* scores. The stylistic scores are based on examination of the actual written responses of an examinee and thus may reflect *how* something was done; for example, an invitation to attend a

141

meeting might be extended courteously or without any particular show of courtesy; it might be done formally or informally; or it might be extended in writing or orally, by telephone or in person. Content scores, on the other hand, are based on a record of the courses of action taken by a respondent rather than on the actual protocol, and they reflect only *what* was done. While the distinction between style and content scores is actually not as clear-cut as the foregoing description implies, there is at least a methodological distinction in the way the scores are obtained that justifies their separate description here.

Scoring for Stylistic Categories of Performance

The scoring form consists of several sheets of paper, each containing a large number of empty cells formed by lines defining rows and columns. (A sample page from the scoring form is shown in Fig. 7-1.) The column heads are the scoring categories, and the rows are numbered to correspond to in-basket items. The scorer reads the response to an in-basket item plus the statements made by the subject in the Reasons for Action form, and then (for most columns) she records a 0 or a 1 in the appropriate cell to indicate the presence or absence of the category of behavior represented by the column heading. In the case of Columns 1, 3, 4, 5, and 6, the entry may be a digit other than 0 or 1. Estimated Number of Words is coded from 0 (for nothing written) to 4 (for a long response, defined as 75 or more words). Entries in Columns 3 to 6 represent the number of subordinates, peers, superiors, or outsiders, respectively, who are involved by the subject in his action or plan for action. Involvement implies that the person involved will at the very least know about the subject's action as a consequence of that action.

The scoring categories used in this study are basically the same as those developed in earlier research involving the in-baskets. Additions to and deletions from the list were made, however, in an effort to profit from the earlier experience. Some categories that were very rarely used and consequently yielded very unreliable scores were dropped. New categories were added in an attempt to reflect more completely the variations in behavior that were found to occur, and certain faults in the early categories were corrected. One fault was due to combining too many ideas in one category. For example, a category used in earlier studies was "Discusses with superiors or outsiders." The two factors that reflect tendency to be concerned with superiors and with outsiders would have been more clearly defined had there been two categories instead of one. In

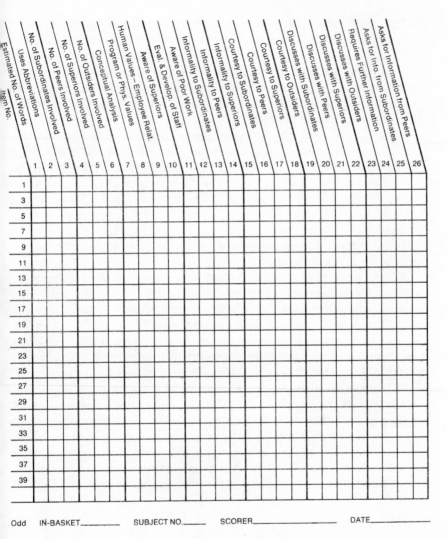

Fig. 7-1 Sample page from scoring form.

the present study care was taken not to combine in one category too wide a variety of behaviors.

An effort was also made to identify and include in the list of scoring categories any additional dimensions of performance that could be perceived. During the training period, the scorers were encouraged to be alert for attributes of behavior that had been overlooked, and a number of new categories were suggested by them and by the supervisor. Several of these new scoring categories proved to be useful; but as more ideas were suggested, they became more and more trivial and the behaviors involved proved to occur rarely in the protocols. The impression of the research staff and of the scorers is that it is unlikely that any major categories of behavior have been overlooked.

The scoring manual previously developed was revised and expanded to accommodate the new scoring categories (Carlton & Brault, 1971). This manual made it possible to require high standards of accuracy on the part of the scorers. The manual consists for the most part of definitions of the scoring categories, and rules and examples to guide the scorer in her decision as to whether or not the behavior defined by the category is present or absent in a response to an item. These rules and examples were developed through experience in scoring more than 600 in-basket protocols in previous studies.

Different scorers specialized in particular parts of the in-baskets, so that they could become completely familiar with the items, the people involved, and the variety of responses encountered. One scorer, for example, scored all the odd-numbered items of the first CDC in-basket, and another scored all the even-numbered items. This method of assigning responsibility for scoring made it possible to compute odd-even reliabilities that reflect both the amount of agreement between different scorers and amount of consistency in performance of the subjects.

Each in-basket item is thought of as providing an opportunity for each category of performance to occur; the number of I's recorded in a column represents the number of times it did occur. Scores are thus obtained merely by summing the columns of the scoring form and then combining these subtotals across in-baskets and parts of in-baskets to obtain a total score. The scoring categories employed in the study are those listed in Table 7-1.

Scoring for Content

Content scores are based on the particular courses of action taken or planned by a subject. On the basis of a content analysis of a sample of the protocols, a list of courses of action that were found to occur was drawn up for each problem. Further additions to the lists were made during the early part of the scoring period. The scorer's task was to decide which, if any, of the courses of action listed were taken by a subject and to record them by placing I's in the appropriate cells of the score sheet.

An example will make this clearer. If you were Art Dodd, you would find near the top of your first CDC in-basket a memo from Ray Loupe, the manager of the Chicago office. The memo states that an Illinois company is considering two sites for a new manufacturing plant, one of which is in California, and that certain information is badly needed in order to make a comparison of the two sites. The cost of getting a print-out of the information from a tape is $250, and a quick authorization for the expenditure is requested. A handwritten note from Loupe is attached which states that Loupe intends to send communications requiring prompt replies directly to you rather than to Jay Capitola, who is Loupe's superior and your subordinate. The strong implication is that Loupe feels that Capitola would not take prompt action. The following courses of action were found to have. been taken (or planned) by varying numbers of subjects:

A. Refer to Capitola with instructions on handling (speed, method, or possible decision).
B. Refer to Capitola with no instructions.
C. Instruct Loupe to send such requests to Capitola in the future.
D. Discuss with Capitola his workload and/or problem of getting things done.
E. Discuss with Capitola, subject not specified.
F. O.K. expenditure.
G. Take definite steps to be sure Capitola does not see Loupe's handwritten memo (destroy, file, detach from other memo, etc.).
H. Discuss with Loupe.
I. Consider general problems of proper channeling or discuss channeling with Regional Managers.
J. Consider possibilities of making this kind of information more readily available in the future.
K. Get authorization for expenditure.

The first page of the score sheet contains 12 columns, with headings A to L that correspond to up to 12 courses of action that might be taken. The scorer's job is to decide which, if any, of these courses of action were taken by each subject and to place a *1* in the cell below the letter corresponding to each course of action taken. Thus, if the subject referred the problem to Capitola without comment and wrote a letter to Loupe telling him to deal directly with Capitola in the future, the scorer would record *1*'s in Columns B and C. When scoring is complete, the first page of the score sheet thus contains a record of all the listed courses of action taken by the subject. If the subject takes actions not listed, the scorer records a *1* in the column for a scoring category called "Unusual action."

The column totals for Columns A–L are of course meaningless because the cells in a column all refer to different courses of action. It is possible, however, to derive several meaningful scores from Columns A–L. One score is the number of *1*'s in all the A–L columns; this number represents the total number of "usual" courses of action taken or planned by a subject and may be thought of as one measure of productivity.

It is also possible to identify courses of action that have particular characteristics and obtain scores that represent the number of courses of action of that particular kind. Two such scores were obtained: one is the number of courses of action judged to be *imaginative*, and the other is the number of courses of action that involve making an *organizational change*, such as a change in personnel, assignment of duties, or procedure that is more than *ad hoc*. An imaginative course of action is one that was judged to represent clearly a good idea that is not directly suggested by the item. In the example above, courses of action I and J were keyed as imaginative. Course of action C was keyed for organizational change, since it results in a procedural change that applies to more than the instance represented by the in-basket item. Three scores are thus directly based on the records of courses of action taken: (1) the number of "usual" courses of action, (2) the number of imaginative courses of action, and (3) the number of courses of action that involve organizational change. In addition, a score called number of unusual (i.e., unlisted) courses of action was obtained.

The Scorers' Ratings

The score sheet also contains a series of rating scales (Figs. 7-2 and 7-3). When the scoring of a subject's protocol was completed, the scorer obviously had a very thorough knowledge and understanding of the subject's performance on the standard set of in-basket tasks. The purpose of the rating scales was to provide an opportunity for the scorer at this moment to record her subjective impressions of the subject's administrative performance.

The first four of the scales shown in Fig. 7-2 have to do with the organizational climates that constitute the experimental treatments. A subject who correctly perceives the climate conditions and tries to conform to them should, insofar as his ability and personality allows, alter his behavior in directions defined by these four rating scales; and if such changes

RATINGS

Encircle the number that best describes the Subject's performance.

1. To what extent did the Subject show in his own behavior and/or encourage in others original, imaginative, innovative, and flexible performance?

| Showed or encouraged innovation | 9 8 7 6 5 4 3 2 1 0 | Did not show or encourage innovation |

2. In his own work, in supervising subordinates, and/or in evaluating the work of others, to what extent did the Subject show concern about the quality of end products of work?

| High concern about quality of end products | 9 8 7 6 5 4 3 2 1 0 | Low concern about quality of end products |

3. In his own work, in supervising subordinates, and/or in evaluating the work of others, to what extent did the Subject emphasize the importance of the details of the work process?

| Emphasized details | 9 8 7 6 5 4 3 2 1 0 | Did not emphasize details |

4. In his own work, in supervising subordinates, and/or in evaluating the work of others, to what extent did the Subject emphasize the importance of strictly following rules, regulations, and standard procedures?

| Emphasized rules and regulations | 9 8 7 6 5 4 3 2 1 0 | Did not emphasize rules and regulations |

5. How well did the Subject perform as the Chief of Field Services?

| Extremely well | 9 8 7 6 5 4 3 2 1 0 | Extremely poorly |

6. How pleased do you think Apex and Veep would be with the Subject's performance?

| Extremely pleased | 9 8 7 6 5 4 3 2 1 0 | Extremely displeased |

Fig. 7-2 Scorers' rating form.

	RATINGS (*Continued*)											
	Encircle the number that best describes the Subject and/or his behavior.											
7.	Compulsive	9	8	7	6	5	4	3	2	1	0	Noncompulsive
8.	Flexible	9	8	7	6	5	4	3	2	1	0	Rigid
9.	Global concerns	9	8	7	6	5	4	3	2	1	0	Specific concerns
10.	Ordinary	9	8	7	6	5	4	3	2	1	0	Creative
11.	Authoritarian	9	8	7	6	5	4	3	2	1	0	Democratic
12.	Careful	9	8	7	6	5	4	3	2	1	0	Careless
13.	Satisfied	9	8	7	6	5	4	3	2	1	0	Disgruntled
14.	Complaisant	9	8	7	6	5	4	3	2	1	0	Rebellious
Odd	IN-BASKET____ SUBJECT NO.____ SCORER_____ DATE_____											

Fig. 7-3   Scorers' rating form.

can be perceived by the scorers, we should expect that the mean ratings would be different for the different treatment combinations. The fifth rating requires the scorer to make an overall evaluation of the subject's performance, and the sixth rating is supposed to provide indirectly an estimate of the extent to which the subject attempted to comply with the climate conditions. The remaining rating scales are defined by adjectives that were thought to be relevant to the climate conditions or the subject's reactions to them.

Training and Supervising Scorers

The responsibility for hiring, training, and supervising the in-basket scorers was put in the hands of a very able person[1] who has been associated with such work from the beginning of the research involving in-basket tests. Scorers were nine female college graduates who worked on a part-time basis. All had had previous work experience; five had had some graduate education. A training program was carried out which required about four hours per day for five days; this was followed by a period of scoring under very close supervision. Only after scorers had demonstrated high competence was the supervision reduced to a spot-checking procedure.

Since each scorer was to specialize in scoring half (the odd- or even-numbered items) of a particular in-basket, it was possible to conduct the training sessions in one group only for the initial sessions. All nine

[1]Mrs. Margueritte Brault.

Ident. # [   ]

RESEARCH PROJECT ON EXECUTIVE SELECTION
Part A — Descriptive Rating Form

Directions: Encircle the number that best describes the subject's performance. If you feel that you cannot make a fair evaluation, put an X in the box.

Rating of _____
My relationship to person being rated:
☐ His Superior
☐ His Co-worker (Peer)

1. ☐ Discussion

```
       9    8    7    6    5    4    3    2    1    0
```

Has many meetings and discussions with associates; prefers face-to-face communication

Has few meetings and discussions with associates; does not necessarily prefer face-to-face communication

2. ☐ Speed of deciding

```
       9    8    7    6    5    4    3    2    1    0
```

Usually decides and takes action quickly

Usually takes plenty of time to decide or to take action

3. ☐ Compliance with suggestions

```
       9    8    7    6    5    4    3    2    1    0
```

Usually follows suggestions made by subordinates

Tends not to follow suggestions made by subordinates

4. ☐ Preparatory action

```
       9    8    7    6    5    4    3    2    1    0
```

Usually obtains information and advice and plans other procedures for deciding before making final decision

Tends to decide with a minimum of information, advice, and other preparatory action

5. ☐ Conceptual analysis

```
       9    8    7    6    5    4    3    2    1    0
```

Usually sees the broader implications of a problem

Tends not to see the broader implications of a problem

Fig. 7-4   Rating form for use by peers and superiors.

6. ☐ Concern with superiors

9   8   7   6   5   4   3   2   1   0

Often shows concern for superiors by involving them in discussions, asking them for information or approval, following their suggestions, doing what would please them

Tends not to show concern for superior by such behaviors

7. ☐ Control of subordinates

9   8   7   6   5   4   3   2   1   0

Tends to control subordinates by such means as giving directions and suggestions, delegating, setting deadlines, and evaluating their work

Tends not to control subordinates

8. ☐ Procrastination

9   8   7   6   5   4   3   2   1   0

Tends to temporize, to postpone action; is slow to go beyond the planning stage

Usually does not temporize or postpone action; quickly goes beyond the planning stage

9. ☐ Orderly routine

9   8   7   6   5   4   3   2   1   0

Tends to follow rules and regulations, to use established procedures, and to schedule his work

Tends not to follow rules and regulations, to use established procedures, or to schedule his work

10. ☐ Informality

9   8   7   6   5   4   3   2   1   0

Frequently uses first names, slang, colloquial expressions

Tends not to use first names, slang, colloquial expressions

11. ☐ Interaction with outsiders

9   8   7   6   5   4   3   2   1   0

Often interacts with people outside the organization by involving them in discussion and by correspondence

Tends not to interact with people outside the organization

Fig. 7-4   *(Continued)*

12. ☐ Constructive action

| | 9 | 8 | 7 | 6 | 5 | 4 | 3 | 2 | 1 | 0 | |

Has many good ideas and acts on them; willing to make organizational changes

Has few good ideas; seldom makes organizational changes

13. ☐ Amount of work

| | 9 | 8 | 7 | 6 | 5 | 4 | 3 | 2 | 1 | 0 | |

Takes many actions, involves many people, deals with many problems, gets out many letters and/or memos

Takes few actions, involves few people, deals with few problems, gets out few letters and/or memos

Fig. 7-4   *(Continued)*

scorers met together for these first training sessions. The training materials provided for each scorer included the following items: (1) An in-basket of the type the scorer would be scoring; (2) a copy of the scoring manual; (3) a set of about 20 responses to items in each in-basket (these responses were especially prepared to illustrate various scoring problems, with every scoring category represented at least once in each set); and (4) a completed in-basket of each type duplicated to provide identical copies for each scorer.

The first task of the scorers was to take the in-basket as if they were subjects in the experiment. This experience not only made the scorers familiar with the content of the background material and the in-basket items, but also gave them some insight into the attitudes and feelings of the subject who is plunged into the problems of managing the Division of Field Services of CDC. The first training session was concerned with discussions of in-baskets and their use in training and research and an explanation of the scoring procedures and the scoring manual. The first homework assignment was to study the manual and write down questions for the next session. This second session continued to dwell on the definitions of categories and courses of action and the scoring rules. After this point in training, separate meetings were held for scorers who specialized on particular in-baskets. Demonstration scoring was done by the supervisor; then the group continued the scoring of the in-basket as a group. Homework consisted in continuing scoring, and in subsequent sessions item-by-item discussions of the scoring were conducted.

Scorers were not told what the major purposes of the experiment were, and they did not know that there were differences in the experimental conditions for subgroups of subjects. Care was taken that experimental treatments were not confounded with scorers. Items that had been placed in the in-basket to reinforce the perception of the organizational climates were removed before assigning protocols to scorers. The omission of items was explained to the scorers in terms of "filler" items intended merely to make the in-basket more realistic.

Three of the nine scorers were assigned to each in-basket. One of the three scored odd-numbered items, one scored even-numbered items, and the third (the one judged to be most proficient) shifted from odd- to even-numbered items somewhere near the middle of the scoring task. Care was taken that she never scored odd and even halves of the same in-basket.

The supervision of the scoring, once it got past the training phase, is best described by the supervisor herself. After the first 10 in-baskets had been scored, checked, and accepted, scorers were given in-baskets in lots of 10. Here is an excerpt from a memorandum from the supervisor describing the amount and kind of checking that was done:

> For each group of 10 I checked one in-basket completely. I found with this method I could get a better feeling for the proficiency of the scorer — whether she tended to drift, how thorough she was, etc. Then I checked six items at random (using a random number table) in each in-basket. I tried taking items randomly from the nine as a whole, but it bothered me when only one item from an in-basket happened to come up .... I believe a random sample of each in-basket gives a better picture of the scorer's work.
>
> So this means I was checking at least 54 items randomly for each batch plus another 20 to 40 on the complete in-basket, depending on which one it was and on how much the subject had completed. I allowed one disagreement per category, but I also considered the total number of errors. If there were two errors in any category, I checked it further, on 10 more items at least. If it was one of the new categories or one that scorers always find difficult, I checked it completely. (There were, even at this point, only a few categories that were causing problems for any one scorer.) There were a couple of cases of confusion on what involved courtesy and abbreviations, but these were easily corrected. Since the first batch was checked so thoroughly, I didn't have any of the scorers redo any — I essentially did it myself, keeping complete notes on each error. I discussed all their disagreements with each scorer after each lot. I had planned to check the first 50 in-baskets of each scorer in lots of 10 in this manner, but it soon became evident that this was unnecessary for some of them. After checking the second lot of 10 (or a total of 30, counting the first two batches of five), I increased the lots to 20 for three of the scorers. The number of items checked remained the same. After the third lot of 10 I increased it to 20 for two others. For one scorer I continued checking in lots of 10 beyond the 50 as I felt she was still a little shaky in some areas.
>
> As a result of having so many people to keep tabs on, I got a little behind, and I had to have two or three scorers redo one category for a couple of lots. These were in all cases one of the infrequently used categories that hadn't come up often enough to indicate that the scorer had a misconception about it.
>
> I kept notes on the work of each scorer and checked more completely (than the 70

items) any category that she seemed to be having trouble with even if it met the standards for that check. I'm afraid I got too compulsive about it sometimes and checked some of the more difficult categories almost completely.

So I never allowed standards any lower than the most rigid setup for the school study (two disagreements for 76 items), and for the most part tried to keep them above that, particularly for the infrequently scored categories. Two disagreements in the conceptual analysis category seemed to me more important than two in the Number of Subordinates Involved category, for example. In fact, it sent me to the phone for an immediate conference.

RELIABILITY OF IN-BASKET SCORES

Reliability of Stylistic and Content Scores

The reliability coefficients are shown in Table 7-1, and frequency distributions of the reliability coefficients are shown in Table 7-2. The first four columns of Table 7-1 contain the reliabilities based on correlations between scores for odd- and even-numbered items. These correlations were corrected for double length by the Spearman–Brown formula. Since odd- and even-numbered items were scored by different scorers, these reliabilities reflect both the consistency in performance of the subjects and the amount of agreement between scorers. The "alternate form" reliabilities, shown in the last four columns, are correlations between scores obtained from different in-baskets. The B and C in-baskets are the two California Department of Commerce in-baskets and the BB is the Bureau of Business in-basket.

The odd-even reliabilities of most of the scores from the combined CDC in-baskets are high enough to justify their use in further statistical analyses. Only seven scoring categories had reliabilities below 0.2. All of these were dropped from further analysis except "Initiates a new structure"; this score was retained for use in the factor analysis of the dependent variables, in spite of its reliability of only 0.17, because it has proved useful in helping to define factors in previous studies and because it had a much larger reliability coefficient (0.48) for the BB in-basket.

The reliabilities of the BB in-basket and the separate B and C in-baskets are somewhat lower, no doubt because of the smaller number of items. The large number of zero or near-zero reliabilities for the BB in-basket can be accounted for in large part by the fact that the in-basket does not elicit certain kinds of behavior that the California in-baskets do; for example, the eight scoring categories that reflect various kinds of interaction with peers all have zero reliabilities for BB because the Bureau of Business situation does not provide any opportunity to interact with peers.

Table 7-1 Reliability of In-Basket Scores

Scoring Category	Odd-Even Reliability*				Alternate-Form Reliability			
	B+C	B	C	BB	B+C vs. BB	B vs. C	B vs. BB	C vs. BB
Number of usual courses of action	0.83	0.71	0.75	0.80	0.60	0.54	0.53	0.53
Number of unusual courses of action	0.34	0.25	0.28	0.28	0.19	0.06	0.18	0.10
Number of imaginative courses of action	0.49	0.08	0.50	0.46	0.34	0.18	0.28	0.26
Organizational change	0.32	—†	0.36	0.18	0.19	-0.01	0.09	0.17
Estimated number of words	0.93	0.86	0.90	0.83	0.60	0.62	0.56	0.54
Uses abbreviations	0.86	0.80	0.74	0.73	0.66	0.63	0.61	0.59
Number of subordinates involved	0.87	0.79	0.82	0.73	0.50	0.55	0.44	0.44
Number of peers involved	0.60	0.38	0.56	0.00	0.01	0.38	0.07	-0.03
Number of superiors involved	0.70	0.48	0.66	0.65	0.26	0.29	0.16	0.24
Number of outsiders involved	0.42	0.08	0.45	0.24	0.18	-0.01	0.16	0.14
Conceptual analysis	0.64	0.46	0.58	0.18	0.24	0.30	0.19	0.19
Program or physical values‡	0.16	0.23	0.05	0.14	0.07	0.00	0.08	0.03
Human values—employee relation‡	0.16	0.17	0.18	0.09	0.17	0.08	0.14	0.12
Aware of superiors‡	0.34	0.10	0.25	0.40	-0.04	0.26	0.00	-0.05
Evaluation and development of staff	0.44	0.60	0.19	0.43	0.25	0.07	0.34	0.03
Aware of poor work	0.47	0.31	0.41	0.54	0.31	0.15	0.16	0.29
Informality to subordinates	0.92	0.90	0.85	0.82	0.20	0.47	0.18	0.16
Informality to peers	0.65	0.71	0.41	0.00	0.01	0.39	-0.02	0.03
Informality to superiors	0.59	0.21	0.54	0.12	0.24	0.35	0.05	0.26
Courtesy to subordinates	0.86	0.76	0.78	0.72	0.51	0.58	0.46	0.45
Courtesy to peers	0.34	0.30	0.25	—†	-0.04	0.20	-0.08	0.02
Courtesy to superiors‡	0.12	0.02	0.12	—†	0.04	0.12	-0.03	0.07
Courtesy to outsiders‡	0.17	0.00	0.13	0.06	0.04	0.09	0.12	0.01
Discusses with subordinates	0.83	0.72	0.75	0.69	0.49	0.47	0.37	0.46
Discusses with peers	0.59	0.55	0.41	—†	0.00	0.23	0.09	-0.09
Discusses with superiors	0.60	0.46	0.52	0.45	0.16	0.26	0.10	0.15

154

Discusses with outsiders	0.31	0.00	0.27	0.42	0.10	0.06	−0.02	0.11
Requires further information	0.70	0.63	0.60	0.55	0.46	0.25	0.43	0.28
Asks for information from subordinates	0.63	0.57	0.47	0.72	0.46	0.29	0.47	0.27
Asks for information from peers	0.44	0.37	0.44	0.00	−0.01	0.11	−0.07	0.07
Asks for information from superiors	0.46	0.19	0.42	0.14	0.14	0.14	0.10	0.11
Gives information to superiors	0.25	0.03	0.31	0.05	0.12	0.08	0.16	0.06
Gives suggestions to superiors	0.77	0.46	0.73	0.14	−0.04	0.39	−0.04	−0.03
Gives directions to subordinates	0.85	0.80	0.76	0.67	0.45	0.50	0.39	0.40
Explains actions to subordinates‡	0.13	0.22	−†	0.16	0.26	0.15	0.25	0.12
Explains actions to peers	0.26	0.14	0.28	0.00	0.00	0.08	0.00	0.00
Explains actions to superiors‡	0.07	0.20	0.00	−†	0.17	0.10	0.04	0.17
Communicates by writing	0.93	0.87	0.90	0.81	0.48	0.61	0.43	0.43
Communicates face-to-face	0.87	0.77	0.78	0.71	0.45	0.58	0.41	0.39
Delays or postpones decision	0.83	0.73	0.74	0.68	0.32	0.48	0.21	0.33
Procedural decision	0.84	0.72	0.75	0.78	0.52	0.51	0.44	0.46
Concluding decision	0.72	0.50	0.65	0.87	0.46	0.45	0.39	0.39
Makes plans only	0.82	0.81	0.72	0.57	0.23	0.33	0.12	0.25
Takes leading action	0.86	0.78	0.74	0.72	0.51	0.53	0.48	0.43
Takes terminal action	0.74	0.54	0.65	0.81	0.43	0.48	0.39	0.36
Schedules work – specific day	0.86	0.81	0.80	0.61	0.28	0.39	0.22	0.25
Schedules work – specific week	0.64	0.44	0.64	0.26	0.14	0.26	0.10	0.11
Indicates time priorities	0.72	0.56	0.69	0.04	0.14	0.44	0.09	0.15
Refers to peers	0.36	0.18	0.24	0.00	0.00	0.20	0.00	0.00
Refers to superiors	0.61	0.21	0.56	0.18	0.04	0.19	0.04	0.02
Follows lead by subordinates	0.48	0.12	0.49	0.58	0.21	0.40	0.11	0.22
Follows lead by peers	0.20	0.23	0.14	0.00	0.00	−0.05	0.00	0.00
Follows lead by superiors	0.29	0.00	0.20	0.74	0.39	0.21	0.28	0.34

Table 7-1 (*Continued*)

Scoring Category	Odd-Even Reliability*				Alternate-Form Reliability			
	B+C	B	C	BB	B+C vs. BB	B vs. C	B vs. BB	C vs. BB
Uses preestablished structure	0.71	0.57	0.67	0.45	0.13	0.38	0.08	0.13
Initiates new structure	0.17	–†	0.17	0.48	0.26	0.13	0.24	0.17
Encourages quickness	0.25	0.35	0.06	0.33	0.21	0.03	0.29	0.02
Sets a deadline	0.46	0.28	0.44	0.35	0.24	0.19	0.10	0.26
Sets up checks on others	0.54	0.43	0.17	0.18	0.09	0.21	0.06	0.07
Sets up checks on himself	0.76	0.61	0.77	0.43	0.14	0.39	0.10	0.13
Concern with proper channels	0.50	0.00	0.44	0.28	0.14	0.27	0.12	0.12
Responds with specificity	0.71	0.41	0.58	0.42	0.29	0.41	0.30	0.20
Number of items attempted	0.96	0.96	0.94	0.93	0.57	0.63	0.54	0.51

*Obtained by computing correlations between scores based on odd- and even-numbered items and correcting for double length by means of the Spearman–Brown formula.

†Reliability not computed because of a negative correlation between scores based on odd- and even-numbered items.

‡Not used in the analysis.

156

Table 7-2 Distributions of Reliability Coefficients

	Frequency							
	Odd-Even Reliability				Alternate-Form Reliability			
Interval	B+C	B	C	BB	B+C vs. BB	B vs. C	B vs. BB	C vs. BB
0.90–0.99	4	2	3	1				
0.80–0.89	12	6	3	6				
0.70–0.79	9	9	12	8				
0.60–0.69	7←	3	7	5	3	4	1	
0.50–0.59	4	6	7←	4	5	7	3	4
0.40–0.49	8	7←	10	9←	8	8	8	7
0.30–0.39	6	5	2	2	4	9←	6	5
0.20–0.29	5	8	7	4	13←	12	7←	11←
0.10–0.19	6	6	7	9	14	10	17←	17
0.00–0.09*	1	10	4	14	11	9	14	14
(−0.01)–(−0.10)	–	–	–	–	4	3	6	4
Median	0.60	0.43	0.52	0.42	0.22	0.27	0.15	0.17

*For odd-even reliabilities, this interval includes instances where the correlation between odd- and even-numbered items was negative.

The most striking finding in Table 7-2 is the difference in magnitude of the odd-even and "alternate-form" reliabilities. The alternate-form reliabilities involving **BB** can no doubt be accounted for by the fact that the situations are quite different and that the in-baskets therefore tend to elicit different behaviors. The correlations between the two CDC in-baskets are noticeably higher than the correlations of B and C with **BB**.

The correlations between B and C are substantially lower than the odd-even reliabilities of B and C, although both in-baskets involve the same general situation and personnel and there is no striking difference between the in-baskets in type of item. A similar result was observed in the school administration study data (Frederiksen, 1961), as is shown in Table 2-4 of Chapter 2. The observation suggests that performance in the simulated job may be influenced by transient variations in attitude or set that occur from day to day as well as by whatever differences in style and content there may have been in the in-baskets.

No information is available as to the proportion of variance contributed by in-basket scorers as opposed to the respondents. Such information would be useful, but because of the cost involved in having protocols scored by more than one scorer, the necessary data have not been collected.

Reliability and Intercorrelations of Scorers' Ratings

The reliabilities and intercorrelations of the scorers' ratings are shown in Table 7-3. The intercorrelations are based on the pooled ratings of four scorers, each of whom saw a different sample of each subject's performance. The reliability coefficients shown on the main diagonal are based on the correlations between the sum of the ratings of the two scorers who scored the odd-numbered CDC items with the sum of the ratings of the two scorers who scored the even-numbered items; these correlations represent the reliability of the pooled rating of two judges. The coefficients shown in the diagonal are the correlations corrected for double length by the Spearman–Brown formula as an estimate of the reliability of the pooled judgment of four scorers. The last column contains the correlations of the pooled judgments of the four CDC scorers with the pooled judgment of the two BB scorers.

Apparently the CDC scorers were able to agree with each other fairly well, especially in judging overall performance and ability to please Veep and Apex (scales 5 and 6). The amount of agreement is remarkable when we recall that reliabilities reflect judgments of scorers who saw completely different samples of each subject's responses. Reliabilities are also quite high for the first three scales (relating to organizational climates) and to several of the adjective scales. The rank order of the CDC–BB correlations is very similar to the CDC reliabilities but somewhat lower, as would be expected because of differences in behavior elicited by the two in-baskets and because only two raters are involved. The *compulsive-noncompulsive* and *authoritarian-democratic* adjective scales were extremely unreliable.

A factor analysis of the intercorrelations of the ratings was carried out, the details of which will not be reported. The results show that one factor accounts for most of the variance in the scorers' ratings. A second very small factor has loadings on *satisfied-disgruntled* and *complaisant-rebellious*, reflecting the correlation of 0.54 between the two scales and their low correlations with other variables. In view of the low reliabilities of these scales, one might assume that the factor reflects the similarity in meaning of the adjacent adjective pairs more than a factor that has a counterpart in performance. With these exceptions, and with the exception of scales 7 and 11 (which have zero reliabilities), all scales load on the one large factor. The scorers were apparently unable to do more than make an overall judgment of the quality of performance.

Table 7-3 Intercorrelations, Reliabilities, Means, and Standard Deviations of Scorers' Ratings of CDC In-Baskets (N = 258)

Variable	1	2	3	4	5	6	7	8	9	10	11	12	13	14	r with BB rating
1. Encouraged innovation	0.63*														0.43
2. Concern about quality of end-products	0.80	0.63													0.35
3. Emphasized details	0.78	0.83	0.60												0.40
4. Emphasized rules and regulations	0.51	0.57	0.57	0.41											0.32
5. Overall performance	0.80	0.81	0.70	0.63	0.70										0.60
6. Pleased Veep and Apex	0.77	0.81	0.69	0.65	0.98	0.67									0.59
7. Compulsive-noncompulsive	0.11	0.26	0.24	0.29	0.15	0.16	0.06								−0.28
8. Flexible-rigid	0.80	0.64	0.59	0.34	0.70	0.67	−0.03	0.57							0.19
9. Global concerns-specific concerns	0.74	0.73	0.67	0.44	0.71	0.70	0.14	0.71	0.54						0.16
10. Ordinary-creative	−0.90	−0.74	−0.73	−0.47	−0.79	−0.76	−0.09	−0.77	−0.77	0.62					0.46
11. Authoritarian-democratic	0.15	0.20	0.12	0.16	0.21	0.19	0.07	0.14	0.25	−0.18	0.02				−0.07
12. Careful-careless	0.53	0.66	0.60	0.35	0.55	0.55	0.35	0.39	0.50	−0.50	0.13	0.43			0.24
13. Satisfied-disgruntled	0.19	0.33	0.29	0.26	0.30	0.32	0.20	0.14	0.21	−0.18	−0.08	0.32	0.25		0.06
14. Complaisant-rebellious	−0.21	−0.07	−0.05	0.06	−0.12	−0.08	0.06	−0.18	−0.18	0.26	−0.15	0.02	0.54	0.32	0.16
Mean	4.9	5.1	5.1	5.1	4.9	4.9	4.7	5.2	5.0	4.9	5.0	5.2	5.2	5.1	
Standard Deviation	3.9	3.6	3.9	3.0	4.2	4.3	2.6	2.9	3.3	3.8	2.7	2.8	1.6	1.4	

*Entries in the diagonal are correlations between odd-item scorers and even-item scorers corrected for double length.

CORRELATIONS OF IN-BASKET SCORES WITH
RATINGS BY PEERS AND SUPERIORS

Evidence so far available pertaining to the question of validity of in-baskets consists mainly of correlations between in-basket scores and various measures obtained from personality inventories, ability tests, and biographical information. These correlations show that some degree of consistency in performance exists across a domain defined by such scores (*see* Chapter 2). One would prefer, however, to have evidence showing that a measure of performance obtained from the simulated job correlated with an analogous measure obtained from performance in a real job. Measures of performance in a real job are of course not easy to obtain. The most feasible method for attempting to get information about real-life performance is to use ratings.

Rating techniques have obvious weaknesses, especially when one wants to get information about a number of related dimensions of behavior for the same individuals. These weaknesses have to do with the well-known halo phenomenon, with the fact that different job situations tend to elicit different behaviors, and with limitations and variations in opportunity for raters to make the observations that are necessary for valid ratings. In spite of such considerations, it was decided to make an attempt to obtain ratings from peers and superiors in order to make possible a study of correlations between ratings and scores on the in-basket tests.

Ratings would be most useful as criteria for validating in-basket scores if they were based on categories of behavior defined to correspond as closely as possible to the in-basket scores to be investigated. A study that employs ratings so defined has not previously been carried out. Ratings were used in the study of elementary school principals (Hemphill, Griffiths, & Frederiksen, 1962), but since the items in the rating scales were chosen before the in-basket scoring procedures had been worked out, there was only fortuitous correspondence in definitions of behavior categories. Most of the correlations between in-basket scores and ratings were quite low. As it turned out, the highest correlation between a rating by superiors and an in-basket "composite" score (one based on the results of a factor analysis) was 0.38 — between a rating of "oral communication (informal)" and a composite score called "Discussing before acting."

In the present study, a rating form was devised for the purpose of obtaining judgments that correspond to 12 first-order in-basket factors (those that were identified in one of the investigations described in Chapter 2) plus the second-order factor of productivity. A copy of the rating form is shown in Fig. 7-4 (*see* pages 149–151). The definitions of the extreme points of the graphic rating scales are based on the interpretations of the factors found in the earlier study.

Not all of these factors were clearly delineated in the new CDC in-baskets with the different subjects. Nevertheless, composite in-basket scores were computed to represent the factors; an initial selection of scores was based on the scoring categories found in the previous study to have high loadings on the factors. The reliabilities of the scoring categories found in the present study were also used in making a final choice of scores to be combined to form each composite. Composite scores were obtained both from the CDC in-basket and from the BB, although in the latter case fewer scores could be used, because of low reliabilities, in forming certain of the composites.

After the Research Institutes had been held, letters were sent to certain of the participants asking them to nominate two or more peers and two or more superiors who they thought were qualified to make judgments about aspects of their administrative work. The request for nominations was sent only to participants below a certain level in the state service, since it was not considered appropriate to ask the more senior people to participate in this part of the study. Of the 127 participants requested to nominate raters, 118 (93%) did so. Letters and forms were then sent to those nominated with a request to fill out the rating scales. Almost 90% of those requested to make ratings returned the completed forms. The rate of return was so high that no follow-up request was made. The number of peer ratings per subject used in the correlations ranged from 1 to 5, with an average of 1.89, and the number of superior ratings ranged from 1 to 4, with an average of 1.94.

Three kinds of measures based on the ratings were constructed: (1) the average of the ratings on each category by the *peers* who rated each subject, (2) the average of the ratings by *superiors* who rated each subject, and (3) the mean of the peers' average rating and the superiors' average rating. Table 7-4 presents the correlations of the average peers' rating with the average superiors' rating on each scale (Column 1), the correlation between the composite scores obtained from the BB and CDC in-baskets (Column 2), and the correlations of peers' ratings, superiors' ratings, and the combined ratings with the composite scores from each in-basket.

The agreement between the peers and superiors is not great, as is shown by the correlations in Column 1 of Table 7-4. The highest correlations are 0.48 for *Informality* and 0.45 for *Orderly routine*. Eight of

Table 7-4 Correlations of Ratings by Peers and Superiors with Composite Scores from In-Baskets ($N = 103$)

Factor	Peers' ratings with superiors' ratings	BB in-basket scores with CDC in-basket scores	Peers' ratings with BB in-basket scores	Superiors' ratings with BB in-basket scores	Combined ratings with BB in-basket scores	Peers' ratings with CDC in-basket scores	Superiors' ratings with CDC in-basket scores	Combined ratings with CDC in-basket scores
1. Discusses	0.21*	0.49†	0.09	0.25*	0.19*	0.26†	0.19*	0.26†
2. Final action	0.27†	0.37†	0.13	0.08	0.15	0.21*	0.14	0.22*
3. Complies with suggestions	0.24*	0.25*	0.04	0.11	0.11	-0.01	-0.10	-0.09
4. Preparation for action	0.42†	0.55†	0.06	0.10	0.09	0.11	0.03	0.06
5. Conceptual analysis	0.40†	0.40†	0.10	0.07	0.08	0.10	0.07	0.11
6. Concern with superiors	0.10	0.11	0.14	0.16	0.19*	0.04	0.09	0.06
7. Control of subordinates	0.22*	0.39†	0.05	-0.08	0.00	0.13	0.01	0.06
8. Procrastination	0.29†	0.41†	-0.21*	-0.13	-0.22*	-0.01	-0.05	-0.06
9. Orderly routine	0.45†	0.33†	-0.07	0.00	-0.03	-0.12	-0.02	-0.11
10. Informality	0.48†	0.34†	0.06	0.08	0.04	0.06	0.06	0.05
11. Interacts with outsiders	0.40†	0.05	-0.01	0.02	-0.02	0.10	0.07	0.11
12. Constructive action	0.37†	0.30†	0.13	-0.04	0.07	0.10	0.08	0.10
13. Amount of work	0.29†	0.52†	0.02	0.02	0.04	0.16	0.11	0.14

*Significantly different from zero at the 5% level.
†Significantly different from zero at the 1% level.

the 13 correlations are lower than 0.40. The correlations between composite scores from BB and CDC in-baskets (Column 2) are a little higher on the average, although the range is greater. The highest correlations in Column 2 are 0.55 for *Preparation for action* and 0.52 for *Amount of work*.

In view of the low correlations found in the first two columns, we probably should not expect to find high correlations between ratings and in-basket scores. The correlations in Columns 3–8 are in fact quite low. The only row containing predominantly significant correlations is the first one, which contains correlations for the performance category *Discusses*. In the second row, for *Final action*, there are a couple of significant correlations; but in general, correlations between ratings and in-basket composite scores are below 0.2. For *Procrastination* the correlations are consistently negative and in a couple of instances they are significant.

On the basis of these results we certainly cannot claim to have validated in-baskets against the rating criteria. But on the other hand, the low correlations do not necessarily mean lack of validity. The lack of agreement might, for example, result from the varied situational influences that affect performance in the real jobs in various ways; the raters may see the subject behaving in a job setting that is quite different from the setting of either the CDC or the Bureau of Business. It is also possible that the paper work corresponding to in-basket performance is a fairly private matter that peers and superiors actually see little of; they tend to see various aspects of one's "public" behavior. The positive correlations with *Discussion* may occur because tendency to discuss is a more public aspect of one's administrative performance than the other categories rated. While we are speculating, we might even guess that the negative correlations with *Procrastination* might result from facades that people successfully use to conceal their deficiencies. At any rate, while the data do not show validity, the correlations cannot be interpreted as proving that the in-basket performance measures are not valid. They might, on the contrary, be interpreted to cast doubt on the validity of ratings.

CHAPTER 8

The Criterion Measures: Factor
Analysis of In-Basket Scores

The scoring of the records of the subjects' administrative paper work, the in-basket protocols, resulted in 55 in-basket performance scores of sufficient reliability for further analysis. The intercorrelations of these 55 scores show that there is a good deal of redundancy in the score matrix. In the interest of parsimony as well as computational efficiency, it is desirable to combine scores in a way which will preserve most of the information and reduce the number of variables appreciably. Factor analysis is of course the statistical method designed to do this job. The particular method of factor analysis employed was chosen because it provides the best way to answer the first of the major questions we have posed: what are the effects of the experimental treatments on the factor structure of the dependent measures?

In this chapter we will be concerned only with the factor analysis of in-basket performance scores for the entire group of 260 subjects. The factors that result from this analysis are important, because they constitute the criterion measures on the basis of which we evaluate the results of the entire experiment on effects of organizational climates.

The method of factor analysis is called within-group covariance factor analysis. The procedure required, first, that the mean of the appropriate treatment group be subtracted from each subject's score. The resulting scores were then standardized for the pooled groups. This procedure thus eliminated any effects of treatments on means but not on variances and covariances. The resulting standard score matrix was then factored by the principal components method, with unity in the diagonal. (The method is described more fully in the appendix.)

164

The first principal component resulting from the analysis is shown in the first column in Table 8-1. This is, of course, the largest of the unrotated factors, accounting for 21% of the total variance. The largest loadings are as follows:

Number of usual courses of action taken	0.92
Takes leading action	0.88
Communicates by writing	0.84
Number of subordinates involved	0.83
Estimated number of words written	0.82
Procedural decision	0.81
Gives directions to subordinates	0.77
Number of items attempted	0.72
Communicates face-to-face	0.69

This is clearly a productivity factor, reflecting the amount of work accomplished by subjects in the simulated job.

In previous studies, amount of work has been identified as a second-order factor. In the present study, it seemed preferable to preserve the productivity factor as a primary factor, setting it orthogonal to all other factors and thus in effect partialing out the effects of general productivity from all the remaining factors. It was hoped that such a procedure would reduce markedly the intercorrelations of the first-order factors.

Several orthogonal (equamax) rotations with varying numbers of factors were tried in order to provide a basis for judging the number of factors to be retained. These rotations did not involve the first principal component described above. The results showed that nine factors were clearly interpretable and represented good simple structure. When larger numbers of factors were tried, the first eight were almost unchanged but the ninth factor was fractionated into smaller factors that did not seem to have clear interpretations. It was therefore decided to work with nine factors plus the first principal component — the productivity factor. These 10 factors account for 61% of the total variance.

Factors II through X were next rotated to an oblique structure, using the promax (Hendrickson & White, 1964) procedure, and maintaining the orthogonal position of Factor I. The factor matrix is shown in Table 8-1. The effect of this rotation on the factor structure is minor. In general, the factor structure was improved in that the largest factor loadings were increased slightly and the low loadings were decreased. Table 8-2 shows that the factors are not highly correlated; the highest correlation is −0.19, between Factor II (*Acts in compliance with suggestions*) and

Table 8-1 Factor Loadings of In-Basket Performance Scores* (Oblique Rotation)

Score	Factor									
	I	II	III	IV	V	VI	VII	VIII	IX	X
1. Number of usual courses of action	0.92	0.09	−0.07	0.02	0.20	0.01	−0.03	−0.12	0.00	0.04
2. Number of unusual courses of action	0.47	0.07	0.19	0.17	−0.18	−0.06	0.00	0.12	−0.10	0.12
3. Number of imaginative courses of action	0.51	−0.00	0.20	0.49	0.02	0.03	−0.05	−0.03	−0.09	0.18
4. Organizational change	0.29	0.36	−0.05	−0.03	−0.12	−0.14	0.12	−0.06	0.11	0.19
5. Estimated number of words	0.82	0.22	−0.11	−0.14	0.01	0.29	0.01	−0.03	−0.01	−0.03
6. Uses abbreviations	0.54	−0.17	0.08	−0.10	−0.11	−0.04	0.13	0.05	0.04	0.02
7. Number of subordinates involved	0.83	−0.14	−0.19	−0.03	0.03	−0.14	−0.27	0.07	0.03	−0.11
8. Number of peers involved	0.59	−0.06	−0.00	−0.20	0.07	−0.12	0.60	−0.04	−0.03	0.04
9. Number of superiors involved	0.52	−0.02	0.78	0.04	−0.05	0.00	−0.08	−0.11	0.00	−0.06
10. Number of outsiders involved	0.29	0.04	−0.06	0.46	−0.09	−0.07	−0.03	−0.07	0.03	−0.42
11. Conceptual analysis	0.39	−0.04	0.15	0.73	0.01	−0.08	−0.05	−0.01	−0.05	−0.04
12. Evaluation and development of staff	0.28	−0.09	−0.01	0.59	0.06	−0.06	−0.02	0.06	0.01	0.03
13. Aware of poor work	0.19	−0.04	0.01	0.30	−0.03	0.15	−0.08	−0.08	−0.10	0.35
14. Informality to subordinates	0.45	−0.14	−0.05	−0.13	−0.27	0.10	−0.16	0.05	0.43	−0.06
15. Informality to peers	0.05	0.06	0.01	−0.01	0.04	0.01	0.13	−0.11	0.81	0.04
16. Informality to superiors	0.07	0.17	0.07	0.01	0.10	−0.00	−0.16	−0.07	0.81	0.11
17. Courtesy to subordinates	0.37	−0.07	−0.24	−0.19	−0.20	−0.19	−0.20	−0.13	0.29	−0.01
18. Courtesy to peers	0.19	−0.14	−0.24	0.11	−0.25	0.01	0.63	−0.08	0.11	−0.04
19. Discusses with subordinates	0.58	−0.16	−0.18	0.05	0.54	−0.08	−0.27	0.18	0.01	−0.06
20. Discusses with peers	0.55	−0.17	0.12	−0.22	0.25	−0.18	0.37	−0.01	0.02	0.02
21. Discusses with superiors	0.39	−0.30	0.45	−0.17	0.24	−0.13	0.10	−0.02	0.12	−0.06
22. Discusses with outsiders	0.12	−0.17	0.10	0.04	−0.01	−0.08	−0.10	−0.28	0.10	−0.09
23. Requires further information	0.17	−0.13	−0.08	0.05	0.27	0.24	−0.10	−0.32	−0.14	0.18
24. Asks for information from subordinates	0.62	−0.21	−0.17	−0.08	−0.25	−0.03	−0.10	−0.18	−0.19	0.13
25. Asks for information from peers	0.41	−0.11	−0.14	0.02	−0.18	0.03	0.67	−0.15	−0.19	−0.04
26. Asks for information from superiors	0.25	−0.23	0.30	0.07	−0.06	0.03	0.12	−0.16	−0.03	−0.39

Item										
27. Gives information to superiors	0.29	−0.22	*0.51*	−0.05	−0.21	0.02	0.00	−0.04	0.13	0.26
28. Gives suggestions to superiors	0.24	0.10	*0.82*	0.14	−0.07	−0.03	−0.11	0.04	−0.03	−0.08
29. Gives directions to subordinates	*0.77*	−0.07	−0.27	−0.21	−0.29	−0.01	−0.22	0.06	0.01	0.02
30. Explains actions to peers	0.09	0.08	−0.21	*0.39*	0.14	0.15	0.17	−0.06	0.20	−0.21
31. Communicates by writing	*0.84*	0.19	−0.05	−0.17	−0.35	0.16	−0.02	0.05	−0.03	−0.06
32. Communicates face-to-face	*0.69*	−0.23	−0.07	−0.05	*0.49*	−0.12	−0.08	0.10	0.07	−0.08
33. Delays or postpones decision	−0.24	−0.00	0.01	−0.14	−0.00	*0.84*	0.04	0.18	0.02	−0.05
34. Procedural decision	*0.81*	−0.22	−0.09	−0.13	0.31	0.08	−0.03	−0.11	−0.11	−0.05
35. Concluding decision	*0.44*	*0.80*	0.04	−0.02	−0.13	0.04	−0.02	−0.02	0.07	0.03
36. Makes plans only	0.00	0.15	−0.07	−0.05	*0.88*	0.15	−0.05	−0.09	0.00	0.09
37. Takes leading action	*0.88*	−0.26	−0.06	−0.06	−0.17	−0.03	−0.01	−0.04	−0.11	−0.05
38. Takes terminal action	0.29	*0.85*	0.06	−0.07	−0.13	0.08	−0.02	−0.04	0.09	−0.03
39. Schedules work — specific day	*0.43*	−0.21	−0.03	0.00	0.09	−0.01	−0.11	*0.63*	−0.08	0.00
40. Schedules work — specific week	0.30	−0.32	−0.19	0.10	0.19	*0.35*	−0.03	−0.22	0.11	−0.12
41. Indicates time priorities	−0.07	−0.21	0.12	0.01	−0.15	*0.71*	−0.01	0.13	0.05	−0.02
42. Refers to peers	0.07	0.21	−0.08	0.02	−0.03	0.11	*0.66*	0.18	0.03	0.00
43. Refers to superiors	0.17	0.23	*0.72*	0.02	−0.09	0.07	−0.11	−0.05	0.03	−0.17
44. Follows lead by subordinates	*0.56*	*0.46*	−0.09	−0.21	0.10	−0.10	0.08	0.01	−0.10	−0.06
45. Follows lead by peers	*0.36*	0.23	−0.03	−0.26	−0.08	−0.19	0.01	0.02	−0.16	−0.23
46. Follows lead by superiors	*0.48*	*0.42*	0.06	−0.01	0.01	0.02	−0.13	−0.16	−0.02	−0.05
47. Uses preestablished structure	0.23	0.01	−0.08	0.04	−0.12	0.13	−0.07	*0.77*	−0.09	−0.10
48. Initiates new structure	0.31	0.20	−0.12	0.16	−0.00	−0.14	−0.06	−0.09	0.11	*0.41*
49. Encourages quickness	0.11	−0.10	−0.10	0.05	0.14	−0.15	0.10	0.05	0.02	*0.51*
50. Sets a deadline	*0.35*	−0.31	−0.05	−0.05	−0.23	0.03	−0.02	−0.16	−0.11	−0.06
51. Sets up checks on others	0.34	−0.04	−0.26	0.25	−0.04	−0.12	0.07	0.21	0.01	0.31
52. Sets up checks on himself	0.28	−0.31	0.02	−0.00	−0.06	*0.36*	0.06	*0.53*	0.10	0.04
53. Concern with proper channels	0.25	−0.00	0.03	−0.18	−0.08	0.05	−0.00	−0.14	0.08	*0.56*
54. Responds with specificity	0.32	−0.07	−0.02	*0.74*	−0.09	−0.24	−0.01	0.04	0.00	−0.08
55. Number of items attempted	*0.72*	0.32	−0.03	−0.18	0.15	*0.54*	−0.02	−0.00	−0.05	−0.04

*Loadings of 0.35 or greater are in italic type.

167

Table 8-2 Variances and Intercorrelations of Factor Scores for Pooled Groups

	I	II	III	IV	V	VI	VII	VIII	IX	X
I. Productivity	1.00									
II. Final action	0.00	1.00								
III. Interacts with superiors	-0.00	0.11	1.00							
IV. Thoughtful analysis	-0.00	-0.01	-0.05	1.00						
V. Plans and discusses	0.00	-0.19	0.09	-0.03	1.00					
VI. Defers	0.00	-0.07	-0.13	0.14	0.08	1.00				
VII. Interacts with peers	-0.00	0.08	0.11	0.17	0.08	-0.01	1.00			
VIII. Orderly work	0.00	-0.09	0.04	-0.03	0.12	-0.07	-0.02	1.00		
IX. Informality	-0.00	-0.12	-0.05	0.15	-0.10	0.03	0.14	0.09	1.00	
X. Accepts administrative responsibility	0.00	-0.00	0.03	0.05	-0.15	-0.01	-0.11	0.03	-0.05	1.00

Factor V (*Plans and discusses*). Removal of the effects of the first principal component, the productivity factor, has apparently removed the main reason for high intercorrelations between factors.

The interpretation of the first factor as a productivity factor has already been presented. The interpretations of the next nine performance factors are as follows:

Factor II. Acts in compliance with suggestions (Final action). The loadings of 0.35 or greater for this factor are as follows:

Takes terminal action	0.85
Concluding decision	0.80
Follows lead by subordinates	0.46
Follows lead by superiors	0.42
Organizational change	0.36

This is the familiar factor reflecting a tendency to make final decisions and take final action in problems during the test period. Presumably the actions are usually those suggested by others, since the two categories of "following leads" have appreciable loadings.

Factor III. Interacts with superiors. The loadings of 0.35 or greater are as follows:

Gives suggestions to superiors	0.82
Number of superiors involved	0.78
Refers to superiors	0.72
Gives information to superiors	0.51
Discusses with superiors	0.45

The interpretation of this factor as interacting with superiors seems obvious.

Factor IV. Thoughtful analysis of problems. The loadings are as follows:

Responds with specificity	0.74
Conceptual analysis	0.73
Evaluation and development of staff	0.59
Number of imaginative courses of action	0.49
Number of outsiders involved	0.46
Explains actions to peers	0.39

Reference to the scoring manual shows that in order for a response to be scored for "Responds with specificity" it must not be a mere generality;

it must contain details that reveal some depth in the analysis of a problem
For example, the instruction "Discuss this with Mr. Veep" would not be
scored, but "Discuss this with Veep and point out A, B, and C" would be
scored. "Conceptual analysis" refers to the recognition by the subject
that a problem has implications beyond those actually stated, such as
noting that the problem is related to another problem in the in-basket or
that the situation may be symptomatic of a bigger or more general problem. "Evaluation and development of staff" is scored when the subject
shows an interest in evaluating staff members or of providing training
opportunities for them. The loading for "Number of outsiders involved"
presumably results from a need to involve people outside the organization
when the broader significance of certain problems is realized; the purpose
of the Department of Commerce is, after all, to influence people outside
the organization. The name *Thoughtful analysis of problems* is intended
to imply a tendency to go beyond a superficial level of analysis in dealing
with in-basket items.

Factor V. Plans and discusses.   The loadings of 0.35 or higher are as
follows:

Makes plans only	0.88
Discusses with subordinates	0.54
Communicates face-to-face	0.49
Communicates by writing	−0.35

An additional loading is 0.31 for "Procedural decision." The factor therefore seems to reflect tendencies to prepare for action rather than to act
However, instructions for scoring state that "Plans only" should not be
scored if the subject takes any action on the item, no matter how trivial
and is not to be scored if "Leading action" is scored. We have avoided
calling the factor "preparatory action" because of the very high loading
on the "Plans only" category.

Factor VI. Defers judgment and action.   The loadings:

Delays or postpones decision	0.84
Indicates time priorities	0.71
Number of items attempted	0.54
Sets up checks on himself	0.36
Schedules work for a specific week	0.35

The first of the five performance categories represents stalling tactic
("I'll think about it") without any steps toward decision and action
"Indicates time priorities" is scored when the subject states the order

n which tasks are to be done, and is also scored when the subject says hat something can wait or is not urgent. Scheduling work for a specific veek contrasts with scheduling work for a specific day because it usually nplies greater delay as well as a much less precise planning of one's ctivities. The positive loading on "Number of items attempted" seems nconsistent, but it probably results from a tendency on the part of some ubjects to get through the final items in the in-basket by saying something like "I'll do this later" or "I'll take this home to work on." The eason for the loading on "Sets up checks on himself" is not clear. The actor might be called "procrastination," but we have chosen a less valuative name, *Defers judgment and action.*

Factor VII. Interacts with peers.   Here are the highest loadings:

Asks for information from peers	0.67
Refers to peers	0.66
Courtesy to peers	0.63
Number of peers involved	0.60
Discusses with peers	0.37

`he interpretation of this factor as *Interacts with peers* seems obvious.

Factor VIII. Orderly work.   The loadings:

Follows a preestablished structure	0.77
Schedules work for a specific day	0.63
Sets up checks on himself	0.53

`he rules for scoring "Follows a preestablished structure" state that any esponse indicating that the subject has, for example, followed a regula- on or rule (without being specifically instructed to do so), made use of an ffice routine (such as filing or distributing forms), or referred a problem to n individual or agency whose assigned function it is to deal with such roblems, should be scored. "Schedules work for a specific day" con- asts with the more vague kind of planning such as "next week" or "when get back from my trip." "Sets up checks on self" is scored when the ubject specifically asks a subordinate to remind him of something or to heck up on him. All these behaviors seem to imply an orderly, systematic nd possibly compulsive) set of work habits. The factor is thus named *rderly work.*

Factor IX. Informality.   Three scores have loadings higher than 0.35:

Informality to peers	0.81
Informality to superiors	0.81
Informality to subordinates	0.43

It is obvious why this factor has been named *Informality*. Informality is scored when the subject uses slang or colloquial language, first names, or makes general inquiries about someone's health or family.

Factor X. Accepts administrative responsibility. These are the loadings of 0.35 or greater:

Concern with proper channels	0.56
Encourages quickness	0.51
Initiates new structure	0.41
Aware of poor work	0.35
Asks for information from superiors	−0.39
Number of outsiders involved	−0.42

A loading of 0.31 on "Sets up checks on others" is also relevant. The category "Concern with proper channels" is scored when the subject shows concern for following administrative channels, e.g., "This is not supposed to come to me," or "Sellers should have gone to Jay with this problem." "Encourages quickness" is scored when the subject notes the need for promptness or encourages someone to be quick. "Initiates a new structure" is scored when the subject does not merely use a routine procedure but rather develops a new administrative arrangement for dealing with a problem or class of problems. Appointing an *ad hoc* committee, changing a subordinate's duties, requiring a subordinate to work with someone with whom he would not ordinarily work, and suggesting new goals for the organization are examples of behavior that would be scored as initiating structure. "Aware of poor work" is scored when the subject corrects or otherwise notes poor work on the part of a subordinate. All these are concerned with developing the organization to perform work more effectively. The categories with negative loadings, on the other hand, involve going outside the organization that is under the subject's control. The factor is named *Accepts administrative responsibility*.

These 10 factors, then, constitute criteria that we will use in studying effects of experimental modifications of organizational climates. We will be interested in comparing the subgroups of subjects who worked under different climates with respect to variances and covariances of factor scores, with respect to correlations of the factor scores with predictor variables, and with respect to the means of the factor scores.

One other criterion measure is the scorers' rating. It will be recalled from Chapter 7 that a factor analysis of these ratings showed that raters were able to make reasonably reliable judgments about overall performance but not about more detailed characteristics such as "authoritarian-democratic." Accordingly the rating of "overall performance," which had a reliability of 0.70, was chosen to represent the scorers' evaluation of performance.

Table 8-3 shows the correlations of scorers' overall rating with factor scores based on the 10 in-basket performance factors. It is apparent that

Table 8-3   Correlations of Scorers' Overall
Rating with In-Basket Factor Scores ($N = 260$)

Factor	r
I. Productivity	0.43†
II. Final action	0.03
III. Interacts with superiors	−0.09
IV. Thoughtful analysis	0.13*
V. Plans and discusses	−0.13*
VI. Defers judgment	−0.08
VII. Interacts with peers	−0.01
VIII. Orderly work	−0.10
IX. Informality	0.05
X. Accepts administrative responsibility	0.19†

*Significantly different from zero at the 5% level.

†Significantly different from zero at the 1% level.

scorers were most impressed with productivity — number of actions taken, number of people involved, number of communications, number of items attempted, and so on. The only other highly significant correlation is 0.19, with *Accepts administrative responsibility*. The signs of the correlations with Factors IV and V showed that scorers tended to prefer subjects who showed evidence of thoughtful analysis and who did more than plan and discuss. The factor scores for Factors II through X, remember, are orthogonal to the *Productivity* factor, and their correlations with ratings reflect that aspect of each factor that is independent of amount of work done.

Since the scorers' rating of overall performance may add some information to the criterion domain, it will be included as an eleventh variable in subsequent analyses having to do with comparisons of the treatment groups.

CHAPTER 9

Effects of Organizational Climates on Factor Structure

The factors just described are based on data for the entire group of 260 participants in the study; the data reflect the influences of the experimental climate conditions on the variances and intercovariances of the dependent measures, but not on the means. Our task now is to inquire into the first of the major questions we have asked—the effect of the experimental treatments on factor structure for subjects in the contrasting organizational climates. Do the same factors appear in the subgroups comprising each treatment dichotomy, and are the intercorrelations of the factors the same?

The next step in the analysis was to compute factor scores for the members of each subgroup, and then, for each subgroup, to compute the variance-covariance matrix of factor scores. (The appendix contains a more detailed description of the procedure.) By this method differences between matrices for two treatment groups are attributable only to differences in performance of the subgroup members, not to differences in factor loadings. If a factor does not exist for one of the subgroups, this fact would be known because of a zero variance for that factor. If two factors merge for one subgroup, the covariance would be very high. The statistical significance of differences between two matrices of variance and covariance can be evaluated by using the Box (1949) test of the homogeneity of variance-covariance matrices.

Variances and covariances of factor scores were accordingly computed for each of the three pairs of treatment subgroups: innovation vs. rules, detailed supervision vs. global supervision, and consistent vs. inconsistent climates. In all three cases, the Box test indicated highly significant differences; the p-value in each case was 0.002, using the more conservative F distribution rather than chi-square, as is recommended by Box (1949).

The results for the innovation-rules dichotomy are shown in Table 9-1. The entries in the diagonal are variances; the entries shown in the off-diagonal cells are correlations, rather than covariances, because it is easier to interpret correlations. The top member of each pair of entries is for the subjects who were assigned to the innovation climate condition, and the lower member of each pair is for subjects in the rules climate. The Box test yields an F of 1.737, which, with 55 and 214,851.1 degrees of freedom, is significant at the 0.002 level of confidence.

We conclude that the experimental treatment involving climates aimed at encouraging innovation vs. following rules and regulations does affect the variability and interrelationships of factors in the domain of administrative behaviors. In the following paragraphs we will see more specifically what these differences are.

Examination of the entries in the diagonal of Table 9-1 shows no large differences in variances. The biggest difference is for Factor VIII, *Orderly work*, where the variances are 0.82 and 1.17 for innovation and rules climates, respectively. (The variance for the pooled groups is 1.00.) Variability in "orderly work" is apparently decreased slightly by the innovation climate and increased by the rules condition.

The significant Box test must, then, be mainly due to differences in covariances rather than variances. We shall be interested in pairs of correlations that differ by 0.30 or more. A difference of 0.25 would be significant at the 5% level and a difference of 0.32 at the 1% level for correlations of about the magnitude of those in the table. The largest differences in correlations are as follows:

1. The largest difference (0.40) is significant at well beyond the 0.01 level. It shows that in the rules climate Factor IV, *Thoughtful analysis*, is associated with Factor X, *Accepts administrative responsibility*, ($r = 0.26$); while there is a small negative correlation ($r = -0.14$) in the innovation climate.

2. *Thoughtful analysis* is positively correlated with *Interacts with superiors* in the rules climate ($r = 0.11$) and negatively correlated in the innovation climate ($r = -0.21$), a difference of 0.32.

3. There is also a difference in sign for the correlations between Factors I and II. *Productivity* is positively associated with *Final action* in the innovation climate ($r = 0.17$) and negatively correlated under the rules condition ($r = -0.16$), the difference being 0.33.

Table 9-1 Variances and Intercorrelations of Factor Scores for Innovation and Rules Climates*

Factor	I	II	III	IV	V	VI	VII	VIII	IX	X
I. Productivity	1.05 / 0.95									
II. Final action	0.17 / −0.16	1.11 / 0.90								
III. Interacts with superiors	−0.04 / 0.04	−0.07 / 0.15	0.86 / 1.14							
IV. Thoughtful analysis	0.10 / −0.10	0.12 / 0.10	−0.21 / 0.11	1.11 / 0.89						
V. Plans and discusses	−0.01 / 0.01	−0.31 / −0.08	0.05 / 0.12	0.05 / −0.10	1.00 / 1.00					
VI. Defers judgment and action	0.09 / −0.09	0.13 / −0.02	−0.13 / −0.17	0.06 / 0.23	−0.15 / 0.03	0.92 / 1.08				
VII. Interacts with peers	0.05 / −0.05	−0.07 / 0.07	0.14 / 0.07	0.27 / 0.07	−0.14 / 0.04	0.01 / −0.02	1.03 / 0.97			
VIII. Orderly work	0.01 / −0.01	−0.01 / −0.19	−0.00 / 0.06	0.01 / −0.06	−0.06 / 0.19	−0.26 / 0.12	0.00 / −0.03	0.82 / 1.17		
IX. Informality	0.03 / −0.03	0.12 / −0.14	−0.06 / −0.00	0.19 / 0.06	0.02 / −0.13	0.01 / 0.06	0.10 / 0.18	−0.02 / 0.18	0.99 / 1.01	
X. Accepts administrative responsibility	−0.12 / 0.12	−0.09 / −0.10	0.06 / −0.04	−0.14 / 0.26	0.12 / −0.15	0.04 / −0.02	−0.16 / −0.08	0.08 / −0.03	0.06 / −0.13	1.02 / 0.98

*The top member of each pair of entries is for subjects in the innovation climate and the bottom member is for subjects in the rules climate.

4. There is a difference of 0.38 between correlations of Factor VI, *Defers judgment and action*, and Factor VIII, *Orderly work*. The two factors are correlated positively in the rules climate ($r = 0.12$) and negatively in the innovation climate ($r = -0.26$).

Table 9-2 is the table of variances and correlations for subgroups working under global and detailed supervision climates. With 55 and 214,851.1 degrees of freedom, the F of 1.766 is significant at the 0.002 level. The experimental treatments have influenced variability with respect to two varieties of performance, those defined by Factors IV, *Thoughtful analysis*, and VII, *Interacts with peers*. In both instances variability was increased by global supervision and decreased by the detailed supervision climate condition, where the subject was expected to monitor in detail the work of his subordinates. The effect was quite substantial, with the variance about 1.25 for the global and 0.75 for the detailed climate.

There are also several substantial differences in correlations.

1. The largest difference (0.44) again involves Factors III and IV. Factor IV, *Thoughtful analysis*, is negatively correlated with Factor III, *Interacts with superiors*, for the global supervision condition ($r = -0.27$) and positively correlated for detailed supervision ($r = 0.17$).

2. Factor IV, *Thoughtful analysis*, is positively correlated with Factor VII, *Interacts with peers*, in the global supervision climate ($r = 0.36$) and about zero in the detailed supervision climate ($r = -0.02$), for a difference of 0.38.

3. Factor IV is negatively correlated with Factor X, *Accepts administrative responsibility*, in the global supervision climate ($r = -0.11$) and positively correlated in the detailed supervision climate ($r = 0.26$), the difference being 0.37.

4. Factor VII, *Interacts with peers*, is negatively correlated with Factor X, *Accepts administrative responsibility*, in the global supervision condition ($r = -0.31$) and positively correlated in the detailed supervision condition ($r = 0.10$), the difference in correlations being 0.41.

Table 9-3 is the variance-correlation table for the interaction of innovation-rules climates with global-detailed supervision climates. This interaction has been interpreted in an earlier chapter in terms of consistent vs. inconsistent climate conditions. The Box test yields an F equal to 1.866, which, with 55 and 214,955.8 degrees of freedom, is again significant at the 0.002 level.

The interaction of the climate conditions affects variability of factor scores primarily. The most striking result is for the variances of scores for

Table 9-2 Variances and Intercorrelations of Factor Scores for Global and Detailed Supervision Climates*

Factor	I	II	III	IV	V	VI	VII	VIII	IX	X
I. Productivity	0.99 1.01									
II. Final action	−0.14 0.14	0.95 1.05								
III. Interacts with superiors	−0.01 0.01	−0.02 −0.20	0.81 1.19							
IV. Thoughtful analysis	0.02 −0.02	0.05 −0.03	−0.27 0.17	1.25 0.75						
V. Plans and discusses	0.09 −0.10	−0.18 −0.22	0.01 0.18	0.06 −0.10	0.94 1.06					
VI. Defers judgment and action	−0.04 0.05	0.04 0.10	−0.22 −0.07	0.23 0.05	−0.09 −0.08	1.11 0.89				
VII. Interacts with peers	0.08 −0.08	−0.03 −0.10	0.17 0.03	0.36 −0.02	−0.15 −0.04	−0.04 0.02	1.24 0.76			
VIII. Orderly work	−0.01 0.01	0.05 0.15	−0.04 0.11	−0.04 −0.02	−0.13 −0.11	−0.03 −0.10	−0.10 0.07	0.97 1.03		
IX. Informality	−0.00 0.00	0.18 0.06	−0.03 −0.02	0.26 0.00	0.14 0.04	0.05 −0.01	0.21 0.08	0.03 0.15	1.12 0.88	
X. Accepts administrative responsibility	−0.04 0.04	−0.01 0.02	0.05 −0.04	−0.11 0.26	0.17 0.12	0.02 −0.03	−0.31 0.10	0.01 0.05	−0.13 0.06	1.06 0.94

*The top member of each pair of entries is for subjects in the global supervision climate and the bottom member is for subjects in the detailed supervision climate.

Table 9-3 Variances and Intercorrelations of Factor Scores for Consistent and Inconsistent Climates*

Factor	I	II	III	IV	V	VI	VII	VIII	IX	X
I. Productivity	0.90 1.10									
II. Final action	−0.01 0.01	0.95 1.05								
III. Interacts with superiors	−0.05 0.05	−0.21 −0.01	1.15 0.85							
IV. Thoughtful analysis	0.11 −0.11	0.02 0.02	−0.08 −0.02	1.33 0.67						
V. Plans and discusses	0.03 −0.03	−0.17 −0.23	0.09 0.07	−0.06 0.04	1.04 0.96					
VI. Defers judgment and action	−0.03 0.03	0.08 −0.06	−0.19 −0.06	0.06 0.20	0.14 0.08	0.95 1.05				
VII. Interacts with peers	−0.00 0.00	0.04 0.17	−0.00 0.21	0.25 0.11	0.12 0.07	−0.01 −0.00	1.12 0.88			
VIII. Orderly work	0.12 −0.12	−0.01 −0.22	0.12 −0.06	−0.06 0.01	0.23 0.01	−0.20 0.06	0.12 −0.16	1.07 0.93		
IX. Informality	0.01 −0.01	−0.29 0.02	−0.06 −0.05	0.13 0.14	0.05 −0.20	0.03 0.06	0.18 0.09	0.03 0.14	0.80 1.20	
X. Accepts administrative responsibility	0.05 −0.05	−0.11 0.07	0.04 0.01	0.01 0.09	−0.21 −0.01	−0.02 0.01	−0.17 −0.06	0.05 0.02	−0.15 0.07	1.26 0.74

*The top member of each pair of entries is for subjects in consistent climates and the bottom member is for subjects in inconsistent climates.

Factor IV, *Thoughtful analysis*; the variability is considerably greater (1.33) for the consistent climate conditions than for the inconsistent climate conditions (0.67). The effects are similar but less extreme for Factor X, *Accepts administrative responsibility*, where the variances are 1.26 and 0.74. The only other effect which is possibly worthy of note is that variability for Factor IX, *Informality*, is greater under the inconsistent climate conditions (variances are 0.80 and 1.20 for consistent and inconsistent climates, respectively).

In only one case do correlations differ by more than 0.30. With consistent climates, Factor II, *Final action*, and Factor IX, *Informality*, correlate negatively ($r = -0.29$), and under the inconsistent climate conditions the correlation is approximately zero ($r = 0.02$).

Before trying to put all these detailed results together to see if more general conclusions can be reached, we should remind ourselves of a kind of similarity between the innovation-rules dichotomy and the global-detailed supervision dichotomy. This similarity is what led us to interpret the interaction of the two treatment dichotomies in terms of consistent vs. inconsistent climate conditions. The similarity has to do with the amount of freedom of thought and action permitted. *Innovation* permits one to seek new, original ways of accomplishing work and solving problems, while *rules* restricts such search. *Global supervision* also encourages employees to solve problems and do work in their own way, while *detailed supervision* implies the need to conform to the supervisor's wishes. Because of such similarities, one might suppose that both treatment dichotomies would have somewhat similar influences on the variance correlation matrices. Do these treatments in fact have similar effects?

We note that *Thoughtful analysis* is involved in many of the instances where large differences in correlation occur. *Thoughtful analysis* is negatively correlated with *Interacts with superiors* in both the innovation and global supervision conditions, and positively correlated with *Accepts administrative responsibility* in both the rules and detailed supervision conditions. Furthermore, *Thoughtful analysis* correlates positively with *Interacts with peers* in both the innovation and global supervision conditions (although the difference was not significant in the case of innovation and rules conditions). It would thus appear that in the freer climates the more thoughtful responses are likely to be associated with attempts to deal directly with peers, while the more restrictive rules and detailed supervision climates tend to produce an association of the thoughtful responses with interactions with the boss and attempts to influence directly one's own administrative organization. The administrators thus seemed to take advantage of their freedom by bypassing superiors in order to deal directly with the source of many of their problems. The more disciplined climates seem necessary in order for the results of the thoughtful analysis to be translated into the normal channels for administrative action.

The negative correlation between *Interacts with peers* and *Accepts administrative responsibility* in the global supervision climate seems consistent with the above interpretation, as does the positive correlation between *Productivity* and *Final action* in the innovation climate.

All factors are present in all the treatment conditions. The most extreme effects on variances were found in the interactions of the climate conditions. *Thoughtful analysis* again figures in the findings, where the variance is much greater for consistent than for inconsistent climates. Much of the effect of our experimental variations in organizational climates thus seems to center on thoughtful analysis and its relationships with other factors.

Discussing variances and correlations of factors without knowing about their means is a little unsatisfying. We will return to the question of means after we have assured ourselves that effects of experimental treatments are relatively the same for all subjects — that the regressions of factor scores on measures of personal characteristics have the same slope for different treatment groups. If they do, one can legitimately compare treatment groups with respect to means of the dependent variables.

CHAPTER 10

Effects of Climates on Means and on Relationships of Performance to Predictor Variables

EFFECTS DUE TO PERSONAL CHARACTERISTICS

In this chapter we shall first be concerned with the relationships between in-basket performance factor scores and the predictor measures that are based on the personality inventories, the biographical questionnaire, and the cognitive ability tests. As is described in Chapter 5, a series of factor analyses was used to reduce a large number of items of information in the predictor domain to 21 scores that represent a set of personal characteristics. The ratings of the organizational climates of the subjects' *real* jobs, on innovation-rules and detailed-global supervision scales, were used as two additional predictor variables. To what extent are these 23 measures predictive of performance in the simulated administrative job, using scores on the 10 in-basket factors and the scorers' rating as criteria?

The Zero-Order Correlations for the Total Group

Table 10-1 contains the zero-order correlations between the criteria and the 23 predictor measures. The first 10 columns represent the 10 in-basket factors and the eleventh column the scorers' overall rating of performance. These correlations were computed using in-basket factor scores based on the total group of 260 subjects, and they reflect whatever influences on means may have been produced by the experimental treatments.

The last two predictor measures are the subjects' ratings of the climates of their real-job organization. A high rating on *Climate Rating-Rules* means that the real job was thought to be characterized by a *rules* climate

Table 10-1 Correlations of Predictor Variables with Performance Factor Scores ($N = 260$)

Predictor	Factor I	II	III	IV	V	VI	VII	VIII	IX	X	Scorers' Rating
Acquiescence	0.13*	0.03	0.05	0.01	-0.05	-0.04	-0.06	0.10	0.05	0.06	0.07
Social Extroversion	0.12	-0.01	-0.08	-0.08	-0.00	-0.10	-0.07	0.05	-0.08	0.02	0.08
Independence	0.12	0.02	0.02	0.11	-0.12	0.02	0.01	-0.02	0.06	0.07	0.08
Maladjustment	0.13*	0.04	-0.01	-0.00	0.05	-0.05	-0.04	0.11	-0.05	0.10	0.03
Rigid Authoritarianism	-0.14*	0.11	0.09	-0.13*	-0.04	-0.07	0.05	0.06	0.05	-0.03	-0.02
Theoretical Education	-0.04	-0.13*	-0.04	0.03	0.07	0.09	-0.14*	0.06	-0.03	0.01	0.03
Years of Military Service	0.06	-0.06	0.04	-0.02	-0.03	0.19†	-0.03	0.03	0.02	-0.05	0.01
Number of Children	0.06	-0.03	-0.06	0.06	0.03	0.08	0.09	-0.03	0.03	0.02	0.07
Educated Institutional Man	0.08	-0.06	0.02	0.02	0.06	-0.01	-0.10	-0.03	-0.09	-0.10	-0.04
Power and Seniority	-0.06	0.04	0.00	-0.03	-0.21†	-0.13*	0.06	0.00	-0.00	-0.13*	-0.08
Dead-End Seniority	-0.15*	0.04	0.04	-0.18†	-0.09	-0.12	0.00	0.07	0.04	-0.04	-0.20†
Staff Officer	0.08	-0.14*	-0.07	0.18†	0.02	0.08	0.08	0.06	-0.02	-0.09	0.08
Hidden Patterns	0.22†	0.11	-0.01	0.19†	0.03	-0.02	0.14*	-0.09	0.04	0.03	0.18†
Memory	0.10	-0.05	-0.09	0.15†	0.15*	0.07	0.07	0.03	0.04	-0.03	0.03
Vocabulary	0.09	-0.04	0.13*	0.21†	-0.07	-0.01	0.14*	-0.09	0.04	-0.02	-0.00
Multiple Analogies	0.10	0.11	-0.01	0.09	0.12*	0.12	0.03	-0.07	-0.12	0.09	0.07
Test S – Successful Strategy	0.09	0.02	0.02	0.14*	0.10	0.18†	0.03	-0.07	0.12	0.14*	-0.04
Test S – Conservative Strategy	0.05	0.07	-0.05	0.04	0.00	0.12	-0.04	-0.15*	0.05	0.12	0.07
Speed of Closure	0.18†	-0.06	-0.03	0.16†	0.10	0.07	0.00	0.01	0.05	-0.00	0.17†
Ideational Fluency	0.22†	-0.01	-0.01	0.06	-0.09	-0.02	0.01	-0.01	-0.02	0.05	0.03
Inductive Reasoning	0.16†	0.01	0.02	0.10	0.11	0.16†	0.09	-0.11	0.10	0.04	0.06
Climate Rating-Rules	0.03	0.01	-0.11	0.08	-0.03	0.04	0.05	-0.08	-0.04	-0.02	0.12
Climate Rating-Global	-0.15*	0.11	0.10	-0.14*	0.04	-0.10	-0.02	0.05	-0.03	-0.08	-0.12*

*Significantly different from zero at the 5% level.
†Significantly different from zero at the 1% level.

rather than an innovation climate. A high rating on *Climate Rating-Global* means that the subject thought his real job was characterized by a *global* supervision climate rather than a detailed supervision climate.

The coefficients are generally quite low. Correlations that are significant at the 1% level occur only for four of the in-basket factor scores and for the scorers' overall rating.

The best predictors of the first in-basket factor, *Productivity*, as judged by the zero-order correlations, are cognitive ability tests—Hidden Patterns, Ideational Fluency, Speed of Closure, and Inductive Reasoning. It is also of interest that the biographical score called Dead-End Seniority correlates negatively with Productivity, as does the personality factor score for Rigid Authoritarianism. The Hidden Patterns test, which is listed with the cognitive tests, is often used as a measure of Witkin's personality construct of field independence. Although the correlations are low, the signs of the correlations generally agree with the theoretical implications of the predictor measures.

Hidden Patterns is also one of the best predictors of Factor IV, *Thoughtful analysis*, along with the Vocabulary test. Dead-End Seniority and Rigid Authoritarianism have negative correlations with Factor IV, while being a Staff Officer is positively correlated with this criterion.

Only one correlation is highly significant for Factor V (*Plans and discusses*): Power and Seniority is negatively related to this criterion measure, a factor which reflects a tendency to refrain from any action more overt than discussing the problem with others.

The best predictor of Factor VI, *Defers judgment and action*, is, interestingly enough, Years of Military Service, and the correlation is positive. The Successful Strategy score on Test S, Analogies, is positively correlated with Factor VI.

The scorers' overall rating of in-basket performance, as shown in the last column, is best predicted by Dead-End Seniority. Those whose in-basket performance was least well regarded by the scorers tended to be the same subjects whose careers suggest that they were not well regarded by their superiors. But the correlation is, of course, quite low. Hidden Patterns and Speed of Closure were the only tests that had significant correlations with the overall rating.

A low correlation for the total group might result from the pooling of two subgroups that differ substantially with respect to the slopes and intercepts of regressions. One of the purposes of the study was to investigate the possibility that the relationships between measures of administrative performance and predictors are different for groups whose organizations differed with respect to climate. The next section is concerned with the zero-order correlations separately for the various treatment groups.

Zero-Order Correlations for Experimental Groups

Correlations of the 23 predictor measures with the 11 criterion measures were computed for the two groups in each of the three experimental dichotomies: innovation vs. rules; global vs. detailed supervision; and the interaction of these two dichotomies, which we have interpreted as consistent vs. inconsistent climate conditions. The correlations were in general quite low, although they ranged somewhat higher than those in Table 10-1. We are particularly interested in *differences* between correlations for the groups comprising a dichotomy, because a large difference indicates a tendency for the climate conditions to produce different results for people with different personal characteristics. For correlations of the generally low magnitude we are dealing with here, a difference in correlation of about 0.32 is significant at the 1% level, and a difference of 0.25 is significant at the 5% level. Among the larger differences in correlation are the following:

1. In the innovation climate, productivity tends to be low for subjects who are rigid-authoritarian ($r = -0.26$); the correlation is about zero ($r = -0.02$) for the rules climate.

2. Again in the innovation climate, productivity is high for those who have experience as staff officers ($r = 0.22$); in the rules climate, the corresponding correlation is -0.07.

3. In the global supervision climate, the correlation of Inductive Reasoning with *Productivity* is 0.34 in the global supervision climate and near zero (-0.02) in the detailed supervision climate. The difference of 0.36 is statistically significant.

4. Tendency to take final action is associated with a high real-job rating on global supervision ($r = 0.24$) for subjects in the global supervision climate; the correlation is slightly negative ($r = -0.06$) for subjects in the detailed supervision climate.

5. Tendency to interact with superiors is associated with high scores on Inductive Reasoning for subjects in the rules climate ($r = 0.19$); for subjects in the innovation climate, the correlation is negative ($r = -0.14$), for a difference in correlation of 0.33.

6. Thoughtful analysis is associated slightly with Maladjustment for subjects in the innovation climate ($r = 0.14$); for subjects in the rules climate the correlation is negative ($r = -0.17$).

7. Deferring judgment and action is negatively related to Maladjustment in the consistent climate conditions ($r = -0.22$); the correlation is positive for inconsistent climates ($r = 0.13$), for a difference of 0.35.

8. Interacting with peers is positively associated with Vocabulary score for subjects in the global supervision climate ($r = 0.28$); the correlation is slightly negative for subjects in the detailed supervision climate ($r = -0.05$).

9. Rigid Authoritarianism is associated with orderly work in the rules climate ($r = 0.18$); in the innovation climate the correlation is negative ($r = -0.09$).

10. Being a Staff Officer is associated with informality in the rules climate ($r = 0.14$); the relationship is negative for those in the innovation climate ($r = -0.19$).

The differences in correlations that have been commented on are of course too tenuous to justify any elaborate attempt to relate them to psychological theory, even though the relationship of certain of the findings to construct validity is often obvious. The differences are too small and too few, in relation to the number of comparisons possible, to attribute much significance to these results. In a later section we will report the results of multivariate statistical tests of the differences in slopes and intercepts of regressions.

Multiple Correlations

The multiple correlations to be discussed in this section are based on the pooled treatment groups, with the influences of the experimental treatments on the means of the in-basket factor scores removed. This is accomplished by working, in effect, with standard scores, the mean of which is set at zero for each group. The correlations described in the preceding section, on the other hand, were based on the total group and were to some extent influenced by the experimental treatments.

Table 10-2 shows the multiple correlations of the 23 predictor variables with each of the in-basket factor scores and with the scorers' overall rating of in-basket performance. The multiple correlations range from 0.28 to 0.42. Three of the R's are highly significant, statistically speaking, and one is significantly different from zero at only a marginal (10%) level.

The most predictable of the 11 criterion measures is the *Productivity* factor score ($R = 0.42$). As is shown in the first column of Table 10-2, regression weights for two of the predictors, Social Extroversion and Hidden Patterns, are significant at the 2% level. Maladjustment,

Table 10-2 Multiple Correlations and Regression Weights

Predictor	I	II	III	IV	V	VI	VII	VIII	IX	X	Scorers' Rating
Acquiescence	0.08	−0.02	0.05	0.01	−0.01	−0.03	−0.09	0.12*	0.08	0.06	0.07
Social Extroversion	0.10‡	0.03	−0.02	−0.03	0.01	−0.10‡	0.00	0.04	−0.06	0.02	0.19
Independence	0.05	0.04	−0.03	0.06	−0.11*	0.01	−0.08	−0.01	0.06	0.10	0.12
Maladjustment	0.09*	0.03	−0.04	−0.04	0.03	−0.08*	−0.04	0.11‡	−0.06	0.04	0.09
Rigid Authoritarianism	−0.03	0.07	0.09*	−0.04	0.02	−0.05	0.07	−0.00	0.01	−0.02	0.11
Theoretical Education	−0.02	−0.12*	−0.07	0.02	0.06	0.07	−0.15†	0.09	−0.04	0.01	0.10
Years of Military Service	0.03	−0.05	0.05	−0.07	−0.06	0.18§	−0.03	0.00	0.03	−0.04	−0.01
Number of Children	−0.03	−0.02	−0.05	0.05	0.01	0.04	0.11	−0.01	0.05	−0.02	0.05
Educated Institutional Man	0.05	−0.00	−0.00	−0.02	0.09	−0.02	−0.10	−0.02	−0.08	−0.12†	−0.03
Power and Seniority	0.02	0.01	−0.05	0.03	−0.11†	−0.04	0.04	0.02	0.01	−0.11†	−0.08
Dead-End Seniority	−0.08	−0.00	−0.04	−0.10	−0.09	−0.06	−0.01	0.05	0.08	−0.02	−0.47‡
Staff Officer	0.05	−0.06	−0.05	0.11§	0.03	0.05	0.06	0.04	−0.03	−0.07*	0.21
Hidden Patterns	0.16‡	0.13*	0.00	0.12*	−0.03	−0.12*	0.13*	−0.05	0.01	−0.01	0.39*
Memory	0.00	−0.06	−0.10	0.07	0.13*	−0.01	0.08	0.08	0.03	−0.07	−0.22
Vocabulary	−0.00	−0.01	0.21§	0.13*	−0.09	−0.11	0.22§	−0.10	0.03	−0.02	−0.04
Multiple Analogies	0.00	0.10*	−0.04	0.04	0.10	0.11*	−0.01	−0.07	−0.16§	0.06	0.17
Test S – Successful Strategy	−0.02	0.03	0.01	0.03	0.00	0.05	−0.00	0.02	0.05	0.07	−0.07
Test S – Conservative Strategy	0.03	0.07	−0.02	0.01	−0.06	0.07	−0.03	−0.14§	0.03	0.06	0.17
Speed of Closure	0.03	−0.10	−0.02	0.07	0.02	−0.00	−0.05	0.04	0.06	−0.08	0.32
Ideational Fluency	0.10*	0.01	0.00	−0.02	−0.12*	−0.01	−0.01	−0.03	−0.03	0.06	−0.09
Inductive Reasoning	0.10*	−0.02	0.00	−0.02	0.08	0.07	0.04	−0.04	0.05	−0.08	−0.00
Climate Rating-Rules	−0.01	0.02	−0.06	0.03	0.02	0.05	0.01	−0.05	−0.04	−0.03	0.12
Climate Rating-Global	−0.03	0.06	0.03	−0.03	0.05	−0.03	0.00	0.01	−0.02	−0.05	−0.10
R	0.42§	0.32	0.28	0.40§	0.36*	0.40§	0.35	0.34	0.29	0.32	0.34

*Significant at the 10% level.
†Significant at the 5% level.
‡Significant at the 2% level.
§Significant at the 1% level.

187

Ideational Fluency, and Inductive Reasoning all have marginally significant regression weights. Most of the predictable variance of *Productivity*, so far as this set of predictor variables is concerned, is associated with a personality inventory score, Social Extroversion, and a cognitive style measure thought to reflect field independence, the Hidden Patterns test.

Factor IV, *Thoughtful analysis*, has a significant R of 0.40 with the 23 predictors, and there is only one highly significant regression weight, that for Staff Officer. This single biographical questionnaire score, reflecting experience in administrative staff work, bears most of the load in predicting the *Thoughtful analysis* factor. Hidden Patterns and Vocabulary tests have marginally significant weights.

Factor V, *Plans and discusses*, has a multiple correlation with the predictors of 0.36, which just misses significance at the 5% level. This factor, it will be recalled, has a high loading on *plans only* and seems to reflect an unwillingness to go much closer to final action than having conversations about the problem. We find the only statistically significant weight is for a biographical variable, Power and Seniority, and the relationship is negative. Other variables with weights that are significant at only the 10% level are Ideational Fluency, Memory, and Independence. The sign is positive in the case of the Memory test.

Factor VI, *Defers judgment and action*, has an R of 0.40 with the predictors. A biographical item, Years of Military Service, has the highest regression weight, and it is positive—many years of military service is associated with postponing judgment and action. Presumably this finding reflects some quirk having to do with the kind of military men who choose to go into state service. Social Extroversion and Maladjustment both have negative weights, as does Hidden Patterns. The weight for the Multiple Analogies test, however, is positive.

We find, then, that several of the in-basket performance factors are moderately predictable by combinations of measures in our predictor battery. *Productivity* is best predicted by cognitive ability tests such as Hidden Patterns and Ideational Fluency, but a personality measure, Social Extroversion, makes an important contribution to the multiple correlation. Hidden Patterns and Vocabulary tests are the best predictors of *Thoughtful analysis*, but the biographical history item Staff Officer makes the greatest contribution to the multiple correlation. Tendency to *Defer judgment and action* for some reason is most closely related (positively) to Years of Military Service, while tendency to do nothing beyond planning and discussing is predicted (negatively) by

Power and Seniority. The scorers' overall evaluation of in-basket performance was most closely related, negatively, to Dead-End Seniority. Differences in correlation associated with the organizational climate treatments were found to occur, and they seem to make theoretical sense, although differences are small.

EFFECTS OF CLIMATES ON THE RELATIONSHIP OF PREDICTORS TO PERFORMANCE AND ON THE MEANS OF PERFORMANCE FACTOR SCORES

In this section we shall deal with the effects of the experimental treatments on the relationships of personal characteristics to performance-factor scores. One of our primary interests is whether or not the different treatments bring about differences in the means of the criteria; however, the simple approach of testing the significance of differences in means might be obscured by differences in the individuals assigned to the treatments. We have already noted a number of intriguing differences among the correlations for different treatment groups, and we might expect the joint effect of the 23 predictors on the criteria to vary from group to group, possibly making a comparison of means misleading. We therefore first address ourselves to this issue:

Is the slope of the regression of each criterion on the 23 personal variables, considered simultaneously, the same for each treatment? If not, then it is clear that certain types of subjects will perform differently under certain conditions, and it is also clear that a simple test of means would be influenced by the types of subjects assigned to the treatment. Put more positively, the treatments would seem to affect persons differently, depending on the values of the personal variables.

If the slopes do not differ, we then attack the second issue: Are the mean scores on the criterion variables the same for the different experimental treatments? If the 23 personal variables do affect the means, then we will want to adjust the means for variations in these variables; if they do not, we may perform a simple analysis of the means. This question finally answers a basic question about the effects of organizational climates on an individual's performance.

The appropriate techniques for investigating these questions are the analysis of variance and covariance. For each criterion, a linear statistical model was developed that included the experimental treatments, the 23 personal variables, and the interaction between the treatments and the personality variables. The model was then fitted, using all 260 cases. The parameter estimates from the fitted model are various functions of the 23-variable regression lines for the four experimental treatment combinations (the cells in Fig. 3-1). The construction of such models and the estimation of their parameters are discussed fully by Beaton (1964).

Effects of Organizational Climate on the Relationship between Predictor Variables and Criteria

The first question can be viewed as a series of hypotheses about similarities and differences among regression lines. The linear model was fitted for each of the 11 criteria, and the slopes of the innovation-rules, global-detailed, and consistent-inconsistent regression lines were compared. The slopes only, not the intercepts, were compared, so as to test the parallelism, not the complete identity, of the regression lines. The results of these 33 tests (3 contrasts × 11 criteria) are shown in Table 10-3. Only one of the 33 comparisons is highly significant (1% level), and the p-value for one other comparison is 0.07. We may conclude that whatever effects the experimental treatments may have produced were in general not specific to certain types of individuals.

The one significant result was for the regression of Factor VII, *Interacts with peers*, on a composite of the predictors for the global-detailed supervision climates. Table 10-4 shows the regression weights for the 23 predictors. Each weight represents the contribution of a variable to the prediction of the criterion for those subjects in a particular experimental condition. The largest regression weight is 0.68, for the Vocabulary test in the global supervision climate, which may be contrasted with the −0.04 weight for the detailed supervision climate. The global supervision climate produced an increase in peer interaction for subjects who had high vocabulary scores. Whatever effect the detailed supervision climate may have had did not depend upon vocabulary level.

Many of the in-basket items are concerned with inter-divisional problems and, therefore, with peer relationships; and in the global supervision climate the subject would presumably feel more free to deal directly with his peers. (Remember that the supervision climates concern how the subject can expect to be treated as well as how he should treat his subordinates.) The verbally brighter subjects, according to this result, are the ones who in fact did take up problems directly with their peers under the global supervision condition, while the less verbally able tended not to do so. But under detailed supervision, where initiative in dealing with others is discouraged, vocabulary level is not related to peer interaction.

Table 10-3 Tests of Equality of Slopes of Regressions of In-Basket Factor Scores on Predictors

Criterion	Row Effects (Innovation-Rules)		Column Effects (Global-Detailed Supv.)		Interaction (Consist.-Inconsist.)	
	F	P	F	P	F	P
I. Productivity	0.93	NS	0.81	NS	0.48	NS
II. Final action	1.41	NS	0.72	NS	1.17	NS
III. Interacts with superiors	1.17	NS	1.13	NS	0.45	NS
IV. Thoughtful analysis	0.86	NS	0.99	NS	1.12	NS
V. Plans and discusses	1.51	0.07	0.73	NS	1.10	NS
VI. Defers judgment and action	1.25	NS	1.06	NS	1.27	NS
VII. Interacts with peers	1.42	NS	1.91	0.01	1.16	NS
VIII. Orderly work	0.81	NS	0.54	NS	0.69	NS
IX. Informality	1.16	NS	0.63	NS	0.80	NS
X. Accepts administrative responsibility	1.02	NS	1.09	NS	0.77	NS
Scorers' Rating	1.00	NS	0.72	NS	1.40	NS

Table 10-4   Regression Weights for Predicting Factor VII, Interacts with Peers, in Global Supervision and Detailed Supervision Climates

	Predictor	Regression Coefficients		
		Global Supervision	Detailed Supervision	Difference Global – Detailed
1.	Acquiescence	0.00	0.06	−0.06
2.	Social Extroversion	−0.02	0.04	−0.06
3.	Independence	−0.17	−0.11	−0.06
4.	Maladjustment	−0.05	0.09	−0.14
5.	Rigid-Authoritarianism	0.05	0.03	0.02
6.	Theoretical Education	−0.11	−0.15	0.04
7.	Years of Military Service	0.12	−0.04	0.16
8.	Number of Children	0.50	−0.02	0.52
9.	Educated Institutional Man	−0.31	−0.11	−0.20
10.	Power and Seniority	0.00	−0.02	0.02
11.	Dead-End Seniority	−0.04	0.06	−0.10
12.	Staff Officer	−0.04	0.08	−0.12
13.	Hidden Patterns	0.04	0.10	−0.06
14.	Memory	0.19	−0.01	0.20
15.	Vocabulary	0.68	−0.04	0.72
16.	Multiple Analogies	−0.13	−0.03	−0.10
17.	Test S – Successful Strategy	0.01	−0.01	−0.00
18.	Test S – Conservative Strategy	−0.03	0.07	−0.10
19.	Speed of Closure	−0.18	0.02	−0.20
20.	Ideational Fluency	0.02	−0.06	0.08
21.	Inductive Reasoning	0.05	0.09	−0.04
22.	Climate Rating-Rules	0.15	−0.05	0.20
23.	Climate Rating-Global	0.07	−0.01	0.08

Our enthusiasm for such an interpretation, however sensible it may seem, will be somewhat cooled when we remember that this is the only significant finding out of the 33 trials.

Effects of Organizational Climates on Means

We now proceed to examine differences in means of the in-basket criterion variable scores that may be attributable to the different organizational climates. The means of the groups we want to contrast are shown in Table 10-5. (The grand mean of all observations was set at zero, and these means are deviations from the grand mean.) Since the number of observations in the various climates varied slightly, the means of the main effects have been "adjusted for disproportionality" in order to assure the statistical independence of the mean comparisons.

Table 10-5 Means of Performance Factor Scores for Treatment Groups

Criterion	Row Effect		Column Effect		Interaction	
	Innovation	Rules	Global	Detailed Supv.	Consist.	Inconsist.
I. Productivity	−0.08	0.08	0.08	−0.08	0.14	−0.14
II. Final action	−0.01	0.01	−0.04	0.04	−0.05	0.05
III. Interacts with superiors	0.00	0.00	−0.07	0.07	−0.12	0.12
IV. Thoughtful analysis	0.08	−0.08	−0.05	0.05	0.00	0.00
V. Plans and discusses	0.04	−0.04	0.00	−0.00	0.01	−0.01
VI. Defers judgment and action	−0.10	0.10	0.02	−0.02	0.08	−0.08
VII. Interacts with peers	0.09	−0.09	−0.07	0.07	−0.02	0.02
VIII. Orderly work	−0.00	0.00	0.01	−0.01	0.02	−0.02
IX. Informality	−0.01	0.01	0.09	−0.09	−0.09	0.09
X. Accepts administrative responsibility	0.08	−0.08	0.07	−0.07	0.05	−0.05
Scorers' Rating	−0.03	0.03	0.11	−0.11	0.26	−0.26

Inspection of the first two columns of the table shows that the innovation climate, in contrast with the rules climate, tends to reduce productivity, to increase thoughtful analysis, to decrease postponement of decisions, to increase interaction with peers, and to increase acceptance of administrative responsibility. The global supervision climate, in contrast with detailed supervision, tends to increase productivity, to decrease interaction with superiors, to increase informality, and to increase acceptance of administrative responsibility. (Since slopes of regression lines seem to be different for Factor VII, we should avoid stating a general effect on interaction with peers.) The biggest differences are found in the last two columns. Consistent climate conditions (as contrasted with inconsistent climates) tend to produce a relatively large increase in productivity, a decrease in interaction with superiors, an increase in postponing, a decrease in informality, and an increase in the favorability of the scorers' ratings. (The increase in scorers' rating is not as large, relatively, as it appears from the means because of much larger variances.)

These are the findings; but before attempting an interpretation we had better compare the magnitude of these criterion differences with the differences we might expect from sampling fluctuations, which could also generate differences in these means. This was done by a two-way non-orthogonal analysis of variance, the results of which are shown in Table 10-6. Most of the differences noted above prove not to be significantly different from zero. Only two differences are significant, and both involve the interaction of the climate dichotomies. Productivity is significantly higher (at the 2% level of confidence) and interaction with superiors is significantly lower (5% level) in the consistent as compared with the inconsistent climate conditions.

The F ratios in Table 10-6 show us that the unexplained or "error" variance, presumably attributable to sampling variations, is large relative to the effects of organizational climates. We know from Table 10-1 that several of the criteria are significantly correlated with the personal variables, variables which were not directly controlled in the assignment of individuals to climates. Perhaps, then, we should adjust the criterion scores for initial differences in the personal variables, making everybody "equal" on these variables in a statistical sense, and then perform the analysis of variance. For such a statistical adjustment to be useful, the slopes of regressions of criteria on personal variables must be the same for all organizational climates, that is, the regression lines must be parallel; otherwise the differences between means would change, depending on the value of the personal variables to which all individuals were adjusted.

Table 10-6 Tests of Equality of Means of Performance Factors

Performance Factor	Row Effects (Innovation-Rules)		Column Effects (Global-Detailed Supv.)		Interaction (Consist.-Inconsist.)	
	F	P	F	P	F	P
I. Productivity	1.50	NS	1.56	NS	5.46	0.02
II. Final action	0.02	NS	0.29	NS	0.65	NS
III. Interacts with superiors	0.00	NS	1.06	NS	3.76	0.05
IV. Thoughtful analysis	1.58	NS	0.61	NS	0.00	NS
V. Plans and discusses	0.40	NS	0.00	NS	0.05	NS
VI. Defers judgment and action	2.38	NS	0.14	NS	1.75	NS
VII. Interacts with peers	1.77	NS	1.04	NS	0.10	NS
VIII. Orderly work	0.00	NS	0.01	NS	0.10	NS
IX. Informality	0.04	NS	1.94	NS	1.87	NS
X. Accepts administrative responsibility	1.58	NS	1.15	NS	0.71	NS
Scorers' Rating	0.03	NS	0.31	NS	1.69	NS

Table 10-7 Tests of Equality of Means of Performance Factors, Allowing for Influence of 23 Predictor Variables

Performance Factor	Row Effects (Innovation-Rules)		Column Effects (Global-Detailed Supv.)		Interaction (Consist.-Inconsist.)	
	F	P	F	P	F	P
I. Productivity	1.02	NS	0.88	NS	2.35	0.02
II. Final action	0.49	NS	0.22	NS	0.94	NS
III. Interacts with superiors	0.07	NS	0.63	NS	1.37	NS
IV. Thoughtful analysis	1.30	NS	1.27	NS	0.20	NS
V. Plans and discusses	0.38	NS	0.44	NS	0.07	NS
VI. Defers judgment and action	2.26	0.05	0.38	NS	0.43	NS
VII. Interacts with peers	1.12	NS	–	*	0.08	NS
VIII. Orderly work	0.61	NS	0.23	NS	0.88	NS
IX. Informality	0.18	NS	1.55	NS	1.27	NS
X. Accepts administrative responsibility	1.01	NS	0.65	NS	0.58	NS
Scorers' Rating	0.01	NS	0.43	NS	0.28	NS

*This test is not appropriate because of a significant difference in slopes.

Earlier in this chapter we found that the regression slopes for the various contrasts were not significantly different (except for the global-detailed contrast of Factor VII, *Interacts with peers*); therefore such an analysis is reasonable.

The appropriate technique for this is the analysis of covariance. The results of the significance tests for such an analysis are shown in Table 10-7. We find that the difference between consistent and inconsistent climate conditions with respect to *Productivity* is still significant at the 2% level when the additional covariates are employed; but the difference with respect to *Interacts with superiors* is no longer significant. Another difference is now found to be significant, that for Factor VI, *Defers judgment and action*, under the innovation-rules climates. The amount of postponing is significantly reduced, according to this finding, in the innovation climate.

Table 10-8 shows the means of the *Productivity* factor score for each of

Table 10-8 Cell Means for Productivity

		SUPERVISORY CLIMATE	
		Global	Detailed
ADMINISTRATIVE CLIMATE	Innovation	0.14	−0.30
	Rules	0.01	0.14

the four cells that contribute to the row, column, and interaction effects we have been describing. This table shows that productivity was particularly depressed in the treatment combination involving both innovation and detailed supervision. The requirement to create new ideas and to translate them into action through detailed instructions to subordinates effectively reduced the number of actions taken, the amount of writing, the number of discussions planned, and other variables contributing to the *Productivity* factor.

The cell means for Factor III, *Interacts with superiors*, are shown in Table 10-9 and for Factor VI, *Defers judgment and action*, are shown in Table 10-10.

Table 10-9 Cell Means for Interacts with Superiors.

SUPERVISORY CLIMATE

		Global	Detailed
ADMINISTRATIVE CLIMATE	Innovation	−0.19	0.19
	Rules	0.06	−0.05

Table 10-10 Cell Means for Defers Judgment and Action.

SUPERVISORY CLIMATE

		Global	Detailed
ADMINISTRATIVE CLIMATE	Innovation	0.01	−0.21
	Rules	0.04	0.16

Summary

The results of the analyses of variance and covariance show that the effects of the experimental variations in organizational climate were, generally speaking, not dependent on the personal characteristics of the subjects, and one can therefore proceed to the investigation of effects on the means of performance measures. The comparison of means showed clearly that productivity is influenced by the joint effects (the interaction) of the treatment dichotomies. More specifically, productivity is depressed under the condition where the subject is expected both to be innovative and to exercise detailed supervision. There are also indications that inter-action with superiors is reduced by consistent climate conditions and that tendencies to postpone judgment and action are reduced when innovation is expected.

CHAPTER 11

The Three-Mode Factor Analysis[1]

The basic idea of this investigation was to study the joint effects of situational and personal variables on performance. The situational variables were defined as the organizational climates, which were manipulated experimentally; and the individual difference measures were provided by a battery of personality inventories, cognitive ability tests, and biographical items. The experimental treatments were found to influence substantially one's productivity and to alter the interrelationships of performance factors. But by and large there was little conclusive evidence of interactions of personal variables with situational variables, when the latter are the experimentally-produced climates.

A possible reason for not finding more striking evidence of interactions involving experimental climate treatments is that the in-basket test is itself rather heterogeneous, from the standpoint of controlling other situational variables. Such heterogeneity would tend to reduce predictability and to dissipate any general effects of climates. We do in fact find that correlations between two different in-basket tests are appreciably lower than the odd-even reliability of either one alone (Chapter 7) and that correlations between in-basket factor scores and predictors are generally low (Chapter 10). Perhaps smaller clusters of in-basket items can be found, using empirical methods for developing taxonomies, that are in some sense more homogeneous than the complete assortment of in-basket problems, and that these clusters of items will more clearly reveal interactions of situations with individual characteristics in predicting performance.

[1]The work in this chapter was supported in part by the National Institute of Child Health and Human Development under Research Grant 1 PO1 HDO1762.

199

Any attempt to identify homogeneous clusters of items by empirical methods requires us to discard the in-basket performance category scores, where we sum across items to obtain a total score, and to go back to the item data—the in-basket score sheets. Each score sheet is an item by performance category matrix. The entry in each cell indicates presence or absence of the behavior defined by a scoring category (or sometimes the extent of the behavior) in response to a particular in-basket item. The complete matrix of data is a stack of such score sheets, one for each subject in the study. In other words, the complete data matrix is a three-dimensional solid, representing 260 subjects, 57 items, and 55 scoring categories. The three dimensions represent (1) individuals, (2) stimulus situations, and (3) categories of performance. Three-mode factor analysis provides one way of searching for meaningful interrelationships in such a data matrix.

THREE-MODE FACTOR ANALYSIS

Three-mode factor analysis was developed by L. R Tucker as a method of searching for relations in a body of data in which three-way cross-ciassifications have been applied. Ordinary two-way factor analysis is a method of searching for relationships in data that have been cross-classified in two ways; in the typical psychological example, two-way factor analysis has been applied to test scores classified by individual and by test. Three-way factor analysis would be applicable when three-way classifications of data are used, e.g., when a group of *individuals* are judged by a number of *raters* in each of a variety of *situations*. The method has been described by Tucker in Harris (1963) and in Frederiksen and Gulliksen (1964). The most recent description of three-mode factor analysis (Tucker, 1966) provides methods applicable to data for large samples of individuals. The choice of which of the three-mode matrices to rotate to simple structure is discussed by Bloxom (1968). In Chapter 1 we have proposed the use of three-mode factor analysis as a method for developing a taxonomy of situations, using the criterion of similarity with respect to the behaviors elicited by the situations.

Tucker has summarized the results of three studies employing three-mode factor analysis (Hoffman & Tucker, 1964; Levin, 1965; Tucker, 1965). Lilly (1965) and Wicker (1966) have also employed three-mode factor analysis in their research. All these studies show that interpretable results can be obtained and that such analyses can reveal some of the more complex interrelationships of individual characteristics, situations, and performance.

The three-mode factor analysis of our data involved the pooling of variance-covariance matrices over all subjects in all treatment groups, using the same origin and same unit of measurement for all categories on all items. Two separate principal component analyses were performed. The first required computing the sums of squares and cross products of performance categories across items, separately for each person in each treatment group. These variance-covariance matrices were pooled to make a total variance-covariance matrix for categories. The analysis of this matrix yielded a factor matrix of loadings of performance scores on factors (principal components) in the performance domain. This analysis is analogous to the one reported in Chapter 8, which yields the factors we have used as dependent variables. The second analysis required computing the sums of squares and cross products of items across performance categories, separately for each person in each treatment group. These variance-covariance matrices were pooled to make a total variance-covariance matrix for items. Each entry in this matrix represents the extent to which the members of a given pair of items tend to elicit the same performance. The analysis of this matrix yields a factor matrix of loadings of items on factors (principal components) in the item domain. A factor in this domain represents a cluster of items that are similar in that they tend to elicit similar behaviors.

Each of these factor matrices was rotated to orthogonal simple structure, using the equamax criterion.

The next step in the procedure was to arrange the data in a super-matrix, with one row for each subject and with columns formed by stringing out the performance categories for each of the items. Tucker's procedure makes it possible to transform this super-matrix into a matrix with one row for each subject and with one column for each performance factor combined with each item factor. This matrix is in turn factored and rotated. The final product of the three-mode factor analysis is a three-dimensional core matrix like the data solid we started with, but with fewer performance variables, fewer item categories, and fewer types of subjects. In the present instance, the number of performance variables was reduced to 11 performance factors, the number of items was reduced to six item factors, and the number of subjects was reduced to six person factors. A separate table will be presented, later on, for each of the six person factors; the entries in that table will show that particular kinds of performance are associated with particular kinds of in-basket items for subjects who represent that particular person factor.

FACTOR ANALYSIS OF THE PERFORMANCE CATEGORIES

Before carrying out the three-mode factor analysis, a conventional principal components analysis of the performance category scores was performed, using data for all 260 cases and using the performance category scores obtained by summing over items, as is described in Chapter 7. For purposes of this analysis, the first principal component or "productivity" factor was not set orthogonal to all other factors, as it was in the analysis reported in Chapter 8. Inspection of the roots showed that 11 seemed to be the correct number of factors. The 11 factors were rotated to the equamax criterion of simple structure. All factors were found to be interpretable and to be more or less similar to factors previously found. In the following listings, loadings of 0.40 or higher are included. (The scores marked by asterisks were used to represent the factors in a procedure to be described in a moment.)

I. Acts in compliance with suggestions. The scoring categories whose loadings on Factor I are 0.40 or higher are as follows:

*Takes terminal action	0.88
*Concluding decision	0.88
Number of items attempted	0.64
*Follows lead by subordinates	0.64
Communicates by writing	0.60
*Follows lead by superiors	0.59
Estimated number of words	0.59
Number of usual courses of action	0.42
Follows lead by peers	0.41
Organizational change	0.40

This factor is very similar to the factor that was given the same name in Chapter 8, except that some of the loadings suggest high productivity as well.

II. Preparatory action. The loadings for Factor II are as follows:

*Communicates face-to-face	0.78
*Discusses with subordinates	0.75
*Makes tentative or definite plans only	0.72
*Arrives at a procedure for deciding	0.71

Number of usual courses of action	0.53
Discusses with peers	0.46
Number of subordinates involved	0.45
Schedules work — specific week	0.44
Discusses with superiors	0.44
Number of items attempted	0.43

This factor clearly involves doing things that are preparatory to decision and action. The factor is similar to *Plans and discusses* in the analysis described in Chapter 8, but is broader. The more general name *Preparatory action* therefore seems preferable.

III. Controls subordinates.   Ten scores had loadings greater than 0.40 on this factor:

*Gives directions and/or suggestions to subordinates	0.73
*Asks for information, opinion, advice, or permission from subordinates	0.63
Takes leading action	0.63
Number of subordinates involved	0.59
*Courtesy to subordinates	0.57
Communicates by writing	0.55
Informality to subordinates	0.51
Sets a deadline	0.48
Arrives at a procedure for deciding	0.41
Makes tentative or definite plans only	−0.42

Because of the two category scores at the top of the list, the factor has been named in terms of controlling subordinates, in spite of the fact that it involves a somewhat wider range of behaviors than controlling. The factor seems to represent accomplishing work through subordinates. Presumably the courtesy and informality implied by two of the scores represent stylistic aspects of attempts to control subordinates. This factor is the one that most closely resembles the *Productivity* factor in Chapter 8.

IV. Interacts with superiors.   The loadings are as follows:

Number of superiors involved	0.87
*Gives suggestions to superiors	0.82
*Refers to superiors	0.68
*Discusses with superiors	0.56
*Gives information to superiors	0.56

This factor is very similar to the one given the same name in the first analysis.

   V. Interacts with peers.   There are five loadings to report:

*Asks for information, opinion, advice, or permission from peers	0.77
Number of peers involved	0.71
*Courtesy to peers	0.67
*Refers to peers	0.62
Discusses with peers	0.47

For a similar reason, this factor is named *Interacts with peers*.

   VI. Orderly work.   There are only four loadings higher than 0.40:

*Follows a preestablished structure	0.81
*Schedules work for a specific day	0.77
*Sets up checks on himself	0.57
Discusses with subordinates	0.44

This factor is very similar to one found in the first analysis and is given the same name.

   VII. Thoughtful analysis of problems.   There are six loadings above 0.40:

*Responds with specificity	0.77
*Conceptual analysis	0.73
Number of outsiders involved	0.66
*Evaluation and development of staff	0.52
Number of imaginative courses of action	0.50
Explains actions to peers	0.44

Again, the factor is very similar to one previously found and is given the same name.

   VIII. Defers judgment and action.   There are four loadings to consider:

*Delays or postpones decision, or temporizes	0.84
*Indicates time priorities	0.81
Sets up checks on self	0.44
*Schedules work for a specific week	0.43

This factor is very similar to the *Defers* factor identified in Chapter 8.

IX. Evaluates work of others.   There are three scoring categories to consider:

*Shows awareness of poor work	0.65
*Requires further information	0.43
*Concern with proper channels	0.43

The extra factor in this analysis apparently resulted from splitting the previous Factor X, *Accepts administrative responsibility,* into two parts; this is one of the parts.

X. Accepts administrative responsibility.   There are four loadings greater than 0.40:

*Encourages or notes need for quickness or promptness	0.70
*Initiates a new structure	0.51
*Sets up checks on others	0.48
Concern with proper channels	0.40

This is the second part of the previous Factor X. It was judged to be sufficiently similar to that factor to retain the name, *Accepts administrative responsibility.*

XI. Informality.   The three loadings for this factor are as follows:

*Informality with peers	0.83
*Informality with superiors	0.78
*Informality with subordinates	0.46

Again, the similarity to the previous factor with the same name is very high.

The three-mode factor analysis is computationally much more complex than ordinary factor studies, and we do not have enough experience with such studies to know how "robust" the method is. With such a method and with the limited amount of data available, one must be particularly concerned about such matters as skewness of distribution, amount of missing data, and use of dichotomous scoring methods. At the item level, scoring of in-baskets for most performance categories is dichotomous. Many of the behaviors are sufficiently rare to produce skewed score distributions. And not all subjects completed their in-baskets; items near the end of the test were particularly likely to be omitted. Before continuing with the three-mode factor analysis, it was judged necessary to make certain modifications in the data in order to reduce skewness and produce continuous variables.

The problem of missing data was dealt with by an "eyeball" technique which resulted in discarding subjects who attempted relatively few items and discarding items that relatively few subjects attempted. This process tended to reduce the skewness of the score distributions. A few more subjects were discarded at random in order to yield equal N's for the four treatment combinations. After discarding subjects and items, 188 subjects (instead of 260) and 37 items (instead of 57) were left. The number of subjects was equal for the four cells of Fig. 3-1.

In order to further reduce skewness and to eliminate dichotomous scores, a new set of 15 performance variables was defined for use in the three-mode factor analysis. These new variables were based on the results of the factor analysis described above and were intended to produce the same 11 factors. Four of the 15 variables are the non-dichotomous items having to do with number of subordinates, number of superiors, number of peers, and number of outsiders involved in the response to an item; these variables are the same as those used in the conventional factor analysis. Eleven new variables were defined, one to represent each of the 11 factors. Each new variable was the sum of several dichotomously-scored variables selected to represent one of the 11 factors; they are marked by asterisks in the listings above. For example, the new variable constructed to represent Factor I was the sum of the scores for "Takes terminal action," "Concluding decision," "Follows lead by subordinates," and "Follows lead by superiors." Table 11-1 shows the 15 new variables.

The 15 new variables were analyzed using the principal components method on the pooled category variance-covariance matrix alluded to in the preceding section. An inspection of the roots suggested that the expected number of factors, 11, appeared, but it turned out that the factors from the new analysis are slightly different. Table 11-1 shows the factor matrix for the performance-category mode that resulted. Seven factors are defined by single variables, as was expected, and these loadings are all at least 0.97. Four factors are each defined by two variables, as had been planned. However, the factor called Factor VII in the first analysis, which was supposed to be defined by two variables, split apart to yield the new Factors V and IX. These two new performance factors we can name *Involves outsiders* (Factor V) and *Thoughtful analysis of problems* (Factor IX). And the two factors previously identified as I (*Acts in compliance with suggestions*) and II (*Preparatory action*) merged to form one bipolar factor (Factor XI in the new analysis), which we call *Prepares for action vs. Takes action in compliance with suggestions*.

Table 11-1 Factor Loadings of Grouped Performance Categories ($N = 188$)

	Factor										
	I	II	III	IV	V	VI	VII	VIII	IX	X	XI
1. Acts in compliance with suggestions	-0.09	-0.04	0.14	-0.18	0.09	-0.04	0.05	0.07	0.03	0.06	-0.68
2. Preparatory action	-0.09	-0.03	0.13	-0.17	0.08	-0.04	0.04	0.06	0.02	0.06	0.73
3. Number of subordinates involved	0.03	-0.06	0.69	-0.02	0.09	-0.06	0.02	0.02	0.05	-0.00	0.07
4. Controls subordinates	-0.02	0.07	0.69	0.04	-0.10	0.07	-0.03	-0.03	-0.05	-0.02	-0.08
5. Number of superiors involved	-0.02	0.02	0.00	0.02	0.00	-0.01	-0.01	0.00	0.03	0.70	-0.03
6. Interacts with superiors	0.03	-0.02	-0.02	-0.01	-0.01	0.01	0.00	-0.01	-0.03	0.70	0.03
7. Number of peers involved	-0.05	-0.04	0.06	-0.01	0.06	0.01	0.01	0.72	-0.03	0.08	0.01
8. Interacts with peers	0.06	0.04	-0.07	0.02	-0.07	-0.00	-0.02	0.69	0.02	-0.09	-0.01
9. Orderly work	0.00	0.00	-0.01	0.01	-0.01	0.00	1.00	-0.01	-0.00	-0.01	-0.00
10. Number of outsiders involved	0.01	0.01	-0.02	0.02	0.98	0.01	-0.01	-0.01	-0.00	-0.02	-0.01
11. Thoughtful analysis of problems	0.00	0.00	-0.00	0.00	-0.01	0.00	-0.00	-0.00	1.00	0.00	-0.00
12. Defers judgment and action	-0.02	-0.01	0.04	0.97	0.02	-0.01	0.01	0.02	0.01	0.02	0.01
13. Evaluates work of others	-0.00	0.99	0.01	-0.01	0.01	-0.01	0.00	0.01	0.00	0.01	0.01
14. Accepts administrative responsibility	-0.00	-0.01	0.01	-0.01	0.01	0.99	0.00	0.01	0.00	0.00	0.01
15. Informality	0.99	-0.00	0.02	-0.01	0.01	-0.00	0.00	0.01	0.00	0.01	-0.00

To summarize, the 11 performance factors to be employed in the three-mode factor analysis are as follows:

Performance Factor I.	Informality
Performance Factor II.	Evaluates work of others
Performance Factor III.	Controls subordinates
Performance Factor IV.	Defers judgment and action
Performance Factor V.	Involves outsiders
Performance Factor VI.	Accepts administrative responsibility
Performance Factor VII.	Orderly work
Performance Factor VIII.	Interacts with peers
Performance Factor IX.	Thoughtful analysis of problems
Performance Factor X.	Interacts with superiors
Performance Factor XI.	Prepares for action vs. takes action in compliance with suggestions

All references to performance factors in the discussion of the three-mode factor analysis will have to do with the 11 factors named above.

FACTOR ANALYSIS OF THE ITEMS

The factor analysis of the in-basket items is based on each person's cross-products matrix across categories. These matrices are pooled across persons to yield a variance-covariance matrix for items. A high covariance between two in-basket items means that the two items tended to elicit similar behaviors. A factor analysis of that matrix thus should produce clusters of items that are similar with respect to the behaviors they elicit.

Inspection of the roots of the factor analysis of the items suggested that there are six factors. Accordingly six factors were retained and rotated orthogonally, using the equamax criterion. The factor matrix is shown in Table 11-2.

The proportion of total variance accounted for by the six item factors is quite small. If one attempts to use loadings of 0.35 or higher in interpreting the factors, he finds that only 19 of the 37 items are involved; the highest loading is 0.56. Such results are perhaps to be expected in view of the fact that the content of the in-baskets was not planned with this kind of analysis in mind. In any future work of this sort, it would seem desirable to employ a more systematic method, such as a facet analysis (Guttman, 1965; Guttman & Schlesinger, 1965), to provide a hypothesis for guiding the selection of stimulus materials used to simulate the executive's paper work.

Table 11-2 Factor Loadings of 37 In-Basket Items
(Equamax Rotation)

Item	Factor					
	I	II	III	IV	V	VI
B3	−0.05	0.17	0.16	0.06	−0.03	0.01
B7	−0.21	0.06	0.22	0.11	0.10	−0.05
B9	0.04	−0.09	*0.42*	0.06	−0.02	−0.02
B11	−0.04´	0.15	0.24	−0.03	−0.06	0.08
B15	0.01	0.30	0.17	−0.07	−0.09	0.04
B19	−0.19	0.23	0.14	−0.00	0.06	0.05
B2	0.08	0.19	0.18	−0.05	−0.08	0.02
B6	−0.28	0.04	0.10	0.00	0.08	0.31
B8	−0.01	−0.07	*0.41*	0.00	−0.02	0.09
B10	−0.07	0.11	*0.39*	0.01	−0.00	−0.10
B12	−0.07	0.09	0.14	−0.07	0.02	*0.37*
B18	0.12	−0.00	*0.37*	−0.07	0.01	0.00
B20	−0.05	0.09	0.07	0.13	0.09	−0.08
C1	0.11	−0.02	0.04	−0.01	−0.00	0.12
C3	*0.42*	0.06	−0.07	−0.07	−0.10	0.26
C7	*0.37*	0.13	0.01	0.01	−0.05	0.02
C9	−0.05	−0.06	−0.07	0.28	0.10	0.16
C11	0.30	−0.06	0.18	−0.09	0.23	−0.15
C15	0.01	−0.08	0.01	0.04	0.03	*0.44*
C17	−0.05	0.13	−0.06	*0.36*	−0.01	0.13
C19	0.11	0.09	−0.06	0.04	0.27	−0.01
C21	−0.06	−0.06	0.00	−0.05	*0.56*	0.06
C23	0.06	−0.08	0.02	*0.47*	−0.01	−0.09
C25	−0.02	−0.13	0.02	−0.07	*0.55*	0.06
C29	0.27	0.07	−0.04	0.05	0.08	0.11
C2	0.07	−0.04	−0.03	−0.00	−0.03	*0.38*
C6	0.21	−0.21	0.17	0.05	0.16	0.03
C8	0.04	0.12	0.03	0.11	−0.03	−0.05
C10	*0.38*	−0.08	0.08	0.08	0.10	−0.08
C12	0.03	−0.04	0.02	*0.43*	−0.06	0.00
C16	0.05	0.33	−0.04	0.21	0.04	−0.09
C18	0.11	−0.07	0.06	*0.40*	−0.01	−0.02
C20	−0.05	*0.47*	−0.14	−0.05	0.20	0.03
C22	0.06	0.02	−0.07	0.07	−0.03	*0.44*
C26	0.25	*0.42*	−0.05	−0.08	0.01	−0.04
C28	−0.11	0.09	−0.03	0.23	0.03	0.03
C30	−0.01	0.21	−0.07	0.09	0.30	−0.09

**Item Factor I.   Items Requiring Evaluation of Procedures for
Accomplishing Organizational Goals**

The first item factor comprises a cluster of three items with loadings
greater than 0.35. Item C3 (the third item in in-basket C, which was given
on the second day) is a memorandum to Art Dodd (the role taken by each
subject) from Mark Hopkins, a Senior Business Development Agent in
the San Francisco office. The memo states that Hopkins had heard an
address by an influential California businessman blasting the California
business climate, taxes, and labor costs. Hopkins feels that something
must be done to combat the unfavorable effects of the speech, by such
means as sending the speaker a letter to "set the record straight" and
having members of CDC's advisory committees talk individually with
businessmen in the bay area. A draft of the proposed letter to the speaker
is attached.

Item C10 is a memorandum to Art Dodd from Chet Brinkley, the CDC
representative in Washington, D.C., strongly urging the development of
a promotional brochure stressing the financial advantages of locating a
business in California, in order to compete with similar items being
circulated by representatives of other states. The memo also contains
a complaint that some of the people from the Governor's office who visit
Washington expect the Washington representative to provide services for
them that he considers menial. (The double-barrelled nature of the item
is unfortunate from the point of view of the present analysis; but of course
the items were not written with the present analysis in mind.)

Item C7 is a memorandum to Art Dodd from Harvey Rush, Special
Representative of the Director of CDC. The note requests Dodd to
provide a pro and con evaluation of the way CDC is organized, the
statement to be incorporated in a reply to an inquiry from another state
that is considering a reorganization of its industrial development and
Department of Commerce activities.

The common aspect of the three items seems to be that all require
evaluation of methods used or proposed for carrying out the mission of
CDC. Inspection of the two items with the next highest positive loadings
are consistent with this interpretation. Item C11 (loading $= 0.30$) is a
recommendation from a subordinate that a Departmental Operations
Notice be issued in order to implement his previously presented plan
for a campaign to attract new companies to California. Item C29 (loading
$= 0.27$) is another memorandum from a subordinate, this one urging that a
campaign be initiated to obtain freight rates for export grain that are

more competitive with rates in effect in other west coast states that store wheat and export it to Japan. The factor, therefore, is named *Items requiring evaluation of procedures for accomplishing organizational goals.*

Item Factor II.   Items Permitting Routine Solutions

There are only two loadings greater than 0.35. One is for Item C20, which is a letter from the Chief Clerk of the Board of Supervisors of a California county requesting information as to the kind and extent of help that could be provided by the CDC Field Services Division to the county in establishing an economic development organization. The other item (C26) is a note to Dodd from Capitola, with an enclosed memo addressed to Capitola from one of his subordinates. The memo indicates that a Chinese food processing company intends to hire only people of Chinese ancestry and asks if CDC would be considered an accessory if CDC helps the company and there is a fair employment practices suit. Capitola merely asks if a check should be made with the Fair Employment Practices Commission.

The common thread in these two items is that they can be treated routinely or nonroutinely. For example, the letter from the county Board of Supervisors represents the kind of request that forms the bulk of the field office mail. Answering such letters is the bread-and-butter field office job. If the subject realizes this fact, he would most probably buck the letter to the appropriate Field Office Chief. On the other hand, if the subject has not attained the necessary awareness of organizational functioning or if he is concerned that Jay Capitola's response may be neither timely nor considered (Jay, the appropriate Field Office Chief, is depicted as a problem child), the subject would probably keep the letter out of normal channels. The same bipolar treatment possibility is characteristic of the fair employment practices item. At the time of the Institute, the State of California had just issued a policy statement on this matter, but not all subjects had been exposed to this statement. Those who had seen the statement could treat the item routinely; for all others it posed a special problem. The two items with loadings in the low thirties also fit this routine vs. nonroutine interpretation. One is a memo asking how to handle a request from a bonding company for information about a former employee known to have misappropriated departmental funds. The other involves a request from a university for help in a research project. In each instance a basis for handling the item routinely has been provided; also built in are specifics from which the need for special handling can readily be inferred. In three of the four items with the highest loadings, the availability of two approaches (with the choice as to which one should be used being left to the inclinations of the subjects) was intentional. The availability of a routine solution to the fair employment problem was accidental, one of the fortunes of basing a simulation on a real, always changing institution. Item Factor II is called *Items permitting routine solutions*.

Item Factor III.   Items Requiring Solution of Interorganizational Problems

There are four items with loadings of 0.35 or greater. All are from the in-basket which was taken on the first day, and all are addressed to the man Dodd replaced as Chief of the Field Services Division.

Item B9 is a memorandum from the Manager of the Coast Region, Herb Bay, complaining that he and his subordinates are being frustrated by a subordinate in another division in their attempts to develop an educational program for new export trade enterprises. Bay asks his Division Chief to try to blast the man out of his position.

Item B8 is also from Herb Bay; he reports on difficulties arising from apparent overlapping of duties between one of his sections and a section in still another division, and asks for clarification.

Item B10 is from Ora Sellers, another Division Chief, to the Chief of Field Services. It is a memorandum asking the Field Services Division to assign people to spend a substantial amount of time helping Sellers' staff to develop a series of reports.

The fourth item, B18, is a memo from Jay Capitola proposing a standard procedure for handling requests for services, the proposed procedure to be followed no matter which division receives the request. It is apparent that all these items represent problems that cut across division lines, hence the title *Items requiring solution of interorganizational problems* was chosen.

Item Factor IV.   Items Requiring Solution of Personnel Problems

There are four items to consider.

Item C23 is a memo to Dodd from Ralph Chavez, the Manager of the Southern Region. Chavez points out that he is losing the third Business Development Agent he has trained and recommends changes in job classification and pay range in order to make possible a more rapid promotion of Business Development Agents.

Item C12 is a memo from Mr. Apex, the Director of CDC, to Dodd stating that he had heard rumors of losing more personnel in the LA region and raising questions about political pressures and about Chavez' management of the operation.

Item C18 is a personal letter to Dodd from a Business Development Agent in the bay area about his dissatisfaction because of salary and his desire to be transferred to a different division in CDC.

Item C17 is a confidential communication from Chavez about plans for replacing a Trade Specialist who is about to retire. Chavez requests approval of an appointment that he defends as sound but which will cause political repercussions.

All the items are concerned with personnel policies and appointments, and the problems are obviously interrelated in various ways in addition to being similar with respect to content. Item C9, with a loading of 0.28, also presents a personnel problem that has political implications. It seems appropriate to label this factor *Items requiring solution of personnel problems*.

Item Factor V.   Items Recommending a Change in Policy

At a divisional staff meeting, Art Dodd had previously asked for proposals regarding needed modifications of programs. The two items with high loadings on Factor V are responses to that request from two Business Development Agents, one from the bay area and one from the valley area. Both suggestions had to do with development work in nonmetropolitan areas. One recommendation (C21) was to put much more emphasis on the nonmetropolitan communities because metropolitan areas do not need state aid. The other (C25) was to reduce the effort in nonmetropolitan areas by using simplified procedures so that effort could be increased in areas where gains in employment are potentially greater. The factor thus seems to present a question of policy with respect to relative amount of support to be given metropolitan and nonmetropolitan communities. Item C30 (loading = 0.30) supports this interpretation. It is a letter to Dodd from a small town Chamber of Commerce study committee which makes a strong case for more support for the small community. The name *Items recommending a change in policy* was therefore chosen. The items pose a fundamental question of policy, with apparently strong arguments on both sides of the issue.

Item Factor VI.   Items Presenting Conflicting Demands for Staff Time

There are four items with loadings greater than 0.35.

Item C22 includes copies of documents showing that Mr. Apex's office has asked Sellers, Chief of another division, to assign someone to appear and give testimony at a committee hearing of the state Assembly. Sellers in turn asks Dodd to have Herb Bay represent the department at the hearing.

Item C15 is somewhat similar; documents show that Sellers has been requested (this time by one of Dodd's subordinates) to provide a conference leader, and Sellers sends the request to Dodd with a note that Herb Bay is the best man for the assignment. (The dates of the two meetings for which Sellers recommends Bay are conflicting.)

Item C2 reveals that Dodd's secretary has been asked to fill in for Mr. Apex's secretary for a period from three weeks to six months; this could be a serious matter, since (as various items make clear) Dodd's secretary must be relied upon not only to serve as secretary but also to fill the role of a fairly responsible administrative assistant.

Item B12 is an official notice that Dodd is expected to attend a series of semi-monthly staff meetings for top administrative personnel in the Director's conference room. (Another item, not scored, indicates that on several of these meeting dates Dodd has been committed by Veep to attend all-day sessions of a specialized management training course.)

All these items thus represent conflicting demands for the time of Dodd or members of his staff. Item B6, with a loading of 0.31, also fits this interpretation; it is a carbon copy of a letter from Sellers (written at the request of Apex) to a local Chamber of Commerce stating that Ralph Chavez (Dodd's subordinate) is available for discussions. No mention of consultation with Chavez is made. This fact coupled with a notation that a carbon copy of the letter is being sent to Chavez implies that Chavez may have some scheduling headaches. The factor is called *Items presenting conflicting demands for staff time*.

These six factors may be viewed tentatively as the categories in a taxonomy of paper-work problems of state service executives.

THE CORE MATRIX

The core matrix was obtained by a principal components analysis, as described earlier. An inspection of the roots suggested that there are six person factors. The core matrix for these factors was rotated to the equamax criterion of simple structure. Tables 11-3 to 11-8 constitute the three-dimensional core box. Each of the six tables is a 6×11 matrix whose entries ("loadings") show the relationships between performance factors and item factors for the members of one of the person factors. Table 11-3, for example, shows the relationship of performance factors to item factors for members of Person Factor I. The interpretations of the person factors which follow are based on information in the core matrix.

Person Factor I

The highest "loading" in Table 11-3 is 1.16, which is found in the cell corresponding to Performance Factor VII (*Orderly work*) and Item Factor IV (*Items requiring solution of personnel problems*). The typical person in Person Factor I, then, is likely to follow rules and employ routine procedures in handling the documents that present problems involving personnel policies and appointments. But the loadings for *Orderly work* are relatively high in all the columns except for Item Factor II (*Items permitting routine solutions*). With the same exception, the loadings tend to be relatively high for Performance Factor III (*Interacting with subordinates*), although this tendency is less consistent. The in-basket scores which load on *Orderly work* and *Interacting with subordinates* include the following: asks for information from subordinates, uses preestablished structure, schedules work for a specific day, gives directions to subordinates, sets up checks on himself. The pattern is similar to the classical depiction of a first or second level supervisor—the person concerned with accomplishment of short-range or day-to-day operational objectives through supervision of subordinate staff. Person Factor I represents the *Systematic supervisor*.

Person Factor II

The largest loading in Table 11-4, 1.41, indicates an association of Performance Factor I (*Informality*) with Item Factor III (*Items requiring solution of interorganizational problems*). But the tendency toward informality is fairly general for persons in Factor II; the highest loading in each column is the one for *Informality*. The second highest loading in four of the six columns is for Performance Factor III (*Interacting with subordinates*). This *Informality, Interacting with subordinates* configuration seems to match what has been dubbed the "country club" manager. The contributory in-basket scores, however, are clearly restricted to informality and interacting with subordinates. Person Factor II, therefore, is called the *Informal communicator*.

P.O.B.—H

Table 11-3 Core Matrix: Person Factor I*

				Item Factor		
Performance Factor	I Items requiring evaluation of procedures	II Items permitting routine solutions	III Items involving interorganiza-tional problems	IV Items involving personnel problems	V Items recommending change in policy	VI Items presenting conflicting demands for staff time
I. Informality	0.24	−0.14	−0.35	0.23	0.45	−0.02
II. Evaluates work of others	0.02	−0.06	−0.02	−0.06	−0.04	0.00
III. Controls subordinates	0.34	0.14	*0.83*	*0.78*	0.53	0.42
IV. Defers judgment and action	0.09	−0.02	−0.19	−0.03	−0.15	0.02
V. Involves outsiders	−0.15	−0.01	0.07	0.04	0.15	0.10
VI. Accepts administrative responsibility	−0.10	0.09	−0.11	0.07	0.02	0.30
VII. Orderly work	0.62	0.10	*0.94*	*1.16*	*0.94*	0.68
VIII. Interacts with peers	−0.10	0.36	−0.05	0.09	0.20	0.17
IX. Thoughtful analysis of problems	−0.09	0.05	0.13	0.17	−0.11	0.01
X. Interacts with superiors	0.19	0.03	0.16	0.05	0.10	−0.25
XI. Prepares for action vs. takes action in compliance with suggestions	0.17	−0.06	0.58	0.64	0.65	0.29

*Entries of 0.75 or greater are in italic type.

Table 11-4 Core Matrix: Person Factor II*

Performance Factor	Item Factor					
	I Items requiring evaluation of procedures	II Items permitting routine solutions	III Items involving interorganizational problems	IV Items involving personnel problems	V Items recommending change in policy	VI Items presenting conflicting demands for staff time
I. Informality	*0.63*	*1.00*	*1.41*	*1.03*	*0.85*	*0.76*
II. Evaluates work of others	-0.09	-0.13	0.02	0.15	-0.02	-0.08
III. Controls subordinates	0.12	0.49	0.68	0.59	0.42	0.24
IV. Defers judgment and action	-0.05	-0.04	0.19	0.17	0.13	-0.14
V. Involves outsiders	0.06	-0.03	-0.05	0.03	0.10	0.00
VI. Accepts administrative responsibility	-0.09	0.18	0.24	-0.13	0.28	0.09
VII. Orderly work	-0.08	0.03	0.36	-0.02	-0.03	-0.01
VIII. Interacts with peers	0.16	0.13	-0.28	-0.07	0.23	0.16
IX. Thoughtful analysis of problems	0.18	0.05	0.04	0.04	-0.03	-0.03
X. Interacts with superiors	-0.12	0.05	0.13	0.38	-0.07	-0.07
XI. Prepares for action vs. takes action in compliance with suggestions	-0.17	0.04	0.00	0.07	-0.08	-0.23

*Entries of 0.75 or greater are in italic type.

Person Factor III

A member of Person Factor III is especially likely to interact with his superiors on questions concerning changes in policy, as shown by the loading of 1.71 for Performance Factor X and Item Factor V (Table 11-5). The tendency to interact with superiors is fairly general except for problems permitting routine solutions, where the loading is slightly negative (−0.28). On matters requiring evaluation of procedures for accomplishment of organizational goals (Item Factor I) the subject avoids going to his subordinates (the loading is −0.46), and he is inclined not to procrastinate on the policy question (the loading is −0.58 for Performance Factor IV and Item Factor V). Most generally, Person Factor II represents persons who tend to interact with superiors on problems other than those with a routine solution. Person Factor III is called the *Superior-centered manager.*

Person Factor IV

The loading of 1.71 for Performance Factor V and Item Factor V is the largest one in Table 11-6; it shows a tendency for subjects to interact with people outside the organization on policy questions. Other comparatively large loadings show a tendency (0.76) to interact with outsiders (Performance Factor V) on problems requiring evaluation of procedures for accomplishing organizational goals (Item Factor I); a slight tendency (0.44) to involve *subordinates* (Performance Factor III) on interorganizational problems (Item Factor III); a tendency (0.53) to interact with *peers* (Performance Factor VIII) in solving personnel problems (Item Factor IV); and a tendency (0.48) to interact with superiors (Performance Factor X) in dealing with conflicting demands for staff time (Item Factor VI). There are also several high loadings on Performance Factor IX (*Thoughtful analysis of problems*). Again, no high loadings are found in the Item Factor II column, representing problems permitting routine and nonroutine solutions. Person Factor IV represents a tendency for a subject to appropriately involve others in the thoughtful analysis of administrative problems. The overall picture is one of a person concerned with probing deeply into problems, with relating the solution of these problems to optimum achievement of organizational goals, and with involving in the decision-making process those who wiil be most affected by a given decision. To the same degree that Person Factor I (*Systematic supervisor*) is similar to the classical description of a supervisor, Person Factor IV is similar to the classical description of an administrator. The

Table 11-5 Core Matrix: Person Factor III*

Performance Factor	Item Factor					
	I Items requiring evaluation of procedures	II Items permitting routine solutions	III Items involving interorganizational problems	IV Items involving personnel problems	V Items recommending change in policy	VI Items presenting conflicting demands for staff time
I. Informality	−0.08	0.06	0.18	−0.05	−0.15	0.03
II. Evaluates work of others	−0.11	0.08	−0.10	−0.06	0.07	0.08
III. Controls subordinates	−0.46	−0.13	0.09	−0.08	−0.05	−0.05
IV. Defers judgment and action	−0.29	−0.05	−0.29	−0.32	−0.58	−0.21
V. Involves outsiders	−0.13	0.05	0.01	−0.04	−0.16	0.06
VI. Accepts administrative responsibility	−0.06	−0.07	0.01	0.36	0.09	0.04
VII. Orderly work	−0.00	−0.09	0.22	−0.17	0.09	0.15
VIII. Interacts with peers	−0.04	0.06	0.03	−0.16	0.33	−0.14
IX. Thoughtful analysis of problems	0.06	0.28	0.09	0.22	0.50	−0.03
X. Interacts with superiors	*0.75*	−0.28	*0.83*	*0.81*	*1.71*	*1.02*
XI. Prepares for action vs. takes action in compliance with suggestions	−0.26	0.13	−0.01	−0.25	−0.25	−0.02

*Entries of 0.75 or greater are in italic type.

219

Table 11-6 Core Matrix: Person Factor IV*

Performance Factor	Item Factor					
	I Items requiring evaluation of procedures	II Items permitting routine solutions	III Items involving interorganizational problems	IV Items involving personnel problems	V Items recommending change in policy	VI Items presenting conflicting demands for staff time
I. Informality	0.05	−0.12	0.07	0.11	−0.08	0.04
II. Evaluates work of others	−0.15	−0.05	0.14	−0.11	−0.06	−0.02
III. Controls subordinates	0.19	0.16	0.44	0.35	0.53	0.01
IV. Defers judgment and action	−0.05	0.07	−0.18	−0.10	−0.01	−0.11
V. Involves outsiders	*0.76*	−0.16	0.28	−0.03	*1.71*	−0.07
VI. Accepts administrative responsibility	−0.01	0.11	0.04	0.03	0.09	−0.01
VII. Orderly work	−0.18	0.17	0.21	−0.11	−0.05	0.09
VIII. Interacts with peers	0.47	0.01	0.22	0.53	−0.14	0.15
IX. Thoughtful analysis of problems	0.53	0.19	0.59	0.48	*0.99*	0.26
X. Interacts with superiors	0.13	0.08	0.01	−0.05	0.13	0.48
XI. Prepares for action vs. takes action in compliance with suggestions	−0.04	0.07	0.34	0.03	0.44	−0.22

*Entries of 0.75 or greater are in italic type.

supervisor is concerned with tactics for cutting through and classifying the daily flux; the administrator is concerned with strategies for shaping and molding overall programs. Person Factor IV is called the *Program-centered manager*.

Person Factor V

The highest value in Table 11-7 is 1.39; it represents an association between *Interacting with subordinates* (Performance Factor III) and the problem of recommending policy changes (Item Factor V). The tendency to involve subordinates extends to some extent to all kinds of problems except personnel problems and problems involving conflicting demands for staff time. On the policy question there is also a tendency not to procrastinate or involve outsiders, and to evaluate staff work. Person Factor V is called the *Subordinate-centered manager*.

Person Factor VI

The highest loading for this person factor is 1.19, which shows an association between Performance Factor XI (*Preparatory action vs. acting in compliance with suggestions*) and Item Factor IV (*Personnel problems*) (Table 11-8). In Column IV we also find a loading of 1.00, showing a tendency to procrastinate. The pattern of deferment of decision and avoidance of final action extends in varying degrees to all problem situations. Person Factor VI, thus, seems to represent the kind of individual who does whatever preliminary work he feels is necessary to avoid the appearance of doing nothing and then sits back and waits for the problem to go away or be solved by others. Person Factor VI is called the *Commitment-avoiding manager*.

The person factors reflect personal operational or performance styles which tend to be consistent across several types of in-basket item situations. Several questions remain to be answered, among which are the following: What are the differential effects of organizational climates on the intercorrelations of person factor scores? Are there styles which are specific to a particular climate or subset of climates? What are the ability, personality, and biographical characteristics of individuals who adopt a given style in a given organizational climate? Are these characteristics similar to or different from the characteristics of those adopting the same style in another climate? These are some of the questions treated in the next two sections.

Table 11-7 Core Matrix: Person Factor V*

Performance Factor	Item Factor					
	I Items requiring evaluation of procedures	II Items permitting routine solutions	III Items involving interorganizational problems	IV Items involving personnel problems	V Items recommending change in policy	VI Items presenting conflicting demands for staff time
I. Informality	−0.01	0.10	0.12	−0.31	0.08	−0.09
II. Evaluates work of others	0.23	−0.04	0.01	0.23	0.50	0.28
III. Controls subordinates	0.54	0.72	*0.99*	0.21	*1.39*	0.25
IV. Defers judgment and action	−0.23	0.00	*−0.78*	−0.04	−0.69	−0.15
V. Involves outsiders	−0.09	0.39	−0.03	0.23	−0.49	0.07
VI. Accepts administrative responsibility	0.02	0.17	0.48	−0.07	0.19	0.03
VII. Orderly work	0.13	0.02	−0.34	−0.19	0.04	−0.04
VIII. Interacts with peers	0.09	−0.64	0.40	−0.05	−0.09	0.00
IX. Thoughtful analysis of problems	0.10	0.04	0.20	0.09	−0.13	−0.03
X. Interacts with superiors	0.22	0.04	0.10	0.14	−0.02	−0.21
XI. Prepares for action vs. takes action in compliance with suggestions	−0.05	−0.31	−0.11	0.05	0.14	0.10

*Entries of 0.75 or greater are in italic type.

222

Table 11-8 Core Matrix: Person Factor VI*

Performance Factor	Item Factor					
	I Items requiring evaluation of procedures	II Items permitting routine solutions	III Items involving interorganizational problems	IV Items involving personnel problems	V Items recommending change in policy	VI Items presenting conflicting demands for staff time
I. Informality	−0.00	0.26	0.16	−0.17	−0.28	−0.01
II. Evaluates work of others	0.00	0.33	0.23	0.02	0.06	0.07
III. Controls subordinates	−0.01	0.27	0.03	−0.50	−0.43	−0.43
IV. Defers judgment and action	0.30	0.54	0.54	*1.00*	0.34	0.46
V. Involves outsiders	−0.02	−0.14	0.02	−0.09	−0.13	−0.01
VI. Accepts administrative responsibility	−0.08	0.40	0.15	−0.20	−0.03	−0.01
VII. Orderly work	0.23	0.39	0.03	0.16	−0.13	0.10
VIII. Interacts with peers	−0.26	−0.07	−0.31	−0.40	−0.15	0.41
IX. Thoughtful analysis of problems	0.03	0.31	0.25	0.11	0.10	0.18
X. Interacts with superiors	−0.38	0.05	−0.00	−0.03	0.16	0.42
XI. Prepares for action vs. takes action in compliance with suggestions	*0.22*	*0.82*	*0.46*	*1.19*	*0.22*	*0.56*

*Entries of 0.75 or greater are in italic type.

INTERCORRELATIONS OF THE PERSON-FACTOR SCORES

In this section we shall examine the intercorrelations of factor scores based on the six person factors. These vectors for factor scores for the total group are orthogonal and are based on data adjusted to have sums of squares equal to one and means equal to zero. Therefore, over all the four treatment groups ($N = 188$), the standard deviations are 0.073, the means are zero, and the intercorrelations are zero.

Since the subjects' ratings of the experimental manipulations indicated the treatments to be primarily additive, it was reasonable to use the following procedures for analyzing the intercorrelations of the person factor scores: The intercorrelations for the innovation climate are compared with those for the rules climate, and the intercorrelations for the global supervision condition are compared with those for detailed supervision. It can then be seen which, if either, of the two climate manipulations had an effect on the intercorrelations. It can also be seen if the two experimental manipulations had an additive effect on performance, as they had on the ratings of the climates.

Table 11-9 shows the means, standard deviations, and intercorrelations of the six person factors for the innovation and rules climates, and Table 11-10 shows analogous information for the global supervision and detailed supervision climates. Table 11-11 is included to help clarify results in the other tables. It shows means, standard deviations, and intercorrelations of the person-factor scores for "consistent" conditions (global supervision in the innovation climate and detailed supervision in the rules climate) and for "inconsistent" climates (global supervision in the rules climate and detailed supervision in the innovation climate). All these tables are of interest because of the information they provide on the effects of the experimental treatments on the factor structure in the person-factor domain.

The most striking finding has to do with the correlation between Person Factor III and Person Factor VI. In the upper entry of the cell in all three tables the correlation is low, but significantly negative (about -0.27); and in the lower cell the correlation is high and positive (nearly 0.60). Reference to Fig. 3-1 will help to see what is happening. For every treatment combination that includes the subjects in the upper left-hand cell in Fig. 3-1 (innovation combined with global supervision treatments), the correlation between Person Factors III and VI is low and negative. For all treatment combinations not involving this cell, the correlation is high and positive. It appears that Person Factor III (the *Superior-*

Table 11-9 Intercorrelations of Person-Factor Scores for Subjects in the Innovation Climate and in the Rules Climate*

	Person Factor					
	I	II	III	IV	V	VI
I		−0.07 0.06	0.15 −0.24†	0.00 −0.00	−0.03 0.02	−0.02 0.02
II	−0.07 0.06		−0.01 0.02	−0.02 0.02	0.20† −0.18	0.07 −0.09
III	0.15 −0.24†	−0.01 0.02		−0.04 0.08	−0.08 0.13	−0.27‡ 0.59‡
IV	0.00 −0.00	−0.02 0.02	−0.04 0.08		−0.09 0.10	−0.07 0.11
V	−0.03 0.02	0.20† −0.18	−0.08 0.13	−0.09 0.10		−0.10 0.11
VI	−0.02 0.02	0.07 −0.09	−0.27‡ 0.59‡	−0.07 0.11	−0.10 0.11	
Mean	−0.001 0.001	0.001 −0.001	0.008 −0.008	0.001 −0.001	0.001 −0.001	−0.002 0.002
S.D.	0.069 0.077	0.074 0.071	0.090 0.050	0.079 0.066	0.068 0.078	0.079 0.066

*The upper entry in each cell is for the innovation climate and the lower entry is for the rules climate. $N = 94$ for each climate group.
†Significantly different from zero at the 5% level.
‡Significantly different from zero at the 1% level.

centered manager) is specific to the innovation-global supervision treatment combination, and that for subjects in all other cells Person Factor III tends to merge with Person Factor VI (*Commitment-avoiding manager*). The differences in the standard deviations of the factor scores bear out this interpretation. The standard deviation for Person Factor III scores is relatively high in the upper part of the cell and low in the lower entry of the cell. Note that large variance is associated with low correlations; the higher correlations appear in spite of decreased variability.

In other words, it appears that the person adopting a superior-oriented style in the innovation and global supervision climates does not tend toward commitment-avoiding behavior. Conversely, those adopting the

Table 11-10   Intercorrelations of Person-Factor Scores for Subjects in Global Supervision Climate and in the Detailed Supervision Climate*

	Person Factor					
	I	II	III	IV	V	VI
I		0.06 −0.06	0.09 −0.15	0.02 −0.01	0.09 −0.07	0.06 −0.05
II	0.06 −0.06		0.07 −0.11	−0.00 0.02	0.30‡ −0.22†	0.19 −0.19
III	0.09 −0.15	0.07 −0.11		−0.04 0.06	−0.11 0.17	−0.27‡ 0.60‡
IV	0.02 −0.01	−0.00 0.02	−0.04 0.06		−0.14 0.10	0.08 −0.12
V	0.09 −0.07	0.30‡ −0.22†	−0.11 0.17	−0.14 0.10		−0.06 0.06
VI	0.06 −0.05	0.19 −0.19	−0.27‡ 0.60‡	0.08 −0.12	−0.06 0.06	
Mean	0.005 −0.005	0.008 −0.008	−0.002 0.002	−0.007 0.007	−0.001 0.001	−0.008 0.008
S.D.	0.069 0.076	0.069 0.076	0.091 0.049	0.070 0.075	0.066 0.079	0.079 0.066

*The upper entry in each cell is for the global supervision climate and the lower entry is for the detailed supervision climate. $N = 94$ for each group.
†Significantly different from zero at the 5% level.
‡Significantly different from zero at the 1% level.

superior-centered style in the rules and detailed supervision climates *do* tend to defer decision and final action.

Although one or two other correlations are significantly different from zero, none are very high. The highest of these correlations is 0.30, between Person Factors II and V in the global supervision climate; the comparable correlation is 0.20 in the innovation climate. Those who appropriately involve subordinates (Person Factor V) tend to do so informally (Person Factor II) when supervision is global rather than detailed and when the administrative press is for innovation rather than for compliance with rules. Consistency of the climate conditions seems to make no difference in correlation between these two person factors.

Table 11-11 Intercorrelations of Person-Factor Scores for Subjects in Consistent Climates and in Inconsistent Climates*

	Person Factor					
	I	II	III	IV	V	VI
I		−0.08 0.05	−0.04 0.03	−0.02 −0.00	−0.07 0.06	−0.14 0.15
II	−0.08 0.05		−0.02 0.01	−0.17 0.17	−0.06 0.08	0.01 0.00
III	−0.04 0.03	−0.02 0.01		−0.09 0.12	0.07 −0.12	−0.28† 0.54†
IV	−0.02 −0.00	−0.17 0.17	−0.09 0.12		−0.05 0.04	−0.08 0.09
V	−0.07 0.06	−0.06 0.08	0.07 −0.12	−0.05 0.04		0.11 −0.15
VI	−0.14 0.15	0.01 0.00	−0.28† 0.54†	−0.08 0.09	0.11 −0.15	
Mean	0.010 −0.010	0.009 −0.009	0.005 −0.005	0.005 −0.005	0.002 −0.001	−0.003 0.003
S.D.	0.067 0.077	0.080 0.064	0.088 0.054	0.068 0.077	0.077 0.068	0.079 0.067

*The upper entry in each cell is for the compatible climates and the lower entry is for the incompatible climates. $N = 94$ for each group.

†Significantly different from zero at the 1% level.

CORRELATIONS OF PERSON-FACTOR SCORES WITH PREDICTORS

Up to this point, the interpretation of person factors has been dependent entirely on the information contained in the core matrix. A considerable amount of additional information is available about the subjects in the form of scores on the 23 predictor variables. By computing the correlations of these predictor scores with the person-factor scores, it is possible to see relationships that will, hopefully, aid in the interpretation of the person factors. Correlations were therefore computed between the six person-factor scores and predictor scores.

Tables 11-12 through 11-17 show the correlations between each person factor and the 23 variables external to the in-basket test. Each table shows correlations for one person factor. The first two columns show correlations for the innovation and rules conditions, respectively. The second pair of columns shows correlations for the global and detailed supervision conditions, and the third pair of columns shows the correlations for the "consistent" and "inconsistent" conditions. The final column shows the correlations for all groups combined.

Table 11-12 shows the correlations for Person Factor I (*Systematic supervisor*). A significant correlation of 0.19 for the total group shows some tendency for these systematic supervisors to be high in speed of closure, i.e., able to "unify an apparently disparate perceptual field into a single percept" (French, Ekstrom, & Price, 1963). Persons who adopt this style of supervision also tend slightly to adopt a risk-taking strategy which emphasizes maximizing gains rather than minimizing losses (a significant relationship for total group of −0.16 with Conservative Strategy on Test S). This set of relationships fits the stereotype for supervisory role-ability interaction: A supervisor is immersed in a continual flux of disparate, concurrent activity. To be successful the incumbent first must be able to organize this field of activity and then, if anything worthwhile is to be accomplished, he must be willing to make decisions and take actions involving the taking of calculated risks.

In the detailed supervision and incompatible climates, a systematic supervisory style is associated with a high score on the First and Last Names Test (*r*'s are 0.24 and 0.21, respectively). Under such climate conditions, a good memory is apparently helpful for successful utilization of a systematic approach to supervisory tasks. In consistent climates, independence (self-sufficiency, activity, reflectiveness, impulsiveness) tends to be associated with the systematic style (*r* = 0.26), while the reverse is true in the inconsistent climates (*r* = −0.21). A "tool vs. crutch" analogy may indicate the nature of this set of relationships.

Table 11-13 shows the correlations for Person Factor II (*Informal communicator*). The pattern of correlations indicates that such behavior is somewhat characteristic of people who describe themselves as socially extroverted. This correlation is especially high in the innovation climate (*r* = 0.30) and low in the rules climate (*r* = 0.07). In the detailed supervision climate combined with rules, subjects who are informal tend to be persons of high educational level who are employed in an institutional setting. The correlations in the last row, when reflected, indicate that subjects who say they work in a detailed supervision climate in their real jobs are relatively "informal" in their in-basket communications,

Table 11-12 Correlations of Factor Scores with Predictors and Climate Ratings
Person Factor I: Systematic Supervisor

Predictors	Treatment Group						Total Group (N = 188)
	Innovation (N = 94)	Rules (N = 94)	Global Supervision (N = 94)	Detailed Supervision (N = 94)	Compatible (N = 94)	Incompatible (N = 94)	
Acquiescence	0.14	0.08	0.06	0.17	0.05	0.16	0.11
Social Extroversion	0.09	0.14	0.07	0.16	0.13	0.10	0.12
Independence	0.06	-0.05	-0.08	0.07	0.26†	-0.21*	-0.00
Maladjustment	-0.07	0.13	0.07	0.00	-0.03	0.10	0.04
Rigid Authoritarian	-0.11	-0.10	-0.10	-0.09	0.02	-0.25*	-0.11
Theoretical Education	0.07	0.03	-0.02	0.11	-0.04	0.13	0.05
Years of Military Service	0.18	-0.02	0.10	0.08	-0.10	0.20*	0.07
Number of Children	0.08	0.09	0.10	0.06	0.07	0.07	0.08
Educated Institutional Man	0.04	0.05	0.10	0.00	-0.07	0.14	0.04
Power and Seniority	0.15	-0.23*	0.03	-0.13	0.02	-0.11	-0.05
Dead-end Seniority	-0.04	-0.08	-0.18	0.04	-0.09	0.00	-0.06
Staff Officer	0.16	-0.01	0.06	0.09	0.16	-0.01	0.08
Hidden Patterns	-0.02	-0.07	0.04	-0.15	-0.02	-0.06	-0.05
First and Last Names	0.03	0.14	-0.06	0.24*	-0.00	0.21*	0.09
Vocabulary	0.03	-0.14	-0.06	-0.06	0.03	-0.11	-0.06
Multiple Analogies Test	0.03	0.23*	0.10	-0.05	-0.06	0.11	0.03
Test S, Successful Strategy	-0.12	0.05	-0.01	-0.05	0.05	-0.10	-0.03
Test S, Conservative Strategy	-0.14	-0.19	-0.12	-0.20*	-0.29†	-0.07	-0.16*
Speed of Closure	0.11	0.27†	0.26†	0.15	0.16	0.20*	0.19†
Ideational Fluency	0.21*	-0.02	0.10	0.05	0.06	0.14	0.08
Inductive Reasoning	-0.04	-0.07	-0.01	-0.11	-0.03	-0.09	-0.06
Climate Rating: Rules	0.09	-0.11	-0.09	0.06	0.10	-0.12	-0.01
Climate Rating: Global Supervision	-0.01	-0.05	-0.04	-0.01	-0.11	0.05	-0.03

*Significantly different from zero at the 5% level.   †Significantly different from zero at the 1% level.

Table 11-13 Correlations of Factor Scores with Predictors and Climate Ratings
Person Factor II: Informal Communicator

Predictors	Treatment Group						Total Group (N = 188)
	Innovation (N = 94)	Rules (N = 94)	Global Supervision (N = 94)	Detailed Supervision (N = 94)	Compatible (N = 94)	Incompatible (N = 94)	
Acquiescence	0.19	−0.15	−0.06	0.10	0.03	−0.01	0.01
Social Extroversion	0.30†	0.07	0.20*	0.17	0.10	0.29†	0.18*
Independence	0.09	−0.02	−0.07	0.13	0.03	0.04	0.04
Maladjustment	−0.02	0.09	0.02	0.06	0.16	−0.16	0.04
Rigid Authoritarian	−0.13	−0.04	−0.20*	0.06	−0.03	−0.17	−0.08
Theoretical Education	−0.03	0.04	−0.11	0.11	0.00	0.02	0.01
Years of Military Service	0.05	−0.03	−0.04	0.05	0.03	−0.02	0.01
Number of Children	0.01	0.12	0.06	0.07	0.01	0.13	0.07
Educated Institutional Man	0.00	0.20*	0.07	0.13	0.23*	−0.07	0.10
Power and Seniority	0.10	−0.10	0.02	−0.01	−0.11	0.17	0.00
Dead-end Seniority	−0.05	0.09	−0.10	0.13	0.14	−0.12	0.02
Staff Officer	0.09	−0.15	−0.06	0.01	0.05	−0.14	−0.02
Hidden Patterns	0.06	0.08	0.11	0.01	0.07	0.09	0.07
First and Last Names	−0.01	0.05	0.00	0.05	0.00	0.09	0.02
Vocabulary	−0.05	−0.12	−0.20*	0.02	−0.02	−0.13	−0.08
Multiple Analogies Test	0.11	−0.11	0.12	−0.09	−0.04	0.07	0.01
Test S, Successful Strategy	−0.00	−0.02	0.01	−0.03	0.05	−0.10	−0.01
Test S, Conservative Strategy	0.04	0.14	0.01	0.17	0.05	0.12	0.09
Speed of Closure	0.02	0.09	0.14	−0.01	−0.01	0.08	0.05
Ideational Fluency	0.01	0.09	−0.03	0.10	0.10	0.03	0.05
Inductive Reasoning	0.07	0.03	0.12	−0.02	0.10	−0.02	0.05
Climate Rating: Rules	0.18	0.02	0.02	0.18	0.11	0.07	0.11
Climate Rating: Global Supervision	−0.31†	0.01	−0.08	−0.21*	−0.22*	−0.05	−0.15*

*Significantly different from zero at the 5% level.   †Significantly different from zero at the 1% level.

especially in the innovation condition $(r = -0.31)$. A contrast between real job and simulated job may account for this.

In other words, the picture is that of contrasting personality types adopting the same operational style under different conditions, and probably for different reasons. In the innovative, global, and incompatible climates the informal style of communication is adopted by the social extrovert (as a device for coping with the unfamiliar or the uncomfortable?). In the rules and compatible climates (in more familiar or comfortable surroundings) the style is adopted (as a means of gaining rapport?) by the educated institutional man, the stereotyped introvert.

Table 11-14 shows the correlations for Person Factor III (*Superior-centered manager*). The pattern of positive correlations shows this performance tendency to be characteristic of staff officers who score high on Hidden Patterns, Vocabulary, and Speed of Closure. The negative correlations indicate these people to be nonrigid and nonauthoritarian $(r = -0.19)$ and not to have dead-end jobs $(r = -0.23)$. The higher correlations are found primarily in the innovation, global, and compatible climates. This result further supports the conclusion in an earlier section that Person Factor III tends to be specific to the innovation-global climate cell. In the combination of these climates, Factor III has its greatest variance, its lowest correlations with other factors, and its highest correlations with the predictor variables. Again, there is the indication that under different organizational climates differing types of individuals will adopt a given operational style.

In the innovative and global supervision climates, the superior-centered style is associated with the successful $(r = -0.26$ and -0.39 for Dead-end Seniority) staff officer $(r = 0.26)$ who is nonrigid and nonauthoritarian $(r = -0.23$ for Rigid Authoritarian) and who has a high speed of closure $(r = 0.21)$. In the rules and detailed supervision climates, where this style merges with Avoiding Commitment (Person Factor VI), a different type of individual tends to be superior centered. In the rules climate, the style is characteristic of the young, junior manager $(r = -0.26$ for Dead-end Seniority and -0.16 for Power and Seniority) with a conservative, albeit successful, approach to risk taking $(r = 0.24$ for Conservative Strategy and 0.20 for Successful Strategy). In the detailed supervision climate, the dependent person $(r = -0.22$ for Independence) tends to be superior centered.

Table 11-15 shows the correlations for Person Factor IV (*Program-centered manager*). The only significant correlation coefficient for the total group is a negative one $(r = -0.15$ for Staff Officer). The pattern of

Table 11-14 Correlations of Factor Scores with Predictors and Climate Ratings Person Factor III: Superior-Centered Manager

Predictors	Treatment Group						Total Group (N = 188)
	Innovation (N = 94)	Rules (N = 94)	Global Supervision (N = 94)	Detailed Supervision (N = 94)	Compatible (N = 94)	Incompatible (N = 94)	
Acquiescence	−0.01	−0.12	−0.05	−0.09	−0.06	−0.07	−0.06
Social Extroversion	−0.03	0.01	0.01	−0.09	−0.02	−0.05	−0.03
Independence	0.02	−0.15	0.05	−0.22*	0.03	−0.18	−0.05
Maladjustment	0.01	−0.15	−0.08	0.05	0.00	−0.10	−0.03
Rigid Authoritarian	−0.23*	−0.11	−0.23*	−0.15	−0.27†	−0.04	−0.19†
Theoretical Education	0.00	0.05	−0.01	0.05	0.00	0.02	0.01
Years of Military Service	0.06	−0.13	−0.01	−0.01	0.00	−0.01	−0.01
Number of Children	0.12	−0.10	0.11	−0.06	0.05	0.03	0.05
Educated Institutional Man	0.06	0.03	0.02	0.11	0.11	−0.03	0.05
Power and Seniority	0.17	−0.16	0.06	−0.01	0.09	−0.04	0.04
Dead-end Seniority	−0.23*	−0.26†	−0.39†	0.00	−0.37†	0.04	−0.23†
Staff Officer	0.26†	0.09	0.26†	0.08	0.24*	0.11	0.19†
Hidden Patterns	0.18	0.17	0.21*	0.13	0.24*	0.12	0.18*
First and Last Names	0.21*	−0.03	0.17	−0.01	0.14	0.09	0.10
Vocabulary	0.20*	0.12	0.17	0.18	0.21*	0.13	0.16*
Multiple Analogies Test	0.11	0.15	0.12	0.16	0.11	0.16	0.13
Test S, Successful Strategy	0.02	0.20*	0.20*	−0.07	0.16	−0.01	0.10
Test S, Conservative Strategy	−0.04	0.24*	0.12	−0.04	0.06	0.05	0.06
Speed of Closure	0.21*	0.06	0.21*	0.08	0.16	0.13	0.15*
Ideational Fluency	0.04	−0.07	−0.04	0.08	0.05	−0.04	0.00
Inductive Reasoning	0.10	0.09	0.15	0.05	0.06	0.20*	0.11
Climate Rating: Rules	0.05	0.12	0.12	0.00	0.09	0.04	0.07
Climate Rating: Global Supervision	−0.07	−0.06	−0.11	−0.02	−0.07	−0.08	−0.08

*Significantly different from zero at the 5% level.   †Significantly different from zero at the 1% level.

Table 11-15 Correlations of Factor Scores with Predictors and Climate Ratings
Person Factor IV: Program-Centered Manager

Predictors	Treatment Group						Total Group ($N = 188$)
	Innovation ($N = 94$)	Rules ($N = 94$)	Global Supervision ($N = 94$)	Detailed Supervision ($N = 94$)	Compatible ($N = 94$)	Incompatible ($N = 94$)	
Acquiescence	0.10	0.04	−0.02	0.15	0.00	0.13	0.07
Social Extroversion	0.21*	−0.03	0.13	0.07	0.06	0.13	0.10
Independence	0.15	0.03	0.21*	−0.02	0.06	0.11	0.09
Maladjustment	−0.07	0.07	−0.05	0.04	0.12	−0.14	0.00
Rigid Authoritarian	0.05	0.08	−0.01	0.11	0.01	0.12	0.06
Theoretical Education	−0.01	−0.24*	−0.18	−0.05	−0.08	−0.15	−0.12
Years of Military Service	0.05	−0.07	−0.00	−0.03	−0.01	−0.01	−0.01
Number of Children	−0.13	−0.03	−0.04	−0.11	−0.04	−0.14	−0.08
Educated Institutional Man	0.15	−0.08	0.11	−0.02	0.14	−0.04	0.05
Power and Seniority	0.20*	0.07	0.08	0.19	0.08	0.20	0.14
Dead-end Seniority	0.02	0.10	−0.01	0.11	0.07	0.07	0.06
Staff Officer	−0.06	−0.26†	−0.23*	−0.07	−0.10	−0.20*	−0.15*
Hidden Patterns	0.19	0.05	0.09	0.17	0.12	0.13	0.12
First and Last Names	−0.13	−0.01	−0.05	−0.09	−0.02	−0.10	−0.07
Vocabulary	−0.06	0.05	0.03	−0.04	0.02	−0.02	−0.01
Multiple Analogies Test	−0.07	0.16	0.04	0.02	−0.07	0.12	0.03
Test S, Successful Strategy	−0.29†	0.06	−0.18	−0.08	−0.04	−0.22*	−0.13
Test S, Conservative Strategy	−0.05	0.04	−0.08	0.06	0.09	−0.12	−0.01
Speed of Closure	−0.24*	0.20*	−0.04	−0.06	−0.02	−0.09	−0.05
Ideational Fluency	0.15	0.08	0.14	0.12	0.21*	0.06	0.12
Inductive Reasoning	−0.31†	0.23*	−0.05	−0.12	−0.10	−0.07	−0.09
Climate Rating: Rules	0.00	0.06	−0.09	0.11	−0.12	0.13	0.02
Climate Rating: Global Supervision	0.05	0.12	0.08	0.07	0.07	0.10	0.08

*Significantly different from zero at the 5% level. †Significantly different from zero at the 1% level.

233

correlations implies that the negative relationship is strongest in the rules-global supervision treatment combination. In an innovative climate combined with detailed supervision, program-centered style appears to correlate with power and seniority. There are substantial differences between program-centered individuals in the innovation vs. rules comparison:

	Innovation	Rules	Difference
Inductive Reasoning	−0.31	0.23	0.54
Speed of Closure	−0.24	0.20	0.44
Test S, Successful Strategy	−0.29	0.06	0.35
Social Extroversion	0.21	−0.03	0.24
Theoretical Education	−0.01	−0.24	0.23
Staff Officer	−0.06	−0.26	0.20

Table 11-16 shows the correlations for Person Factor V (*Subordinate-centered manager*). Once again there is only one significant correlation coefficient in the total group column, 0.16 with Hidden Patterns. The relationship, it can be inferred, is strongest in the rules-detailed supervision climate combination.

In spite of the correlation between Person Factor V and Person Factor II (*Informal communicator*) in the innovation climate, none of the predictors of the latter are correlated with subordinate-centeredness. For example, social extroversion correlates with Person Factor II in the innovation climate, but not with Person Factor V.

Table 11-17 shows the correlations for Person Factor VI (*Commitment-avoiding manager*).

From the total group column, it is apparent that a commitment-avoiding style is associated with being dependent ($r = -0.18$ for Independence) and with readily seeing multiple relationships ($r = 0.18$ for Multiple Analogies). In an innovative climate the avoidance of commitment is associated with being an older man in a dead-end job ($r = 0.22$ for Dead-end Seniority). In the rules climate the opposite is true; it is the young junior manager ($r = -0.21$ for Power and Seniority and Dead-end Seniority) who avoids making commitments. This is partly consistent with the findings in Table 11-14 for Person Factor III, the superior-centered manager.

In the rules climate, both superior-centeredness and avoidance of commitments are characteristic of young individuals. In those climates in which Person Factors III and VI have a negative relationship (innovation and global supervision), a superior-centered style is characteristic of the successful staff officer.

Table 11-18 Correlations of Factor Scores with Predictors and Climate Ratings
Person Factor V: Subordinate-Centered Manager

Predictors	Treatment Group						Total Group (N = 188)
	Innovation (N = 94)	Rules (N = 94)	Global Supervision (N = 94)	Detailed Supervision (N = 94)	Compatible (N = 94)	Incompatible (N = 94)	
Acquiescence	0.10	0.02	0.01	0.09	0.06	0.05	0.05
Social Extroversion	-0.01	-0.05	0.11	-0.16	-0.08	-0.02	-0.03
Independence	0.01	0.04	0.11	-0.03	-0.06	0.12	0.03
Maladjustment	0.18	0.08	0.11	0.15	0.11	0.14	0.13
Rigid Authoritarian	-0.15	-0.11	-0.17	-0.11	-0.18	-0.07	-0.13
Theoretical Education	0.07	-0.05	0.00	0.01	-0.03	0.03	0.00
Years of Military Service	0.01	-0.02	-0.05	0.01	0.04	-0.05	-0.01
Number of Children	-0.03	0.10	0.13	-0.02	0.02	0.07	0.04
Educated Institutional Man	0.02	0.03	0.07	-0.01	0.05	0.00	0.03
Power and Seniority	-0.15	-0.07	-0.14	-0.08	-0.13	-0.07	-0.11
Dead-end Seniority	-0.04	-0.21*	-0.08	-0.17	-0.18	-0.06	-0.13
Staff Officer	-0.04	-0.02	-0.03	-0.03	-0.01	-0.05	-0.03
Hidden Patterns	0.14	0.17	0.11	0.21*	0.23*	0.10	0.16*
First and Last Names	-0.01	-0.03	0.00	-0.05	-0.04	0.00	-0.03
Vocabulary	0.14	0.08	-0.05	0.24*	0.18	0.03	0.11
Multiple Analogies Test	0.01	0.00	-0.12	0.12	0.08	-0.08	0.01
Test S, Successful Strategy	0.22*	0.04	0.04	0.19	0.19	0.04	0.13
Test S, Conservative Strategy	0.06	0.01	0.10	-0.01	0.00	0.07	0.04
Speed of Closure	0.01	0.15	0.09	0.07	0.15	0.00	0.08
Ideational Fluency	0.13	0.10	0.09	0.14	0.09	0.14	0.11
Inductive Reasoning	0.11	-0.01	0.17	-0.04	0.05	0.06	0.05
Climate Rating: Rules	0.12	-0.12	-0.02	0.02	0.01	-0.02	0.00
Climate Rating: Global Supervision	-0.17	-0.03	-0.28†	0.09	-0.07	-0.12	-0.10

*Significantly different from zero at the 5% level. †Significantly different from zero at the 1% level.

235

Table 11-17 Correlations of Factor Scores with Predictors and Climate Ratings
Person Factor VI: Commitment-Avoiding Manager

Predictors	Treatment Group						Total Group (N = 188)
	Innovation (N = 94)	Rules (N = 94)	Global Supervision (N = 94)	Detailed Supervision (N = 94)	Compatible (N = 94)	Incompatible (N = 94)	
Acquiescence	0.02	-0.02	0.04	-0.05	0.06	-0.05	0.01
Social Extroversion	-0.01	0.14	0.17	-0.08	0.10	0.01	0.06
Independence	-0.17	-0.19	-0.15	-0.22*	-0.13	-0.22*	-0.18*
Maladjustment	0.17	-0.02	0.02	0.15	0.11	0.03	0.08
Rigid Authoritarian	0.10	-0.14	0.08	-0.15	0.00	-0.01	-0.01
Theoretical Education	0.08	0.04	0.08	0.04	0.12	-0.02	0.06
Years of Military Service	0.03	-0.06	-0.01	-0.03	0.02	-0.04	-0.01
Number of Children	0.04	-0.08	-0.06	-0.03	-0.01	-0.02	-0.02
Educated Institutional Man	0.01	0.05	-0.06	0.10	0.03	0.01	0.02
Power and Seniority	-0.07	-0.21*	-0.19	-0.06	-0.15	-0.10	-0.13
Dead-end Seniority	0.22*	-0.21*	0.08	-0.05	0.00	0.05	0.02
Staff Officer	0.11	-0.07	-0.07	0.15	0.01	0.06	0.03
Hidden Patterns	-0.16	-0.03	-0.16	0.00	-0.15	-0.06	-0.10
First and Last Names	0.05	-0.04	-0.06	0.07	-0.15	0.17	0.00
Vocabulary	-0.07	0.07	-0.14	0.15	0.02	-0.05	-0.01
Multiple Analogies Test	0.14	0.26†	0.14	0.25*	0.20*	0.16	0.18*
Test S. Successful Strategy	-0.15	0.18	-0.07	0.09	0.01	-0.01	-0.00
Test S. Conservative Strategy	-0.12	0.10	0.01	-0.06	-0.04	0.01	-0.02
Speed of Closure	0.08	0.01	-0.03	0.12	-0.01	0.13	0.05
Ideational Fluency	0.15	-0.13	-0.05	0.12	0.01	0.01	0.02
Inductive Reasoning	0.02	0.05	0.01	0.04	0.03	0.02	0.03
Climate Rating: Rules	-0.13	-0.07	-0.17	-0.04	-0.12	-0.07	-0.10
Climate Rating: Global Supervision	0.03	0.04	0.08	-0.06	0.11	-0.05	0.04

*Significantly different from zero at the 5% level   †Significantly different from zero at the 1% level

DISCUSSION OF THE RESULTS

A major problem in large correlational analyses such as those conducted in this study is the problem of statistical confidence in the results.
Tables 11-12 through 11-17 contain a large number of correlations, all
of which were tested for statistical significance by a conventional method
(Edwards, 1960). By chance, there were surely a number of Type I
errors. On the other hand, the method of principal components, which
was employed here to obtain subjects' scores on the in-basket test and on
most of the predictors, generally yields scores which in turn yield more
reliable beta weights in prediction problems than do scores on single
variables (Burket, 1964). The implication of this is that the correlations
between the in-basket factors and the 23 predictor factors should be more
replicable than if manifest scores had been used in these analyses. Thus
it may be justifiable to consider at least tentatively all the significant
correlations reported.

It was suggested at the beginning of this chapter that the heterogeneity of in-basket items may have dissipated any effects of the experimental climates and attenuated correlations with other variables to an
extent that makes it difficult to find evidence that climates affect the
relationships of performance with potential predictors of performance.
Such an interpretation is consistent with the suggestion of Bracht and
Glass (1968) that the "molarity" (as opposed to "molecularity") of
variables might obscure interactions that would be observable if person
variables and treatments were more narrowly defined. They point out
that in educational research treatments often consist of broadly defined
curricula, and that research aimed at more narrowly defined treatments
might be more likely to yield significant interactions with personal
characteristics. The purpose of the three-mode factor analysis was to
look again for interactions of situational and individual variables using a
method that would define situations in terms of homogeneous subsets of
items.

The new method of analysis did provide clusters of in-basket items
that are homogeneous in the sense that they tend to elicit similar behaviors. Six clusters of items were found that had to do with (1) evaluation
of procedures for accomplishing organizational goals, (2) routine handling of problems, (3) solution of interorganizational problems, (4) solution of personnel problems, (5) recommendations of a change in policy,
and (6) conflicting demands for staff time. These six categories by no
means exhaust the variance found in the data, but they do represent

homogeneous subsamples of items. A study that was planned specifically to deal with this aspect of the problem, possibly one based on a theory stemming from a facet analysis, would presumably be more successful in finding major factors in the domain of stimulus materials. The criterion of similarity with respect to behaviors elicited appears to be a reasonable one for use in the empirical development of a taxonomy of situations.

The core matrix demonstrated that subgroups of individuals can be identified who are characterized by the exhibition of particular patterns of performance in response to particular clusters of items. Six such person factors were found. The intercorrelations of scores on these person factors for subjects who experienced different climate conditions showed that the climates do influence interrelationships of person factors. In fact, one of the person factors exists primarily in a particular climate condition. This factor is Person Factor III; subjects who represent this factor tend to interact with superiors (particularly on items involving a major policy question) provided they are in a climate condition that encourages innovation and global supervision. In other climate conditions the factor tends to merge with another person factor that seems to reflect a tendency to avoid rather than take action on problems.

The correlations of person-factor scores with scores on predictor variables show a number of instances where the correlations are different for different climate conditions. One finds, for example, (a) that under consistent climate conditions, *independence* of thought and action is associated with a tendency to utilize a systematic approach to supervisory problems, but under inconsistent climate conditions, *dependence* is associated with this same operational style; (b) that in the rules climate a tendency to involve others in the solution of problems is predicted by the Inductive Reasoning test, but in the innovation climate the direction of the prediction is reversed; and (c) that in an innovation, global supervision, and compatible climate, those scoring high on social extroversion tend to be informal communicators, but in the rules and compatible climates (and to a lesser extent in the detailed supervision climate) the same style is characteristic of the educated institutional man.

The correlation of operational style and climate conditions with conventional criterion measures suggests the following sets of relationships: The successful senior line manager tends to adopt a program-centered style, especially in innovation, detailed supervision, or incompatible climates. The successful senior staff officer tends to adopt a superior-centered style, especially in innovation, global supervision or compatible climates. The effective junior manager tends to adopt a systematic super-visory style, especially in a rules climate. The dead-end manager, on the other hand, tends to adopt a commitment-avoiding style, especially in an innovation climate. This same commitment-avoiding behavior, often coupled with a reliance on superiors, is typical of the dependent, in-effective junior manager, especially in the rules climate.

Of the various personality and cognitive predictors employed in the study, Test S (risk-taking styles) and Speed of Closure (ability and tendency to quickly unify a disparate field into a single percept) seem to be most closely related to style of in-basket performance. They con-tribute an equal number of significant coefficients and in total they account for almost one-half of the significant correlations between cogni-tive variables and operational styles. Test S has at least one significant coefficient in each of the seven climate conditions; Speed of Closure has at least one in five of the seven climate conditions. Test S relates to Person Factors I, III, IV, and V, while Speed of Closure relates to Person Factors I, III, and IV. In other words, in-basket performance, as defined by person-factor scores, is most closely related to (a) willing-ness and ability to quickly perceive the "gestalt" of the task and (b) willingness and ability to adopt a risk-taking strategy commensurate with that perception.

Although this discussion points up relationships of in-basket perform-ance measures to scores on other measures, the reader should not regard this as indicating the in-basket test to be a good predictor of job performance. Previous studies as well as the present study show correla-tions between work criteria and in-basket performance that are quite low. Also, the design of the study is such that work experience is brought to and hence confounded with in-basket performance. In the ideal predic-tion study, the predictors should be administered to subjects long before their performance on the job. This problem is best pointed up in the per-formance of subjects who consistently avoid the making of commitments (Person Factor VI) in the innovation climate. These subjects tend to be ones who hold positions with dead-end seniority. This could be because (a) they had always been "hemmers and hawers," or (b) prolonged execu-tive employment without hope of promotion made them less inclined to show initiative or to take action.

Even though this study is not immediately applicable to the prediction of job performance, it suggests a qualification to be placed on future predictive studies. It indicates that regression equations used in such studies may vary widely from "office" to "office," even within one organization. Assuming two offices differ in the extent to which the supervisors encourage strict adherence to routines, the predictors of performance in one office would not apply to performance in the other office. Thus, the regression equation for predicting performance would differ for the two offices.

CHAPTER 12

The Findings and Their Implications

In this chapter we will summarize the major findings of the research and discuss some of their implications with respect to possible applications, models for human behavior, and methodology.

The research was performed in a simulated organization, which made possible a rigorous experiment in the sense that subjects could be assigned to experimental treatments according to plan, and identical work situations could be maintained in spite of the fact that a good deal of the complexity and realism of a working organization was retained. The experimental treatments involved two dichotomies of organizational climate, arranged in a 2×2 design. One dichotomy contrasted a climate in which innovation and originality are encouraged with a climate that encourages following rules and standard procedures. The second dichotomy was concerned with supervisory practices. One organizational climate condition encouraged "global" supervision, in which work is assigned and the subordinate allowed freedom in carrying out the assignment; and the contrasting condition encouraged detailed supervision, in which the supervisor is expected to monitor in detail the work of a subordinate. These experimental conditions were presented in subtle and not-so-subtle ways as part of the background information about the simulated organization. The perceptions of the climates were kept alive, while subjects performed their duties, by including appropriate documents in the subjects' in-baskets.

The situational test that was the vehicle for the simulation required each subject to perform the paper work of an administrator, responding to documents in his in-basket as though he were actually on the job. Methods of scoring the resulting protocols have been developed in previous studies; they produce reasonably reliable scores on a wide variety of behaviors identifiable in the protocols. The dependent variables are based on these scores. Additional information about the subjects was obtained by using biographical questionnaires, personality inventories, and cognitive ability tests. A series of factor analyses reduced this "predictor" domain to 23 measures.

The purpose of the study was to look for person-situation interactions in an examination of the effects of the organizational climates on the administrative performance of executives. More specifically, the aim was to answer three general kinds of questions: (1) What are the effects of situational variables—the organizational climates and their inter-action—on the means of the dependent variables? (2) What are the effects of the climates, and their interaction, on the factor structure in the domain of the dependent variables? (3) What are the effects of the organizational climates on the correlations between dependent variables and measures of personality, ability, and background characteristics of the subjects? The following section describes the salient findings of the study with respect to these and other questions.

SUMMARY OF MAJOR FINDINGS

Dimensions of Performance in an Executive's Paper Work

The method of scoring in-basket protocols that has evolved over several years of work with this type of situational test comes close, we feel, to exhausting the types of variability that can be perceived in the records of performance. In this study, 55 in-basket scores were judged to be sufficiently reliable to include in a factor analysis. The purpose of the factor analysis was to remove most of the redundancy in the information, to reduce the number of variables to a manageable size, and to verify or add to our knowledge about factor structure in a domain of such performance variables.

The first unrotated performance factor was interpreted as *Productivity*; it represents the amount of work accomplished during the hours spent in dealing with problems represented by the in-basket items. It is a large factor, accounting for 21% of the total variance. In previous studies, a large second-order factor has been interpreted as amount of work. In this study, we felt it would be better to retain the primary factor as a measure of productivity while keeping it orthogonal to all other factors, thus in effect removing the influence of productivity from all the remaining factors. This procedure was expected to reduce the intercorrelations of the factors and therefore to make it unnecessary to deal with a second-order factor structure.

Nine additional performance factors were identified. When rotated to an oblique structure, their intercorrelations were indeed low, the highest correlation being −0.19. There were no surprises in the list of factors identified; all were similar to factors found in previous work with in-basket protocols. The 10 factors accounted for 61% of the total variance. The names assigned to the 10 factors are as follows:

1. Productivity
2. Acts in compliance with suggestions
3. Interacts with superiors
4. Thoughtful analysis of problems
5. Plans and discusses
6. Defers judgment and action
7. Interacts with peers
8. Orderly work
9. Informality
10. Accepts administrative responsibility

Scores representing these 10 performance factors served as dependent variables in our investigation of effects of organizational climates on performance. An additional variable, the average of the in-basket scorers' rating of overall quality of performance, constitutes the eleventh criterion. Correlations of this rating with the 10 in-basket performance factor scores show that scorers were most impressed with *productivity* ($r = 0.43$); no other correlation was higher than 0.19. There seemed to be a sufficient amount of variance in the average rating that is independent of the factor scores to justify its inclusion as another criterion variable. The criteria of performance used in studying effects of organizational climates, then, are the 10 in-basket performance factor scores and the average rating by the in-basket scorers of quality of performance.

Effects of Climates on Means of the Dependent Variables

In considering the effects of the experimental treatments, we are concerned with three kinds of comparison. One involves the *row* effects in our 2 × 2 design (*see* Fig. 3-1), which for the purposes of this section involves a comparison of subjects in the innovation climate with subjects in the rules climate in regard to means of the dependent variables. A second kind of comparison involves the *column* effects, or a comparison of subjects in the global supervision climate with subjects in the detailed supervision climate in regard to the means. And the third involves the *interaction* of rows and columns, or a comparison of subjects in the climate combinations represented by the cells in the two diagonals of the 2×2 table. Subjects in the upper left and lower right cells are in climate combinations that appear to be consistent or compatible: innovation combined with global supervision, and rules combined with detailed supervision. Subjects in the lower left and upper right cells, on the other hand, are in climate combinations that are inconsistent: global supervision with rules, and detailed supervision with innovation. It is possible to interpret significant interactions in terms of this consistency or inconsistency of climate conditions.

One procedure for comparing treatment groups with respect to means uses only the criterion score information. This method assumes that the assignment of subjects to experimental treatments was unbiased. Another procedure does not assume that the assignment method worked perfectly and uses a statistical method which takes account of and corrects for any differences between the groups with respect to the various predictor measures of personality, ability, and background measures that were obtained. Both methods were used.

The major finding is that the mean *Productivity* score is significantly affected by the consistency of the climate conditions. The difference in means is significant (2% level of confidence) whether one does or does not control on the 23 predictor measures. Productivity is increased when climate conditions are consistent, and decreased when climate conditions are inconsistent. (The means are 0.14 and -0.14, respectively, where the mean for the combined groups is zero and the standard deviation is 1.00.) If we look at the means for the treatment combinations represented by the four cells in our 2×2 table, we find that the effect is most pronounced in the *innovation-detailed supervision* combination, where the mean is -0.30. The amount of work accomplished, as measured by such things as number of actions taken, amount written, number of subordinates involved, and number of items attempted is appreciably reduced when subjects are asked to work under climate conditions that simultaneously encourage innovation and detailed supervision of subordinates.

There are suggestions of other effects of climates on means, but significance levels depend upon whether or not the control measures are employed. There is a suggestion that *Interaction with superiors* is decreased by consistent climate conditions (especially in the innovation-global supervision cell, where the mean is -0.19) and increased by inconsistent climate conditions. And there is also some evidence that *Deferring judgment and action* is decreased by the innovation climate and increased by the rules climate.

The means of none of the other criterion variables were significantly affected by the climate conditions. The consistency of the climate dichotomies turned out to be of greater importance, from this point of view, than either climate dichotomy considered alone.

A number of previous studies have dealt with climate variables that are somewhat similar to one or the other of the two dichotomies we have used. Katz, Maccoby, and Morse (1950) employed a method that first involved identifying office work groups characterized by high and low productivity, and then, on the basis of interviews with workers and supervisors, discovering the leadership styles used by supervisors. They found that the heads of high-producing sections were more likely to give *general* rather than *close* supervision. (They also spent more time in supervision and tended to be employee-oriented rather than production-oriented.) The *general-close* supervision dichotomy used by Katz *et al.* appears to be rather similar to our *global-detailed* supervision. Day and Hamblin (1961) investigated effects of close and punitive styles of supervision. Their hypothesis was that such supervision would produce aggressive feelings; lowered productivity and overt verbal aggression were used as indicators of aggressive feelings. The results supported their hypothesis. Argyle, Gardner, and Cioffi (1958) used as a measure of productivity the ratio of time taken to time allowed to complete a task. They found that "nonpunitive" supervision was associated with increased productivity, although "democratic" supervision was only slightly related. Comrey, Pfiffner, and Beem (1952) used a questionnaire approach in studying forest-management work groups; they found that the supervisors of more effective work groups were more democratic in dealing with their assistants, allowing them greater participation in decision making. Thus several studies seem to show that styles of supervision more or less resembling our "detailed" supervision are associated with low productivity. Our study showed results that were in the same direction (means were 0.08 and -0.08 for global and detailed supervision climates, respectively) but were not significant. Our 2×2 design, in which two climate dichotomies were used, may have obscured the results somewhat for the global-detailed supervision dichotomy considered alone.

Pelz (1957) and Meltzer (1956) have studied variables that appear to be related to our innovation-rules climate dichotomy, working in research organizations. Their findings show that the productivity of a research scientist is greater in climates where greater freedom is permitted. Our result was in the opposite direction for the innovation-rules comparison; however, if we interpret greater freedom in terms of the global-detailed supervision dichotomy, the results are in agreement, at least with respect to direction of difference. Considering both climates together, the greatest amount of freedom would seem to be associated with Cell A of Fig. 3-1 (innovation combined with global supervision). For subjects in this cell, productivity is indeed above average; but it is equally high for Cell D (rules with detailed supervision). For our study, *consistency* of climate conditions is the salient determiner of productivity.

The interaction of our two climate dichotomies, which we have interpreted in terms of consistency of climate conditions, is similar to the notion of ambiguity of role expectations, which has been the subject of several investigations. Smith (1957) and Steiner and Dodge (1956) used small group situations where vagueness of roles could be controlled experimentally, and their results appear to show that productivity and effectiveness in problem solving are adversely affected by lack of clarity of roles; these results are consistent with our finding of depressed productivity when the two climates are incompatible.

Kahn *et al.* (1964) used interview and survey methods in a study directly concerned with role clarity among salaried employees. Unfortunately, productivity was not one of the dependent variables. Their results showed that ambiguity or vagueness of occupational role was associated with job dissatisfaction, increased tension, and lowered self-confidence. It is tempting to assume that these effects would be accompanied by reduced effectiveness, but such an assumption would not necessarily be supported by findings from investigations of that relationship. Vroom (1964) summarized the results of 20 studies reporting correlations between measures of job satisfaction and various criteria of effectiveness and found no consistent relationship.

Effects of Climates on Factor Structure of Dependent Variables

The method used to study effects of climates on factor structure is based on the factor analysis of in-basket performance that was described in a preceding section. That analysis made use of scores for subjects in all the climate conditions combined. The next step was to compute factor scores for all subjects and then to compute the variance-covariance matrix of these factor scores for subjects in each treatment group separately. Following the pattern dictated by our 2×2 design, comparisons are made for innovation vs. rules climate groups, global vs. detailed supervision groups, and compatible vs. incompatible climate groups. The variance-covariance matrices of performance factor scores were found to be significantly different ($p = 0.002$) in all three of these comparisons; the organizational climates clearly do influence the interrelationships of the performance factor scores.

The performance factor that figures most strongly in the findings is *Thoughtful analysis of problems*. The row and column treatments influence especially the correlations of *Thoughtful analysis of problems* with other performance factors, and there is a degree of similarity in the pattern of differences found. In both innovation and global supervision climates (as contrasted with rules and detailed supervision) *Thoughtful analysis of problems* is negatively correlated with *Interacts with superiors* and with *Accepts administrative responsibility*, and positively correlated with *Interacts with peers*. It would appear that the climates that provide more freedom of thought and action to employees — innovation and global supervision — tend to send the more thoughtful subjects out to deal directly with their peers (heads of other divisions, who happen to be the source of many of the in-basket problems). In the more restrictive and controlled climates — rules and detailed supervision — the thoughtful people are, on the other hand, constrained to work through their superiors and through that part of the organization for which they are responsible. Other differences in correlations of factors seem consistent with this interpretation.

The consistency of climate conditions has more influence on variability than on intercorrelations of factors, particularly for *Thoughtful analysis of problems*; the variance of factor scores for thoughtful analysis is about twice as great for consistent as for inconsistent climate conditions.

In no case does a variance decrease to the vanishing point, nor are any correlations large enough to suggest that two factors merge in any of the treatment conditions. We judge, therefore, that all factors are present in all the organizational climates.

Most behavioral science researchers confine their attention to effects of experimental treatments on the means of their dependent variables, although there is a growing tendency to look for differences in slopes of regressions of dependent variables on personal characteristics of subjects. It is rare to find a report of a study in which the effects of experimental treatments on the *interrelationships* among a set of dependent variables is investigated. Our finding of significant differences in variance-covariance matrices for dependent variables suggests that treatments may produce important differences in *patterns* of performance even in instances where means are not significantly affected, and that these differences in patterns of performance may be of considerable importance, both practically and theoretically.

Effects of Climates on Slopes of Regressions

The question to be answered in this section has to do with the possibility that organizational climates do not have uniform effects on all individuals, but that people will be differentially influenced, depending upon their personal characteristics. The answer to the question is provided by comparing slopes of regressions of in-basket performance factor scores on measures of personal characteristics – the scores on personality, ability, and background tests and questionnaires. If slopes of regressions are significantly different, we may assume that the effect of an experimental treatment depends on one or more of these personal characteristics, and an examination of the regression weights for our measures of these characteristics will reveal which characteristics are involved.

For each pair of contrasting groups – innovation and rules, for example – 11 comparisons were made, one for each of the 11 criterion variables. In each comparison, the slopes of two regression lines were compared; for example, the regression of *Productivity* on the best-weighted combination of predictors for subjects in the innovation climate is compared with the corresponding regression for subjects in the rules climate. In all, therefore, 33 statistical tests were made.

The results were almost completely negative. In only one of the 33 instances was the difference in slopes found to be significant, and the importance of this finding is reduced because of the large number of tests that were made and thus the possibility that a "significant" difference might have arisen by chance. The obvious conclusion from these results is that the hypothesis of differential susceptibility to influences of the organizational climates is not supported. Examination of zero-order correlations between criterion and the predictor measures, however, reveals a number of instances of sizable and individually significant differences in correlations that seem to make theoretical sense. The possibility remains that another study with more subjects, a better selection of predictors, more reliable criteria, or better control of treatments would provide statistically convincing evidence of differential treatment effects.

The finding of generally insignificant differences in slopes of regressions does justify the previously discussed investigation of effects of treatments on the *means* of criterion variables. If the effects were radically different for different kinds of individuals, statements about a general effect of an experimental treatment would be inappropriate.

In view of the difficulty that has been encountered in finding clear instances of person-situation interactions in education and in organizational performance, as was described in Chapter 1, we should perhaps not be surprised that significant differences in slopes were not found in this investigation. If our intuitive judgment is correct, that performance is a function of both one's personal characteristics and the situation one encounters, there must be something wrong in the approach to the study of person-situation interactions that has commonly been employed. The next section describes the results of a somewhat different method of looking for person-situation interactions.

The Results of a Three-Mode Factor Analysis

Another approach to the problem of investigating interactions of situations and personal characteristics in influencing performance is to employ more elementary units as situational variables. Instead of the very general and pervasive organizational climates, we may use in-basket items, or clusters of in-basket items, to define situational variables. This approach requires us to go back to data showing how responses to individual items were scored.

The data we have obtained in this study may be thought of as a three-dimensional matrix based on classification of data by subject, by in-basket item, and by performance category. An appropriate method of analysis of such a data matrix is three-mode factor analysis. The expected result of such an analysis would be factors in each of three modes — performance factors, item factors, and person factors. The *performance* factors are clusters of in-basket performance categories comparable to those listed in an earlier section. The *item* factors are clusters of in-basket items that are similar in that they tend to elicit similar categories of performance. The *person* factors are clusters of individuals who are alike in that they tend to show similar relationships between performance factors and item factors. If only one person factor is found, there is no person-situation interaction, since the relationship between situations and performance is the same for all subjects. Finding more than one person factor demonstrates the existence of person-situation interaction.

The factors identified in the performance mode were very similar to those found in the main analysis, except that the method used did not take out productivity as a separate orthogonal factor.

Six interpretable item factors were found that may be considered tentatively as a taxonomy of paper-work problems of state service executives. The item factors were given the following names:

1. Items requiring evaluation of procedures for accomplishing organizational goals
2. Items permitting a routine solution
3. Items requiring solution of interorganizational problems
4. Items requiring solution of personnel problems
5. Items recommending a change in policy
6. Items presenting conflicting demands for staff time

Six person factors were found, indicating the presence of person-situation interactions. The interpretation of each person factor is based on its corresponding performance-factor by item-factor matrix. Person Factor I, for example, is represented by individuals who tend to be orderly and systematic in their work, particularly on personnel problems but *not* on problems permitting choice of routine or nonroutine solutions. Without spelling out all these interpretations, it can be concluded that groups of individuals can be identified who differ with respect to their *performance factor-item factor* interrelationships. To put it another way, the relationship of type of task to performance is not uniform across all subjects but varies in accordance with one's resemblance to an idealized representative of one person factor or another. The person factors were named as follows:

Person Factor I:	Systematic supervisor
Person Factor II:	Informal communicator
Person Factor III:	Superior-centered manager
Person Factor IV:	Program-centered manager
Person Factor V:	Subordinate-centered manager
Person Factor VI:	Commitment-avoiding manager

Factor scores on person factors were computed for each subject, and variance-covariance matrices of person-factor scores were computed for the groups of subjects represented by the rows, columns, and interaction in our 2 × 2 treatment design. Thus the innovation group was compared with the rules group, the global-supervision group with the detailed-supervision group, and the consistent-climate group with the inconsistent-climate group, with respect to variances and covariances of person-factor scores.

The most striking finding from these comparisons was that one of the person factors (Person Factor III, the superior-centered manager) exists primarily in a particular climate combination, and under other conditions it combines with another person factor. Person Factor III is interpreted as a tendency to interact with superiors on problems other than those that permit a routine solution. This factor exists separately in the climate combination of innovation with global supervision, and under other climate conditions it merges with Person Factor VI, reflecting a tendency to avoid making commitments. These results demonstrate a sort of second-order interaction, in the sense that the nature of the interaction of items and personal characteristics in influencing behavior is in turn modified by a more general situational variable, the organizational climate condition.

The correlations of person-factor scores with the various measures of personality, cognitive, and background characteristics were computed, in hopes that interpretations of the person factors would acquire more psychological meaning in the light of these relationships. The correlations for the total group were in general too low to permit such interpretations to be made with much confidence. There are, however, a number of instances in which individual correlations, or patterns of correlations, are different for contrasting climate conditions. Inspection of individual coefficients reveals, for example, that in the rules climate a high score on *Inductive Reasoning* is associated with a tendency to be a program-centered manager ($r = 0.23$), but in the innovation climate the direction of relationship is reversed ($r = -0.31$). Although the correlations are not high, the difference in correlation is substantial (0.54). We also find that successful staff officers tend to adopt a superior-oriented managerial style in the innovative climate, but ineffective junior managers are the ones most likely to adopt a superior-centered style in a rules climate.

Although no overall tests of significance are possible, the obtained differences in correlation suggest that climate variations influence the relationships between types of problem and type of performance differently for subsets of individuals with different personal characteristics.

The Prediction of In-Basket Performance

For the total group of 260 subjects, multiple correlations of the predictors (cognitive, personality, and biographical scores) with the 11 criterion measures ranged from 0.28 to 0.42. Only three R's, those of 0.40 or greater, are highly significant. The three most predictable performance-factor criteria are *Productivity, Thoughtful analysis of problems*, and *Defers judgment and action.*

Productivity is the most predictable of the criteria. The highest regression weights are for the Hidden Patterns test (a presumed measure of field independence) and Social Extroversion. Maladjustment, Ideational Fluency, and Inductive Reasoning have marginally significant weights. All weights are positive.

Thoughtful analysis of problems has only one highly significant regression weight, that for Staff Officer. This is a factor from the biographical questionnaire reflecting managerial experience in nonline, administrative service functions. Hidden Patterns and Vocabulary tests have marginally significant weights.

Defers judgment and action also has only one highly significant regression weight, that for Years of Military Service. The weight is positive, indicating that many years of military service is associated with a tendency to postpone. This relationship presumably results from selective factors of some sort having to do with the kind of retired officers who go into state service. Social Extroversion has a negative weight. Marginally significant weights are found for Maladjustment and Hidden Patterns (both negative) and the Multiple Analogies test (positive).

Zero-order correlations between predictors and performance factor criteria are quite low for the entire group of subjects; no correlation is higher than 0.22. The Hidden Patterns test turns out to be the test that is potentially more useful than any other one of the 23 predictors; it is significantly correlated with more criterion variables (for the various treatment groups) and has more significant regression weights in the multiple correlations. It has the largest weight in predicting *Productivity* and makes important contributions in the prediction of *Defers judgment and action* and *Thoughtful analysis of problems*. This is a surprising finding; at present it is probable that no test battery for selection of administrative personnel contains a test like Hidden Patterns. These relationships are of interest also because of their theoretical implications. Hidden Patterns has been used as a practical substitute for the rod and frame test (Witkin *et al.*, 1962), which is thought to provide a measure of field independence. The correlations appear to be consistent with the theoretical thinking about field independence.

Among the inventory measures, Social Extroversion and Maladjustment would seem to be the most useful as judged by regression weights in multiple correlations. Maladjustment tends to be associated with high productivity and low tendency to defer action. The measure of Rigid

Authoritarianism has many significant zero-order correlations with the criterion scores. Among the biographical scores, being a staff officer has most to do with *Thoughtful analysis of problems*. Dead-end Seniority has a number of significant negative correlations with *Productivity* and *Thoughtful analysis*. By and large, the cognitive tests were usually among the best predictors; in addition to the Hidden Patterns test, Vocabulary, Speed of Closure, and Inductive Reasoning are relatively good predictors.

When correlations for the contrasting treatment groups are examined, a number of differences in correlation are found that are individually significant and theoretically interesting. But since the multivariate tests of slopes showed few significant differences, we must be careful in our interpretations based on comparisons of zero-order correlations.

IMPLICATIONS FOR PERSONNEL PRACTICE

Any inclination to put into immediate practice personnel procedures that appear to be desirable on the basis of findings reported here will presumably be inhibited if one recalls that the study is based on performance in a simulated job. There is no denying the likelihood that to some degree subjects will perform differently in a situational test than they do in a real job, knowing as they do that decisions are not "for real" and that no one's career would really be influenced by any action taken. The reason for doing the study in a simulated job was to make possible a more rigorous study, through ability to assign subjects to treatments and to control conditions more completely. The penalty that must be paid is the doubt about external validity—about the generality of findings. We shall have more to say on this point in a later section.

Having stated this *caveat*, we will nevertheless proceed to consider some of the implications of the study for personnel practices.

Use of Multiple Criteria

This investigation, in common with several previous studies in which in-baskets were used as the basis for a situational test, showed that an appreciable number of factors is needed to account for the common variance in a score matrix. When productivity is controlled, as it was in this study, the performance factors have quite low intercorrelations. In view of such results, the common practice of trying to evaluate administrators in terms of one overall criterion variable seems highly questionable. If the situational test could somehow be broadened to reflect behavior in interpersonal situations and to involve problems that unfold over a longer span of time, the criterion space would undoubtedly be still more complex. Evaluation of the performance of administrators requires the use of a variety of criteria, whether they are to be used for research purposes or as the basis for personnel decisions. One's performance as an administrator can vary in many ways, and the interpretation of each criterion in terms of "good" or "bad" may be specific to a particular situation.

Selection of Administrative Personnel

Before choosing a test battery for the selection of managers, one needs to give thought to two considerations: (1) what criteria of performance are considered important and (2) in what kind of situation or organization will the candidate work. As we have pointed out, one should think in terms of multiple criteria rather than a single criterion of quality of administrative performance. Furthermore, the value assigned to a particular dimension of performance might vary considerably, depending upon the requirements of a certain job assignment.

The results from the multiple correlations with the 23 predictors used in this investigation suggest that if productivity is thought to be an important criterion of successful performance, regardless of administrative style, one would choose candidates who are socially extroverted and field independent; in addition, it would be desirable for them not to feel too secure — to be somewhat "maladjusted" — and to have good ideational fluency and inductive reasoning ability.

With respect to Maladjustment, we should be reminded that this is a factor score based on inventory scales that purport to measure anxiety, maladjustment, and instability (*see* Chapter 5). A number of the items were originally from the Minnesota Multiphasic Personality Inventory, by way of the Taylor Manifest Anxiety Scale. The latter scale has been widely used in studies of learning as a measure of emotionally-based drive, and it is probably in this sense that the Maladjustment variable should be interpreted here. Since it is not unusual to find curvilinear relationships between anxiety and cognitive performance, especially on complex tasks (Klein *et al.*, 1969), it would perhaps be prudent to seek a moderate but not an extreme amount of maladjustment.

If thoughtful analysis of problems is an important criterion, again regardless of other aspects of administrative style, one would seek someone with the background of a successful staff officer who is high in verbal ability and field independence. If it is felt to be important that the administrator not procrastinate by deferring judgment and action, one should seek a candidate who is socially extroverted, somewhat maladjusted, and field independent.

On the question of the influence of the particular situation or organization on the predictive value of a test, this study gives two kinds of results, depending upon the generality of the situational variable employed. The multivariate study comparing slopes of regressions of performance factors on predictors for contrasting climate groups have generally negative findings; the same regression formula would do about equally well for all the climate conditions. The three-mode factor analysis, on the other hand, showed that the relationships of performance factors to factorially "pure" in-basket item clusters were different for different groups of individuals. Furthermore, the number of such groups and their interrelationships were influenced by the experimental climate conditions. Assuming that the groups of individuals differ with respect to measurable psychological characteristics, there is at least a strong possibility that the predictive value of a test will vary from one situation to another when *situation* is defined in terms of a cluster of similar problems. It seems likely that the low validities often found in prediction studies are the result of combining subjects whose work is influenced by varying situational conditions. Until more information is available, it seems wise to assume that validities of tests will vary considerably from one job situation to another, and that prediction formulas need to be determined separately for homogeneous groupings within an organization. Eventually it may be possible to measure situational variables well enough to put them into an appropriate prediction equation along with measures of personal qualities, and come out with better predictions.

Management of Organizational Climates

The foregoing discussion assumed that the problem is to identify appropriate people to work in an existing organization, given its climates and other situational characteristics. In the present section we will assume that administrative employees are already on the staff and the problem is how to modify the climate conditions in such a way as to maximize the performance of an employee with respect to selected criteria of good administrative behavior.

The most obvious recommendation is that in order to increase productivity of an administrative staff, the climate conditions should be made consistent, at least so far as the *innovation-rules* and *global supervision-detailed supervision* climates are concerned. One should particularly avoid the combination of innovation climate with detailed supervision, according to our results. The extent to which the relationship between climate compatibility and productivity is specific to the climate dichotomies under investigation here is anybody's guess, but one might speculate that the effect on productivity results from an uncertainty on the part of the subject as to what kind of performance will be approved. If this speculation is correct, then productivity could be improved by reducing as much as possible any influences leading to conflicting expectations about the desirability of various modes of behavior.

The finding that regressions of productivity scores on predictor measures are not significantly different in slope would permit the above recommendation to stand without qualification. But the results of the three-mode factor analysis, which show that interrelationships of person factors are influenced by the experimental climates, lead us to a word of caution; the relationships of categories of administrative performance to personal characteristics may vary with the situation.

Other suggestions can be made, based on the effects of climates on the intercorrelations of administrative performance factors. One's management of the organizational climate would again depend upon what outcome is preferred. If it is desired that thoughtful analysis of problems be associated with efforts to deal directly with the people who are responsible for the problems (for this experiment, the subject's peers) rather than with superiors, then the climate should be one that provides freedom of thought and action on the part of one's staff. If, on the other hand, it is desired that thoughtful analysis be associated with efforts to work through one's own organization, then an organizational climate that implies a higher degree of control, such as the rules or detailed supervision climate, should be established.

Limitations of the Rating Method

Ratings were involved in this study in two ways. (1) Scorers were asked to rate each subject on a variety of characteristics, as the last step in their scoring procedure. The ratings were thus made immediately after the scorers' attention had necessarily been directed to detailed examination of the protocol. A factor analysis showed that one factor accounted for almost all the reliable variance in the ratings. In spite of the analytic attitude toward the protocol that was required in order to score it for all the performance categories, scorers were unable to do more than make an overall judgment of the quality of performance. This overall rating was found to correlate with productivity, the factor reflecting amount of work done, and little else. (2) The other ratings in the study were made by peers and superiors of the subjects in their real job, on categories of performance similar to the in-basket performance factors. Correlations between average ratings and the in-basket scores on these factors were in general extremely low. Consistent positive correlations were found only for a "discussion" factor, which is a fairly public kind of behavior. The correlations for a "procrastination" factor tended to be negative, as though subjects in their real jobs succeeded in setting up facades that concealed their tendency to postpone action. The general lack of agreement can of course be interpreted as lack of validity for the in-basket performance scores, but the reverse interpretation is logically just as sound.

It is well known that raters differ significantly as to (a) their sensitivity, (b) their opportunity for observation, (c) the representativeness of their sampling of ratee behaviors, (d) the kinds of performances and administrative styles they prize, and (e) the effects of the interactions of their own individual needs and goals with the institutional needs and goals they are supposed to represent. Until rater behavior is systematically analyzed and categorized, and until rater evaluations are based on situationally defined man-job-situation interaction configurations (Tagiuri, 1961), ratings, whether for use in research or personnel decisions, are not likely to be dependable and frequently will be misleading.

IMPLICATIONS FOR A MODEL OF HUMAN BEHAVIOR

The first and simplest statement of a model of human behavior is no doubt the old $S \rightarrow R$ formulation, which implies that the organism responds predictably to a given stimulus. The fact of individual variations in response to a stimulus, such as those related to age, sex, or amount of training, was of course known, and such variation was recognized by Woodworth (1934), for example, when in the third edition of his textbook he inserted an O (for *organism*) to produce the more adequate formulation $S \rightarrow O \rightarrow R$. The more recent development of mathematical models has ordinarily been based on either the S or the O but not on both together. The regression formula typically used by the personnel psychologist predicts behavior only from the O or individual difference variables, and the mathematical models for predicting learning, for example, make use of S variables but use O variables only in a very general way or not at all.

The concept of differential predictability and the use of moderator variables in the prediction formula of the personnel psychologist recognize a greater degree of complexity. The notion is that the predictive value of one variable may be influenced by another variable, the moderator variable. For example, the value of aptitude tests for predicting academic achievement is moderated by the sex of the student, and the value of interest tests for predicting grades in engineering are moderated by compulsiveness. While most studies of moderator variables have employed measures of individual differences as the moderators, there is no reason why the moderator variable cannot be a situational variable. The use of situations as moderators of predictions based on personal characteristics permits us to write a type of regression formula (Saunders, 1955a) that recognizes one kind of interaction between situational and personal variables. It is also reasonable to turn it around and consider personal characteristics as moderators of predictions based on situational variables. Still better might be a more complete curvilinear model which considers the cross products and squares of a set of predictors, including both personal and situational variables.

Important interactions of situational and personal variables are suggested by the three-mode factor analysis. There are other aspects of the study which lead us to believe that a model of still greater complexity is needed. One is the finding that the factor structure in the domain of dependent variables is influenced by the experimental treatments. Situational variables (such as organizational climates) thus may not only influence performance on a single dependent variable, but they may influence the *interrelationships* of a number of dependent variables. Thus our model of human behavior should be one that can consider a variety of relevant criterion variables simultaneously and consider effects on variability and intercorrelations of the dependent variables.

The other result which has a bearing on this discussion is the finding that the factor structure of person-factor scores (from the three-mode factor analysis) is altered by the organizational climates. This suggests a sort of higher-order interaction: the nature of the interaction between personal and situational variables is influenced by still other situational variables of a broader and more general nature.

Most theories of organizational behavior place great stress on the importance of interactions. Schein (1965), for example, speaks of an organization as a system with multiple purposes and functions, which involve multiple interactions with the environment, and with many sub-systems that are in dynamic interaction with one another. The findings of this investigation suggest that organization theorists are correct in stressing the importance of interactions. Hopefully, the study has contributed something toward a methodology for identifying and measuring some of the variables involved in organizational behavior and toward development of a better understanding of some of their interactions.

METHODOLOGICAL IMPLICATIONS

The chief methodological innovation in this study is the simulation of an organization as the vehicle for a social-psychological experiment. However, every experiment involves some degree of simulation in the sense that some aspect of the environment is abstracted and brought under laboratory control. In this experiment, a complex organization was simulated and controlled, while certain aspects of the organization were systematically varied and the influences on performance observed. In a more typical laboratory experiment, the aspects of the environment that are specifically brought under control are much more limited; for example, the background conditions of illumination and noise might be controlled while experimental variations in pitch of a sound or number of dots on a screen are introduced. In the case of either kind of experiment, we have the problem of generalizing to other situations. What are the advantages or disadvantages of the complex simulation from the point of view of generalization of results to other situations, including real-life settings?

In the case of many laboratory experiments the question does not seem to arise, possibly because it is taken for granted that the results will hold under a variety of conditions, or perhaps because the laboratory findings are of scientific interest whether or not they may be generalized. Why does the problem seem to be more serious in the case of the simulation of an organization? The answer may be that the simulation of the organization necessarily makes specific a good many details, any one of which could conceivably influence the outcome of the experiment. In the laboratory experiment, fewer attributes of the environment are specifically brought under control; therefore there is less reason to suspect that the findings are specific to a given set of background conditions.

This question of generality is the problem of external validity posed by Campbell (1957) and discussed by Campbell and Stanley in their article on "Experimental and Quasi-Experimental Designs for Research," in the *Handbook of Research on Teaching* (1966). Bracht and Glass (1968) have elaborated and extended that discussion of sources of external invalidity, and their classification of ways to go wrong may provide a good outline for an evaluation of the external validity of experiments based on simulations of an organization.

Bracht and Glass suggest that questions about external validity are of two main classes: (1) *population validity* (what population can be expected to behave like the experimental subjects?) and (2) *ecological validity* (in what settings or under what conditions can we expect people to behave like the experimental subjects?).

Population validity   Strictly speaking, one can generalize from an experiment only to that population from which the experimenter has drawn his sample, and then only if the sample has been drawn randomly. It is, however, rarely possible to draw a really random sample of human subjects for participation in an experiment, and one can therefore rigorously generalize only to something Bracht and Glass call the "experimentally accessible" population. Membership in this accessible population is restricted by a large number of considerations such as willingness to serve as subject and freedom to participate at a particular time and place. We do not usually know in detail what differentiates the accessible population from the target population that we would like to sample. Since we can rigorously generalize an experimental finding only to the accessible population and not to the target population, we are usually in the awkward position of not even knowing accurately the nature of the population to which we *can* generalize.

Any psychological research with human subjects is likely to involve this problem of the accessible population, although it is perhaps less serious in certain educational investigations where the target population might be a "captive" population, such as all third-graders in the public school system of a certain city. The problem may be more serious when the target population is composed of adult subjects who are relatively free from administrative control and who may have many conflicting demands on their time, as was true in the present study. Usually we assume that differences between the accessible population and the target population are of minor importance, and we tend to generalize to any group judged to be "like" the group studied. We know that in some instances such an assumption is dangerous; good illustrations are provided by polls that went wrong because of bias in sampling. A partial solution is to compare the accessible populations with the target population on whatever variables are available, in order to find out what kinds of bias were produced by the sampling procedures. Another method is to replicate the study in situations where the factors limiting participation are presumed to be different, using the same target population. A better method would be somehow to induce an unbiased sample of the non-respondents to participate in the experiment to see if they differ from the accessible group with regard to experimental results.

In the study here reported, our target population was all those employed at certain levels as administrators by the State of California (*see* Chapter 4). We know very little about all the decisions that went into determining the accessible population. Some were administrative decisions and some were personal decisions. The biases with respect to certain gross indicators, such as agencies in which subjects were employed, are shown in Chapter 4, but we can only guess as to the personal considerations that entered into the many decisions as to participation. Hence, generalization of research findings to all subjects in state service in California is risky, to say nothing of generalization to administrators in public service in other states or in the federal government, or to administrators in schools or in profit-making organizations. One would hope that in general outline the findings would apply quite broadly; but one must await the completion of other similar research projects before we know the limitations in population validity.

Ecological validity   The preceding discussion has to do with limitations in generality attributable solely to the selection of subjects. Ecological validity has to do with limitations attributable to the environment, i.e., to the situation in which the experiment was conducted. In this instance, we will be particularly concerned about the fact that the data were obtained in a simulated job in a simulated organization, using simulated organizational climates. To what extent is one justified in generalizing from data obtained in such a setting to performance in other settings, especially real-life jobs?

The first consideration discussed by Bracht and Glass has to do with the need to specify accurately the set of operations involved in the experiment. They were interested primarily in educational research, where there is often difficulty in specifying exactly what an experimental treatment is. If, for example, the "discovery" method is used as an experimental teaching method, the operations involved in teaching by that method should be specified so clearly and completely that another investigator could repeat the study with a high degree of fidelity. From this point of view, simulations such as that employed in our study would get high marks, since it is possible to replicate the materials used with a high degree of accuracy and completeness, using apparatus no more complicated than a printing press and a tape recorder. Simulation makes feasible a high degree of accuracy in replication of the experimental conditions, which makes it quite easy to check on external validity from the point of view of replication of the experiment itself. A more important question, however, has to do with generalization to real-life work situations.

Another consideration discussed by Bracht and Glass is the effect on behavior of a subject's knowledge that he is participating in an experiment. Under this heading they discuss the possibility that anxiety will be generated by the experience, that subjects will exhibit "social desirability" bias, and that subjects will try to behave in accordance with what they perceive to be the experimenter's hypotheses or in accordance with their own "lay theory" about behavior in the experimental setting as they perceive it.

With regard to anxiety, subjects in our experiment were given assurances that their protocols would be identified only by number and that there would be complete anonymity in reporting data. These statements no doubt reduced anxiety, but we would not expect to completely eliminate anxiety by such means. In fact, we would not want to, since a real job is anxiety-generating, probably to an even greater degree than the simulated job; the anxiety presumably adds to the realism of the situation. We did, in fact, find some relationships between measures of trait anxiety and performance in the simulated job, suggesting that anxiety may serve as an emotional drive state (Taylor, 1956).

Social desirability bias is usually interpreted as a tendency for a person responding to a questionnaire or personality inventory to choose responses that tend to put him in a good light. We should no doubt assume that subjects in the situational test try to put themselves in a good light, just as candidates do in taking an arithmetic test or in any situation in which they expect their work to be critically examined and evaluated. But the subject taking an in-basket test cannot anticipate the specific ways in which his protocol will be scored. Unlike the inventory or the arithmetic test, the situational test provides no hints as to what facets of behavior the scorers will look for, and the examinee must spontaneously produce the ideas and words that to him represent "putting himself in a good light." While the subject will no doubt assume that such characteristics as high productivity and good judgment are important, it is not always clear what constitutes good judgment. It is unlikely that the subject will specifically anticipate most of the attributes of behavior that form the basis of in-basket scoring. Correlations of social desirability measures with in-basket scores suggest that the response bias is associated with a generally high level of performance, both in terms of quality and quantity, and with attempts to make a good impression on persons in positions of authority—which is just about what one would expect a person with high need for approval to do in a real job (Frederiksen, 1965).

For similar reasons, one would not expect that lay theories of organizational behavior or subjects' perceptions of the hypotheses being tested would influence subjects' behavior in any systematic way. The stimulus materials do not suggest that any particular behaviors are of interest, the task is unstructured, and the dependent variables are numerous and varied. It is extremely unlikely that hypotheses as complex as those involved in person-situation interactions or factor structure in the domain of the dependent variables would have occurred to the subjects.

A third source of ecological invalidity discussed by Bracht and Glass is the effects of novelty and disruption. They suggest that an experimental educational treatment may be effective the first time it is used because of its novelty to the learners, but if the method is adopted and used routinely it may lose its effectiveness. Conversely, a treatment might not be effective the first time it is used because the disruption and confusion associated with the installation of new procedures interferes with its effectiveness. The solution is, of course, to extend the treatment for a longer period of time so that these effects are overcome, and to measure the dependent variables at appropriate intervals so that one can track the changes (compared with appropriate control groups) associated with disruption or novelty.

Since Bracht and Glass were concerned with educational research primarily, the particular effects they had in mind would presumably be associated with educational innovations imposed on school classes in regular sessions. Our data, on the other hand, were obtained in a so-called "research institute" held outside the place of regular employment of subjects. There was certainly disruption of the regular work routine, but there was for most subjects no disruption so far as the simulated job was concerned. The experimental situation was in a sense novel, but the actual simulation of the organization and of the paper work was made as realistic as possible. The new organization was put in the familiar state setting, and the in-basket items were adapted largely from real documents from the files of people in state service. Subjects apparently had no difficulty in settling in to the job situation. Many subjects in the CDC setting, as well as in other in-basket situations, have volunteered the opinion that the experience was just like being at one's own desk.

On the other hand, the effects of the simulated climate conditions might change with time as subjects either adapt to them or become increasingly sensitive to them. Such questions can only be answered by continuing the experiment for a longer period of time.

We shall not discuss in detail all of the factors described by Bracht and Glass that might limit ecological validity, since the general nature of the problem has been sufficiently indicated by the above paragraphs. Other factors they consider are multiple-treatment interference (where two or more treatments are administered consecutively to the same subjects), experimenter effects (the experimenter may unintentionally influence the behavior of subjects), pretest sensitization (administration of a pretest may make the subject aware of the dependent variable of interest to the experimenter), interaction of treatments with events occurring simultaneously in the world or local community, choice of method for measuring the dependent variable, and interaction of treatment effects with time of measurement.

So far as our specific experiment is concerned, perhaps the most important single question has to do with the operations used to represent the organizational climates (described in Chapter 6). Any generalizations about the effects of climates having to do with innovation vs. rules, global vs. detailed supervision, and the consistency of these climate conditions would, strictly speaking, apply only to organizations that used the methods of communicating climate conditions that were used in the simulation. Other methods might be more or less effective, or might carry different nuances in communicating the meaning and implications of the climate conditions.

We have evidence of some degree of consistency in performance between the one simulated job and another through a variety of low but significant correlations between scores based on different in-baskets (Tables 2-4 and 7-2). We also have some evidence of consistency in performance in simulated jobs and real jobs through use of biographical data (Chapter 10; Frederiksen, 1966). It is not inconceivable that the correlations between measures of performance in different *real* jobs (if we could get them) would not be much higher than the relationships of similar measures across real and simulated jobs.

The question of generality will ultimately be settled only by more studies, both experimental and in field settings, which tend to agree in showing that certain relationships appear consistently. A good example is a field study of 24 hospitals by Rosner (1968), in which relationships between administrative controls and innovation, as measured by frequency and latency in trying new drugs, was investigated.

The feasibility of doing social-psychological experiments in simulated settings appears to have been amply demonstrated by this experiment. The variations in settings, experimental treatments, and dependent variables that might be employed are limited only by the experimenter's imagination. The use of a complex situational test as a device for performing experiments in the behavioral sciences obviously has advantages over field studies from the standpoint of experimental controls, and should be used more extensively as an investigative technique.

References

Abelson, R. P. Sex differences in predictability of college grades. *Educational and Psychological Measurement*, 1952, **12**, 638–644.

Adorno, T. W., Frenkel-Brunswik, E., Levinson, D. J., & Sanford, R. N. *The Authoritarian Personality*. New York: Harper, 1950.

Argyle, M., Gardner, G., & Cioffi, F. Supervisory methods related to productivity, absenteeism and labour turnover. *Human Relations*, 1958, **11**, 23–41.

Aronson, E., & Carlsmith, J. M. Experimentation in social psychology. In G. Lindzey and E. Aronson (Eds.), *The Handbook of Social Psychology*, Vol. II. Reading, Mass.: Addison-Wesley, 1969. Pp. 1–79.

Astin, A. W. An empirical characterization of higher educational institutions. *Journal of Educational Psychology*, 1962, **53**, 224–235.

Barron, F. Complexity-simplicity as a personality dimension. *Journal of Abnormal and Social Psychology*, 1953, **48**, 163–172.

Beaton, A. E. The use of special matrix operators in statistical calculus. Research Bulletin 64–51. Princeton, N.J.: Educational Testing Service, 1964.

Bloxom, B. A note on invariance in three-mode factor analysis. *Psychometrika*, 1968, **33**, 347–350.

Box, G. E. P. A general distribution theory for a class of likelihood criteria. *Biometrika*, 1949, **36**, 317–346.

Bracht, G. H., & Glass, G. V. The external validity of experiments. *American Educational Research Journal*, 1968, **5**, 437–474.

Bray, D. W., & Grant, D. L. The assessment center in the measurement of potential for business management. *Psychological Monographs: General and Applied*, 1966, **80** (17, Whole No. 625).

Brown, R. Models of attitude change. In R. Brown, E. Galanter, E. H. Hess, and G. Mandler (Eds.), *New Directions in Psychology*. New York: Holt, Rinehart and Winston, 1962. Pp. 1–85.

Budner, S. Intolerance of ambiguity as a personality variable. *Journal of Personality*, 1962, **30**, 29–50.

Burket, G. R. A study of reduced rank models for multiple prediction. *Psychometric Mono-graph No. 12*. Richmond, Va.: Wm. Byrd Press, 1964.

Campbell, D. T. Factors relevant to the validity of experiments in social settings. *Psychological Bulletin*, 1957, **54**, 297–312.

Campbell, D. T., & Fiske, D. W. Convergent and discriminant validation by the multitrait-multimethod matrix. *Psychological Bulletin*, 1959, **56**, 81–105.

Campbell, D. T., & Stanley, J. C. *Experimental and Quasi-Experimental Designs for Research*. Chicago: Rand McNally, 1966. [Reprinted from N. L. Gage (Ed.), *Handbook of Research on Teaching*. Chicago: Rand McNally, 1963.]

Carlton, S., & Brault, M. In-Basket Scoring Manual. Research Memorandum 71–13. Princeton, N.J.: Educational Testing Service, 1971.

Carroll, J. B. Biquartimin criterion for rotation to oblique simple structure in factor analysis. *Science*, 1957, **126**, 1114–1115.

Cattell, R. B. *The Description and Measurement of Personality*. New York: World, 1946.

Cattell, R. B. *Personality and Motivation Structure and Measurement*. New York: World, 1957.

Cattell, R. B. Theory of fluid and crystallized intelligence: A critical experiment. *Journal of Educational Psychology*, 1963, **54**, 1–22.

Cattell, R. B. Estimating modulator indices and state liabilities. *Multivariate Behavioral Research*, 1971, **6**, 7–33.

Chapman, R. L., Kennedy, J. L., Newell, A., & Biel, W. C. The Systems Research Laboratory's air-defense experiments. In H. Guetzkow (Ed.), *Simulation in Social Science: Readings*. Englewood Cliffs, N.J.: Prentice-Hall, 1962. Pp. 172–188.

Christie, R. Authoritarianism re-examined. In R. Christie and M. Jahoda (Eds.), *Studies in the Scope and Method of "The Authoritarian Personality."* Glencoe, Ill.: Free Press, 1954. Pp. 123–196.

Cleary, T. A. An individual differences model for multiple regression. *Psychometrika*, 1966, **31**, 215–224.

Cohen, K. J., Cyert, R. M., Dill, W. R., Kuehn, A. A., Miller, M. H., Van Wormer, T. A., & Winters, P. R. The Carnegie Tech management game. *The Journal of Business*, 1960, **33**, 303–321.

Coleman, J. S., *et al. Equality of Educational Opportunity*. Washington, D.C.: U.S. Government Printing Office, 1966.

Comrey, A. L., Pfiffner, J. M., & Beem, H. P. Factors influencing organizational effectiveness: I. The U.S. forest survey. *Personnel Psychology*, 1952, **5**, 307–328.

Corey, S. M. Professed attitudes and actual behavior. *Journal of Educational Psychology*, 1937, **28**, 271–280.

Cronbach, L. J. Response sets and test validity. *Educational and Psychological Measurement*, 1946, **6**, 475–494.

Cronbach, L. J. Further evidence on response sets and test design. *Educational and Psychological Measurement*, 1950, **10**, 3–31.

Cronbach, L. J. The two disciplines of scientific psychology. *American Psychologist*, 1957, **12**, 671–684.

Cronbach, L. J. *Essentials of Psychological Testing*. (2nd ed.), New York: Harper, 1960.

Cronbach, L. J. How can instruction be adapted to individual differences? In R. M. Gagné (Ed.), *Learning and Individual Differences*. Columbus, Ohio: Charles E. Merrill, 1967. Pp. 23–39.

Cronbach, L. J., & Gleser, G. C. Assessing similarity between profiles. *Psychological Bulletin*, 1953, **50**, 456–473.

Cronbach, L. J., & Snow, R. E. *Individual Differences in Learning Ability as a Function of Instructional Variables*. Stanford, Calif.: Stanford University, School of Education, 1969.

Day, R. C., & Hamblin, R. L. Some effects of close and punitive styles of supervision. ONR Contract 81611 Technical Report #8. August 1961. (AD264837).

Dunnette, M. D. A modified model for test validation and selection research. *Journal of Applied Psychology*, 1963, **47**, 317–323.

Edwards, A. L. The relationship between the judged desirability of a trait and the probability that the trait will be endorsed. *Journal of Applied Psychology*, 1953, **37**, 90–93.

Edwards, A. L. *The Social Desirability Variable in Personality Assessment and Research*. New York: Dryden Press, 1957.

Edwards, A. L. *Experimental Design in Psychological Research*. (2nd ed.) New York: Holt, Rinehart and Winston, 1960.

Endler, N. S., Hunt, J. McV., & Rosenstein, A. J. An S-R inventory of anxiousness. *Psychological Monographs*, No. 536, 1962, **76**, No. 17.

Evan, W. M., & Zelditch, M., Jr. A laboratory experiment on bureaucratic authority. *American Sociological Review*, 1961, **26**, 883–893.

Eysenck, H. J. *The Structure of Human Personality*. London: Methuen, 1953 (New York: Wiley).

Eysenck, H. J. *Dynamics of Anxiety and Hysteria*. London: Routledge & Kegan Paul, 1957.

Festinger, L. Behavioral support for attitude change. *Public Opinion Quarterly*, 1964, **28**, 404–417.

Fiedler, F. E. Situational factors related to leadership effectiveness. In E. A. Fleishman (Ed.), *Studies in Personnel and Industrial Psychology*. Homewood, Ill.: Dorsey, 1967. Pp. 426–436. (a)

Fiedler, F. E. *A Theory of Leadership Effectiveness*. New York: McGraw-Hill, 1967. (b)

Findley, W. G., Frederiksen, N., & Saunders, D. R. An analysis of the objectives of an executive-level educational program. Maxwell Air Force Base, Alabama: ARDC, Human Resources Research Institute Technical Research Report No. 22, January 1954 (Contract AF 33(600)-5833).

Fisher, R. A. The use of multiple measurements in taxonomic problems. *Annals of Eugenics*, 1936, **7**, 179–188.

Fleishman, E. A. Predicting advanced levels of proficiency in psychomotor skills. In *Proceedings of the Symposium on Human Engineering*. Washington, D.C.: National Academy of Science, 1956.

Fleishman, E. A., & Hempel, W. E., Jr. Changes in factor structure of a complex psychomotor test as a function of practice. *Psychometrika*, 1954, **19**, 239–252.

Forehand, G. A. Assessments of innovative behavior: Partial criteria for the assessment of executive performance. *Journal of Applied Psychology*, 1963, **47**, 206–213.

Forehand, G. A., & Gilmer, B. von H. Environmental variations in studies of organizational behavior. *Psychological Bulletin*, 1964, **62**, 361–382.

Frederiksen, N. Consistency of performance in simulated situations. ONR Technical Report and Research Bulletin 61-22. Princeton, N.J.: Educational Testing Service, 1961.

Frederiksen, N. Factors in in-basket performance. *Psychological Monographs: General and Applied*, 1962, **76** (22, Whole No. 541). (a)

Frederiksen, N. Proficiency tests for training evaluation. In R. Glaser (Ed.), *Training Research and Education*. Pittsburgh: University of Pittsburgh Press, 1962. Pp. 323–346. (b) [Reprinted by Wiley & Sons (Science Editions), 1965.]

Frederiksen, N. Response set scores as predictors of performance. *Personnel Psychology*, 1965, **18**, 225–244.

Frederiksen, N. Validation of a simulation technique. *Organizational Behavior and Human Performance*, 1966, **1**, 87–109.

Frederiksen, N., & Gilbert, A. C. F. Replication of a study of differential predictability. *Educational and Psychological Measurement*, 1960, **20**, 759–767.

Frederiksen, N., & Gulliksen, H. (Eds.) *Contributions to Mathematical Psychology*. New York: Holt, Rinehart and Winston, 1964.

Frederiksen, N., & Melville, S. D. Differential predictability in the use of test scores. *Educational and Psychological Measurement*, 1954, **14**, 647–656.

Frederiksen, N., & Messick, S. Response set as a measure of personality. *Educational and Psychological Measurement*, 1959, **19**, 137–157.

Frederiksen, N., Saunders, D. R., & Wand, B. The in-basket test. *Psychological Monographs: General and Applied*, 1957, **71** (9, Whole No. 438).

Frederiksen, N., & Schrader, W. B. *Adjustment to College: A Study of 10,000 Veteran and Nonveteran Students in Sixteen American Colleges*. Princeton, N.J.: Educational Testing Service, 1951.

French, J. W., Ekstrom, R., & Price, L. A. *Manual for Kit of Reference Tests for Cognitive Factors*. Princeton, N.J.: Educational Testing Service, 1963.

Freud, S. Libidinal types. *Psychoanalytic Quarterly*, 1932, **1**, 3–6.

Friedman, H. P., & Rubin, J. On some invariant criteria for grouping data. *Journal of the American Statistical Association*, 1967, **62**, 1159–1178.

Gaylord, R. H., & Carroll, J. B. A general approach to the problem of the population control variable. *American Psychologist*, 1948, **3**, 310. (Abstract)

Getzels, J. W., & Jackson, P. W. *Creativity and Intelligence*. New York: Wiley, 1962.

Ghiselli, E. E. The forced-choice technique in self-description. *Personnel Psychology*, 1954, **7**, 201–208.

Ghiselli, E. E. Differentiation of individuals in terms of their predictability. *Journal of Applied Psychology*, 1956, **40**, 374–377.

Ghiselli, E. E. The prediction of predictability. *Educational and Psychological Measurement*, 1960, **20**, 3–8.

Gough, H. G., & Sanford, R. N. Rigidity as a psychological variable. Unpublished manuscript, University of California Institute of Personality Assessment and Research, 1952.

Graen, G., Alvares, K., Orris, J. B., & Martella, J. A. Contingency model of leadership effectiveness: Antecedent and evidential results. *Psychological Bulletin*, 1970, **74**, 285–296.

Grayson, H. M. A psychological admissions testing program and manual. Los Angeles: Veterans Administration Center Neuropsychiatric Hospital, 1951.

Green, B. F. Attitude measurement. In D. N. Jackson and S. Messick (Eds.), *Problems in Human Assessment*. New York: McGraw-Hill, 1967. Pp. 725–736.

Griffiths, D. E. *Administrative Theory*. New York: Appleton-Century-Crofts, 1959.

Guetzkow, H. A use of simulation in the study of inter-nation relations. *Behavioral Science*, 1959, **4**, 183–191.

Guetzkow, H. (Ed.) *Simulation in Social Science: Readings*. Englewood Cliffs, N.J.: Prentice-Hall, 1962.

Guilford, J. P. The structure of intellect. *Psychological Bulletin*, 1956, **53**, 267–293.

Guilford, J. P. *Personality*. New York: McGraw-Hill, 1959.

Guilford, J. P. *The Nature of Human Intelligence*. New York: McGraw-Hill, 1967.

Gulliksen, H., & Wilks, S. S. Regression tests for several samples. *Psychometrika*, 1950, **15**, 91–114.

Guttman, L. The structure of interrelations among intelligence tests. In *Proceedings of the 1964 Invitational Conference on Testing Problems*. Princeton, N.J.: Educational Testing Service, 1965. Pp. 25–36.

Guttman, L., & Schlesinger, I. M. A faceted definition of intelligence. *Scripta Hierosolymitana: Studies in Psychology*. Jerusalem, Israel: The Hebrew University, 1965. Pp. 166–181.

Harris, C. W. (Ed.) *Problems in Measuring Change*. Madison: University of Wisconsin Press, 1963.

Helm, C. Simulation models for psychometric theories. In *Proceedings of the American Federation of Information Processing Societies*, Vol. 27, Part 1. Washington, D.C.: Spartan Books, 1965.

Hemphill, J. K. *Leader Behavior Description*. Columbus, Ohio: Personnel Research Board, Ohio State University, 1950.

Hemphill, J. K. Administration as problem solving. In A. W. Halpin (Ed.), *Administrative Theory in Education*. Chicago: Midwest Administration Center, University of Chicago, 1958.

Hemphill, J. K. Job descriptions for executives. *Harvard Business Review*, 1959, **37**, 55–67.

Hemphill, J. K., Griffiths, D. E., & Frederiksen, N. *Administrative Performance and Personality: A Study of the Principal in a Simulated Elementary School*. New York: Columbia University, Teachers College Bureau of Publications, 1962.

Hendrickson, A. E., & White, P. O. Promax: A quick method for rotation to oblique simple structure. *British Journal of Statistical Psychology*, 1964, **17**, 65–70.

Heron, A. A two-part personality measure for use as a research criterion. *British Journal of Psychology*, 1956, **47**, 243–251.

Hoepfner, R., & Klein, S. P. Elementary School Evaluation Kit. Booklet IV. Collecting Information. Los Angeles: University of California, 1970.

Hoffman, E. L., & Tucker, L. R. Three-way factor analysis of a multitrait-multimethod matrix. ONR Technical Report, Contract Nonr 1834 (39). Urbana: University of Illinois, 1964.

Jackson, D. N., Messick, S., & Myers, C. T. Evaluation of group and individual forms of embedded-figures measures of field-independence. *Educational and Psychological Measurement*, 1964, **24**, 177–192.

Jacobs, P. I., Maier, M. H., & Stolurow, L. M. *A Guide to Evaluating Self-Instructional Programs*. New York: Holt, Rinehart and Winston, 1966.

Jensen, A. R. How much can we boost IQ and scholastic achievement? *Harvard Educational Review*, 1969, **39**, 1–123.

Johnson, P. O., & Neyman, J. Tests of certain linear hypotheses and their application to some educational problems. *Statistical Research Memoirs*, University of London, 1936, **1**, 57–93.

Johnson, S. C. Hierarchical clustering schemes. *Psychometrika*, 1967, **32**, 241–254.

Jung, C. G. *Psychological Types*. New York: Harcourt, Brace, 1922.

Kahn, R. L., Wolfe, D. M., Quinn, R. P., Snoek, J. D., & Rosenthal, R. A. *Organizational Stress: Studies in Role Conflict and Ambiguity*. New York: Wiley, 1964.

Katz, D., Maccoby, N., & Morse, N. *Productivity, Supervision and Morale in an Office Situation. Part 1*. Ann Arbor, Mich. (Survey Research Center): Darel Press, 1950.

Klein, S. P., Frederiksen, N., & Evans, F. R. Anxiety and learning to formulate hypotheses. *Journal of Educational Psychology*, 1969, **60**, 465–475.

Kogan, N., & Wallach, M. A. *Risk Taking: A Study in Cognition and Personality*. New York: Holt, Rinehart and Winston, 1964.

Krause, M. S. Use of social situations for research purposes. *American Psychologist*, 1970, **25**, 748–753.

Kropp, R. P., Nelson, W. H., & King, F. J. Identification and definition of subject-matter content variables related to human aptitudes. Report of Cooperative Research Project No. 2914. Tallahassee, Fla.: Florida State University, 1967.

Kruskal, J. B. Multidimensional scaling by optimizing goodness of fit to a nonmetric hypothesis. *Psychometrika*, 1964, **29**, 1–27.

LaPiere, R. T. Attitudes vs. actions. *Social Forces*, 1934, **14**, 230–237.

Levin, J. Three-mode factor analysis. *Psychological Bulletin*, 1965, **64** (6), 442–452.

Likert, R. A technique for the measurement of attitudes. *Archives of Psychology*, 1932, **22**, No. 140.

Lilly, R. S. A developmental study of the semantic differential. ETS Research Bulletin 65-28 and doctoral dissertation, Princeton University, Princeton, N.J.: Educational Testing Service, 1965.

Lopez, F. M., Jr. *Evaluating Executive Decision Making: The In-Basket Technique*. New York: American Management Association, 1966.

Mahalanobis, P. C. On the generalized distance in statistics. *Proceedings of the National Institute for Science, India*, 1936, **12**, 48–58.

Maier, M. H., & Jacobs, P. I. Programed learning—some recommendations and results. *Bulletin of the National Association of Secondary School Principals*, 1964, **48**, 242–255.

March, J. G., & Simon, H. A. *Organizations*. New York: Wiley, 1958.

McQuitty, L. L. Agreement analysis: Classifying persons by predominant patterns of responses. *British Journal of Statistical Psychology*, 1956, **9**, 5–16.

Meltzer, L. Scientific productivity in organizational settings. *Journal of Social Issues*, 1956, **12**, 32–40.

Messick, S. Dimensions of social desirability. *Journal of Consulting Psychology*, 1960, **24**, 279–287.

Messick, S., & Jackson, D. N. Acquiescence and the factorial interpretation of the MMPI. *Psychological Bulletin*, 1961, **58**, 299–304.

Milgram, S. Behavioral study of obedience. *Journal of Abnormal and Social Psychology*, 1963, **67**, 371–378.

Norman, W. T. Toward an adequate taxonomy of personality attributes: Replicated factor structures in peer nomination personality ratings. *Journal of Abnormal and Social Psychology*, 1963, **66**, 574–583.

Orne, M. On the social psychology of the psychological experiment: With particular reference to demand characteristics and their implications. *American Psychologist*, 1962, **17**, 776–783.

Osgood, C. E., & Suci, G. A measure of relation determined by both mean difference and profile information. *Psychological Bulletin*, 1952, **49**, 251–262.

Pace, C. R. The measurement of college environments. In R. Tagiuri and G. H. Litwin (Eds.), *Organizational Climate: Explorations of a Concept*. Boston: Graduate School of Business Administration, Harvard University, 1968. Pp. 129–147.

Pearson, K. On the coefficient of racial likeness. *Biometrika*, 1926, **18**, 105–117.

Pelz, D. Motivation of the engineering and research specialist. *American Management Association, General Management Series*, 1957, No. 186, 25–46.

Rao, C. R. The utilization of multiple measurements in problems of biological classification. *Journal of the Royal Statistical Society*, Series A, 1948, **103**, 159–203.

Riecken, H. W. A program for research on experiments in social psychology. In N. F. Washburne (Ed.), *Decision, Values, and Groups*, Vol. 2. New York: Pergamon Press, 1962.

Rock, D. A., Barone, J. L., & Linn, R. L. A Fortran computer program for a moderated stepwise prediction system. *Educational and Psychological Measurement*, 1967, **27**, 709–713.

Rosner, M. M. Administrative controls and innovation. *Behavioral Science*, 1968, **13**, 36–43.

Rubin, J. Optimal classification into groups: An approach for solving the taxonomy problem. *Journal of Theoretical Biology*, 1967, **15**, 103–144.

Saunders, D. R. The moderator variable as a useful tool in prediction. In *Proceedings of the 1954 Invitational Conference on Testing Problems*. Princeton, N.J.: Educational Testing Service, 1955. (a)

Saunders, D. R. Some preliminary interpretive material for the PRI. Research Memorandum 55-15. Princeton, N.J.: Educational Testing Service, 1955. (b)

Saunders, D. R. Moderator variables in prediction. *Educational and Psychological Measurement*, 1956, **16**, 209–222.

Saunders, D. R. The contribution of communality estimation to the achievement of factorial invariance, with special reference to the MMPI. Research Bulletin 60-5. Princeton, N.J.: Educational Testing Service, 1960.

Schein, E. H. *Organizational Psychology*. Englewood Cliffs, N.J.: Prentice-Hall, 1965.

Sells, S. B. An interactionist looks at the environment. *American Psychologist*, 1963, **18**, 696–702. (a)

Sells, S. B. (Ed.) *Stimulus Determinants of Behavior*. New York: Ronald, 1963. (b)

Shepard, R. N. The analysis of proximities: Multidimensional scaling with an unknown distance function I. *Psychometrika*, 1962, **27**, 125–140.

Sherif, M., & Sherif, C. W. *An Outline of Social Psychology*. (Rev. ed.) New York: Harper, 1956.

Smith, E. E. The effects of clear and unclear roll expectations on group productivity and defensiveness. *Journal of Abnormal and Social Psychology*, 1957, **55**, 213–217.

Snow, R. E., Tiffin, J., & Seibert, W. F. Individual differences and instructional film effects. *Journal of Educational Psychology*, 1965, **56**, 315–326.

Sokal, R. R., & Sneath, P. H. A. *Principles of Numerical Taxonomy*. San Francisco: Freeman, 1963.

Spranger, E. *Types of Men: The Psychology and Ethics of Personality*. New York: Steckert, 1928.

Steiner, I. D., & Dodge, J. S. Interpersonal perception and role structure as determinants of group and individual efficiency. *Human Relations*, 1956, **9**, 467–480.

Stricker, L. J. Compulsivity as a moderator variable: A replication and extension. *Journal of Applied Psychology*, 1966, **50**, 331–335.

Stricker, L. J. The true deceiver. *Psychological Bulletin*, 1967, **68**, 13–20.

Tagiuri, R. (Ed.) *Research Needs in Executive Selection*. Boston: Graduate School of Business Administration, Harvard University, 1961.

Tagiuri, R. Research in executive selection: Some needed directions of effort. In R. Tagiuri (Ed.), *Research Needs in Executive Selection*. Boston: Graduate School of Business Administration, Harvard University, 1961. Pp. 31–44.

Taylor, J. A. A personality scale of manifest anxiety. *Journal of Abnormal and Social Psychology*, 1953, **48**, 285–290.

Taylor, J. A. Drive theory and manifest anxiety. *Psychological Bulletin*, 1956, **53**, 303–320.

Thurstone, L. L. Attitudes can be measured. *American Journal of Sociology*, 1928, **33**, 529–554.

Thurstone, L. L. Primary mental abilities. *Psychometric Monographs*, 1938, No. 1.

Thurstone, L. L., & Chave, E. J. *The Measurement of Attitude*. Chicago: University of Chicago Press, 1929.

True, D. L., & Matson, R. G. Cluster analysis and multidimensional scaling of archeological sites in northern Chile. *Science*, 1970, **169**, 1201–1203.

Tryon, R. C., & Bailey, D. E. The BC TRY computer system of cluster and factor analysis. *Multivariate Behavioral Research*, 1966, **1**, 95–111.

Tucker, L. R. Implications of factor analysis of three-way matrices for measurement of change. In C. W. Harris (Ed.), *Problems in Measuring Change*. Madison: University of Wisconsin Press, 1963. Pp. 122–137.

Tucker, L. R. The extension of factor analysis to three-dimensional matrices. In N. Frederiksen and H. Gulliksen (Eds.), *Contributions to Mathematical Psychology*. New York: Holt, Rinehart and Winston, 1964. Pp. 109–127.

Tucker, L. R. Experiments in multi-mode factor analysis. In *Proceedings of the 1964 Invitational Conference on Testing Problems*. Princeton, N.J.: Educational Testing Service, 1965. Pp. 46–57.

Tucker, L. R. Some mathematical notes on three-mode factor analysis. *Psychometrika*, 1966, **31**, 279–311.

Vroom, V. H. Some personality determinants of the effects of participation. *Journal of Abnormal and Social Psychology*, 1959, **59**, 322–327.

Vroom, V. H. Some personality determinants of the effects of participation. Englewood Cliffs, N.J.: Prentice-Hall, 1960.

Vroom, V. H. *Work and Motivation*. New York: Wiley, 1964.

Vroom, V. H. Industrial social psychology. In G. Lindzey and E. Aronson (Eds.), *The Handbook of Social Psychology*, Vol. V. Reading, Mass.: Addison-Wesley, 1969. Pp. 196–268.

Ward, J. H., Jr. Hierarchical grouping to optimize an objective function. *Journal of the American Statistical Association*, 1963, **58**, 236–244.

Ward, L. B. The Business In-Basket Test: A method of assessing certain administrative skills. Research Bulletin 59-8. Princeton, N.J.: Educational Testing Service, 1959.

Weber, M. Bureaucracy. In *From Max Weber: Essays in Sociology*. Translated and edited by H. H Gerth and C. W. Mills. New York: Oxford University Press, 1946.

Wicker, F. W. A scaling study of synesthetic thinking. ETS Research Bulletin 66-25 and doctoral dissertation, Princeton University. Princeton, N.J.: Educational Testing

Wicker, F. W. (*Continued*)
   Service, 1966. [Published in part in: Mapping the intersensory regions of perceptual space. *American Journal of Psychology*, 1968, **81**, 178–188.]
Witkin, H. A., Dyk, R. B., Faterson, H. F., Goodenough, D. R., & Karp, S. A. *Psychological Differentiation*. New York: Wiley, 1962.
Wolff, W. M. Certainty: generality and relation to manifest anxiety. *Journal of Abnormal and Social Psychology*, 1958, **50**, 59–64.
Woodworth, R. S. *Psychology*. (3rd ed.) New York: Henry Holt, 1934.

APPENDIX A

Group Principal Components Factor Analysis

Since the number of predictor variables was too large to handle effectively, the number of variables was reduced by a group principal components method. This method uses *a priori* information about the interrelationships among variables to guide in the identification of interpretable factors. The data analyst divides his variables into subsets, each of which is believed to correspond to a factor. The factors within any single set are orthogonal, but the relationship among sets of factors may be oblique. The method was due to Herbert Gerjuoy, who performed the analysis.

The procedure can be described in several steps.

(1) Compute a correlation matrix of all of the variables included in the analysis.

(2) Decide which subsets of the variables should represent a single factor. This was initially done on the basis of a conventional principal components analysis.

(3) Perform a principal components analysis on each subset of variables. (This factoring was done both with unities in the diagonal and with estimates of communality. The solution with unities in the diagonal seemed preferable and was used.)

(4) Decide on the number of factors in each subset. Hopefully, each set of variables should have one factor, thus be of unit rank. In the case of more than one factor, the set is divided into sub-subsets and Step (3) repeated with each. If, however, the variables in a subset do not break naturally into sub-subsets, then all significant factors are retained. Factors within a subset are mutually orthogonal.

(5) Compute the intercorrelations of the factors and the correlations between these factors and all of the original variables.
(6) If the solution seems satisfactory, compute individual factor scores; if not, then perform Step (2) again.

Within-Group Covariance Factor Analysis

A factor analysis was performed in order to reduce the number of criterion variables to a much smaller number of interpretable factors. Ordinary factor analytic methods were not appropriate because of the need to find a single set of factors which could be applied to all four treatment groups while temporarily disregarding differences in the means of factor scores. Differences in relationships among the factors for different treatment groups were of particular interest. The most appropriate factor analytic technique was an adaptation of the within-group factor analysis developed by Tucker and Messick.

The technique is justified as follows: Since the individual subjects were assigned to treatment groups in an unbiased manner, there is no reason to expect differences among the four groups, with respect to their means, standard deviations, intercorrelations, or factor structure, except for experimental treatments and sampling fluctuations. Differences in the means of factor scores are of course of considerable interest, but a prior question reflects importantly on the comparisons of means: do the factors have the same meaning for the different treatments? If a factor had a different meaning under one treatment condition than under another, a comparison of means would be dubious. We, therefore, first wish to see if there is a common factor structure for the four groups.

First, we set the means of the 55 criterion variables and of the factor scores (which are linear combinations of the 55 original variables) to zero. This in effect partialed out any effect of the treatments on the means of the four groups. Now, if the treatments had no effect at all, or an effect only on the means, then the deviations of the raw or factor scores from the group means would have the same variances and covariances (but for sampling error) in the four groups. The sum of these matrices, weighted by group sample size, is the within-group covariance matrix. This matrix was standardized in such a way that the diagonal elements were unity. In fact, this matrix is the equivalent of a partial correlation matrix, with the linear effect of the treatments removed.

This correlation matrix was then factor analyzed by the principal components method and rotated to an oblique structure. Unities were used in the diagonal, since our aim was prediction of as much criterion variance as possible, rather than common variance only. A variance/covariance matrix of factor scores was computed for each group.

These group factor variance/covariance matrices were then examined, and the results are discussed in Chapter 8. If the factor structure were the same in the four groups, then these matrices would be identity matrices, but for sampling variation.

The procedure used for this analysis is as follows:

(1) Compute a cross-products matrix for each group.
(2) Convert the cross-products matrix into a covariance matrix.
(3) Compute a within-group covariance matrix

$$W = (n_1C_1 + n_2C_2 + n_3C_3 + n_4C_4)/N$$

where n_k is one less than the number of persons in the kth group and C_k is the covariance matrix of that group, and $N = \Sigma_k n_k$.

(4) Standardize the matrix by dividing the i,j^{th} element by the square root of the ii^{th} and jj^{th} diagonal elements. Call this matrix R.
(5) Factor the matrix R by principal components method.
(6) Decide on the number of factors.
(7) Rotate the factors to oblique simple structure.
(8) Compute a "composite" score for each subject on each factor.
(9) Compute variance/covariance matrix of composite scores for each treatment group.

Department of Commerce In-Basket B

(This version of In-Basket B contains climate items for Rules and Global Supervision climates.)

Item 1 Appointment Calendar

A P R I L   1 9 6 5

Sunday	Monday	Tuesday	Wednesday	Thursday	Friday	Saturday
				1	2	3
4	5	6	7	8	9	10
11	12	13	14	15	16 GOOD FRIDAY	17
18	19	20	21	22	23	24
25	26	27	28	29	30	

MAY 1965

Sunday	Monday	Tuesday	Wednesday	Thursday	Friday	Saturday
						1
2	3	4	5	6	7	8
9	10	11	12	13	14	15
16	17	18	19	20	21	22
MEMORIAL DAY 23/30	24/31	25	26	27	28	29

281

Item 2

STATE OF CALIFORNIA

OFFICE MEMO

Date __April 9, 1965__

To_____ Art Dodd

From_____ Mary Staffer

Subject_____ Attendance at Training Sessions

I understand you will be in your office this Sunday.
So, rather than going around you, I'll leave this
problem for you.

I have just received a telphone call from Jay Capitola,
saying that Walt Union is not going to be able to go to
the Health Benefit training session. He said, "We have
too much other work to be done because of our
reorganization and because of workload. So Walt can no
longer serve, nor can anyone in my region serve. Since
this is personnel work, your office should handle it."

I have asked your secretary to attach a copy of
Mr. Veep's Memo of March 1, 1965.

Please advise.

STD FORM 100

CALIFORNIA DEPARTMENT OF COMMERCE

California
FIRST
In Population

DATE: March 1, 1965

MEMO TO: Frank Fields

FROM: John Veep

SUBJECT: Health Benefit Program

As you know, the state recently put into effect the new Health Benefit Program. Under this program it will be necessary to have one employee in each Region serve as the Assistant Health Benefit Officer for that division. As per your nominations, the following are named as Assistant Health Benefit Officers for the Field Service Division.

    Walt Union, Valley Region
    Jack Tarr, Coast Region
    Jose Olvera, Southern Region

Procedures for initial sign up of employees under the new program will be set forth by the Personnel Section. The Assistant Health Benefit Officers are to attend a training session explaining the new program to be conducted by the Retirement System. This program is to be held in the Auditorium of the Employment Building on Tuesday, April 13, 1965.

The Chief of Division of Administration, Mary Staffer, will have responsibility for coordination of the program.

283

Item 3

STATE OF CALIFORNIA

OFFICE MEMO

Date_____

To_____

From_____

Subject_____

Frank –

Unless you tell me you object, I'm going to send hot items, of which the attached is an example, directly to you.

If the length of time it takes to get a reply out of Jay is any guage, he doesn't put his finger in his inbasket until all the material therein has reached room temperature.

Ray

STD FORM 100

284

CALIFORNIA DEPARTMENT OF COMMERCE

MEMO TO: Frank Fields, Chief Division of   **DATE:** April 7, 1965
              Field Services
FROM: Ray Loupe, Chicago Office Manager

SUBJECT: Approval of $250 expenditure.

      The Electronic Division of the Delta-Y Corporation is going to build a new manufacturing plant west of the Rockies. This plant will cost between 1-1/4 and 1-1/2 million dollars and will employ between 500 and 600 people.

      My company contact informs me that the company has narrowed the choice to two sites, one in California the other in Arizona. Walton of the Sacramento Chamber of Commerce called me last week to thank me for the work I had done and to tell me that the company appeared ready to buy a 14 acre site in Sacramento County.

      Yesterday a representative of the company asked if I could supply data on Illinois (location of company's only present electronics plant) comparable to the data we supplied in Delta-Y Report 2A. I said that I'd check to see what Illinois data was available. I knew that if we had the asked-for-data it would have been in Report 2A, so I called the Industrial Planning and Development Division of the Illinois Department of Registration and Education and found that they have the raw data on cards and tape and that we can obtain a print-out for $250 (cost of set up and running time).

      The company appears to be in the middle of making a series of detailed comparisons -- probably the two sites remaining in the running are neck and neck.

      Continued good service on our part could tip the scale in favor of California.

cc:Jay Capitola

I can get the info. to Delta-Y within one week of their request -- if I receive the go-ahead by Mon P.M.

                  Ray

California
FIRST
In Population

CALIFORNIA DEPARTMENT OF COMMERCE

MEMO TO: Art Dodd   **DATE:** April 9, 1965

FROM: John Veep

SUBJECT: Request to reinstate Mike Johnson.

Last week Sellers submitted a memorandum to Administrative Services Division in which he inquired about the possibility of reinstating Mike Johnson, a former Sr. B.D.A. in Field Services Division. This memo is to inform you of the action taken on this request and to remind you that in the future, whenever an individual being considered for reinstatement is a former employee of your division, you will be asked to participate in the reinstatement determination.

Previous to coming to work for us Johnson was employed as a B.D.A. with San Francisco Port Authority. We appointed him as a Sr. B.D.A. in August 1962. Johnson resigned in November of 1963 in order to accept a job in private industry. This job was eliminated in a reorganization following a recent merger.

While he was employed by the Department, Johnson was most noteworthy for his continual preference for generating his own blue sky approaches to assignments -- rather than following established standards and authorized procedures. While he was often quite ingenious and on occasion got the job done quite well, most of the time he left a broad wake of turmoil and confusion. The request for reinstatement was denied.

Geniuses who will both work within a given framework and submit suggestions for changing the framework through channels -- we can use.

Geniuses who continually remake the framework without authorization -- we can do without.

CALIFORNIA DEPARTMENT OF COMMERCE

California
FIRST
In Population

MEMO TO: All Division and Bureau Chiefs   **DATE:** April 9, 1965

FROM: John Veep

SUBJECT: Functional Time Reporting.

It has been pointed out by several of you that it is impractical for division and bureau heads to distribute their time spent on supervision among the various functions delineated on the functional time report form. As individuals at the division bureau head level should be devoting a large percentage of their time to general supervisory activities--guiding, planning, and serving as a consultant to their staffs--rather than themselves performing production functions, the following modification of the time report appears to be more in accord with out actual work situation. For division and bureau heads only, Section 11 on the functional time report form should be changed to "General Supervision." Only time worked directly on operational projects is to be recorded in the other categories.

JV:MS

287

Item 6

Art Dodd

April 9, 1965

Mr. David E. Rabb, Manager
Industrial Commercial Department
Fullerton Chamber of Commerce
219 East Commonwealth Avenue
Fullerton, California

Dear Mr. Rabb:

      Mr. Apex has asked that I write you about your letter of the 5th to him concerning services of the Department of Commerce to communities desiring to develop action programs to attract new business and industry.

      As part of an accelerated economic development program, the Agency is preparing a comprehensive publication called "California Profit Plus" designed to attract new industries and stimulate expansion of existing ones. This publication will present California's resources available for profit opportunities by stressing "cost of doing business" factors.

      Another closely related part of that accelerated program will be our counseling service to communities that wish to relate and gear their development approach and activities to this "profit opportunities" publication by preparing similar type local information to more effectively service their industrial inquiries. Additional counseling services of the Department in helping communities further develop their economy are

    1. Assistance in identifying community development problems, evaluating present activities, and formulating specific priority development activities or projects.

    2. Assistance on special projects or problems pertaining to the attraction of a particular industry.

    3. Assistance in establishing a local development company as a tool to aid in the attraction of new industry or expansion of existing ones.

    4. Serve as liaison contact with other state agencies on a specific problem affecting economic development of an area.

    5. Assistance in helping local organizations and industries consider the possibilities for foreign export of products now manufactured in the area and not presently exported.

      Mr. Ralph Chavez, Southern Regional Manager, in the State Building at 217 West 1st Street, Los Angeles, Telephone 620-2970, will be glad to discuss the services of the Department with you, if you desire.

                  Sincerely,

                  ORA SELLERS
                  Chief, Economic Development Division

OS:aj
cc:George Apex
    Art Dodd
    Ralph Chavez

STATE OF CALIFORNIA

OFFICE MEMO

Date__ April 7, 1965 __

To (Frank Fields,) Herb Bay, Ralph Chavez, Jay Capitola

From_ Alden Bee _

Subject__ Immediate campaign to attract new companies to California and encourage expansion of existing companies. ____

Please review critically the attached proposed immediate action plan for "attracting new companies to California and encouraging expansion of existing companies." The members of the task force which developed this proposal are: Roy Steel, task force leader; Alden Bee, F.S.D. representative; Lynn Rust, Econ. Develop. Div. representative.

Comments may be written on the copy of the proposal or on separate sheets of paper which are then attached to the proposal. Two weeks from today's date the task force will meet for the purpose of reviewing the suggestions received from the various divisions and developing the draft to be submitted to the Director. All comments and suggestions should be submitted to me within the next ten days.

A first draft of the long range action plan will be ready for division review within six weeks.

STD FORM 100

Rough Draft

       With necessity to create 240,000 new jobs annually to sustain yearly 600,000 population increase, it is proposed Department of Commerce immediately initiate vigorous campaign to attract investment in new and expanded enterprises. Campaign will include two immediate actions:

A. As a first step in series of aids to business locations, there is proposed for national and international distribution, a quality publication, California Profit Plus, which briefly but concisely depicts California profit advantages and resources.

B. Prearranged meetings throughout the United States and major foreign cities by Governor and leading California businessmen to discuss with interested responding company executives profit advantages from California business locations.

California Profit Plus

Publication is primarily for company senior executives responsible for plant location, with minimum narrative and statistics and liberal use of such visual aids as charts and maps to depict California profit advantages and resources:

1. 1,000 copies first minimum printing with type to be held by printer for production of sections and additional complete copies.

2. Less than 100 pages with each major subject outlined in appropriate section.

3. Folio size, 10 x 14 inches.

4. Soft cover; quality paper stock.

5. All elements carefully co-ordinated and integrated, including art, composition, copy, etc. to assure excellence.

6. First 1,000 copies estimated to cost $5,300 (including $1,000 for art costs and $4,300 for composition and printing). Each 500 copies thereafter could be produced at estimated cost of $500.

Contents of <u>California Profit Plus</u> will include four major divisions:

1. Orientation.

2. Markets.

3. Cost Factors.

4. Environment.

Four major divisions will outline in 15 sections California plant location factors:

1. <u>Orientation</u>:

    <u>Part I</u>   - Location, history, geography, topagraphy, meteorological climate.

2. <u>Markets</u>:

    <u>Part II</u> - Markets -- California, regional, national, - world wide - consumer, industrial.

3. <u>Cost Factors</u>:

    <u>Part III</u> - Water -- Existing and planned distribution.

    <u>Part IV</u> - Raw Materials - Agriculture, fish, forests, minerals (metals, non-metals, gas, oil).

    <u>Part V</u>   - Manufacturers -- Service and Supply complexes.

    <u>Part VI</u> - Transportation -- Airlines, airports, railroads, water, ports, trucks, freeways.

    <u>Part VII</u> - Communications -- Newspapers, radio, television, telephone, telegraph, and others.

    <u>Part VIII</u> - Labor Force -- Availability, concentration, skills, training programs, productivity, rates (statewide - regional variations), disability insurance, unemployment compensation, workmen compensation, laws, regulations, safety codes, work stoppages, unions, total costs.

    <u>Part IX</u> - Taxes and Services -- Digest and comparisons.

Part X   - Industrial Land -- Sites, buildings, industrial parks, zoning,
            building codes.

Part XI   - Financing -- Capital and credit, banks, local development
            companies, investment brokers, insurance companies, saving and
            loan associations, etc.

Part XII - Fuel, Energy, and Power -- Atomic, Electricity, Gas, Oil, others.

4. Environment:

Part XIII - Culture, education, government services, medical, public health,
            recreation.

Part XIV - Horizons -- Future.

Part XV   - Index to principle sources of information.

Distribution of California Profit Plus will include mailing to selected
companies with letter from Governor. (Major utilities and Chambers of Commerce
have offered select prospect lists from their files). Follow-up communications
will be made by Department.

As the second major part of the campaign, it is proposed select group of
California businessmen accompany Governor to out-of-state metropolitan centers to
present "California Story" at invitational meetings with leading Industrialists
who have responded with interest in California locations. Foreign contacts
similarly could be undertaken to stimulate world markets for California products,
for example, "California Week in Stockholm" June 15-22 of last year.

CALIFORNIA DEPARTMENT OF COMMERCE

DATE: April 5, 1965

MEMO TO: Frank Fields

FROM: Herb Bay

SUBJECT: Clarification of Duties.

There seems to be a definite overlapping of duties between the Bureau of Local Liaison and the tasks assigned to my Planning and Development Section. I would appreciate it if you and I could get together and discuss where the duties assigned to my Planning and Development Section end and those of Charlie Middleman's Bureau begin.

During recent months, members of the Bureau of Local Liaison have been advising county personnel on how our program is supposed to be carried out. I am under the impression that this is not one of their functions, as Middleman's Bureau is responsible for developing statewide planning standards and for specifically assigned, joint, state-local Planning and Development projects only.

Of course, the program that we are carrying out and those of other units are bound to overlap at times, but it's my opinion that the day-to-day liaison between the Department and county and city people should be carried out through the field offices. If I am wrong about this, we have been traveling on the wrong track for a long time.

I've discussed the situation with Charlie more than once, and we don't seem to be able to see eye-to-eye about the duties of our units and the status of the men assigned to Planning and Development work in the field offices. I'd like to get it straight.

HAB:sf

Item 9

California FIRST in Population

CALIFORNIA DEPARTMENT OF COMMERCE

MEMO TO: Frank Fields   **DATE:** April 5, 1965

FROM: Herb Bay

SUBJECT: Export Trade Promotion.

Keith Giant, Trade Specialist in this region, is convinced that the statewide program for stimulating export trade being developed by the Bureau of Business Services and Trade will backfire on us unless it is accompanied by a full scale educational program for all businesses entering the export field. To date, he hasn't been able to convince Don Solon that we need to do anything more than indicate our willingness to help any business that requests aid regarding particular export sales problems.

Keith states (and I concur) that as a bare minimum we should publish and distribute in conjunction with the promotional program a "Do's and Don'ts of Export Sales" -- a set of basic tenets (example attached).

Will you see what you can do to blast Solon out of his position. My motives in this case are far from pure -- all of us in the field will get it seven ways from Sunday from each business that fails in its attempt to enter the export field.

HAB:sf

294

Basic export sales tenets.

1. Explore and analyze the market thoroughly with respect to your own particular product; (use rifle approach rather than shotgun technique.)

2. Take full advantage of U.S. Foreign Service and U.S. Department of Commerce—an extensive volume of information is available through these agencies. Commercial departments of U.S. and foreign banks or previously established U.S. Firms are also valuable.

3. Make early and adequate provision for fully satisfactory maintenance, repair, and sales service.

4. Use language of country as fully as possible. Salesmen should be fluent; sales literature, maintenance and operating manuals should be in the native tongue.

5. Wherever possible use foreign materials for local appeal and easier acceptance. Avoid agent and sub-agent arrangements because of high sales mark up.

6. As far as possible adapt or modify products to meet domestic preferences and to conform to local custom or use.

7. Make use of trade fairs and exhibits. In Europe these are highly important direct sales activities and quite different from the usual U.S. exhibitions.

8. Don't underestimate the sales effort required to be successful in foreign markets; use every sales tool available.

Item 10

CALIFORNIA DEPARTMENT OF COMMERCE

MEMO TO: Frank Fields   **DATE:** April 6, 1965

FROM: Ora Sellers

SUBJECT: Participation in development of essential new publications.

The Economic Development Division has primary responsibility for the preparation
of reports outlining the Department's contribution and role with respect to

Topic	Project Supervisor
Increasing utilization of California raw materials and technical services	Roy Steel
Attracting more tourists to California	Fred Jett
Increasing California exports and foreign trade	Don Solon
Developing economic opportunities for women	Don Solon
Special aids to small business	Don Solon
Business information for California Executives	Don Solon
Automation	Don Solon

These reports should be ready for publication within the year. We want to obtain
as wide a spectrum of viewpoints as possible and yet meet deadlines and keep costs
down. To these ends we would like you to designate one individual for each topic
to be your division representative on the task force preparing the report.

The representative would have the responsibility of polling other employees in
your division as well as participating in the planning and preparation of the
actual report. It is estimated that .1 of a man-year per topic or a total of .7
of a man-year will be required. There is considerable leeway as to the
scheduling of this participation; this can be worked out on an individual by
individual basis.

As we want to start as soon as possible, I would appreciate receiving your list
of representatives by the end of this month.

OS:aj

Item 11

```
┌─────────────────────────────┐
│  ROUTE SLIP                 │
│  TO:  Mr. Dodd              │
│  ───────────────────────    │
│                             │
│  FROM: ──────────────────── │
│                    (DATE)   │
│  CALIFORNIA STATE DEPARTMENT OF COMMERCE │
│  REMARKS:                   │
│    The attachment referred to in │
│  this letter did not arrive with │
│  the letter.                │
│      I called Mr. Capitola's │
│  secretary. She will send a │
│  copy of the folder as soon as │
│  she can obtain one from    │
│  Mr. Capitola.    Marjorie  │
│  CSDC 190/9/59              │
└─────────────────────────────┘
```

To: Jay Capitola
     701 O Street
     Sacramento, California

(check as many boxes as appropriate)

☐ Enroll me as a member of the Statewide Conference of State and
   Local Economic Development Professional Employees

   ☐ enclosed is $10.00; payment of annual dues in full

   ☐ initiate appropriate payroll deduction

☐ Have a representative call on me

──
         (Time)   (Date)

I am particularly interested in obtaining more information regarding

──

──

──

                         (Signature)   (Date)

Address to which notices   ──────────────────────────────
should be sent: ──────────────────────────────

297

Mr. Arthur Dodd   April 5, 1965
Chief, Field Services Division
Department of Commerce

Dear Mr. Dodd:

          As Chairman of the Statewide Conference of State and Local
Economic Development Professional Employees, may I take this
opportunity to welcome you on your return to the profession and
to extend an invitation for you to join the Sacramento Area Chapter
of the Statewide Conference.

          The folder attached sets forth the Conterence objectives
and by-laws.

          Sacramento Chapter meetings are held on the second Monday
of the month at the Elbo Bender, 6:30 to 9:00 p.m. -- cocktails,
dinner, business meeting, speaker. The speaker for the April 12th
meeting will be R. Permin Everett, Chief of Standards and Surveys
Division of the State Personnel Board. Mr. Everetts' topic is "The
S.P.B. Salary Survey Process." Annual Statewide Conference is held
on three consecutive days starting the third Saturday in June -- on
odd numbered years the conference is held in Los Angeles, on even
numbered years it is held in San Francisco.

          Field Service Division Employees who are members of the
Conference include Alden Bee, Jay Capitola, Norman Dodger,
Dick Fairmont, Jose Olvera, Dave Pasadena, Dick Pico, and Walt Union.

          Ora Sellers, his three bureau chiefs, and six of the
Specialists in the Economic Development Division are also members
of the Conference.

                              Sincerely,

                              Jay Capitola

                              Jay Capitola

JDC:dm
Attachment

California
FIRST
In Population

CALIFORNIA DEPARTMENT OF COMMERCE

MEMO TO: All Administrative Personnel

DATE: April 5, 1965

FROM: Grace Pryor

SUBJECT: Administrative Staff Meetings.

Commencing with the April 19 meeting at 10:00 o'clock in the Director's conference room, we will initiate a series of semi-monthly staff meetings for the top administrative personnel. The schedule calls for meetings (10:00 a.m. to noon) on the first and third Monday of each month, to be attended by all division chiefs, bureau chiefs and regional managers.

Please mark your calendar so you will be available for these meetings.

GP:lk

299

Item 13   Climate Item—Rule

California
FIRST
In Population

CALIFORNIA DEPARTMENT OF COMMERCE

DATE: April 2, 1965

MEMO TO: All Division Chiefs

FROM: John Veep

SUBJECT: Grievance Procedure Statement.

I recently had occasion to review that part of Administrative Memo #7 concerned with departmental grievance procedures. This memo section did not appear to me to be consistent with out general approach to personnel management.

Having come to this conclusion, I had ASD draft a revision. A copy of this proposed replacement is attached. I think they did a pretty good job, but I'd like you to review it and then submit your suggestions for additions, deletions, and modifications to Carl Trainor.

300

Grievance Procedure. In accordance with Rule No. 540 of the State Personnel Board, the Department provides the following grievance procedure which shall be available to all employees.

1. The grievance procedure is governed by the following:
   a. Grievances are resolved through normal supervisory channels to the maximum extent possible.
   b. Grievances are acted upon without delay.
   c. Each employee has the right to assistance by a representative of his own choosing in preparing and presenting his grievance.
   d. Employees and their representatives are free from reprisal of any kind for using the grievance procedure.
   e. Each employee and his representative (if in the Department) is privileged to use a reasonable amount of time as determined by the Department, in preparing and presenting his grievance.
   f. Resolution of a grievance does not include the use of legal forms and procedures.

2. It is the responsibility of the employee (a) to discuss the grievance with his immediate supervisor without undue delay and before filing the grievance in writing and (b) to initiate a formal written grievance if he is dissatisfied with the results of the discussion with his supervisor and desires to pursue the grievance.

3. It is the responsibility of managers and supervisors to explain the grievance procedure to employees, inform employees of the names of the persons at the various levels of review, and make decisions without undue delay, including promptly informing an employee what alternative action he may take if the grievance is not of the type that should be processed through the departmental grievance procedure.

4. It is the responsibility of the Administrative Services Division to maintain an overall review of the operation of the grievance procedure, keep adequate records of the use of the grievance procedure and evaluate its effectiveness.

5. Grievances in any of the following matters normally should be appealed directly to the State Personnel Board without the use of the departmental grievance procedure:
   a. AWOL separation
   b. demotion or transfer for medical reasons
   c. punitive action
   d. rejection during probationary period
   e. separation by resignation
   f. termination of Limited Term employment for cause while TAU or Emergency employee still working
   g. written examination or Qualification Appraisal Panel appeal
   h. rejection of application to take an examination or withhold from certification

Appeals to the State Personnel Board must be filed within specified time limits, which vary depending on the nature of the matter being appealed. State Personnel Board Rule 541 provides, however, for a suspension of the time limit for filing an appeal to the State Personnel Board on matters subject to appeal to the Board during any period when the matter is under consideration as a written grievance within an agency.

CALIFORNIA DEPARTMENT OF COMMERCE

California FIRST In Population

MEMO TO: Chief FSD and Chief EDD   **DATE:** April 5, 1965

FROM: John Veep

SUBJECT: Change of office practice.

Ever since this Department was established, it has been the practice of the line division staffs to make a third copy of all correspondence, memos, etc., for the unit supervisor's file. We have finally realized that this practice is unnecessary and wasteful -- the duplication of filing chores and the failure of the staff to make significant use of these files should have resulted in the abandonment of this practice long ago.

Another point is relevant. The implication involved in requiring the third copy -- the implication that the staff needs to have every detail checked and managed by the supervisor -- is derogatory to the staff and could lead to a significant decline of effort. Let's continue to maintain check points and be available for advice, remembering that the development and expansion of the staff's overall competence is our most vital concern.

Each supervisor is expected to take the steps necessary to stop the practice of making third copies and to purge third copy files.

Abolishing the supervisor's third copy is a concrete action in line with our principles of supervisor-employee relationships. If any of you have other suggestions, please submit them.

Item 15

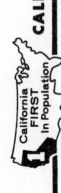

California
FIRST
In Population

CALIFORNIA DEPARTMENT OF COMMERCE

DATE: April 5, 1965

MEMO TO: Frank Fields

FROM: Jay Capitola

SUBJECT: Albert Spooner.

In view of the fact that Mr. Albert Spooner was voluntarily separated from our Fresno office as a result of suspicion of misappropriating departmental funds in the amount of $50 for personal reasons, I would appreciate your advice on how to handle the attached.

For your information, Spooner's shortage was discovered through normal internal auditing procedures, and when confronted with the evidence he made full restitution. In my opinion, Mr. Spooner is basically honest and not criminally inclined. I considered him to be one of our better agents.

JDC:dm

303

MUTUAL BONDING
COMPANY

March 24, 1965

Mr. Jay Capitola
Regional Manager
Department of Commerce
Sacramento, California

Dear Mr. Capitola:

    Mr. Albert Spooner has applied to the Home Appliance Company for a position as a clerk in the payroll section of the finance department. As this position involves the daily handling of a considerable amount of money, Mr. Spooner will be bonded by our organization. Accordingly, I should appreciate your completing the attached form and returning it to us at your earliest convenience.

Sincerely yours,

Albert Bigger
Mutual Bonding Company
Los Angeles, California

AB:ca

- -

1. Name of Employee _____

2. Company _____

3. Was employee discharged or requested to resign?

       _____ Yes.   _____ No.

4. Do you consider him honest?

5. Did he handle money in your employ?

6. Was he in debt to you at the time of leaving?

Signature _____

Title _____

304

CALIFORNIA DEPARTMENT OF COMMERCE

California FIRST In Population

MEMO TO: All Staff Members

FROM: John Veep

SUBJECT: Use of stock items.

DATE: April 2, 1965

I transmit the following memorandum from Administrative Services:

"The results of our third quarter inventory have indicated that our standard stock items are being depleted too rapidly. We must ask that each staff member exercise far more care in the use of office supplies, and we must remind you that the removal of supplies from the premises is a criminal act.

"We suggest, for example, that each of you limit yourselves to one pencil and writing pad per month, that you use scrap paper for such things as notes, messages, and first drafts of letters and reports, and that you re-use paper clips, rubber bands, and file folders. We ask that you follow other economies wherever possible."

We should, of course, cooperate as fully as possible.

California
FIRST
In Population

CALIFORNIA DEPARTMENT OF COMMERCE

MEMO TO: All Staff Members **DATE:** April 2, 1965

FROM: John Veep

SUBJECT: Extended lunch hours.

Once again I am forced to bring up the subject of lunch scheduling. A number of staff members have not been adhering to their allocated lunch shifts. Moreover, many employees appear to be spending more than the alloted 45 minutes for lunch.

Employees have the responsibility not to be absent from duty unnecessarily. In the future all staff members will be expected to rectify this situation and conform to the established schedule.

Also, the staff is reminded that no gambling or card playing of any kind is allowed on State premises during the lunch hour or at any other time. A word to the wise should be sufficient--the poor impression these practices have upon visitors is particularly relevant to the Department of Commerce.

Item 18

CALIFÓRNIA DEPARTMENT OF COMMERCE

MEMO TO: Frank Fields   **DATE:** April 2, 1965

FROM: Jay Capitola

SUBJECT: Inquiries from manufacturing concerns regarding new plants or plant expansions.

1. Requests for information as to possible California locations for manufacturing operations are received in any one of several headquarters offices and in each of the field offices. To date, we have no standard procedure for handling these requests. This lack occasionally results in gaps in our coverage of the clients needs or in duplication of coverage.

2. I hereby suggest that a Department Operations Notice be developed and promulgated which spells out the steps that must be followed when such an inquiry is received.

3. As a minimum the Operations Notice should make the following actions mandatory:

   a. Person receiving inquiry must fill out a <u>Manufacturing Company New Plant or Plant Expansion Inquiry Form</u> (proposed form is attached)

   b. If person completing form is not a bureau chief in Economic Development Division or Regional Manager in Field Services Division then the person completing the form must route the completed form to his bureau chief or regional manager.

   c. Bureau chief or regional manager must outline how request is to be filled and assign one individual as coordinator.

   d. Coordinator must log actions taken, attaching listings of materials sent.

   e. On terminating action on a request the coordinator must state the reason for termination. If reason is other than company occupation of new or expanded facilities in California, he must state (1) why company decided not to locate in California (or to expand their California facilities) and (2) how our service might be improved.

JDC:dm
Attachment

Manufacturing Company New Plant or Plant Expansion Inquiry Form

A. General Information

    1. Name of Company:
    2. Location of Company Headquarters:
    3. Date Inquiry Received:
    4. How Inquiry Received:
    ☐ a. correspondence (attach)
check one ☐ b. phone; name and title of caller:
    ☐ c. personal call; name and title of caller:
    5. Name of Person Receiving Inquiry and Completing Form:

B. Nature of Request (state specifically and completely)

C. Confidentiality (to whom, if any, can disclosures be made, time during
                    which inquiry must be kept confidential)

D. Information on Product(s) to be Manufactured

E. Requirements

    1. Labor:
    2. Land:
    3. Building:
    4. Climate:
    5. Community:
    6. Transportation:
    7. Water, Utility, and Waste Disposal:
    8. Financing:
    9. Other:

Item 19

STATE OF CALIFORNIA

OFFICE MEMO

Date___ April 2, 1965

To_____ Frank Fields

From___ Mary Staffer

Subject___ Letter to Governor's Office.

The following letter was received at the Governor's office and sent to our department for reply. As the certification lists in question refer to appointments being made in your division, will you please give me any thoughts you might have on how this letter should be answered?

FSD appointed Fairmont, Tarr, Wilshire (resigned 12/63) and Union off of the 1962 list for BDA; S.F. Port Authority made no appointments from this list.

FSD appointed Olvera off the 1964 list for BDA; S.F. Port Authority has made two appointments from this list.

With the exception of Olvera (Spanish-American, Catholic) all seven appointees appear to be white, Anglo-Saxon, protestants.

STD FORM 100

TRANSMITTAL OF CORRESPONDENCE

Date: **March 31, 1965**

To: George Apex
         Director, Department of Commerce

From:

         Departmental Secretary
         Governor's Office

This office has received the following:

Protest letter

☐ Please reply to the correspondent.

☐ This is transmitted to you for your information and files.

☒ Please furnish this office a suggested reply as promptly as possible and return the attached correspondence at the same time.

☐ This is transmitted to you for such attention as in your judgment it may require or merit.

☐ Please make an immediate investigation of this matter and furnish this office a report of your findings and recommendations.

☐ Please furnish this office a brief memorandum and return attached correspondence at the same time.

REMARKS:

   Please prepare a reply for my signature in response to the attached protest.

Enclosures: **Protest letter mentioned**

310

The Honorable Edward G. Green
Governor of California
State Capitol
Sacramento, California

March 29, 1965

Dear Governor Green:

     I wish to call to your attention a clear case of racial
discrimination in State Government.

     James Grover, age 34, Negro, graduate of the University
of California, placed number one on the last two civil service
examinations for Business Development Agent. Mr. Grover has had
considerable experience in industrial sales which clearly qualifies
him for Business Development Agent work.

     However, seven people have been appointed from these two
lists and Mr. Grover has been bypassed on each occasion. We think
that this is a clear violation of your "Governor's Code of Fair
Practices" and believe that you should take some corrective action
in this case.

                      Sincerely,

                      Robert Grove

                      Robert Grove
                      Secretary, California Chapter
                      Equal Rights Action Committee

RG:mn

311

P.O.B.—L

Item 20

CALIFORNIA DEPARTMENT OF COMMERCE

MEMO TO: All Division Chiefs   **DATE:** April 2, 1965

FROM: John Veep

SUBJECT: Space Activity and Nuclear Energy.

Space Activity: Between now and 1970 the National Aeronautics and Space
     Administration (NASA) will spend $20 billion on space activities. For
     continued economic well being, California must get her fair share of
     projects and funds.

Nuclear Energy: Electrical energy demand is expected to multiply 10 times over
     the next 40 years, and the Atomic Energy Commission believes nuclear power
     will capture 1/2 of projected increase. The rapid expansion of indistrial
     use of neclear energy and of the number of manufacturing processes
     incorporating atomic research developments will in the torseeable future
     bring about an industrial revolution matching or exceeding the current
     automation revolution.
     Maximum realization of the potential ot California as the number one state
     in the Union can be achieved only if this industrial revolution is
     systematically nourished and regulated at the state and local level.

Question: Is it in the best interest of the people of the state to establish a
     California Atomic Energy and Space Authority for the purpose of promoting
     and regulating space and atomic business and industry in California, or
     should these powers and duties be added to the State Department of Commerce?

We must evaluate the pros and cons of both alternatives and develop a recommendation
within six months.

I am asking each Division Chief to submit his ideas to me as to how we should go
about making the necessary evaluations by April 15.

The material submitted by the Division Chiefs will provide a starting point for
the task force assigned to this project. Task force selections will be made at
the Administrative Staff Meeting on April 19.

Item 21 Climate Item — Rules and Global Supervision

(This item was enclosed in a sealed envelope marked
CONFIDENTIAL and addressed to Art Dodd)

STATE OF CALIFORNIA

OFFICE MEMO

Date___4/2/65_____

To_____Art Dodd_____

From____John Veep_____

Subject___Attached probationary report_____

———

Art: For your information.

Since the normal alternates for Chief, Division of Field
Services (Capitola, Sellers) were unavailable when this
came up, the attached probationary report was submitted
to me for review.

Giant appears to be a valuable addition to our staff --
one worth some extra attention. Bay, in my opinion, is
one of our top supervisors with the potential to go all
the way to the top.

STD FORM 100

STATE OF CALIFORNIA	REPORT OF PERFORMANCE FOR PROBATIONARY EMPLOYEE	☐ FIRST ☑ SECOND ☐ FINAL

Giant	Keith	H.	4/2/65
Last Name	First Name	Initial	Date of Report

Trade Specialist
Civil Service Title

Position Number: 1   Date of Report: 8/3/65

Department of Commerce
State Agency

Subdivision of Agency: FSD   Date Probation Ends

Headquarters of Employee: S.F.

To assist you in your efforts to do a good job, conclusions based upon the way you have been learning and doing your work are summarized below. Your work performance will determine whether you attain permanent civil service status.

The ratings and comments on the copy you receive are the same as shown on the copies I am forwarding.

QUALIFICATION FACTORS:

RATINGS ARE INDICATED BY "X" MARKS

		UNACCEPTABLE	IMPROVEMENT NEEDED	STANDARD	OUTSTANDING
1.	SKILL—Experience in doing specific tasks; accuracy; precision; completeness; neatness; quantity.				X
2.	KNOWLEDGE—Extent of knowledge of methods, materials, tools, equipment, technical expressions and other fundamental subject matter.			X	
3.	WORK HABITS—Organization of work; care of equipment; safety; punctuality and dependability; industry.			X	
4.	RELATIONSHIPS WITH PEOPLE—Ability to get along with others; effectiveness in dealing with the public, other employees, patients or inmates.				X
5.	LEARNING ABILITY—Speed and thoroughness in learning procedures, laws, rules and other details; alertness; perseverance.				X
6.	ATTITUDE—Enthusiasm for the work; willingness to conform to job requirements and to accept suggestions for work improvement; adaptability.				X
7.	PERSONAL FITNESS—Integrity; sobriety; emotional stability; physical condition; appearance and habits.			X	
8.	ABILITY AS SUPERVISOR—Proficiency in training employees and in planning, organizing, laying out and getting out work; leadership.				
9.	ADMINISTRATIVE ABILITY—Promptness of action; soundness of decision; application of good management principles.				
10.	FACTORS NOT LISTED ABOVE (Use additional sheets if more space is needed).				

COMMENTS TO EMPLOYEE: (Supervisor should include comments on work especially well or poorly done and give suggestions as to how performance can be improved. Factor and over-all ratings of Unacceptable and over-all ratings of Outstanding must be substantiated. Use additional sheets if more space is needed.)

314

The overall quantity and quality of your work has been above average; the quantity of work has been exceptionally high for a new employee. I have been impressed by your ability to grasp and apply departmental routines and procedures. Also, your ability in controversial matters to consistently grasp the main point at issue and to suggest an appropriate action has left little need to exercise supervisor criticism. Keep up the good work.

The ratings and comments on this report are made primarily to summarize for higher management review my evaluation of your work to date. But such periodic summaries are of limited usefulness to you and me. Attitudes and work habits are established, maintained, or modified on the basis of day-to-day contacts and tasks. I feel that no individual learning can take place and no institutional progress can be made if there is little opportunity to deviate from the norm. Therefore, I shall continue to exercise my supervisor's prerogative in the form of occasional gentle pushes intended to point you in a general direction -- rather than attempting to keep you on the tag end of a short leash and pull you along the well trodden path.

Rater Discussed Report with Employee. ☑Yes ☐ No

OVER-ALL RATING: (The over-all rating must be consistent with the factor ratings and comments, but there is no prescribed formula for computing the over-all rating.)

	Unacceptable	Short of Standard	Standard	Outstanding
				X

☐ I recommend that you be granted permanent civil service status. (To be checked only on final report. If the probationer is rejected, notification must be given as prescribed by Government Code Section 19173.)   ☐ I recommend that you not be granted permanent civil service status.

Signature of RATER _Robert A. King_   Title _Supervising Bud. Develop. Agent_   Date _3/31/65_

In signing this report I do not necessarily agree with the conclusions of the rater.

Signature of EMPLOYEE _K. A. Grant_   Date _3/31/65_

☐ I would like to discuss this report with the Reviewing Officer.

I concur in the ratings given by the rater. I have made no change in the report.

Signature of REVIEWING OFFICER ___   Date _4/2/65_

As requested, Reviewing Officer discussed report with employee on ___ (Date) ___ (Initials)

(Form No. 636j - Revised 1-63) $

(Official Copy - Departmental Files)

CALIFORNIA DEPARTMENT OF COMMERCE

California
FIRST
In Population

MEMO TO: Frank Fields

FROM: Ralph Chavez

DATE: March 26, 1965

SUBJECT: Need to review and revise Department and Division Operation Notices.

Most of the Department and Division Operation Notices were promulgated at the time Field Services Division was created. They have never been systematically reviewed. Some are not in accord with current actual-practice. Coverage is incomplete, and the general tone and style used makes the Notices difficult to understand and encourages slavish, rather than critical, application of the standards they set forth.

As presently constituted, the Notices do not provide the guidelines needed for training new personnel nor the comprehensive list of joggers that everyone needs when faced with one of our many complex procedural or information gathering problems.

I suggest that we devote a major part of each division staff meeting for the next year or so (until the job is done) to hammering out the needed revisions and new approaches and guidelines.

REC:la

Item 23

STATE OF CALIFORNIA

OFFICE MEMO

Date___ March 25, 1965

To___ Art Dodd

From___ John Veep

Subject___ Applications of Decision Theory to Management
Problems.

_____

The Training Division of the State Personnel Board is

conducting in Sacramento a three-day training workshop

on "Applications of Decision Theory to Management

Problems" May 3, 4 and 5, 1965. We are invited to

send one Division Chief.

I am submitting your name.

STD FORM 100

317

Item 24

California FIRST In Population

CALIFORNIA DEPARTMENT OF COMMERCE

MEMO TO: Frank Fields   **DATE:** March 22, 1965

FROM: Al Smith

SUBJECT: New York-California Competition for Engineers and Scientists.

As you know, New York and California are 1-2 in the nation in research and development activity, and as both engineers and scientists are in short supply, New York and California firms are continually raiding one another.

This competition is wonderful from the standpoint of the person sought after; he gets exceedingly rapid advancements, free transportation and moving expenses from one side of the country to the other, and next-to-complete freedom of choice regarding projects to work on.

From the standpoint of the welfare of the nation, this situation is disastrous. The waste is tremendous, and output is neither adequate nor appropriate. Too much employee time is spent on travel and orientation. The projects which most interest the employee are not necessarily the ones most needed, etc.

I personally know ot a score of cases in which the person involved has made the New York-California shift five or more times in a ten-year period, getting a healthy promotion each time.

This type of raiding does not add to the total number of filled positions in New York and California; it merely redistributes the vacancies, increases the operational costs to all firms, and decreases total research and development output.

Both the New York State Department of Commerce and the California Department of Commerce have R and D Advisory Committees. How about putting them to work on a joint project? If you agree, I can approach management of the New York Department of Commerce regarding their feelings and ideas on the topic. I know from my contacts with the manager of their New York City Office that there has been some

318

(This item was enclosed in a sealed envelope marked
CONFIDENTIAL and addressed to Frank Fields.)

California
FIRST
In Population

CALIFORNIA DEPARTMENT OF COMMERCE

DATE: March 25, 1965

MEMO TO: Frank Fields

FROM: Ora Sellers

SUBJECT: Rotation - Roy Steel.

Frank, I'm writing you this letter because I believe our rotation program is setting up more problems than it is solving. As you are well aware, Roy Steel rotated to my division last year, and Herb Bay, my right hand man, took his place as Manager of the Coast Region.

While Steel probably did a good job for you, he just doesn't fit into the pattern of my organization and losing Bay has been a real detriment to our unit. Steel just isn't working out.

I don't know what your feelings are about this rotation program, but personally I think we should seriously question the value of the program to the organization. I'm not sure what we can do to bring about re-evaluation of the program, but I'm anxious to sit down and talk to you about this. How do you feel about this entire program?

OS:aj

Item 26

CALIFORNIA DEPARTMENT OF COMMERCE

California
FIRST
In Population

DATE: March 24, 1965

MEMO TO: Frank Fields

FROM: Jay Capitola

SUBJECT: Sr. Business Development Agent Bee -- Drunk Driving.

I thought you should know that Alden Bee, a Sr. Business Development Agent in the Sacramento office was arrested for drunk driving yesterday. It appears that he was on his way home from an evening meeting of the Stockton Chamber of Commerce. The arresting officer reported that he was weaving badly and was argumentative when apprehended. He was driving a State car at the time. At present he is still being detained by the Sheriff's office at Lodi.

JDC:dm

ROUTE SLIP

TO: *Frank Field*

FROM: *Jay Capitola* _____ (DATE)

CALIFORNIA STATE DEPARTMENT OF COMMERCE

REMARKS: *How can I keep ahead of the work in this region if Plan & Rulerd. Division not only keeps changing standards and upsetting clients but frirls up in its interpretation of its standards to our client?*

Maybe you can talk Hiroshima into more quality control regarding work of Bureau of Local Liaison?

CSDC 190/9/59

Charles Middleman, Bureau of Local Liaison   March 24, 1965

Bill Manoogian, Fresno Office Manager

Billboard Regulations.

        Some weeks ago members of your bureau held a two-day meeting with
representatives of the Billboard and Sign Industry in the Fresno vicinity.
While this was a well attended meeting, I have since had several comments
from those who attended indicating that they were in complete disagreement
with interpretations which members of your staff gave to certain regulations
regarding signs. As you recall, I attended some of the meetings and during
those times did not overhear anything that supports the contention of the local
representatives. However, there is reason to believe that the interpretation
given by your staff people to certain questions raised by the industry
(apparently on the day I could not attend because of illness) are subject to
further review and clarification.

        I wonder if you would mind stopping in my office the next time you
are in this area so that we can go over some of the points involved so I can
give correct information to those who have raised questions regarding the
material your men presented. I try to maintain very close relationships with
members of industry here and when there appears to be a difference of opinion
among members of the Department staff I feel it's my responsibility to help
get it clarified as soon as possible.

cc:Jay Capitola

Item 28

CALIFORNIA DEPARTMENT OF COMMERCE

California
FIRST
In Population

MEMO TO: Frank Fields   **DATE:**   March 22, 1965

FROM: Ralph Chavez, Southern Regional Manager

SUBJECT:

Last week after the southern regional staff meeting, an old sore was rubbed raw again -- the equating of Business Development Specialist I with Senior Business Development Agent.

The Seniors see the Specialist I's as having less responsible work and no supervisory responsibility. The Business Development Agents see the Specialist I's as performing parallel work at an equivalent level but having far less travel and troubleshooting headaches.

This is getting to be a major morale problem and soon will become a major turnover problem. The Business Development Agent is low man on the totem pole; not only are local agencies and corporations paying more for similar jobs, but the Economic and Development Division of our own Department appears to be paying more for a less responsible job.

For the first time since I took this regional manager position, I'm pushing the panic button!

CALIFORNIA DEPARTMENT OF COMMERCE

California
FIRST
In Population

MEMO TO: All Division Chiefs

DATE: March 22, 1965

FROM: Mary Staffer

SUBJECT: Management Development.

As you know, the Governor has recommended that each agency establish a management development program. Age profiles have shown that this is a particularly pertinent problem in the Department of Commerce.

In order to build a sound management development program in this department, we are requesting that all division chiefs submit recommendations for the expansion of our program. Please forward any ideas you have on this subject to the Administrative Services Division by April 23, 1965.

Up to date, Department of Commerce has only one program under way in the area of management development:

The rotational program which is aimed at giving personnel in each division an opportunity to rotate with other people at their level in order to broaden their experience pattern.

Director Apex had indicated that he believes that this is only a start in management development and that we should expand on this program. What are your ideas on this subject?

Index

Abelson, R. P., 5, 266
Acquiescence response set, 39, 98, 100
Acquiescence scale, 100, 102, 113
Activity scale, 100, 105
Adorno, T. W., 15, 100, 112, 266
Air Force In-Basket Test, 48–51
Alvares, K., 14, 269
Analogies, *see* Test S, Analogies
Analysis of covariance, 19–20, 78, 189–190, 197, 198
Analysis of variance, 137–138, 189–190, 194
Anderson, G. L., 10
Anxiety, 262
Anxiety scale, 100, 104, 105
Aptitude-treatment interaction, 4–12, 18–19, 90
Argyle, M., 245, 266
Aronson, E., 45, 266, 273
Astin, A. W., 29, 266
ATI, *see* Aptitude-treatment interaction
Attitude scales, 38–40
Authoritarianism scale, *see* California F Scale

Background variables, 106–110
  factor analysis of, 107–110
  factor loadings for, 109
  factors,
    dead-end seniority, 110, 112, 113, 184, 189, 231, 234, 253
    educated institutional man, 107, 110, 112, 113
    intercorrelations of, 107, 110
    number of children, 110
    power and seniority, 110, 112, 113, 184, 188, 189, 231, 234
    staff officer, 110, 184, 186, 188, 231, 234, 252, 253
    theoretical education, 110, 234
    years of military service, 110, 184, 188, 252
  intercorrelations of, 108
  questionnaire, 106
Bailey, D. E., 32, 273
Barone, J. L., x, 20, 272
Barron, F., 101, 266
BB In-Basket Test, *see* Bureau of Business In-Basket Test
Beaton, A. E., 19, 266
Beem, H. P., 245, 267
Biel, W. C., 43, 267
Biographical variables, *see* Background variables
Bloxom, B., ix, x, 200, 266
Box, G. E. P., 174, 175, 177, 266
Box test, 174, 175, 177
Bracht, G. H., 237, 260, 261, 262, 263, 264, 266
Brault, M., x, 144, 148, 267
Bray, D. W., 69, 266
Brown, R., 46, 266

Brown, W., 55, 96, 102
Bryan, G. L., ix
Budner, S., 102, 266
Bureau of Business In-Basket Test, 50,
  53–66, 68, 139, 153–158, 161, 163
  factor analysis of, 53–64
  factors,
    acting in compliance with suggestions,
      54, 59, 60, 63
    analyzing the situation, 61, 63–64
    concern with outsiders, 62–63
    concern with public relations, 54, 63
    concern with superiors, 54, 61
    constructive action, 59, 63
    controlling subordinates, 54, 61–62
    discussing, 54, 57, 59, 60
    final action, 59–60, 63
    informality, 54, 62
    intercorrelations of, 58
    orderly work, 62, 84
    preparatory action, 54, 60
    procrastinating, 54, 62, 68
  reliabilities of scores, 55–57, 65–67
  scoring of, 53–56
Burket, G. R., 237, 267

California Department of Commerce
  In-Basket Test, 116–163
  description of, 116–130, 138–140
  factor analysis of, 164–173, 202–208,
    242–243; see also Factor analysis
  factors, see Item factors, Performance
    factors, and Person factors
  items, sample of, 279–323
  organizational climates of, see Organiza-
    tional climate
  scorers' rating form, 146–148; see also
    In-basket scorers' ratings
  scoring form, sample of, 143
  scoring manual for, 144
  scoring methods for, 141–148
  setting for, 116–121
  subjects, 80–86
    assignment of to treatment groups,
      82–83
    comparison of climate groups with
      respect to predictors, 83–84

  computer-generated reports to, x,
    84–86
  description of, 80–82
  perception of climate by, 135–138
  training and supervising of scorers for,
    148–153
California F Scale, 15, 16, 100, 101, 102,
  105
California State Personnel Board, ix, 80,
  88, 91, 94, 102
Campbell, D. T., 25, 45, 64, 259–260, 267
Carlsmith, J. M., 45, 266
Carlton, S., x, 144, 267
Carroll, J. B., 5, 54, 91, 267, 269
Cattell, R. B., 4, 24, 27, 68, 90, 267
CDC In-Basket Test, see California
  Department of Commerce In-Basket
  Test
Chapman, R. L., 43, 267
Chave, E. J., 40, 273
Christie, R., 112, 267
Cioffi, F., 245, 266
Cleary, T. A., 5, 267
Climate ratings, see Organizational
  climate
Cluster analysis, 31–34
Cognitive abilities,
  classification of, 23–24
  factors, 96–98, 113
    inductive reasoning, 98
    intercorrelations of, 99
    Multiple Analogies Test, 98
    speed of closure, 98, 113
    Test S, Conservative Strategy, 98
    Test S, Successful Strategy, 98
  tests of, 88–94
    Concealed Words Test, 88–89
    description of, 88–94
    factor analysis of, 96–98
    factor loadings for, 97
    First and Last Names Test, 90–91,
      98, 188, 228
    Gestalt Completion Test, 88–89
    Hidden Patterns Test, 89, 90, 98,
      184, 186, 188, 231, 234, 252, 253
    intercorrelations of, 95
    Locations Test, 90, 98

Mathematics Test, 91, 98
Multiple Analogies Test, 94, 98, 188, 234, 252
reliabilities of, 96
Test S, Analogies, 91–94, 96, 98, 184, 239
Thing Categories Test, 90, 96, 98
Vocabulary Test, 91, 98, 113, 184, 186, 188, 190, 231, 252, 253
Cohen, K. J., 43, 267
Coleman, J. S., 30, 267
College environments, 29
College and University Environment Scales, 29
Comrey, A. L., 245, 267
Concealed Words Test, 88–89
Construct validity, 67
Contingency model of leadership, 13–14, 18
Core matrix, 214–215
Corey, S. M., 40, 267
Correlational psychology, 3
Creativity, 41–42
Criterion measures, 164
Cronbach, L. J., 3, 4, 8, 9, 10, 11, 18, 32, 47, 65, 90, 267, 268
CUES, see College and University Environment Scales
Cyert, R. M., 43, 267

Damarin, F., x
Data collection, methods of, 37–48
  administering attitude scales, 38–40
  eliciting lifelike behavior, 43
  eliciting related behavior, 41–42
  eliciting "what-I-would-do" behavior, 42–43
  measuring knowledge, 40
  observing real-life behavior, 43–44
  soliciting opinions, 37–38
Davis, M., x
Day, R. C., 245, 268
Deception, 45–48
Defensiveness, 5
Dependent variables, 141
Differential predictability, 5–6, 258
Dill, W. R., 43, 267
Discriminant analysis, 31

Dodge, J. S., 246, 272
Dominance scale, 100, 104, 105
Dunnette, M. D., 12, 268
Dyk, R. B., 90, 252, 274

Ecological validity, 260–265
Edwards, A. L., 39, 65, 101, 237, 268
Edwards Social Desirability Scale, 101
Ekstrom, R., 24, 88, 89, 90, 228, 269
Endler, N. S., 34, 268
Evan, W. M., 43, 268
Evans, F. R., 41, 254, 271
Experimental realism, 45
External validity, 45, 64–65, 69–70, 253, 259–260
Extroversion, 23
Eysenck, H. J., 4, 24, 268

F Scale, see California F Scale
Facet analysis, 23, 27–28, 238
Factor analysis, 24, 27, 29
  of background variables, 107–110
  of Bureau of Business In-Basket Test, 53–64
  of CDC in-basket items, 208–214
  of CDC in-basket scores, 164–173, 202–208, 242–243
  of cognitive tests, 96–98
  group principal components method of, 96, 237, 275–276
  inverse, 31–34
  of personality inventories, 104–105
  of school principals' in-baskets, 52–53
  of scorers' ratings, 158
  three-mode, 20–21, 34–36, 78, 199–240, 249–251, 255, 256, 258
  within-group covariance, method of, 77–78, 164, 277–278
Factor structure, effects of organizational climates on, 174–181, 246–248
Faterson, H. F., 90, 252, 274
Festinger, L., 40, 268
Fiedler, F. E., 13, 14, 268
Field independence, 90, 184, 252
Findley, W. G., 48, 268
First and Last Names Test, 90–91, 98, 188, 228

Fisher, J. F., ix
Fisher, R. A., 31, 268
Fiske, D. W., 25, 267
Fleishman, E. A., 4, 268
Forehand, G. A., 16, 17, 72, 268
Frederiksen, N., 5, 37, 41, 43, 48, 50, 53, 65, 67, 68, 157, 160, 200, 254, 263, 264, 268, 269, 270, 271, 273
French, J. W., 24, 88, 89, 90, 228, 269
Frenkel-Brunswik, E., 15, 100, 112, 266
Freud, S., 23, 269
Friedman, H. P., 32, 269

Gage, N. L., 267
Gagné, R. M., 267
Galanter, E., 266
Gardner, G., 245, 266
Gaylord, R. H., 5, 269
Generosity error, 38
Gerjuoy, H., ix, 275
Gerth, H. H., 273
Gestalt Completion Test, 88–89
Getzels, J. W., 41, 269
Ghiselli, E. E., 5, 102, 104, 269
Gilbert, A. C. F., 5, 269
Gilmer, B. von H., 72, 269
Glaser, R., 269
Glass, G. V., 237, 260, 261, 262, 263, 264, 266
Gleser, G. C., 32, 268
Goodenough, D. R., 90, 252, 274
Gottschaldt Figures Test, 89
Gough, H. G., 101, 269
Graen, G., 14, 269
Grant, D. L., 69, 266
Grayson, H. M., 101, 269
Green, B. F., 40, 269
Griffiths, D. E., 43, 50, 51, 67, 160, 269, 270
Group principal components method, see Factor analysis
Guetzkow, H., 43, 267, 270
Guilford, J. P., 11, 23, 24, 41, 270
Gulliksen, H., 19, 200, 269, 270, 273
Guttman, L., 23, 28, 208, 270

Halo effect, 38
Halpin, A. W., 270

Hamblin, R. L., 245, 268
Harris, C. W., 200, 270, 273
Helm, C., x, 84, 270
Hempel, W. E., Jr., 4, 268
Hemphill, J. K., 13, 32, 33, 43, 50, 51, 67, 160, 270
Hendrickson, A. E., 165, 270
Heron, A., 101, 270
Hess, E. H., 266
Hidden Patterns Test, 89, 90, 98, 184, 186, 188, 231, 234, 252, 253
Hoepfner, R., 30, 31, 270
Hoffman, E. L., 200, 270
Hunt, J. McV., 34, 268

Ideational fluency, 23
Ideational Fluency Test, 184, 188, 252
Impulsiveness scale, 101, 105
In-basket factor scores (CDC),
    correlations of with predictors, 182–189
    correlations with scorers' overall rating, 173
    intercorrelations of, 165, 168, 174, 180–181
        for consistent and inconsistent climates, 177–180
        for global and detailed supervision climates, 177–178
        for innovation-rules climate, 175–177
    means of, 192–198
In-basket item factors, see Item factors (CDC)
In-basket performance factors, see Performance factors (CDC)
In-basket person factors, see Person factors (CDC)
In-basket scorers' ratings, 146, 148, 172–173, 182, 184
    factor analysis of, 158
    form for, 147–148
    intercorrelations of, 158–159
    reliabilities of, 158–159
In-basket test factors, see Bureau of Business In-Basket Test, Item factors (CDC), Performance factors (CDC), Person factors (CDC), School Administrator In-Basket Test

In-basket test scores (CDC),
  correlations of with predictors, 182–189
  correlations of with ratings, 160–163
  factor analysis of, 164–173, 202–208,
    242–243
  reliabilities of, 153–157
  validity of, 160–163
In-basket tests, 47–70; *see also* Situational
    tests
  industrial applications of, 68–70
  prediction of performance on, 251–253
  reliabilities of, 52, 55–57, 65–67,
    153–157
  scoring form, sample page from, 143
  scoring manual for, 144
  scoring methods for, 51–52, 141–163
  scoring of, 51–52, 54–57, 76, 141–163,
    242
    for content, 141–142, 144–146
    for stylistic categories, 141–144
  validity of, 64–68, 160–163
Independence factor, 105, 113, 188, 228,
    231, 234
Inductive Reasoning Test, 184, 185, 188,
    234, 238, 251, 252, 253
Internal validity, 45
Inverse factor analysis, *see* Factor analysis
Item factors (CDC), 208–214, 249–250
  items permitting routine solutions, 211–
    212, 215, 218, 250
  items presenting conflicting demands for
    staff time, 214, 218, 250
  items recommending a change in policy,
    213, 218, 221, 250
  items requiring evaluation of procedures
    for accomplishing organizational
    goals, 210–211, 218, 250
  items requiring solution of inter-
    organizational problems, 212, 215,
    218, 250
  items requiring solution of personnel
    problems, 212–213, 215, 218, 221,
    250

Jackson, D. N., 65, 90, 269, 270, 271
Jackson, P. W., 41, 269
Jacobs, P. I., 8, 270, 271
Jahoda, M., 267

Jensen, A. R., 7, 270
Johnson, P. O., 10, 270
Johnson, S. C., 32, 271
Johnson–Neyman method, 10
Jung, C. G., 23, 271

Kahn, R. L., 73, 246, 271
Karp, S. A., 90, 252, 274
Katz, D., 245, 271
Kennedy, J. L., 43, 267
King, A., x
King, F. J., 11, 271
Kit of Reference Tests for Cognitive
    Factors, 24, 88, 89, 90, 91, 94, 96;
    see also Cognitive abilities, tests of
Klein, S. P., 30, 31, 41, 254, 270, 271
Kogan, N., 5, 271
Krause, M. S., 28, 29, 271
Kropp, R. P., 11, 271
Kruskal, J. B., 32, 271
Kuehn, A. A., 43, 267

Laboratory methods, use of, 44–48
  deception and role-playing in, 45–47
  realism in, 44–45
LaPiere, R. T., 40, 271
Lenz, L., x
Levin, J., 35, 200, 271
Levinson, D. J., 15, 100, 112, 266
Likert, R., 39, 271
Likert Scale, 39
Lilly, R. S., 200, 271
Lindzey, G., 266, 273
Linn, R. L., 20, 272
Litwin, G. H., 272
Locations Test, 90, 98
Lopez, F. M., Jr., 68, 69, 271

Maccoby, N., 245, 271
Mahalanobis, P. C., 32, 271
Maier, M. H., 8, 270, 271
Maladjustment factor, 105, 185–186,
    188, 252, 254–255
Maladjustment scale, 101, 104, 105
Mandler, G., 266
Manifest Anxiety Scale (Taylor), 100,
    101, 254
March, J. G., 25, 271

Marks Test (Thurstone), 90
Martella, J. A., 14, 269
Mathematics Test, 91, 98
Matson, R. G., 32, 273
McQuitty, L. L., 32, 271
Meltzer, L., 245, 271
Melville, S. D., 5, 269
Memory Test, *see* First and Last Names Test
Messick, S., 40, 65, 90, 269, 270, 277
Milgram, S., 46, 271
Miller, M. H., 43, 267
Mills, C. W., 273
Minnesota Multiphasic Personality Inventory, 100, 101, 254
MMPI, *see* Minnesota Multiphasic Personality Inventory
Moderator variables, 5–6, 20, 258
Morse, N., 245, 271
Multiple Analogies Test, 94, 98, 188, 234, 252
Multitrait-multimethod approach, 25
Myers, C. T., 90, 270

Nagay, J. A., ix
Nelson, W. H., 11, 271
Newell, A., 43, 267
Neyman, J., 10, 270
Norman, W. T., 24, 271

Oblimin rotation program, 54
Organizational climate, 16–17, 72–76, 110–112, 122–138, 174–181, 185–186, 189–198, 224–234, 238–239, 243–251, 256, 264, 279–323
    definition of, 72–74, 122
    effects on correlations, 189–198
    effects on factor structure, 174–181, 246–248
    effects on means, 189–198, 243–246
    effects on slopes of regressions, 190–192, 248–249
    management of, 255–256
    perceptions of, 135–138
    perceptions of innovative behavior and, 16–18
    presentation of, 122–130
    ratings of, 110–112, 135–138, 182, 184

Orne, M., 46, 271
Orris, J. B., 14, 269
Osgood, C. E., 32, 272

Pace, C. R., 29, 272
Pearson, K., 31, 272
Pelz, D., 245, 272
Performance factors (CDC), 164–173, 249–250, 253–256
    accepts administrative responsibility, 172, 173, 175, 177, 180, 181, 205, 208, 243, 247
    acts in compliance with suggestions, 165, 168, 169, 175, 180–181, 202, 206, 208, 243
    amount of work, 163
    controls subordinates, 203, 208, 215, 221
    defers judgment and action, 170–171, 177, 184, 188, 197, 198, 204, 208, 243, 245, 252
    discusses, 163
    evaluates work of others, 205, 208
    final action, 163
    informality, 161, 171–172, 180, 205, 208, 215, 243
    interacts with peers, 171, 177, 180–181, 190, 192, 197, 204, 208, 218, 243, 247
    interacts with superiors, 169, 175, 177, 180, 197, 198, 203, 208, 218, 243, 244–245, 247
    involves outsiders, 206, 208, 218
    orderly work, 161, 171, 175, 177, 204, 208, 215, 243
    plans and discusses, 169, 170, 184, 188, 203, 243
    preparation for action, 163
    preparatory action, 202–203, 206
    prepares for action vs. takes action in compliance with suggestions, 208, 221
    procrastination, 163
    productivity, 165, 169, 173, 175, 181, 184, 185, 186, 188, 197, 202, 203, 242, 243, 244, 248, 252, 253
    thoughtful analysis of problems, 169–170, 175, 177, 180, 181, 184, 188, 204, 206, 208, 218, 243, 247, 252, 253

Person-factor scores,
  correlations of with predictors, 227–236
  intercorrelations of, 224–227
Person factors (CDC), 21, 214–223, 256
  commitment-avoiding manager, 221, 223, 224, 225, 231, 234, 239, 250–251
  informal communicator, 215, 217, 226, 228, 231, 234, 250
  program-centered manager, 218, 220, 221, 231, 238–239, 250–251
  subordinate-centered manager, 221–222, 226, 234, 239, 250
  superior-centered manager, 218–219, 224–225, 231–232, 234, 238–239, 250–251
  systematic supervisor, 215–216, 218, 228, 239, 250
Person-situation interaction, 1–3, 242, 249–250, 263
  design for experimental study of, 71–79
  evidence of, 6–18
  statistical models of, 19–21
Personality inventory,
  description of, 98, 100–102
  factor analysis of, 104–105
  factors,
    independence, 105, 113, 188, 228, 231, 234
    intercorrelations of, 106
    maladjustment, 105, 185–186, 188, 252, 254–255
    rigid authoritarianism, 105, 113, 184, 186, 231, 252–253
    social extroversion, 105, 113, 186, 188, 234, 252
    reliabilities of, 104
  scales, 98–102
    Acquiescence, 100, 102, 113
    Activity, 100, 105
    Anxiety, 100, 104, 105
    Authoritarianism, 100, 105
    Dominance, 100, 104, 105
    Impulsiveness, 101, 105
    intercorrelations of, 103
    Maladjustment, 101, 104, 105
    Preference for Complexity, 101, 104, 105
    Reflectiveness, 101, 105

    Rigidity, 101, 102, 104, 105
    Self-sufficiency, 101, 105
    Sociability-H, 101, 105
    Sociability-T, 101, 104, 105
    Social Desirability, 101, 102, 104, 105
    Stability, 102, 105
    Tolerance for Ambiguity, 102, 105
Personality Research Inventory, 100, 101
Pfiffner, J. M., 245, 267
Population validity, 260–261
Predictor variables, 83–84, 87–113, 275; see also Cognitive abilities, Background variables, and Personality inventory
  correlations with performance factors, 182–189
  intercorrelations of, 112–115
Preference for Complexity scale, 101, 104, 105
Price, L. A., 24, 88, 89, 90, 228, 269
Programmed instruction, 8–9
Promax rotation procedure, 165

Quinn, R. P., 73, 246, 271

Rao, C. R., 31, 272
Rating form for executive selection, 149–151
Rating method, limitations of, 256–257
Rating scales, 37–38
Reasons for Action form, 51, 139, 140, 142
Reference Tests for Cognitive Factors, see Kit of Reference Tests for Cognitive Factors
Reflectiveness scale, 101, 105
Reliability of in-basket scores, see In-basket test scores
Research Institutes, 74–75, 138–140
Response set, 65
  acquiescence, 39, 98, 100
  social desirability, 39–40, 65, 262–263
RFA form, see Reasons for Action form
Richardson, F., x
Riecken, H. W., 46, 272
Rigid Authoritarianism factor, 105, 113, 184, 186, 231, 252–253
Rigidity scale, 101, 102, 104, 105

Rock, D. A., 20, 272
Rod and frame test, 90
Role playing, 45–47
Rosenstein, A. J., 34, 268
Rosenthal, R. A., 73, 246, 271
Rosner, M. M., 265, 272
Rote Memory Test, *see* First and Last Names Test
Rubin, J., 32, 269, 272

Sanford, R. N., 15, 100, 101, 112, 266, 269
Saunders, D. R., 5, 20, 48, 50, 57, 100, 258, 268, 269, 272
Schein, E. H., 6, 12, 258, 272
Schlesinger, I. M., 23, 208, 270
School Administration In-Basket Test, 50–53, 65–68
  description of, 50–51
  factor analysis of, 52–53
  factors,
    amount of work done in handling items, 53
    analyzing the situation, 52, 54
    complying with suggestions made by others, 52, 54, 59–60
    directing the work of others, 52, 61–62
    discussing before acting, 52, 54
    exchanging information, 52, 60
    maintaining organizational relationships, 52, 61
    organizing work, 52, 54, 62
    preparation for decision vs. taking final action, 53
    responding to outsiders, 52, 63
  reliabilities of, 52, 66–67
  scoring categories for, 51–52
  scoring methods for, 51–52
Schrader, W. B., 5, 269
Scorers' ratings, *see* In-basket scorers' ratings
Seibert, W. F., 4, 272
Self-Description Inventory, 102, 104
Self-sufficiency scale, 101, 105
Sells, S. B., 4, 6, 12, 26, 28, 29, 272
Shaffer, F., x
Shepard, R. N., 32, 272

Sherif, C. W., 28, 272
Sherif, M., 28, 272
Simon, H. A., 25, 271
Situation,
  attributes of, 33
  definition of, 21–22
Situational tests, 43, 64–65, 116–122, 241–242, 253; *see also* In-basket tests
  in-basket test as a, 47–48
  realism in, 44–45
Situational variables, 2–3, 6, 71–72, 258
16 Personality Factor Questionnaire (Cattell), 68
Smith, E. E., 246, 272
Sneath, P. H. A., 32, 272
Snoek, J. D., 73, 246, 271
Snow, R. E., 4, 8, 9, 10, 11, 18, 90, 268, 272
Sociability-H scale, 101, 105
Sociability-T scale, 101, 104, 105
Social-desirability response set, 39–40, 65, 262–263
Social Desirability scale, 101, 102, 104, 105
Social Extroversion factor, 105, 113, 186, 188, 234, 252
Sokal, R. R., 32, 272
Spearman, C., 14, 55, 96, 102
Spearman–Brown formula, 55, 96, 102
Spearman's rho, 14
Speed of Closure Test, 184, 231, 234, 239, 253
Spranger, E., 23, 272
S-R Inventory of Anxiousness, 35
Stability scale, 102, 105
Stallings, J. A., 9
Stanley, J. C., 259–260, 267
Steiner, I. D., 246, 272
Stolurow, L. M., 8, 270
Stricker, L. J., 5, 46, 273
Strong Vocational Interest Blank, 68
Structure-of-intellect model (Guilford), 11, 23–24
Subjects, *see* California Department of Commerce In-Basket Test
Suci, G., 32, 272
SVIB, *see* Strong Vocational Interest Blank

Tagiuri, R., 12, 257, 272, 273
Taxonomies,
  of attributes, 22–25, 36
  of college environments, 29
  of individuals, 22–23, 36
  methods for developing, 26–27
  of situations, 4, 22–36, 72, 237–238
Taylor, J. A., 100, 101, 254, 262, 273
Taylor, V. R., ix
Test anxiety, 5
Test S, Analogies, 91–94, 96, 98, 184, 239
  description of, 91
  sample answer sheet for, 92
  scoring of, 92–94
    accuracy score, 93–94
    confidence index score, 93, 98
    conservation index, 93, 98
    efficiency index, 93
    number right score, 92, 98
    plunger index, 93
    strategy score, 92
Test S, Conservative Strategy, 228, 231, 239
Test S, Successful Strategy, 184, 231, 234, 239
Thing Categories Test, 90, 96, 98
Three-mode factor analysis, see Factor analysis
Thurstone, L. L., 24, 27, 28, 39, 40, 68, 89, 90, 100, 101, 102, 273
Thurstone, T. G., 27
Thurstone scale, 39
Thurstone Temperament Schedule, 68, 100, 101, 102
Tiffin, J., 4, 272

Tolerance for Ambiguity scale, 102, 105
True, D. L., 32, 273
Tryon, R. C., 32, 273
Tucker, L. R, x, 20, 34, 35, 77, 200, 201, 270, 273, 277

Validity of in-basket tests, see In-basket tests
Van Wormer, T. A., 43, 267
Variables, see Predictor variables and Situational variables
Vocabulary Test, 91, 98, 113, 184, 186, 188, 190, 231, 252, 253
Vroom, V. H., 14, 15, 45, 246, 273

Wallach, M. A., 5, 271
Wand, B., 50, 269
Ward, J. H., Jr., 32, 273
Ward, L. B., 69, 273
Washburne, N. F., 272
Weber, M., 25, 26, 273
Wexler, N., x
White, P. O., 165, 270
Wicker, F. W., 200, 273
Wilks, S. S., 19, 270
Winters, P. R., 43, 267
Within-group covariance factor analysis, see Factor analysis
Witkin, H. A., 90, 184, 252, 274
Wolfe, D. M., 73, 246, 271
Wolff, W. M., 101, 274
Woodworth, R. S., 257, 274

Zelditch, M., Jr., 43, 268

TITLES IN THE PERGAMON GENERAL PSYCHOLOGY SERIES

Vol. 1.   J. WOLPE – *The Practice of Behavior Therapy*
Vol. 2.   T. MAGOON *et al.* – *Mental Health Counselors at Work*
Vol. 3.   J. McDANIEL – *Physical Disability and Human Behavior*
Vol. 4.   M. L. KAPLAN *et al.* – *The Structural Approach in Psychological Testing*
Vol. 5.   H. M. LaFAUCI & P. E. RICHTER – *Team Teaching at the College Level*
Vol. 6.   H. B. PEPINSKY *et al.* – *People and Information*
Vol. 7.   A. W. SIEGMAN & B. POPE – *Studies in Dyadic Communication*
Vol. 8.   R. E. JOHNSON – *Existential Man: The Challenge of Psychotherapy*
Vol. 9.   C. W. TAYLOR – *Climate for Creativity*
Vol. 10. H. C. RICKARD *et al.* – *Behavioral Intervention in Human Problems*
Vol. 11. P. EKMAN, W. V. FRIESEN & P. ELLSWORTH – *Emotion in the Human Face: Guidelines for Research and an Integration of Findings*
Vol. 12. B. MAUSNER & E. S. PLATT – *Smoking: A Behavioral Analysis*
Vol. 14. A. GOLDSTEIN – *Psychotherapeutic Attraction*
Vol. 15. F. HALPERN – *Survival: Black/White*
Vol. 16. K. SALZINGER & R. S. FELDMAN – *Studies in Verbal Behavior: An Empirical Approach*
Vol. 17. H. E. ADAMS & W. K. BOARDMAN – *Advances in Experimental Clinical Psychology*
Vol. 18. R. C. ZILLER – *The Social Self*
Vol. 19. R. P. LIBERMAN – *A Guide to Behavioral Analysis & Therapy*
Vol. 22. H. B. PEPINSKY & M. J. PATTON – *The Psychological Experiment: A Practical Accomplishment*
Vol. 23. T. R. YOUNG – *New Sources of Self*
Vol. 24. L. S. WATSON, JR. – *Child Behavior Modification: A Manual for Teachers, Nurses, and Parents*
Vol. 25. H. L. NEWBOLD – *The Psychiatric Programming of People: Neo-Behavioral Orthomolecular Psychiatry*
Vol. 26. E. L. ROSSI – *Dreams and the Growth of Personality: Expanding Awareness in Psychotherapy*
Vol. 27. K. D. O'LEARY & S. G. O'LEARY – *Classroom Management: The Successful Use of Behavior Modification*
Vol. 28. K. A. FELDMAN – *College and Student: Selected Readings in the Social Psychology of Higher Education*
Vol. 29. B. A. ASHEM & E. G. POSER – *Adaptive Learning: Behavior Modification with Children*
Vol. 30. H. D. BURCK *et al.* – *Counseling and Accountability: Methods and Critique*
Vol. 31. N. FREDERIKSEN *et al.* – *Prediction of Organizational Behavior*
Vol. 32. R. B. CATTELL – *A New Morality from Science: Beyondism*
Vol. 33. M. L. WEINER – *Personality: The Human Potential*

ENCOUNTERS IN ORGANIZATIONAL BEHAVIOR: PROBLEM SITUATIONS
Pergamon Management and Business Series, Volume 2
By Robert D. Joyce, President, Innovative Management, Huntington Beach, California
and Supervisor, Management and Professional Training, Douglas Aircraft Company,
Long Beach, California

Robert Joyce has broken down barriers to innovation in the classroom setting by introducing a book that replaces the dull and the out-dated with unique and insightful
problem cases relating to Management and the Behavioral Sciences as they exist today.
Fifty-four significant problem situations are included in 10 major sections which in-
corporate such contemporary topics as pollution, drugs, four-day weeks, hippies, mod
clothing and non-conformists. Each problem situation is supplemented with instructional
aids to maximize its benefit to both instructor and students.

THE PRACTICE OF MANAGERIAL PSYCHOLOGY
Concepts and Methods for Manager and Organization Development
Pergamon Management and Business Administration Series, Volume 1
By Andrew J. DuBrin, College of Business, Rochester Institute of Technology, New York

Based upon the author's research and practical experience as a consultant, this volume presents a variety of innovative, conceptual schemes to enable the practitioner, student, and manager to understand the underlying factors that will determine if and to what degree psychological intervention will be beneficial, meaningless, or harmful to an organization. Requiring only a basic background in business or psychology, the book offers such new conceptualizations as a list of behavioral changes needed by managers, the Conflict Matrix, the developmental Goal X Level Integrator, managerial motivational schema, and helpful interventions for managerial obsolescence. A unique Managerial Psychology Matrix specifies the proper conditions for applying such techniques as sensitivity training, performance appraisal, psychological assessment, team development meetings, organizational analysis, and super-subordinate counseling.

CLIMATE FOR CREATIVITY
Report of the Seventh National Creativity Research Conference held in Greensboro,
North Carolina. Supported Jointly by the National Science Foundation and the Smith
Richardson Foundation, Inc.
Pergamon General Psychology Series, Volume 9
Edited by Calvin W. Taylor, the University of Utah

This volume offers a multidimensional investigation of the problems of identifying and
establishing proper "climates" or settings for creativity. Part I concentrates on organizational
settings for creativity, including papers on the identification and use of creative abilities
in industry, scientific organizations, major weapon systems innovations, and the U.S. Civil
Service Commission. Part II examines more general creativity climates and studies, discussing
predictors and criteria of creativity; the maintenance of creative output through the years;
programming creative behavior; intellective, non-intellective, and environmental correlates
of mechanical ingenuity; and a holistic approach to creativity.

STUDIES IN DYADIC COMMUNICATION: Proceedings of a Research Conference on the Interview
Pergamon General Psychology Series, Volume 7
Edited by Aron W. Siegman, University of Maryland (Baltimore County Campus) and the
Psychiatric Institute, University of Maryland School of Medicine and Benjamin Pope,
The Sheppard and Enoch Pratt Hospital, Towson, Maryland

The result of a special conference held at the Psychiatric Institute of the University of
Maryland in 1968, this volume includes a number of diverse studies based on both experimental and naturalistic interviews, experimental dialogues and free speech samples. The
papers explore such aspects of the interview as the effectiveness of various interviewing
styles, the role of the interviewer-interviewee relationship, the synchrony phenomenon
or reciprocal modeling, the role of auditory feedback in the control of spontaneous speech,
and speech patterns in patient groups. **Studies in Dyadic Communication** will be a valuable
textbook and reference source for graduate students and research workers in psychology,
communication, psycholinguistics, interviewing, psychotherapy, and counseling.

THE PSYCHOLOGICAL EXPERIMENT: A Practical Accomplishment
Pergamon General Psychology Series, Volume 22
Edited by Harold B. Pepinsky, The Ohio State University, and Michael J. Patton,
University of Utah

Based on the thesis that the reality of an empirical world exists for the participant only
through the methods he and others use to make that world evident to each other, this
volume focuses on reports of six psychological experiments involving counseling processes
and negotiation. The editors examine each of these experiments in retrospect and analyze
how the experimenter and fellow participants contrived to develop the experiment from
its original prospectus into a completed, published document.

PHYSICAL DISABILITY AND HUMAN BEHAVIOR
Pergamon General Psychology Series, Volume 3
By James W. McDaniel, University of Colorado

This textbook and reference concerning the psychological effects of chronic illness and physical disability covers all important aspects of human behavior influenced by illness and physical impairment, as well as the implications of behavioral factors for treatment and rehabilitation processes. Unique in his approach to the subject, the author treats basic psychological processes such as learning, perception, motivation, and emotion as central characteristics which all human beings have in common, and which are subject to predictable changes with illness and permanent disability. The volume collates and critically evaluates for the first time both the theoretically and experimentally relevant work on these problems from the medical and behavioral sciences. Also included are several novel definitions and conceptual models for the study of human behavior in relation to physical disability.

OPERATIONAL RESEARCH QUARTERLY

Editor: R.A. Cuninghame-Green

"Operational research is the attack of modern science on complex problems arising in the direction and management of large systems of men, machines, materials and money in industry, business, government and defence." The Journal examines the broad scope of operational research as the application of scientific analysis to management problems; it covers all aspects of management including administration, organization, economics, workflow, measurement and productivity. The Journal reaches top-level management in building, health engineering, construction, fuel, power, local government, banking and commerce.